THOMISTIC PHILOSOPHY

BY

Rev. HENRI GRENIER, Ph.D., S.T.D., J.C.D.,
Professor of Philosophy, Laval University.

Translated from the Latin of the original
CURSUS PHILOSOPHIAE (Editio tertia)
by
Rev. J. P. E. O'HANLEY, Ph.D.

IN THREE VOLUMES

VOLUME III
MORAL PHILOSOPHY

First English Edition

Published by
ST. DUNSTAN'S UNIVERSITY
CHARLOTTETOWN, CANADA

1949

Nihil obstat:

GAVAN P. MONAGHAN, Ph.D., Paed.D.,
Censor deputatus.

Die 21 Julii, 1948.

Imprimatur:

† JACOBUS BOYLE, D.D.,
Episcopus Carolinapolitanus.

Carolinapoli, die 15 Augusti, 1948.

ALL RIGHTS RESERVED

Des ateliers de L'ACTION CATHOLIQUE, Québec.

To

ST. DUNSTAN

Scholar Statesman Saint

TABLE OF CONTENTS

I

GENERAL INTRODUCTION

Introduction.................................... 3

II

MONASTICS

BOOK I

ULTIMATE END OF HUMAN ACTS

CHAPTER I. Man's ultimate end in general......... 20

    Art. I. End of human acts................... 21
    Art. II. Ultimate end...................... 24

CHAPTER II. Happiness........................... 33

    Art. I. Natural happiness.................. 35
    Art. II. Perfect beatitude.................. 47

Book II

HUMAN ACTS IN THEIR PSYCHOLOGICAL ASPECT

THE ONLY CHAPTER. **Human acts in their psychological aspect**................ 53
    Art. I. Voluntariness....................... 55
    Art. II. Involuntariness.. 58
    Art. III. Elicited and commanded acts of the will 66

BOOK III

HUMAN ACTS IN THEIR MORAL ASPECT

CHAPTER I. **Morality**........................... 74
    Art. I. Morality in general.................. 76
    Art. II. Goodness and malice of human acts...... 80
    Art. III. Intrinsically good and intrinsically evil human acts....................... 82
    Art. IV. Rule of morality..................... 87
    Art. V. Sources of morality................... 93

CHAPTER II. **Consequences of morality**............ 103
    Art. I. Sin............................... 104
    Art. II. Imputability and responsibility 106
    Art. III. Merit and demerit................... 109

BOOK IV

PRINCIPLES OF MORAL ACTS

CHAPTER I. **Laws**.............................. 114
   Art. I. Law in general...................... 116
   Art. II. Eternal law........................ 122
   Art. III. Natural law....................... 124
   Art. IV. Positive law....................... 139
   Art. V. Conscience........................ 147

CHAPTER II. **The virtues**......................... 150
   Art. I. The virtues in general............... 153
   Art. II. Prudence........................... 166
   Art. III. Right............................. 178
   Art. IV. Justice............................ 195
   Art. V. Fortitude.......................... 215
   Art. VI. Temperance........................ 229
   Art. VII. Friendship........................ 255

III

ECONOMICS

Introduction...................................... 273

BOOK I

SOCIETY IN GENERAL

The only chapter. **Society in general**............ 275
    Art. I. Society............................ 276
    Art. II. Authority......................... 287

BOOK II

DOMESTIC SOCIETY

Chapter I. **Matrimonial society**.................. 297
    Art. I. Origin of matrimony................ 298
    Art. II. Precept of matrimony............... 310
    Art. III. Unity of matrimony................. 313
    Art. IV. Indissolubility of matrimony......... 316

Chapter II. **Parental society**..................... 323
    Art. I. Parental authority.................. 324
    Art. II. Education of children............... 330
    Appendix. Herile society..................... 342

IV

POLITICS

Introduction.................................. 347

BOOK I

CAUSES OF CIVIL SOCIETY

CHAPTER I. **End and origin of civil society**......... 350
    Art. I. End of civil society................... 351
    Art. II. Origin of civil society................. 358

CHAPTER II. **Material cause of civil society**........ 363
    Art. I. Relation of persons and families to civil society.......................... 365
    Art. II. Private ownership................... 374
    Art. III. Nationality........................ 388

CHAPTER III. **Civil authority**..................... 396
    Art. I. Origin of civil authority............... 397
    Art. II. Subject of civil authority............. 402

BOOK II

RESTORATION OF SOCIETY

Chapter I. Professional associations 413

    Art. I. End of professional associations. 415
    Art. II. Lawfulness of professional associations. ... 418
    Art. III. Complete professional associations. 421
    Art. IV. Salary or wages...................... 426
    Art. V. Capitalism.......................... 438

Chapter II. Errors in regard to society. 441

    Art. I. Communism......................... 442
    Art. II. Socialism............................ 450
    Art. III. Economic Liberalism.................. 453

BOOK III

RELATIONS BETWEEN SOCIETIES

Chapter I. Relations between civil societies. 458

    Art. I. International law..................... 459
    Art. II. International society.................. 462
    Art. III. War.............................. 465

Chapter II. Relations between Civil Society and the Church 467

    Art. I. The State and religion................. 468
    Art. II. Relations between the State and the Church 471

MORAL
PHYLOSOPHY

GENERAL INTRODUCTION

815. Moral Philosophy, speculative philosophy, and mechanical arts.— 1° The knowledge of order properly appertains to human reason, for this is the only faculty of man which can have knowledge of the relation of one thing to another.

But yet man's reason is not of itself determined to the consideration of one order rather than another. Therefore, when the consideration of a particular order presents special difficulties, reason requires a habit to determine it for this consideration. For a habit is destined to remove the indifference of a faculty, so that the faculty may be able to perform its act without difficulty.

Therefore, in order to know the different sciences, i.e., the division of the sciences, we must divide order according to the special difficulties which each kind of order presents to the consideration of reason.

Under this aspect, order is of four kinds.

2° *a)* There is a kind of order which reason *does not establish*, but only *considers*. This kind of order is the object of real speculative philosophy, i.e., of Philosophy of Nature and of Metaphysics.

b) There is another kind of order which reason, *by its act of knowledge, establishes in its own act*, as, for example, when it gives order to its concepts, or to the signs of its concepts, as it does when it gives order to the words which signify these concepts. This kind of order is the object of rational philosophy, that is to say, of the liberal arts, as, for example, Logic.

c) There is a third kind of order which reason, *in its act of knowledge, establishes in the operations of the will*. It is with this kind of order that Moral Philosophy is concerned.

d) Finally, there is a kind of order which reason, *in its act of knowledge, establishes in external things* constituted by human reason. This kind of order is the concern of the mechanical arts ([1]).

816. Definition of Moral Philosophy. — Moral Philosophy is concerned with the kind of order which reason, by its act of knowledge, establishes in the operations of the will.

Two kinds of order are found in things:

the order of the parts of a whole, i.e., of a multitude, to each other;

the order of things to their end.

The order of things to their end is a higher order than the order which exists between the parts of a whole or multitude, for the former is the end of the latter.

Hence Moral Philosophy may be defined: *the science which deals with the acts of the will in their order to each other and in their order to their end;* or, more briefly, *the science which deals with human acts as directed to their end;* or again, *the science which deals with man as acting voluntarily for an end* ([2]).

From these definitions we learn the material object, the formal object *quod*, and the formal object *quo* of Moral Philosophy.

a) The material object is all human acts.

A human act is an act which proceeds from the will of man according to the order of reason, i.e., an act which is subject to the will and to reason.

Hence acts which are not subject to the will and to reason are not human acts, but natural acts, as, for example, the operations of the vegetative soul, the study of which is alien to Moral Philosophy.

b) The formal object *quod* is human acts as directed to their end.

c) The formal object *quo* is the end to which human acts are directed. Moral Philosophy deals with all human acts

---

(1) *In Ethic.*, l. I, l. 1, n. 1 et 2 (Pirotta).
(2) *In Ethic.*, l. I, l. 1, n. 3 (Pirotta).

as directed to their end, i.e., in relation to their end, and therefore it receives its unity and specification from this end. Hence the end to which human acts are directed is the formal object *quo* of Moral Philosophy, because all sciences receive their unity and specification from their formal object *quo* (n. 184).

817. Moral Philosophy is an essentially practical science.— 1° A science is speculative or practical according to its end.

A speculative science is a science whose end is the contemplation of truth.

A practical science is a science whose end is work, i.e., a science which directs the knowledge of truth to work, that is to say, to operation, or to the object of operation.

2° A practical science may be *radically practical, essentially*, i.e., *formally, practical*, or *completely practical*([1]).

A *radically practical science* is a science which deals with operables, i.e., operations and objects of operation, in a speculative manner; v. g., the knowledge by which a man knows what a house is. Science of this kind is purely speculative, because it proceeds in a speculative manner: its end is the knowledge of the nature of things. But yet it is radically practical, because, in manifesting the nature of an operable, it is the measure of practical knowledge, as the speculative is the measure of the practical: for the practical is radicated in the speculative and measured by it.

An *essentially* or *formally practical science* is a science which is practical both as regards the matter with which it deals and as regards the manner in which it deals with this matter; v.g., a science which deals with how a house is built, or with how a human act is performed. An essentially or formally practical science, then, considers operables in a practical manner, that is, it is a science whose object is not the contemplation of operables, but the knowledge of how they can be performed, or of how they can be attained. Example:

---

(1) NAZARIUS, in I, q. 14, a. 16.— CAJETANUS, supra eumdem articulum.

a man who considers how he can attain God, Who is the ultimate end, has an essentially practical knowledge or science of God, for he considers God as an operable, i.e., an object of his operation, and, moreover, considers Him in a practical manner.

A *completely*, i.e., *perfectly, practical science* is a science which is practical not only as regards its matter and its manner of dealing with this matter, but also as regards the end of the possessor of this knowledge; v.g., the science of a man who considers how to build a house, with a view to building a house.

This division of practical science may be presented in schematic outline as follows:

Science
- a) *radically practical:* practical in its matter, in as much as it deals with operables, v. g., with things which are objects of operation, in a speculative manner;
- b) *essentially practical:* practical in its matter and in its manner of dealing with this matter;
- c) *completely practical:* practical not only in its matter and its manner of dealing with this matter, but also in the end of its possessor.

3° Some modern scholastic philosophers, as Gredt (¹), hold that Moral Philosophy is a speculative science, but concede that it may be regarded as practical in a wide sense, in as much as it is concerned with an operable object. They maintain that it is speculative, because it is not *operably* concerned with its object.

Others, as Maritain (²) and Macquart (³), teach that Moral Philosophy is a speculativo-practical science, for, in their opinion, it is practical as regards its object, but speculative as regards its manner of dealing with that object, i.e., it deals with operables as removed from operation.

4° Moral Philosophy, we maintain, is an essentially or formally practical science.

---

(1) *Elementa Philosophiae Aristotelico-Thomisticae*, n. 103 (edit. 5a).
(2) *Les degrés du Savoir*, pp. 618-621, et pp. 874-896, Desclée de Brouwer et Cie, 1932 (edit. 1a).
(3) *Elementa Philosophiae*, t. I, pp. 200 et 201, Blot, 1937.

Moral Philosophy considers operables, i.e., human acts, in the universal, as the foregoing authors point out; but every science as such considers its object in the universal. Nevertheless, Moral Philosophy not only deals with operables, i.e., with human acts, but it investigates how human acts, though only in the universal, ought to be regulated. Moral Philosophy, therefore, is practical from the point of view of its matter, and also from the point of view of the manner in which it deals with its matter. Hence it is an essentially or formally practical science.

818. Method of Moral Philosophy. — 1° Moral Philosophy, from the point of view of its manner of dealing with things, is a practical science. Hence the method it uses in the study of things differs from that employed by speculative sciences (n. 183).

The end of a speculative science is the manifestation of truth. Hence a speculative science abstracts from existence, and resolves composite realties into simple principles. Therefore the method of a speculative science is *resolutory*, i.e., the method of resolution.

The end of a practical science is something to be done, i.e., an operation, an operable object to be attained or produced. Hence a practical science does not abstract from existence, but rather is concerned with the existence of its object. Therefore the method of a practical science, and, in particular, of Moral Philosophy, is *composite*, i.e., the method of composition, in as much as a practical science is concerned not with simple and universal principles for their own sake, but with their application for the regulation of operations.

2° The kind of demonstration proper to Moral Philosophy is not demonstration *by proper cause* (*demonstratio propter quid*), but rather demonstration *of the mere existence of truth* (*demonstratio quia*) and *a posteriori* ([1]).

For, in the demonstration *by proper cause*, the properties of a thing are deduced from its essence. But Moral Philosophy

---
(1) *In Ethic.*, l. I, l. 4, nn. 51-52.

is not concerned with the knowledge of the quiddity of things, but rather with showing how human acts should be regulated.

3° Since the kind of demonstration proper to Moral Philosophy is demonstration *of the mere existence of truth*, we are not concerned in Moral Philosophy with that absolute certitude found in the speculative sciences, whose conclusions are deduced by means of the demonstration *by proper cause*.

Absolute certitude is impossible of attainment in Moral Philosophy, because Moral Philosophy applies its principles to human acts, which, in the concrete, are very variable and contingent ([1]).

4° Moral Philosophy, though based on universal principles, must, in so far as possible, show the application of these principles to things in their existence. This is necessary in every practical science ([2]).

5° Moral Philosophy is not a perfect science, for it is not based on demonstration *by proper cause*, i.e., its object is not properly scientific, and therefore, in the order of science, it is not an intellectual virtue, but rather an imperfect habit (n. 180).

6° The end of Moral Philosophy is not solely knowledge, but the regulation of human acts. Hence, in our study of it, we should aim at acquiring not mere knowledge, but knowledge destined for virtuous operation.

819. Moral Philosophy and speculative philosophy.—

1° Is Moral Philosophy subalternate to speculative philosophy, and, in particular, to Philosophy of Nature?

2° Some modern scholastic philosophers ([3]) affirm that Moral Philosophy is subalternate to the part of special Philosophy of Nature which deals with the soul, because Moral Philosophy, they claim, adds the accidental differentia of morality to the object (partial) of Philosophy of Nature, i.e,. to human acts.

---

(1) *Ibid.*, l. I, l. 3, n. 35 (Pirotta).
(2) *In Politic.*, l. I, Prologus, sub fine.
(3) GREDT, *op. cit.*, t. II, n. 879.

3° Since Moral Philosophy is essentially a practical science, it is not, we maintain, subalternate to speculative philosophy: Moral Philosophy is possessed of its own self-evident principles, which it does not borrow from speculative science (1).

Indeed, speculative principles and practical principles, in sciences of the natural order, are in opposition to each other (n. 183), and therefore no practical science derives from speculative principles.

4° Nevertheless, since the practical is rooted in the speculative, certain speculative notions are necessary in a treatise on Moral Philosophy; v.g., the moral philosopher must have a knowledge of the nature of the ultimate end, of justice, etc. Moral Philosophy does not seek these notions for their own sake, but only in so far as they are requisites of practical knowledge.

Hence Moral Philosophy, though not subalternate to speculative philosophy, is *subordinate* to it in as much as the practical *is regulated by* the speculative, in which it is radicated.

820. Moral Philosophy and Sacred Theology.—
1° Sacred Theology is a science based on the principles of faith, and, in its moral part, deals with human acts as destined for a supernatural end, i.e., for the intuitive vision of God.

Moral Philosophy is based on the principles of natural reason, and therefore is concerned with human acts as directed to a natural end.

2° Man, because of his elevation to the supernatural order, should direct all his acts to a supernatural end.

Some modern scholastic philosophers, as Deman (2) and Ramirez (3), hold that, in consideration of man's state of elevation, Moral Philosophy is not specifically distinct as a science from Moral Theology.

---
(1) *De Veritate*, q. 16, a. 1.— I, q. 79, a. 12.
(2) *Revue des Sciences philosophiques et théologiques*, 1934, pp. 258-280.
(3) *Bulletin thomiste*, avril-juin, 1935.

Others, as Maritain (¹) and Macquart (²), teach that Moral Philosophy as a science is specifically distinct from Moral Theology, provided that it is considered as subalternate to Theology.

3° Moral Theology and Moral Philosophy are specifically distinct sciences, as is evident from the principles on which they are based. For Moral Theology is founded on the principles of divine faith, whereas Moral Philosophy is founded on the principles of natural reason (³).

4° There is no true subalternation of Moral Philosophy to Sacred Theology, because Moral Philosophy does not borrow its principles from Sacred Theology.

There is, however, an improper mode of subalternation of Moral Philosophy to Sacred Theology, in as much as the end considered by Moral Philosophy is subordinate to the end considered by Sacred Theology (n. 193). For, because of man's elevation to the supernatural order, all human acts are directed to their supernatural end as their ultimate end.

Therefore we may conclude that Moral Philosophy, even though it is a practical science, is not, as a science, sufficient for the regulation of human acts. For man must direct his acts, according to the principles of faith, to their supernatural end.

821. Division of Moral Philosophy.—1° Moral Philosophy, as a practical science, is specified by its end, which is the principle of human acts and the formal object *quo* of moral science, i.e., of the science of human operations.

2° Man is a social animal, and, in the natural order, is a part, i.e., a member, of two societies: domestic society and civil or political society.

---
(1) *Science et Sagesse*, pp. 228-339, (Labergerie, Paris, 1935).
(2) *Elementa Philosophiae*, t. I, p. 243 (Blot).
(3) Ad moralem philosophiam proprie et directe spectat de jure et justitia quaestiones definire quatenus homo ordinatur ad convictum politicum et finem naturalem. Ad sacram theologiam maxime pertinet de jure perscrutari usque ad minima respectu boni spiritualis et finis supernaturalis. Ad hunc itaque modum sacra Theologia, cum sit practica, saltem eminenter considerat omnia quae philosophus moralis multo altius et divinius quam ille.— BANNEZ, *De Jure et Justitia*, Prooemium.

3° Society is a whole of which man is a part.

But a whole can be *absolutely one*, i.e., can have *absolute unity*, or it can have *relative unity*, i.e., unity of order, as, for example, the order of an army.

In a whole which has absolute unity, the operation of the whole and of the part is one and the same; v.g., vision, which is the operation of the sense of sight, is the operation of a man. Therefore, when a whole has absolute unity, the science of the whole and of the part is one and the same. Thus Philosophy of Nature, which deals with man, deals also with the human intellect and will.

In a whole which has only unity of order, the part can have operation which is not the operation of the whole, as a soldier in an army has operation which is not the operation of the whole army. Moreover, a whole can have operation which is not proper to any of the parts, but to the whole, as, for example, the conflict of an army as a whole. Therefore, when a whole has only unity of order, the science of the whole and of the part is not one and the same.

4° Society, which is a multitude characterized by order, is a whole which has not *absolute unity*, but only *unity of order*. Therefore the science which deals with the operations of a single man is not the same as the science which deals with the operations of the whole of society.

Hence Moral Philosophy is divided into three parts.

The first part deals with the operations of individual man as directed to their end, and is called *Ethics* or *Monastics*.

The second part treats of the operations of the domestic multitude, i.e., of the family, and is called *Economics* or *Moral of the family*.

The third part is concerned with the operations of the civil multitude, i.e., of civil society, and is called *Politics* [1] or *Moral of civil society*.

---

(1) *In Ethic.*, l. I, l. 1, a. 6 (Pirotta).

Monastics, Economics, and Politics are not material parts of one and the same science, but are essentially distinct practical sciences, for the end of individual man, the end of domestic society, and the end of civil society are specifically distinct from each other.

Hence Moral Philosophy is divided into the following distinct parts:

Moral Philosophy
- Ethics or Monastics: Moral of individual man.
- Economics: Moral of domestic society.
- Politics: Moral of civil or political society.

822. Politics is wisdom in the order of the practical sciences.— 1° A science is wisdom when it considers things according to their first principles. But the ends of the practical sciences are their principles. Therefore the science which considers human acts in relation to their ultimate end is wisdom in the order of the practical sciences. But Politics deals with human acts as related to their ultimate end, i.e., to happiness.

Since it is only in civil or political society that man can attain natural happiness, happiness is the end with which Politics is properly concerned. Hence, just as Metaphysics is wisdom in the order of the speculative sciences, so Politics is wisdom in the order of the practical sciences ([1]).

2° Certain scholastics, as Liberatore and Zigliara, distinguish between two aspects of human acts. They maintain that a human act may be considered *a*) either in itself, i.e., in relation to its ultimate end, *b*) or in its relation to persons other than its author.

Because of these two aspects of human acts, they divide Moral Philosophy into two parts:

a) *Ethics*, whose object is human acts in themselves, i.e., in relation to their ultimate end;

b) *Natural Law* (*Jus Naturale*), whose object is the moral relations between different persons, i.e., human acts as just or unjust.

---

(1) *In Politic.* Prooemium, circa finem.

This division is inadmissible because there is no opposition between the parts, and especially because it destroys the nature of political science, which is concerned with human acts in relation to their natural end.

3° Certain other philosophers, as Kant, hold that Natural Law (*Jus Naturale*) is not only distinct from Ethics but independent of it, and consequently is not concerned with morality. This opinion is, of course, untenable, because Politics, which is concerned with civil society, deals with the mutual relations of men (Natural Law), and is at the same time the principal part of Moral Philosophy, for it deals with human acts in relation to their ultimate natural end.

POINTS FOR REVIEW

1. With what kind of order is each of the following concerned: real speculative philosophy, liberal arts, mechanical arts, Moral Philosophy?

2. Define Moral Philosophy, state its formal object *quo*, and explain why it is a formally practical science.

3. Define: radically practical science, formally practical science, and completely practical science.

4. Describe the method employed by Moral Philosophy.

5. Explain why Moral Philosophy is not subalternate, and whether it is subordinate, to speculative philosophy.

6. Are Moral Philosophy and Moral Theology specifically distinct sciences? Explain.

7. Is Moral Philosophy subalternate to Moral Theology? Explain.

8. Name the parts of Moral Philosophy, and explain why these parts are specifically distinct sciences.

9. Explain why Politics is wisdom in the order of the practical sciences.

MONASTICS

INTRODUCTION

823. Definition of Monastics.— Monastics, also called Ethics ([1]), etymologically signifies the science of individual man.

Monastics is defined: *the practical science which deals with the human acts of individual man in relation to their end.*

Monastics is distinct from Economics, which deals with the operations of domestic society, and from Politics, which is concerned with the operations of civil or political society.

Monastics, Economics, and Politics are, as we have already pointed out, specifically, i.e., essentially, distinct sciences.

824. Division of Monastics.— Monastics is formally only one science, which deals with the operations of individual man. And, as a practical science, it deals with human operations in relation to their end. The ultimate end to which human operations are directed is happiness. But, since happiness is the common good, the study of it belongs to Politics, because happiness is the end proper to the civil multitude, i.e., to civil society. There are two reasons, however, why we should deal with it at the beginning of Monastics:

first, the ultimate end of all human acts, even of the acts of individual man, is happiness;

secondly, Monastics is related to Politics, which is the principal part of Moral Philosophy and wisdom in the order of the practical sciences, and therefore should deal with the first elements of political science ([2]).

When we have completed our study of the ultimate end of human life, we shall discuss human acts, by which man

---

(1) *In Ethic.*, l. I, l. 1, nn. 6 and 7 (Pirotta).
(2) *In Ethic.*, l. I, l. 2, n. 31 (Pirotta).

attains this ultimate end. Human acts may be considered in their psychological aspect and in their moral aspect. After we have studied human acts under their moral aspect, we shall discuss the principles of moral acts, which are law and the virtues.

Hence Monastics will contain four books.

Book   I: Ultimate end of human acts.

Book II: Human acts in their psychological aspect.

Book III: Human acts in their moral aspect.

Book IV: Principles of moral acts.

BOOK I

Ultimate end of human acts

Prologue.— There are two questions in regard to the ultimate end of human acts with which we are at present concerned: first, the question of whether man acts for an ultimate end; secondly, the question of man's ultimate end in particular, i.e., of happiness. Hence there will be two chapters in this book.

Chapter I: Man's ultimate end in general.

Chapter II: Happiness.

CHAPTER I

MAN'S ULTIMATE END IN GENERAL

Prologue.— In this chapter, we shall show first that every human act is directed to an end; secondly, that every human act is directed to an ultimate end. Hence there will be two articles in this chapter.

End of human acts
- Statement of the question
- Adversaries
- Thesis: Man, in all his human acts, acts for an end in a manner proper to man

Ultimate end
- Statement of the question
- Thesis: Man, in all his human acts, acts for an ultimate end, at least virtually
- There really is an ultimate end of human life
- The ultimate end is the same for all men
- No man can act for more than one ultimate end
- Difficulties

ARTICLE I

END OF HUMAN ACTS

825. Statement of the question.— 1° An end is that towards which an appetite tends, i.e., *that for which an agent operates*.

An end and a good are materially the same, for an appetite is moved or attracted only by a good, true or apparent; an end and a good, however, are formally different, for a thing is a good as the object of the appetite, and an end as it moves the appetite.

2° A distinction must be made between acts of man and human acts.

Acts of man are any acts whatsoever which proceed from man.

Human acts are acts which proceed from man as man, i.e., in as much as he differs from irrational creatures, not only as regards nature but also as regards mode of operation.

Since man differs from irrational creatures as regards mode of operation, in as much as he acts freely, human acts are defined: *acts which proceed from the deliberate will of man*. Thus indeliberate acts of the intellect and will, though in nature proper to man, are not human acts, but acts of man, because such acts, in mode of operation, are not proper to man; but man's acts of eating, drinking, and walking, though in nature common to man and animals, are human acts when they proceed from man's deliberate will.

3° In the thesis, we state that man, in all his human acts, acts for an end *in a manner proper to man*, because man, as a rational agent, is free and of his own accord moves to an end, whereas irrational agents are moved by nature towards their end. Moreover, since man acts for an end in a manner proper to man, his acts possess a special kind of goodness, namely, morality, i.e., moral goodness.

826. Adversaries.— The adversaries of this doctrine are all philosophers, as Spinoza, Buffon, Comte, Bain, Taine, Huxley, Lamarck, Buchner, etc., who hold that the concept of finality originates in the prejudices of the wise and the ignorance of the illiterate.

827. Statement of the thesis.

  THESIS.— MAN, IN ALL HIS HUMAN ACTS, ACTS FOR AN END IN A MANNER PROPER TO MAN.

First part.— *Man, in all his human acts, acts for an end.* All acts which proceed from the deliberate will are for an end. But all human acts are acts which proceed from the deliberate will. Therefore all human acts are for an end, i.e., man, in all his human acts, acts for an end.

Major.— Every act which proceeds from a power is related to the object of the power, i.e., an action which proceeds from a power can be directed, i.e., tend, only to the formal object by which the power is specified; thus vision is concerned only with something visible, intellection only with being. But the object of the will is an end and a good. Therefore.

Second part.— *Man acts for an end in a manner proper to man.*— An agent which has dominion over its acts in virtue of free will acts for an end in a manner proper to man. But man, in virtue of free will, has dominion over his acts. Therefore man acts for an end in a manner proper to man.

Major.— An agent which, in virtue of free will, has dominion over its acts not only moves itself towards its object which is an end, but properly and formally acts for an end, in as much as it chooses and determines an end for itself, i.e., is active in relation to the end.

Minor.— Man, as a being endowed with reason, not only has knowledge of the object which is an end, but has knowledge of it as an end, in as much as he knows and evaluates the worth of the object which is the end, and also the proportion between the end and the act required for its attainment.

ARTICLE II

ULTIMATE END

828. Statement of the question.— 1° An ultimate end is an end to which all other ends are subordinated, and which itself is not subordinated to any other end.

An ultimate end is absolutely ultimate, if it is such in all orders; and it is relatively ultimate, if it is such in a particular order, as health in relation to medicine.

The absolutely ultimate end, then, is the good which can completely and ultimately perfect, i.e., satisfy, the appetite. It is with this end that we are concerned at present.

The absolutely ultimate end that can be formally and electively desired is happiness, of which only an agent endowed with an intellect is capable.

2° The ultimate end of an agent endowed with an intellect has a twofold aspect: *a)* a *formal aspect*, under which all things are desired, and which is good in general and in the abstract; for an appetite which follows an intellect desires a thing only because and in as much as it is a participation of this general aspect of good; *b)* a *material aspect*, which is *the thing desired*, i.e., the good which moves the appetite and is its end.

In the thesis, we are concerned with the ultimate end under its material aspect, i.e., as the thing desired.

3° The ultimate end, under the aspect of the thing desired, may be the *true* ultimate end, i.e., that good which really can completely and perfectly satisfy the appetite; or it may be an *apparent* ultimate end, i.e., something which in reality is not the ultimate end, but which is considered as the ultimate end, i.e., which a person regards as the term of all his desires.

4° In acting for an end, an agent necessarily has the intention of attaining that end. Now there are four ways in which an end may be intended: actually, virtually, habi-_ tually (¹), and interpretatively.

1) *Actual intention* is an intention by which an agent tends to an end as a result of an actual and express act of the will.

There are three elements in actual intention:

a) actual knowledge of the end;

b) actual willing of the end;

c) choice of means and express direction of them to the end.

2) *Virtual intention* is of two kinds: explicit virtual intention and implicit virtual intention.

Explicit virtual intention is an intention by which an agent, in virtue of an intention formed in the past and not retracted, acts and chooses means for an end, without actually thinking of the end; v.g., a doctor gathers herbs for medicine as a result of an intention formed earlier, but of which he does not think while he is gathering them; a person takes a resolution to take daily walks for his health, and takes them without giving any thought to the end he had earlier proposed to himself.

There are three elements in explicit virtual intention:

a) absence of actual consideration of the end;

b) actual willing of the end in the past;

c) real influence of previous volition on present acts which includes real direction of means to the end.

Implicit virtual intention is an intention by which an agent does something which, as an imperfect good, of its nature is destined for and tends to a more perfect good as to an end, of which he may or may not have knowledge, unless perchance he, violently and contrary to the nature of his operation, directs his operation to some other end; v.g., an inferior artificer performing some work according to the rules of his inferior art, but on the orders of a superior artificer, virtually

---

(1) CAJETANUS, in II-II, q. 24, a. 10, n. IV.

intends the end of this supérior artificer, even though he may have no knowledge of this end.

3) *Habitual intention* is an intention which connotes coexistence with an act of a habit which exercises no actual or virtual influence on the act; v.g., a person in the state of grace who recites prayers in his sleep does not act in virtue of the habit of charity which he possesses. Hence there is this difference between habitual intention and explicit virtual intention: in the case of the latter, the agent acts in virtue of a previous intention, whereas, in the case of the former, he possesses during his action a habit which resulted from a former intention, but which has no influence on his present act.

4) Interpretative *intention* is an intention which does not exist and never did exist, but which presumably would exist if the agent were to think of the end, or if certain circumstances were to present themselves; v.g., a child born of Christian parents is said to have an interpretative desire for Baptism, even before he attains the use of reason ([1]).

5° Since there is no real direction of means to an end in the case either of habitual intention or of interpretative intention, man, in all his human acts, acts for an ultimate end in as much as he acts with at least an implicit virtual intention of an ultimate end. Therefore the ultimate end to which all human acts are directed is either the end of the agent or the end of the work (cf. n. 700, 3°). For, in the case of implicit virtual intention, the act is directed to the end of the work rather than to an end actually intended by the agent.

829. Statement of the thesis.

THESIS.— MAN, IN ALL HIS HUMAN ACTS, ACTS FOR AN ULTIMATE END, AT LEAST VIRTUALLY.

First part.— *Man, in all his human acts, acts for an ultimate end.*— 1° An agent which acts for an end acts for an

---
([1]) JOANNES A. SANCTO THOMA, *Cursus Theol.*, t. V, pp. 109-113 (Vivès). — BILLUART, *Summa Sancti Thomae*, t. II, pp. 162-163 (Palmé).

ultimate end. But man, in all his human acts, acts for an end. Therefore man, in all his human acts, acts for an ultimate end.

Major.— The end for which an agent acts is either an end desired for its own sake and in view of which all other ends are desired; or it is an end which is sought in view of another end, and, in this case, is sought in view of the ultimate end, for, just as an infinite series of essentially subordinated efficient causes is impossible, so too is an infinite series of essentially subordinated ends impossible: intermediate ends move, i.e., attract, the appetite and exercise their causality only when dependent upon the ultimate end to which they tend.

The *minor* is evident from what has been already said.

2° An agent which acts either for a perfect good or for an imperfect good which tends to a perfect good acts for an ultimate end. But man, in all his human acts, acts for either a perfect good or for an imperfect good which tends to a perfect good. Therefore man, in all his human acts, acts for an ultimate end.

The *major* is self-evident, for an ultimate end is a perfect good.

Minor.— Since the object of the will is good, man, in all his human acts, acts either for a perfect good or for an imperfect good. But man cannot act for an imperfect good as such, for to do so would be to act for evil; rather he acts for an imperfect good which tends to a perfect good, in as much as he strives, in so far as possible, to attain the perfect good by means of an imperfect good. Therefore.

Second part.— *Man, in all his human acts, acts at least virtually for an ultimate end.*— An agent which really acts for an ultimate end acts at least virtually for this end, i.e., with at least a virtual intention of attaining this end. But man, in all his human acts, really acts for an ultimate end. Therefore man, in all his human acts, acts at least virtually for an ultimate end.

Major. — To truly act for an ultimate end is to be moved by this ultimate end. But, in the case of either habitual intention or interpretative intention, the end does not really move, i.e., exercises no influence on the act; in the case of actual intention, the end really does actually move, as is evident; in the case of virtual intention, the ultimate end truly moves either in virtue of a previous intention which has not been revoked, or in virtue of the essential connexion which obtains between the intermediate end and the ultimate end, i.e., between the imperfect good and the perfect good. Therefore.

The *minor* is evident from the proof of the first part of the thesis.

830. There really is an ultimate end of human life. —

1° *Preliminaries.* — *a)* The ultimate end of which we are speaking now is the ultimate end in the concrete, that is to say, that object which is capable of perfectly satisfying all human desires, and which every man can attain. *b)* This assertion is made in condemnation of the teaching of certain philosophers, as Kant, who hold that man's ultimate end consists in indefinite, i.e., unlimited, human progress, and of the teaching of others, as Schleiermacher, Wundt, and certain evolutionists of our day, who teach that it consists in the cultural progress of the human race. If man's ultimate end consists in indefinite progress, it is not possible of attainment by individual men.

2° *Proof.* — An end which is naturally desired really exists. But man naturally desires an ultimate end. Therefore man's ultimate end really exists, i.e., there really is an ultimate end of human life.

The *major* is evident from the principle of finality, for a natural desire for what is non-existent would be absurd and contradictory.

Minor. — Man, in all his human acts, necessarily acts for an ultimate end.

831. The ultimate end is the same for all men.—
To answer the question of whether the ultimate end is the same for all men, we must distinguish between the formal aspect of the ultimate end and its material aspect, i.e., that in which the formal aspect is realized.

The ultimate end, in its formal aspect, i.e., the act by which the ultimate end is attained, is the same for all men, because all men desire that their perfection be completely attained.

The ultimate end, in its material aspect, i.e., the good in which the formal aspect is realized, is the same for all men, namely, happiness. Nevertheless, all men are not in agreement as regards the good which really constitutes their happiness: some desire riches as their highest good, others desire bodily pleasure, others desire honor, etc.

832. No man can act for more than one ultimate end.
— 1° *Preliminaries.*— *a)* We are not concerned with good in general, i.e., with good in the abstract, which, as is evident, cannot be multiple, but with the good which, in the concrete, is the ultimate end.

b) We are not dealing with the ultimate end of the work, which is determined by nature, but with the ultimate end of the agent.

c) The ultimate end with which we are concerned is the total ultimate end, or, if you will, the formal constituent of the ultimate end in the concrete, not partial ultimate ends, i.e., different things in which the formal constituent of the ultimate end can be found. The pleasure-seeker, for example, can seek pleasure in many things. Pleasure is his total ultimate end, and the different things in which he finds pleasure are his partial ultimate ends.

d) When we say that no man can act for more than one ultimate end, we mean that man cannot act for more than one ultimate end at one and the same time.

e) An ultimate end may be desired either efficaciously and absolutely (simpliciter), or inefficaciously and relatively (secundum quid).

An ultimate end is desired efficaciously and absolutely, if the one desiring it turns completely to it.

An ultimate end is desired inefficaciously and relatively, if the one desiring it does not turn completely to it, but directs some determinate act of the will and operation to it; v.g., a person in the state of grace who commits a venial sin inefficaciously desires a created good as his ultimate end, because he remains turned to God in virtue of his habit of charity; similarly, a person in the state of mortal sin who performs a good act inefficaciously desires God as his ultimate end, because, in virtue of his habit of sin, he remains turned to created good as his ultimate end.

Therefore an ultimate end is efficaciously intended not in as much as the end moves the agent to act, but in as much as it subjects all acts and habits of the will to itself and removes any that are contrary to it; and it is inefficaciously intended in as much as it fails to subject all acts and habits of the will to itself and to remove any that are contrary to it.

2° *In the light of the foregoing remarks,* we may now set forth two propositions which contain the answer to the question of whether a man can act for more than one ultimate end.

First proposition.— *No man can at one and the same time act for two total ultimate ends which he efficaciously desires.*— No man can at one and the same time act for two ends which are wholly incompatible with each other. But two total ultimate ends which are efficaciously desired are wholly incompatible with each other. Therefore no man can at one and the same time act for two total ultimate ends which he efficaciously desires.

The *major* is evident from its terms.

Minor.— A total ultimate end which is efficaciously desired is a good which perfectly satisfies and dominates the will, and in view of which all other ends are desired, and therefore it does not admit of any other ultimate end.

Second proposition.— *A man can actually desire one ultimate end in an inefficacious and relative manner and at the same time remain habitually turned to another ultimate end.*— A man can actually desire one ultimate end in an inefficacious and relative manner and at the same time remain habitually turned to another ultimate end, if, disregarding the good which he generally desires in an efficacious and absolute manner as his ultimate end, he can, in a last practical judgment, judge that something else is a good for him. But a man, disregarding the good which he habitually desires in an efficacious and absolute manner, can, in a last practical judgment, judge that something else is a good for him. Therefore a man can actually desire one ultimate end in an inefficacious and relative manner and at the same time remain habitually turned to another ultimate end in an efficacious and absolute manner.

Major.— The appetite is dependent on knowledge.

The *minor* is proved from the imperfection of the human intellect. In the process of reasoning, the human intellect acquires knowledge of principles independently of knowledge of conclusions, and knowledge of ends independently of knowledge of means. Hence it can actually propose something as man's good, i.e., can, in a last practical judgment, judge something as a good, completely disregarding, because of the lack of sequence, what it habitually judges to be the absolute good, in as much as it does not reduce its last practical judgment to the ultimate end which, though only habitually intended, is desired in an absolute and efficacious manner.

NOTE.— The true ultimate end of a man in the state of grace who commits venial sin is God, to Whom he remains habitually turned. God, in this case, exercises a real influence, though only in a negative manner, on the act of the sinner, because the sinner is inordinately attached to the creature only on condition that he is not turned away from his true ultimate end. It is as the ultimate end of the agent, not as the ultimate end of the work, that God exercises this influence: the sinner would not commit venial sin, if he knew that it would turn him away from God, his true ultimate end.

833. Difficulties.— 1° A man who does not direct all his acts to God as to his ultimate end does not act for his ultimate end. But men do not direct all their acts to God as to their ultimate end. Therefore men do not act for their ultimate end.

Major.— Does not act for his real ultimate end, *I concede*; does not act for an end which he falsely proposes to himself as his ultimate end, *I deny*.

I concede the minor, and distinguish in the consequent.

2° But man sometimes does not act for an ultimate end.

Proof.— A man who desires an imperfect good does not act for an ultimate end. But men sometimes desire an imperfect good. Therefore men sometimes do not act for an ultimate end.

Major.— A man who desires an imperfect good as not tending, i.e., as not directed, to a perfect good, *I concede*; an imperfect good as tending to a perfect good, *I deny*.

Minor.— A man desires an imperfect good which is not directed to a perfect good, *I deny*; which is directed to a perfect good, *I concede*.

Man cannot desire an imperfect good as such, because to do so would be to desire evil, which, of course, is impossible.

3° A man who does not know the ultimate end does not act for the ultimate end. But often men do not know the ultimate end; v.g., when a man does not actually think of the ultimate end. Therefore often men do not act for the ultimate end.

Major.— A man who has no knowledge whatsoever of the ultimate end, *I concede*; who has no explicit and distinct knowledge, but has implicit and confused knowledge, *I deny*.

Minor.— Often men have no knowledge whatsoever of the ultimate end, *I deny*; often have no explicit and distinct knowledge, but only implicit and confused knowledge, *I concede*.

4° But a man who does not actually think of the ultimate end does not act for the ultimate end. Therefore the difficulty remains.

Proof.— An agent on whose action the ultimate end exercises no influence does not act for the ultimate end. But the ultimate end exercises no influence on the action of a man who does not actually think of the ultimate end. Therefore.

Major.— On whose action the ultimate end exercises no influence whatsoever, *I concede*; on whose action it exercises no actual influence, but does exercise a virtual influence, *I deny*.

Minor.— The ultimate end exercises no influence whatsoever, *I deny*; does not exercise an actual influence, but does exercise a virtual influence, *I concede*.

CHAPTER II

HAPPINESS

Prologue.— All men, the illiterate as well as the wise, admit that the ultimate end of human acts, i.e., the highest human good, is happiness. Moreover, all agree that happiness consists in good acts and a good life — *bene vivere et bene operari idem esse quod esse felicem* (¹).

Happiness is of two kinds: first, happiness which is proportionate to human nature, because natural powers are sufficient for its attainment; secondly, happiness whose attainment is beyond man's natural powers and which is promised to man solely as a gift of God.

It is with the study of the first kind of happiness, called the natural and imperfect happiness of this life, that the philosopher is concerned. The study of the second kind of happiness, namely, supernatural and perfect beatitude, is the concern of the theologian.

First, we shall discuss natural happiness; secondly, we shall deal with supernatural beatitude, even though the study of it does not properly belong to the philosopher.

Hence there will be two articles in this chapter.

Natural happiness
- Statement of the question
- Opinions of adversaries
- Thesis: Natural happiness consists in virtuous operation proper to man in a perfect life
- Delight is found in happiness
- Speculative happiness, active happiness
- Goods of the body and the society of friends are quasi-instrumental requisites of natural happiness
- Natural happiness and divine good
- God's glory

---

(1) *In Ethic.*, l. I, l. 4, n. 45 (Pirotta).

Perfect beatitude { Objective beatitude
Corollary
Difficulties
Formal beatitude
Corollary
Difficulties

ARTICLE I

NATURAL HAPPINESS

834. Statement of the question.— 1° There is no one who denies that happiness is the ultimate end of all human acts.

The ultimate end, i.e., happiness, is characterized by two conditions: it must be *a)* a perfect good; *b)* a self-sufficient good, i.e., a good sufficient of itself to completely satisfy all human desires.

2° Happiness must be a perfect good because it is the ultimate term of man's natural desires. The ultimate end of man's natural desires is not chosen or sought for the sake of another, but for its own sake. Therefore it must be a good which perfectly satisfies man's natural desires, i.e., it must be a perfect human good.

3° Since happiness is the ultimate term of man's natural desires, it must be an integral good, because nature is never deficient in necessities. Therefore happiness is self-sufficient: for a self-sufficient good must be an integral good, a good that admits of no deficiency, a perfect good.

4° Natural happiness is a perfect and self-sufficient good, but not in the sense that it is an infinite good, i.e., a good whose goodness cannot be increased by the addition of another good. Natural happiness is human happiness. But human happiness does not embrace every good possible to man, but comprises only those goods necessary for him. Hence happiness is said to be self-sufficient not because it is an infinite good, as, for example, God, but because it is sufficient to satisfy all man's necessities.

Such happiness satisfies man's natural desires, because

human desires which are ruled by reason are not concerned with goods which, *though possible*, are not necessary.

5° Man of his very nature is a civil or social animal. Therefore the *self-sufficient good* which constitutes his happiness is not a good which is sufficient solely for one man living a solitary life, but rather a good sufficient for himself, his parents, his children, his wife, his friends, and his fellowmen. Man, as a social animal, can attain the complete satisfaction of his desires not in providing for himself alone, but in being able to provide also for others.

6° There are two reasons why happiness is a common good.

a) Man can attain happiness only by common means and as a member of society. For, to attain happiness, a man needs the help of others: he needs others who will act in the capacity of servants, counsellors, and teachers.

b) Man naturally desires happiness not only for himself, but also for others, i.e., for those committed to his care and for his fellowmen.

7° Happiness, as defined by Aristotle, *is the virtuous operation proper to man in a perfect life.*

a) *Operation*, i.e., second act of the operative faculties.

b) *Virtuous operation:* act whose principle is either an intellectual virtue, as wisdom, or a moral virtue, as justice, temperance, etc.

c) *Operation proper to man*, that is to say, either the operation of reason, as the act of reasoning and intellection, or operation governed by reason, as the act of willing what is just.

d) *In a perfect life*, i.e., throughout the whole of man's life, in so far as this is possible in man's present state of life. In other words, the virtuous operation proper to man which constitutes man's natural happiness is characterized by the most perfect continuity possible in this life.

835. Opinions of adversaries. — The opinions of philosophers on happiness are almost innumerable, and some of them are wholly absurd. Hence it will be sufficient for us to examine only the principal opinions on the subject.

1° Some hold that happiness is found in riches, because there are no temporal goods which cannot be obtained by riches.

This opinion is false, of course, because riches are only a means to an end, and therefore not man's ultimate end, i.e., happiness (¹).

2° Others hold that happiness consists in pleasure, i.e., in the delight of the senses. This opinion is supported not only by unenlightened voluptuaries, but even by some men eminent for their superior knowledge and integrity of life. The Epicureans, indeed, who believed that pleasure is the highest good, carefully cultivated virtues which would serve their pleasure; or, in other words, they cultivated virtues so that their vices would not be obstacles to their pleasure (²).

Happiness cannot consist in pleasure, for happiness is a good proper to man, whereas pleasure, i.e., delight of the senses, is common to man and irrational animals.

3° Others teach that happiness consists in power. But this is impossible for two reasons:

a) power is a principle, whereas happiness is an ultimate end;

b) power has relation to good and evil, i.e., may serve as a means to good and evil, whereas happiness is man's proper and perfect good (³).

4° Certain others maintain that happiness consists either in earthly fame or glory, or in honor.

---

(1) *In Ethic.*, l. I, l. 5, n. 70.
(2) *Ibidem*, n. 57.
(3) I-II, q. 2, a. 4, c.

Fame, i.e., glory, consists in a person's being greatly renowned and praised because of some perfection which he possesses.

Honor is a sign or attestation given to a person on account of some excellence in him.

Fame and honor cannot constitute happiness, because happiness is man's perfect good, i.e., the good which constitutes man as perfect, whereas fame and honor presuppose a man's excellence or perfection.

5° The Pessimists, as Schopenhauer and Edward von Hartmann, teach that happiness consists in ransom from the miseries of life by the suppression of existence.

The suppression of existence cannot be a condition of happiness, for happiness is the ultimate end of man's natural desires, whereas the suppression of existence is directly opposed to man's natural desires.

836. Statement of the thesis.

THESIS.— NATURAL HAPPINESS CONSISTS IN VIRTUOUS OPERATION PROPER TO MAN IN A PERFECT LIFE.

First part.— *Natural happiness consists in operation proper to man.*— Man's final good is his proper operation. But natural happiness is man's final good. Therefore natural happiness consists in operation proper to man.

Major.— The final good of a thing which has operation proper to it is this operation: for a final good is an ultimate perfection, and the ultimate perfection of a thing is its proper operation, because form is first perfection, and operation is second perfection. But man has proper operation, which is the operation of reason, or operation according to reason: man is a *rational animal*. Therefore man's final good is his proper operation.

Minor.— Happiness is the ultimate term of man's natural desires, and therefore is man's final good, i.e., his ultimate perfection.

Second part.— *Natural happiness consists in virtuous operation proper to man.*— Operation proper to man which is good and most perfect is virtuous operation. But natural happiness consists in operation proper to man which is good and most perfect. Therefore man's natural happiness consists in virtuous operation.

Major.— Good and most perfect operation of any agent is virtuous operation; v.g., a horse's virtue consists in his being a good runner. Hence operation proper to man which is good and most perfect is virtuous operation.

Minor.— Happiness is man's ultimate perfection. Therefore it does not consist in any kind of operation proper to man, but in operation proper to man which is good and most perfect.

Third part.— *Man's natural happiness is realized in a perfect life.*— Natural happiness is realized in a perfect life, in as much as it necessarily has the most perfect continuity and permanence possible in this life. But man's natural happiness necessarily has the most perfect continuity and permanence possible in this life. Therefore man's natural happiness is realized in a perfect life.

The *major* is evident: happiness is realized in a perfect life, in as much as it is enjoyed as much as this is possible in the present life, throughout the whole of a man's life.

Minor.— It is as the ultimate perfection of man's natural desires that happiness is their ultimate term. But man naturally desires his ultimate perfection as continuous and permanent: for, since man's appetite follows his intellect, the scope of human desires is proportionate to man's intellective knowledge, according to which man apprehends existence and happy life not as being realized in the present moment only, but conceives it in an absolute and simple manner, i.e., as having the most perfect continuity and permanence possible in this life. Therefore natural happiness necessarily has the most perfect continuity and permanence possible in this life.

837. Delight is found in happiness.— 1° Delight is the perceived complacency of the appetitive power in a good proper to it (¹), or the repose of the appetite, tending to an end, on account of the presence of the end (²).

Since delight is a perceived repose or complacency, it cannot exist in beings which have no knowledge.

2° Delight is found in both the sensitive and intellective appetite.

3° Certain philosophers, as the Epicureans, held that pleasure, i.e., the delight of the senses, was required for happiness, and they tried to live virtuously with a view to the delight of the senses.

In reality, delight is found in a virtuous life, the kind of life in which happiness consists. Moreover, the delight found in virtuous operation, i.e., in the performance of acts of virtue, is superior to all other kinds of delight.

4° We may now set forth the true teaching on this matter in two propositions.

a) Happiness, which consists in the performance of virtuous acts, has delight in itself.— Delight is the complacency of the appetite on account of the presence of a good loved by it, i.e., to which it is inclined. But a happy man, who is a virtuous man, loves virtuous operation, because he is inclined to it. Therefore a happy man finds delight in virtuous operation; or, in other words, happiness, which consists in the performance of virtuous act, has delight in itself (³).

b) Delight found in the performance of virtuous acts is superior to all other kinds of delight.— Delight which is in conformity with nature is superior to all other kinds of delight. But

---

(1) I-II, q. 11, a. 1, ad 3.
(2) I-II, q. 31, a. 1, ad 2.
(3) *In Ethic.*, l. I, l. 13, n. 155.

delight found in the performance of virtuous acts is in conformity with nature. Therefore delight found in the performance of virtuous acts is superior to all other kinds of delight.

Major.— Delight which is in conformity with nature is common to all men, whereas other kinds of delight are enjoyed only by certain men whose desires are depraved, i.e., not in conformity with man's nature.

Minor.— Delight found in the performance of acts of virtue is the kind of delight which is in most perfect conformity with the nature of man as endowed with reason. But reason is a perfection of human nature: man is a rational animal. Therefore delight found in the performance of acts of virtue is in conformity with nature (¹).

838. Speculative happiness, active happiness. — 1° Happiness consists in the performance of acts of virtue. But virtue may be intellectual or moral. Therefore there are two kinds of happiness; first, happiness which consists in acts of intellectual virtue; secondly, happiness which consists in acts of moral virtue.

2° Speculative happiness is ascribed to wisdom, because an act of wisdom is the most perfect act of the intellect, i.e., the act by which the intellect attains its most perfect object, namely, the most intelligible things, and especially God.

Hence speculative happiness may be defined: *the most perfect act of the intellect;* or, *the act of man's noblest faculty,* i.e., of the intellect, *as concerned with its noblest object,* which is God.

Active happiness is ascribed to prudence, because prudence regulates all the other moral virtues, viz., justice, temperance, fortitude, etc.

Hence active happiness may be defined: *happiness which consists in acts of the moral virtues* (²).

---

(1) *Ibidem,* n. 156.
(2) *In Ethic.,* l. X, l. 12, n. 2111.

3° Speculative happiness is man's primary or chief happiness, because it consists in acts of the faculty of reason, which is the faculty proper to man; active happiness is a secondary kind of human happiness, because it consists in acts of the appetite as directed and regulated by reason ([1]).

839. Goods of the body and the society of friends are quasi-instrumental requisites of natural happiness.— 1° Goods of the body comprise the following:

a) good health of the body, which is said to exist in as much as it makes the body adaptive to the service of the soul while the soul perform acts of the intellectual and moral virtues;

b) material goods which are useful to man; v.g., food and clothing.

2° Goods of the body and the society of friends are quasi-instrumental requisites of natural happiness, not in as much as they are essential constituents of happiness, but in as much as they are required as means for its attainment.

3° Man requires bodily health for acts of the intellectual and moral virtues, because the sensitive powers, which are used by man in speculation, i.e., in acts of the intellectual virtues, and in acts of the moral virtues, are weakened by sickness.

Similarly, for the attainment of happiness, man requires all the necessities of human life, as food, clothing, servants, money, etc.

Material or external goods are not so necessary for speculative happiness, as they are for active happiness.

Man requires many things for acts of the moral virtues, which constitute active happiness; and, moreover, the number of things he requires is proportionate to the number and quality of his virtuous acts; v. g., a generous person needs money, in order to practice liberality, just as a just person needs it to pay his debts.

---

(1) *In Ethic.*, l. 1, l. 10, n. 126, et ll. X-XII.

Acts of wisdom, i.e., of the intellectual virtues, which constitute speculative happiness, do not of themselves require material goods. The necessities of life are sufficient for a man who lives an exclusively contemplative life, unless he lives with others whom he must sometimes help, i.e., unless the man of contemplation performs acts of the moral virtues by helping others. In this case, of course, he requires greater material goods (1).

4° It must be observed that great riches are not required for the enjoyment of human happiness.

Two reasons may be offered in proof of this.

a) First, a happy man is a man who is self-sufficient, i.e., who can provide for his own needs. But no man requires great riches to provide for his own needs, for nature has need of only a few things.

Moreover, an abundance of wealth lessens a man's self-sufficiency, for a man of great riches requires the help of others to look after and to guard his wealth.

b) Secondly, rectitude of judgment of both speculative and practical reason and also external acts of virtue are possible without an abundance of wealth (2).

5° The society of friends is a requisite of happiness.

First, the wise man, i.e., the man who enjoys speculative happiness, has need of others not only to provide him with the necessities of life but also to cooperate with him in the contemplation of truth, so that he may arrive at a more perfect contemplation, i.e., a more perfect understanding of truth (3).

Secondly, the prudent man, i.e., the man who enjoys active happiness, has need of the society of friends for the practice of the moral virtues, even though he is sufficiently supplied with life's necessities. Justice, for example, which is one of the moral virtues, is exercised towards others. Moreover, in order to perform works of justice, temperance, fortitude,

---

(1) *In Ethic.*, l. X, l. 12, nn. 2117-2120.
(2) *In Ethic.*, l. X, l. 13, n. 2128.
(3) *In Ethic.*, l. X, l. 10, n. 2096.

and the other moral virtues, a man often requires the assistance of others (¹).

840. Natural happiness and divine good.— 1° Natural happiness is man's ultimate perfection of the natural order, and therefore consists in man's perfect operation, i.e., in acts of virtue.

But yet man's ultimate natural perfection, i.e., man's highest natural good, is not the absolutely greatest good, for, if it were, man himself would be the most perfect good. But, in addition to man and human good, there exists divine good, i.e., God Himself, Who is the most perfect good, a good which, from the point of view of the natural order, is extrinsic to man and the universe.

Since an inferior good is related to a superior good as the imperfect to the perfect, it follows that the absolutely ultimate end of natural happiness, even though considered only in the natural order, is God.

Hence happiness is the ultimate end of man's natural desires, for it is man's most perfect good, i.e., the greatest of all goods of the natural order.

But God is the absolutely ultimate end, because He, as the ultimate end of the whole universe, is, even from the point of view of the natural order, the ultimate end of happiness, which is man's highest good.

2° In addition to natural happiness, there exists supernatural happiness, by which God is given to man as the object of his happiness. This happiness, which is eternal life, cannot be attained by man by his natural powers, but is bestowed upon him as the gift of divine munificence (²).

Hence natural happiness not only is directed, from the point of view of the natural order, to God naturally known, as to the absolutely ultimate end, but, since natural happiness is a good of a lower order than supernatural happiness, it is

---
(1) *Ibid.*, n. 2094.
(2) *De Veritate*, q. 14, a. 3, c.

directed also to supernatural happiness, i.e., to God as lovable, knowable, and attainable,i.e., as He is the author and object of supernatural happiness.

841. God's glory.— 1° Glory, *in its formal aspect*, is defined by St. Thomas (¹): « great renown accompanied by praise » — *clara notitia cum laude*. In other words, it is a knowledge of a being's perfection such as engenders love, veneration, and praise (²).

Glory, *in its objective aspect*, is the perfection of a being which engenders love, veneration, and praise in one who has knowledge of it.

2° God's glory, considered formally, is of two kinds: *intrinsic* and *extrinsic*. God's intrinsic glory is the knowledge and love which God has of His own perfection. God's extrinsic glory is the knowledge and love which creatures endowed with intelligence have of God's perfection.

God's glory, considered objectively, is also of two kinds: *in Himself* and *in His effects*.

God's glory in Himself is the perfection which God possesses in Himself.

God's glory in the divine effects is God's perfection as manifested in creatures.

3° In the light of the foregoing remarks, *first*, we may now state that the world was created for God's glory (³), i.e., that the ultimate end of the whole world is God's glory. For God, in creating the world, could intend no ultimate end other than His own goodness and perfection, which is the proper end of the divine will. Moreover, since the end of the agent and of the patient as such is the same, the ultimate end of the world is not God's goodness and perfection as intrinsically increased, but as manifested externally, i.e., in creatures, which is God's glory in an objective sense, namely, God's glory in His effects.

---
(1) I-II, q. 2, a. 3.
(2) LESSIUS, *in* I-II, q. 1, a. 8.
(3) Conc. Vaticanum, *Constitutio de Fide Cathol.*, cap. I, can. 5.

Secondly, creatures endowed with intelligence, and therefore man, are directed in a special way to God's glory as to the ultimate end. For man not only is an effect of God which manifests God's perfection, but he is also the *image* of God, in as much as he knows, loves, and praises His perfection.

4° It is evident from what we have just said that God's glory is man's *extrinsic* ultimate end. For natural happiness, even though it is the greatest human good, is not the absolutely ultimate end. Moreover, man's absolutely ultimate end is the absolutely ultimate good. Hence man's ultimate end is the manifestation of God's glory; or, in other words, man's absolutely ultimate end, even in the natural order, is God's extrinsic formal glory.

POINTS FOR REVIEW

1. Natural happiness is described as a perfect good, a self-sufficient good, a common good, as consisting in operation proper to man which is virtuous and realized in a perfect life. Explain each member of this description.

2. Define delight, explain why it is found in natural happiness, and why delight found in happiness is superior to any other kind of delight.

3. Define speculative happiness and active happiness, state to what virtues they are ascribed, and explain whether or not active happiness is higher than speculative happiness.

4. Explain why material goods are not so necessary for speculative happiness as they are for active happiness, and why man does not need great riches in order to be happy.

5. Is the society of friends a requisite of either speculative or active happiness? Give reasons for your answer.

6. Explain whether or not natural happiness is man's absolutely ultimate end, and how God's goodness and supernatural happiness consitute man's ultimate end.

ARTICLE II

PERFECT BEATITUDE

842. Objective beatitude.— 1° Perfect beatitude is distinct from natural happiness.

Natural happiness is the ultimate human perfection, and is of itself sufficient for man whose appetite is ruled by reason. Therefore natural happiness does not comprehend every good, but is merely the highest which man, according to his human condition, can possess.

Perfect beatitude is happiness which completely satisfies the desires of intellectual agents.

It is only by faith that man can know or desire perfect beatitude.

2° Since natural happiness is the ultimate human perfection, it does not consist in man's operation absolutely considered; it consists rather in a good whose attainment surpasses the powers of man, but which can be attained by human operation (¹).

Hence we may distinguish two elements in perfect beatitude:

a) the extrinsic good which completely satisfies man's appetite, i.e., desires; this good is called *objective beatitude*.

b) the operation by which man attains this good, and which is called *formal beatitude*.

The distinction between objective beatitude and formal beatitude is not applicable to natural happiness, for, *first*, natural happiness consists in operation absolutely considered, as it perfects man's faculties; *secondly*, God is not the object

---
(1) *De Veritate*, q. 14, a. 3, c.

of acts of the moral virtues, which constitute active happiness, although He is the absolutely ultimate end of active happiness; *thirdly,* natural speculative happiness attains God only as He shines forth in creatures, but does not unite man to God, i.e., it does not attain God as the object which beatifies, i.e., gives happiness.

3° Objective beatitude is that perfect good which so completely satisfies the desires of man, i.e., of intellectual agents, that there is no other good which he can desire.

Nevertheless, the argument which follows does not prove that man naturally tends to God as to the object of his perfect beatitude. The act of tending to God under the aspect of beatifying object is completely beyond the powers of nature, and therefore can neither be naturally known nor desired by man.

The argument is a proof of the following points:

a) if, in virtue of divine munificence, man attains God as his objective beatitude, i.e., as the object in which his happiness is realized, his desires are completely satisfied;

b) because of the amplitude of man's desires, there is nothing repugnant in man's attaining God as He is in Himself, i.e., as the object in which man's beatitude is found; in other words, there is nothing repugnant, as there would be in the case of the brute, in man's attainment of the beatific vision (¹).

4° **Statement of the thesis.**

THESIS.— God alone is objective beatitude.

God is the only good which can completely satisfy man's desires. But objective beatitude is that good which can completely satisfy man's desires. Therefore God alone is objective beatitude.

Major.— Only infinite good can completely satisfy man's desires: for man's desires follow, i.e., are proportionate to, the knowledge of his intellect, which conceives universal and

---

(1) Joannes a Sancto Thoma, *Cursus Theol.*, t. II, pp. 139-145 (Solesm.)

HAPPINESS

infinite good; and, moreover, the amplitude of the elicited appetite is measured by the knowledge which it follows. But God alone is infinite good. Therefore God alone can completely satisfy man's desires.

843. Corollary.— Man's reason and will are naturally directed to God as He is the author and end of nature [1], in this sense: human reason, in virtue of its natural light, can know God as He is the first principle and ultimate end of nature; and man's will, in virtue of its own principles, can direct itself to God as He is the ultimate end of all natural things. But man's reason and will cannot, in virtue of their natural principles, be directed to God as He is the object which beatifies, i.e., the object of supernatural happiness. Hence, in order that man's reason and will be directed to God as He is the object of supernatural beatitude, there is required God's gratuitous assistance, i.e., grace and the supernatural virtues, as faith, hope, charity, etc.

844. Difficulties.— 1° A finite appetite can be satisfied by finite good. But man's appetite is finite. Therefore man's appetite, i.e., desires, can be satisfied by finite good.

Major.— An appetite which is finite both in its being and in its appetition, *I concede*; which is finite in its being, but infinite in its appetition, *I deny*.

Minor.— Man's appetite is finite both in its being and in its appetition, *I deny*; is finite in its being, but infinite in its appetition, *I concede*.

Man's appetite, as a faculty of a finite being, is finite in its being; but, since it follows the knowledge of the intellect, which apprehends universal good, it is objectively infinite, i.e., infinite in its appetition.

2° An appetite which attains good in a finite manner finds its satisfaction in finite good. But man's appetite attains good in a finite manner. Therefore man's appetite finds its satisfaction in finite good.

Major.— Which attains finite good in a finite manner, *I concede*; which attains infinite good in a finite manner, *I deny*.

Minor.— Man's appetite attains only finite good in a finite manner as its proper object and ultimate end, *I deny*; attains infinite good in a finite manner as its proper object and ultimate end, *I concede*.

845. Formal beatitude.— 1° Objective happiness is that object which perfectly satisfies the desires of an agent endowed

---

(1) I-II, q. 62, a. 1, ad 3.

with an intellect. Formal beatitude is the attainment and possession of this object.

2° Formal beatitude may be considered under two aspects: *in its essence* and *as a state*.

Formal beatitude, *in its essence*, is the act by which objective beatitude, i.e., infinite good, is attained and possessed.

Formal beatitude, *as a state*, is the state which results from the attainment of infinite good, and which includes, in addition to the possession of infinite good, all other goods which have their source in and result from the possession of infinite good. It is defined by Boethius: a perfect state in which all goods are possessed — « Status bonorum omnium aggregatione perfectus ».

It is with formal beatitude in its essence that we are at present concerned.

3° Since formal beatitude is man's ultimate perfection, it must consist in operation: for operation is the ultimate perfection of every being. Moreover, since the operation by which man attains God, Who is a spiritual being, must be the operation of a spiritual faculty, formal beatitude must consist in an act of the intellect, an act of the will, or an act of the intellect and will. Therefore the question arises: is formal beatitude, in its essence, an act of the intellect, an act of the will, or an act of both?

4° *a)* St. Albert the Great, St. Bonaventure, and Suarez hold that formal beatitude, in its essence, consists in an act of the intellect and will, i.e., in the knowledge and love of God.

b) Scotus maintains that it consists in an act of the will, i.e., in an act of love.

c) St. Thomas and his disciples teach that formal beatitude, in its esssence, consists in an act of the intellect, i.e., in an act of knowledge. According to this opinion, the acts of the will, i.e., joy and delight in the possession of infinite good, are resultant properties of the act of knowledge, i.e., of formal beatitude in its essence, just as beauty is a resultant ornament of youth.

5° Statement of the thesis.

THESIS.— FORMAL BEATITUDE CONSISTS ESSENTIALLY IN AN ACT OF THE INTELLECT.

The attainment and possession of the highest good, i.e., of God, does not consist in an act of the will, but in an act of the intellect. But formal beatitude consists essentially in the attainment and possession of the highest good, i.e., of God. Therefore formal beatitude consists essentially in an act of the intellect.

Major.— The attainment and possession of the highest good does not consist in an act of a faculty which is drawn by things, but in an act of a faculty which draws things to itself. But the will, as an appetitive faculty, is drawn by things, whereas the intellect, as a cognitive faculty, draws things to itself in an intentional manner, as we know from Philosophy of Nature. Therefore.

The *first part of the major* may also be proved from an examination of the acts of the will. The acts of the will are *love*, which is the inclination of the will to a good as simply apprehended, i.e., as present or absent (n. 386); *desire*, which is the inclination of the will to a good apprehended as absent; and *delight*, which is the joy of the will in a good which it possesses.

The *minor* is evident from the statement of the question.

846. Corollary.— Formal beatitude, in its essence, is not complete and absolute ultimate perfection, but essentially and radically ultimate perfection.

Joy and delight of the will, and, in the state of the union of soul and body, goods which appertain to the sensitive appetite and, in general, to the well-being of the body are resultant properties of formal beatitude in its essence. In a word, the satisfaction of all desires, i. e., « the perfect state in which all goods are possessed, » results from formal beatitude in its essence.

847. Difficulties.— 1° Man's ultimate perfection does not consist solely in an act of the intellect. But formal beatitude in its essence is man's ultimate perfection. Therefore formal beatitude in its essence does not consist solely in an act of the intellect.

Major.— Man's ultimate perfection considered in its essence and in its root, *I deny*; considered also as regards what is accidental to it, *I concede.*

Minor.— Is man's ultimate perfection considered in its essence and in its root, *I concede*; considered also as regards what is accidental to it, *I deny.*

2° What is concerned with the object of the will, i. e., with good, does not consist in an act of the intellect. But formal beatitude in its essence is concerned with good. Therefore formal beatitude in its essence does not consist in an act of the intellect.

Major.— With good as desired, *I concede;* with good as apprehended and possessed, *I deny.*

Minor.— With good as desired, *I deny;* with good as apprehended and possessed, *I concede.*

BOOK II

Human acts in their psychological aspect

THE ONLY CHAPTER

Prologue.— In the last chapter, we dealt with the ultimate end. We shall now turn our attention to human acts, which are the steps, as it were, by which man advances to his ultimate end.

First, we shall deal with human acts in their psychological aspect, which constitute the matter of morality, of which we shall treat in Book III.

Since a human act proceeds from man's free will, it may be considered under two aspects: as it proceeds immediately from the will, and is called an *elicited* act; and as it proceeds from some other power under the command of the will, and is called a *commanded* act.

First, we shall deal with two conditions common to all human acts; namely, voluntariness (the voluntary) and involuntariness (the involuntary), and, afterwards, with elicited and commanded acts. Hence there will be three articles in this chapter.

Voluntariness { Notion of voluntariness
{ Division of voluntariness

Involuntariness	Notion and sources of involuntariness Violence Fear Concupiscence Ignorance
Elicited and commanded acts of the will	Elicited and commanded acts of the will Enumeration of the acts elicited by the will Necessity of command Relation of command to the intellect and will Relation between command and commanded acts

ARTICLE I

VOLUNTARINESS

848. Notion of voluntariness.— Voluntariness is defined: the condition in virtue of which an act proceeds from an intrinsic principle with knowledge of its end.

a) Condition... from an intrinsic principle: a voluntary act in thus distinguished from an act done as a result of violence, whose principle is extrinsic; and from a willed object, which does not necessarily result from any influence of the will, but is its object and term extrinsically denominated from volition; thus, for example, rain is willed by the farmer, but is not voluntary.

b) With knowledge of its end: a voluntary act is an act of the elicited appetite, not of the natural appetite, and hence presupposes knowledge of its end.

849. Division of voluntariness.— 1° Voluntariness is *essentially* divided, in virtue of knowledge, into perfect voluntariness and imperfect voluntariness.

a) Perfect voluntariness is voluntariness in virtue of which an act proceeds from the appetite with formal knowledge of its end, i.e., with knowledge of the end as such. Formal knowledge is found only in the intellect, and hence only an agent endowed with an intellect is capable of a perfectly voluntary act.

Imperfect voluntariness is voluntariness in virtue of which an act proceeds from the appetite with only material knowledge of its end, i.e., with knowledge only of the thing which is the end, not of the end as an end. Thus an irrational animal is capable of an act which is imperfectly voluntary.

b) Perfect voluntariness is divided into *necessary* voluntariness and *free* voluntariness.

Necessary voluntariness is the voluntariness of an act which proceeds from the will with formal knowledge of the end, but without indifference of the will, v.g., in the beatific vision, an act of love of God is necessarily voluntary.

Free voluntariness is the voluntariness of an act which proceeds from the will with formal knowledge of the end, and with indifference of the will.

c) Free voluntariness is *perfectly* or *imperfectly* free as it results from perfect or imperfect deliberation.

2° Voluntariness is accidentally divided, in virtue of the intention of the will, as follows:

a) Voluntariness may be *immediate* (in se) or *mediate* (in causa).

Immediate voluntariness (voluntarium in se) is the voluntariness of an act which is so intended that the will is directly and immediately concerned with it; v.g., the voluntariness of an act of theft.

Mediate voluntariness (voluntarium in causa) is the voluntariness of an act which is not intended in itself, but results from an act intended in itself; v.g., quarrels caused by a person who deliberately becomes drunk, foreseeing that he will be quarrelsome, are mediately voluntary (voluntary in their cause).

In order that an act be mediately voluntary, i.e., voluntary in its cause, three conditions must be fulfilled:

1) the agent must foresee, at least in a confused manner, what effect will result from the cause, because a voluntary act presupposes knowledge;

2) the agent must be able not to place the cause, or, if it is placed, to remove it, because inability to act destroys voluntariness;

3) the agent must be under obligation not to place the cause, or, if it is already placed, to remove it: for, if a person is justified in placing a cause, the effect which results, contrary to his intention, from this cause is not voluntary.

b) Voluntariness may be *positive* or *negative*. Positive voluntariness is the voluntariness of an act of commission, whereas negative voluntariness is the voluntariness of a deliberate act of omission.

c) Voluntariness may be *direct* or *indirect*.

Direct voluntariness is the voluntariness of an act which proceeds from the will as *acting*.

Indirect voluntariness is the voluntariness of an act which proceeds from the will *not as acting*, but indirectly *in as much it ought to prevent it*, but *fails* to do so, i.e., in as much as it *does not act when it ought to act;* v.g., the sinking of a ship because of the pilot's abandoning the helm is indirectly voluntary.

Indirect voluntariness is the effect of the voluntariness of the omission of an act, i.e., of negative voluntariness. The effect of the omission of an act is voluntary if it *a)* could (moral possibility) and ought (obligation) to have been foreseen; *b)* could have been avoided; *c)* ought to have been avoided.

d) Voluntariness may be *absolute* or *relative*.

Absolute voluntariness (*voluntarium simpliciter*) is the voluntariness of an act as it exists in itself.

Relative voluntariness (*voluntarium secundum quid*) is the voluntariness of an act as it exists only in the mind.

Thus, for example, the casting of merchandise into the sea to save a ship is an act which is absolutely voluntary, because it is willed as it exists in the concrete with all its attendant circumstances, but relatively involuntary, because, considered in itself without its attendant circumstances, it is repugnant to the will.

Authors of recent years speak of an absolutely voluntary act as an act which is not involuntary under any aspect, and of a relatively voluntary act as an act which is involuntary under some aspect. Thus the casting of merchandise into the sea to save a ship is an act which is relatively voluntary and relatively involuntary.

ARTICLE II

INVOLUNTARINESS

850. Notion and sources of involuntariness.—Involuntariness is the privation of voluntariness (¹).

The privation of voluntariness derives from the lack of some condition of voluntariness. Thus an act done contrary to the intrinsic inclination of the will is *positively* and *contrarily* involuntary; and an act done without knowledge, i.e., through ignorance, is *negatively* and *privatively* involuntary, i.e., non-voluntary (²).

Therefore violence and fear, the causes which lead man to the performance of acts which are contrary to the inclination of his will, and concupiscence and ignorance, the causes which disturb or destroy the knowledge of the intellect, nullify voluntariness. Hence the sources of involuntariness are four in number: violence or force, fear, concupicence, and ignorance (³).

851. Violence.— 1° Violence, i.e., the violent, may be defined: *that whose principle is extrinsic and in which the patient does not cooperate.*

Hence violence requires the fulfillment of two conditions: *a*) it must derive from an extrinsic agent; *b*) it must be imposed without the cooperation and with the positive resistance of the patient.

Violence occurs even in inanimate things, as when a stone is thrown upwards. As opposed to voluntariness, it is more properly called *coaction.*

---

(1) *In Ethic.*, l. III, l. 1.
(2) *De Malo*, q. 3, a. 8.
(3) I-II, q. 6, a. 4-8.

2° Violence is *absolute* when the patient gives absolutely no cooperation; and *relative* when the will offers positive resistance, but yet gives a certain cooperation.

Relative violence is usually moral violence, and may be reduced to fear.

3° The elicited acts of the will cannot suffer violence because these acts derive from an intrinsic principle and cannot derive from an extrinsic principle; but the commanded acts of the will can be subject to violence; v.g., the limbs of the body can be prevented by means of violence from carrying out the commands of the will.

4° We shall now prove the proposition which follows.

Absolute violence renders an act wholly involuntary.

An act performed contrary to the inclination of the will is wholly involuntary. But absolute violence renders an act contrary to the inclination of the will. Therefore absolute violence renders an act wholly involuntary.

The *major* is immediately evident.

The *minor* is evident from the definition of absolute violence.

852. Fear.— 1° Fear is *a disturbance of the mind caused by the apprehension of some present or future evil or danger.* Fear results from the apprehension of evil, and it moves the will, by depressing its strength, to flee the evil.

2° Fear may be divided in consideration of *the evil feared, the cause of the fear,* and *the influence of fear on action.*

a) In consideration of the evil feared, fear is *grave* or *light* according as the evil feared is grave or light.

Both grave and light fear are absolutely or relatively such in as much as they are such in themselves or in relation to persons. Absolutely grave fear in law is fear which can influence a resolute man. *Reverential fear,* i.e., fear of giving offense to a superior, (even though light in itself) may be reduced to relatively grave fear.

b) In consideration of its cause, fear is of two kinds: fear *from an intrinsic cause;* v.g., the fear of death because of serious sickness;

fear *from an extrinsic cause* ⎰ fear *from a necessary cause;* v.g., the fear of shipwreck;
fear *from a free cause* ⎰ *justly excited;* v.g., the fear excited in a robber by a policeman's threats;
unjustly excited; v.g., the fear excited in a person by a robber's threats.

c) In consideration of its influence on action, fear may be *antecedent* or *concomitant.*

Antecedent fear is fear which moves a person to action, and is the cause of his action. Such an action is said to proceed from fear. Example: the fear of shipwreck which moves a merchant to throw his merchandise into the sea.

Concomitant fear is fear which accompanies an action, but is not the cause of its performance. Such an action is said to be done with fear. Example: the fear of arrest which fills a thief while he carries out an act of larceny.

3° *In the light of the foregoing remarks,* we shall now prove the proposition which follows.

An action done under stress of fear is absolutely voluntary, and relatively involuntary.

Action is absolutely voluntary when it is willed as it exists in itself, and relatively involuntary when it is willed only as it exists in the mind. But an action done under stress of fear is willed as it exists in itself. Therefore an act done under stress of fear is absolutely voluntary, and relatively involuntary.

Major.— An action which is willed as it exists in itself, i.e., in the concrete with all its attendant circumstances, is absolutely voluntary; an action as it exists in the mind, i.e., without its attendant circumstances, which is repugnant to the will is relatively involuntary. But an action done under stress of fear is willed as it exists in itself, and, as it exists in the mind, is repugnant to the will. Therefore an action done under stress of fear is absolutely voluntary and relatively involuntary.

The *minor* may be established by an example. A merchant who because of fear of shipwreck throws his merchandise into the sea actually wills to do so, and therefore his action is actually voluntarily; nevertheless, his action of throwing away his goods, as it exists in his mind, i.e., without its attendant circumstances, is contrary to the inclination of his will, for, if he were not under stress of fear, he would not abandon his merchandise to the waves, and therefore his action is relatively involuntary.

853. Concupiscence.— 1° Concupiscence, in our present use of the term, is defined: *a movement of the sensitive appetite in pursuit of a good*. As *pursuing* a good, concupiscence is concerned with sensible good in as much as it attracts the appetite to itself ([1]), and thus it is opposed to fear [2].

2° Concupiscence may be *antecedent* or *consequent*.

Antecedent concupiscence is concupiscence which antecedes all movements of the will, and is their cause; v.g., the movement of the sensitive appetite which, when aroused by the sight of a beautiful object, moves the will to strive after it.

Consequent concupiscence is concupiscence which follows the act of the will, either because the will purposely and directly excites, or at least fosters, the movement of the lower appetite, or because the vehemence of the will redounds upon it.

3° *In the light of the foregoing explanations*, we shall now prove the propositions which follow.

1) *Antecedent concupiscence increases voluntariness, but lessens liberty.*

First part.— The interior inclination of the will to its act is intensified by antecedent concupiscence.

---

(1) I-II, q. 30, a. 2.
(2) I-II, q. 30, a. 2, ad 3.

Second part. — Whatsoever disorders the judgment of reason lessens liberty. But antecedent concupiscence disorders the judgment of reason. Therefore antecedent concupiscence lessens liberty.

The *major* is evident: liberty results from the indifferent judgment of the will.

Minor.— Antecedent concupiscence applies reason to a more intense consideration of the sensible good which attracts the appetite, and turns it away from the consideration of those motives which could withdraw it from this object.

2) *Consequent concupiscence neither lessens nor increases the voluntariness of a free act, but is the sign of its intensity.*

First part.— The voluntariness of a free act can be lessened or increased only by its cause. But consequent concupiscence is not the cause, but rather the effect, of the voluntariness of a free act. Therefore.

Second part. — A cause is known from its effect. But consequent concupiscence is the effect of the voluntariness of a free act. Therefore the intensity of the consequent concupiscence of a free act is a manifestation of the intensity of its voluntariness.

854. Ignorance.— 1° Ignorance is the lack of knowledge. The lack of undue knowledge is called *nescience*; v.g., lack of egal knowledge in a musician as such. The lack of due knowledge is properly *ignorance*; v.g., the lack of legal knowledge in a judge.

Error, which involves a judgment contrary to truth, and *inadvertence*, which is a lack of actual attention, are both reducible to ignorance.

2° Ignorance may be divided by reason of its *object*, its *influence on action*, and its *subject*.

a) By reason of its *object*, ignorance is divided into *ignorance of law*, which is ignorance of the existence of the law, as, for example, the ignorance of a person who has no knowledge of the law of fasting on ember days; and *ignorance of fact*, which is ignorance of the existence of the fact, as, for example, the ignorance of a person who does not know that a certain day is an ember day.

b) By reason of its *influence on action*, ignorance is *antecedent*, *concomitant*, or *consequent*.

Antecedent ignorance is ignorance which antecedes the act of the will (thus it is not voluntary) and is the cause of the performance of an action which, in its absence, would not be done; in other words, if the agent had knowledge, he would be unwilling to do what he did out of ignorance; v.g., a person, intending to shoot a deer, shoots his friend whom he mistook for a deer.

Concomitant ignorance is ignorance which antecedes the act of will (thus it is not voluntary), but, nevertheless, is not the cause of the performance of an action which, in its absence, would, nevertheless, have been done; in other words, the agent, even though free from ignorance, would have performed the action; v.g., a person, intending to shoot a deer, shoots his enemy whom he would have shot, even though he had not mistaken him for a deer.

Consequent ignorance is ignorance which is directly or indirectly willed, and which is the reason for the performance of an action which, in its absence, would not have been done. Ignorance which is directly willed is called *affected* ignorance, for it is willed with a view to greater freedom from restraint in sinning. Ignorance which is willed indirectly is called crass or *supine* ignorance if it results from serious negligence, and *light* ignorance if it results from negligence which is not serious.

c) By reason of its *subject*, ignorance may be *invincible* or *vincible*.

Invincible ignorance is ignorance which cannot be removed by the exercise of moral diligence. Moral diligence is such diligence as prudent persons, in consideration of the gravity of the matter, are wont to use in similar circumstances. Invincible ignorance is not voluntary, and therefore is either antecedent or concomitant.

Vincible ignorance is ignorance which can and ought to be overcome by the exercise of moral diligence. Three conditions are required for vincible ignorance:

1° doubt concerning the matter of which knowledge is lacking; 2° advertence to the obligation of seeking enlightenment; 3° neglect in seeking enlightenment.

3° *In the light of the foregoing explanations*, we shall now prove the propositions which follow.

1) *Antecident ignorance causes involuntariness.*

An act which results from antecedent ignorance not only is not willed, — a voluntary act presupposes knowledge, — but is contrary to the inclination of the will. Therefore antecedent ignorance causes involuntariness.

2) *Concomitant ignorance causes neither voluntariness nor involuntariness, but non-voluntariness.*

First part.— An act which is done with concomitant ignorance is not done with the knowledge required for voluntariness.

Second part.— An act which is done with concomitant ignorance is not contrary to the inclination of the will.

Third part.— An act which is done with concomitant ignorance, though not contrary to the inclination of the will, is not done with the knowledge required for voluntariness.

3) *Consequent ignorance does not take away voluntariness, but lessens it, if it is not affected.*

First part.— An act which is the effect of willed ignorance is voluntary: he who wishes the cause wishes the effect. But an act which is done because of consequent ignorance is the effect of willed ignorance. Therefore an act which is the effect of consequent ignorance is voluntary, i.e., consequent ignorance does not take away voluntariness.

Second part. — An act which is done because of consequent ignorance is to some extent contrary to the inclination of the will: it is supposed that the agent would not perform the act if he had knowledge of it.

Third part. — If ignorance is directly willed, i.e., is affected, it is a manifestation of the inclination of the agent to the act performed because of it.

ARTICLE III

ELICITED AND COMMANDED ACTS OF THE WILL

855. Elicited and commanded acts of the will.— A human act is an act which proceeds from man's free will, and therefore is an act which can proceed immediately from the free will, as the act of loving or hating, or mediately, i.e., by means of some power under the command of the will, as the act of studying or walking. Hence we make a distinction between elicited acts and commanded acts of the will.

An *elicited* act of the will is an act which proceeds immediately from the will; v.g., the act of loving.

A *commanded* act of the will is an act which proceeds from the will by means of some other power, i.e., an act which proceeds from a power under the command of the will; v.g., the act of walking.

856. Enumeration of the acts elicited by the will.— The acts elicited by the will are six in number: three are concerned with the end, and three with the means. They are the following.

1. *Concerned with the end*, in as much as the will:

    a) tends to the end *absolutely*......simple volition
    b) *rests* in the end............enjoyment (fruition)
    c) tends to the end *as attainable by means*...intention

2. *Concerned with the means*, in as much as the will:

    a) wills means *absolutely*.................consent
    b) wills *one* means in preference to others...election
    c) *applies* the means to the end................use

HUMAN ACTS IN THEIR PSYCHOLOGICAL ASPECT

Since the appetite follows knowledge, the act of the intellect which directs the will and moves it objectively precedes the acts of the will. Therefore there are *twelve* partial movements, of which six are acts of the intellect and six acts of the will, which constitute the integrity of a perfect or complete human act.

These partial movements are always found in the process of a complete human act, but sometimes more or less explicity; and, when they take place and succeed each other suddenly, often they can scarcely be distinguished by the agent itself. The following is an outline of the partial acts of which we have just spoken.

Acts of the intellect │ Act of the will

I

Order of intention

1. *Concerned with the end*

1. Simple apprehension of good
3. Judgment proposing the end
2. Simple volition of good
4. Intention of the end

2. *Concerned with the means*

5. Counsel
7. Last practical judgment
6. Consent
8. Election

II

Order of execution

9. Command
11. Passive use
10. Active use
12. Enjoyment

We shall add a few words of explanation on each of these partial acts.

a) Simple apprehension has been sufficiently treated in Logic.

b) Simple volition is the simple complacence of the will in the good presented by the intellect.

In the order of knowledge, the act of the intellect which deals with truth in an absolute manner, i.e., without discourse, is called *apprehension;* and, in the appetitive order, the simple movement of the will towards good in an absolute manner, i.e., without relation to means, is called *volition* (¹).

Finally, simple volition follows the nature of the object proposed by the intellect. If the object is good, the volition, i.e., the movement, will be a tendency, as love or desire; if the object is evil, the movement will be a flight or a repulsion, as fear.

c) *The judgment proposing the end* is the act of the intellect by which the end is proposed as worthy of being sought in an efficacious manner. In the judgment proposing the end is terminated the operation by which the intellect gives greater consideration to the good which is the object of simple volition, investigates its excellence, and learns the possibility of its attainment.

d) *Intention* is defined: the efficacious desire of attaining the end by the means. In as much as it is efficacious, the intention is concerned with the end as attainable by the means, and thus it differs from the simple volition of the end, which is only *velleity*, and is concerned with the end in an absolute manner.

e) *Counsel* is defined: the inquiry, i.e., the deliberation, concerning the choice of the means. Counsel appertains to the practical intellect, and hence does not consist in a single simple act, but often comprises a number of distinct acts.

f) *Consent,* in its present meaning, is defined: the special act of the will concerning the means which reason proposes and judges to be suitable. Sometimes consent is used to signify any act by which the will accepts the good proposed to it; v.g., sin is said to be completed by consent.

g) *Last practical judgment*, i.e., the second part of counsel, is the act by which reason, after having deliberated concerning the various means presented to it, reaches a conclusion as to the choice of the determinate means most suited for the attainment of the end.

---

(1) I-II, qq. 8-10

h) Election is defined: the discreet acceptance of one thing (means) in preference to another. Election differs from consent. In each of these acts, the appetite is concerned with means destined for the attainment of the end: in consent, it is concerned with means in general, i.e., without discrimination; but, in election, with that determinate means which is preferable to all others. Hence, when numerous means are proposed to the will, consent precedes election; but, if only one means is proposed to it, consent and election do not differ in reality, but are only logically distinct: consent has reference to means suitable for action, and election to means which are preferred to those which are not suitable (¹).

i) Command is the act of the intellect by which a man is directed, by a certain motion of intimation, to do something (²).

j) Use, in general, is defined: the application of the thing to operation. It is of two kinds: active use and passive use.

Active use is the application considered on the part of the power applying, and is an act of the will, to which the application of the other powers appertains.

Active use differs from election: election belongs to the order of intention, and is directed by the second part of counsel, i.e., by the last practical judgment, whereas use belongs to the order of execution, and is directed by command.

Passive use is the application considered on the part of the power applied. It belongs to any power, and is not one simple act, but often comprises several acts of different powers, which must make use of the whole series of means.

k) Enjoyment is defined: rest in the good possessed, i.e., the happy possession of and delight in the end attained.

857. Necessity of command.—1° *Preliminaries.*—Suarez, Vasquez, and others affirm that the movement of the will which results from election is sufficient for the transition from the order of intention to the order of execution. Hence they do

---
(1) I-II, q. 15, a. 3, ad 3.
(2) I-II, q. 17, a. 2.

not include command and active use among the integrant parts of the complete act of the will.

All Thomists and many others affirm the necessity of command from the necessity of active use.

2° *Proof of the Thomistic opinion.*— Every special act of the will is governed by a previous special act of the intellect. But active use is a special act of the will distinct from election. Therefore there is a special act of the intellect, called command, which precedes and governs active use.

The *major* is evident from the subordination of the will to the intellect.

Minor.—Acts are distinguished by formally distinct objects. But the object of election and the object of active use are formally distinct: both have the same material object, i.e., means; but election is concerned with means in the order of intention, i.e., as it exists in the future, whereas active is concerned with means in the order of execution, i.e., as it exists in the present and must be applied in the present. Therefore active use is a special act of the will distinct from election.

858. Relation of command to the intellect and will. 1° Command, considered either as the act by which a man commands himself or as the act by which he commands other men, appertains to both the intellect and will. For three elements are found in the act of command: the directing of someone to do something, intimation, and movement. Thus in the command: *Thou shalt love God,* a) a person is directed to love God; b) this is intimated to him; c) and the person commanded is moved by the person commanding.

But *a)* the act of directing appertains to the intellect, for it implies the comparing of one thing with another, which is properly an act of reason; *b)* similarly, intimation appertains to the intellect, since it is an act by which the reason of one person directs the reason of another person; *c)* movement, however, appertains to the will: the will moves the other powers of the soul in respect to the exercise of their acts, because the will, in as much as it intends universal good, pursues man's total good (¹).

Hence it is evident that command appertains to both the intellect and will.

2° There is diversity of opinion in regard to the manner in which command appertains to the intellect and will: Suarez identifies command with election, and therefore maintains that command is essentially an act of the will, whereas St. Thomas holds that it is essentially an act of the intellect, which, however, presupposes an act of the will (²). Since law is a kind of command, Suarez affirms that it appertains to the will, whereas St. Thomas holds that it appertains essentially to the intellect.

That command appertains essentially to the intellect is evident from the fact that command proceeds from the will as from a superior power, and from the intellect as from an inferior power: for command belongs to the order of execution, in which order the will is the superior power, for it is the first mover. But, when an act proceeds from two powers, one of which is subordinate to the other, it belongs essentially to the inferior power; thus, for example, the act of writing proceeds from the hand and from the will, but, even though it proceeds from the will as from the superior power, it belongs essentially to the hand. Hence it is evident that command is essentially an act of the intellect.

Therefore command is essentially an act of directing by intimation, which is capable, in virtue of the previous election of the will which virtually remains, of moving (the power) to the execution of what is intimated by the act of directing (³). It is in this sense that it presupposes an act of the will.

859. Relation between command and the commanded act.— 1° Command and the commanded act, considered in an absolute manner, are in themselves two distinct acts, for

---
(1) I-II, q. 9, a. 1.
(2) I-II, q. 17, a. 1.
(3) I-II, q. 17, a. 1.— CAJETANUS, *supra eumdem articulum*.

they appertain to different powers. Moreover, command presupposes at least two acts, namely, an act of the will and an act of reason, and quite often the commanded act is composed of many distinct acts.

2° Command and the commanded act, considered under the aspect of human act, form only one human act. For the commanded act proceeds from the commanded power, which power is moved by reason and the will. Hence the commanded power is the instrumental cause of the commanded act, and reason and the will, in virtue of which the commanded power acts, are its principal cause. But the act of the instrumental cause and the act of the principal cause as such are one and the same act, i.e., the act of the mover and the act of the thing moved as such are one and the same act.

BOOK III

Human acts in their moral aspect

Prologue.— We turn now from the study of human acts in their psychological aspect to the consideration of them in their moral aspect. First, we shall discuss morality ; and, secondly, the consequences of morality. Hence there will be two chapters in this book.

Chapter I. Morality.

Chapter II. Consequences of morality.

CHAPTER I

MORALITY

Prologue.— First, we shall deal with morality in general; secondly, with the existence of good and evil in human acts; thirdly, with essentially good and essentially evil human acts; fourthly, with the rule of morality; fifthly, with the sources of morality, i.e., with the elements by which a human act is constituted morally good or morally evil. Hence there will be five articles in this chapter.

Morality in general
- Notion of morality
- Formal constituent of morality
- Division of morality

Goodness and evil of acts
- Statement of the question
- Opinions
- Thesis: Some human acts are morally good, and others are morally evil
- Scholia
- Difficulty

Intrinsically good and intrinsically evil human acts
- Statement of the question
- Opinions
- Thesis: Some actions are intrinsically good and others are intrinsically evil, independently of any will, human or divine
- Scholia
- Difficulty

Rule of morality
- Statement of the question
- Opinions
- Thesis: The proximate rule of morality is right reason, and its remote rule is the eternal law
- The essential order of things, human nature, and the ultimate end may be called the fundamental rules of morality
- Difficulty

MORALITY

Sources of morality
- Notion and division of the sources of morality
- The primary goodness or evil of a human act is derived from its object
- Human acts derive a certain morality from their circumstances
- Moral circumstances sometimes increase or lessen the goodness or evil of an act without changing the species of its morality
- Moral circumstances sometimes give an act an essential or accidental species in the genus of morality
- The morality of human acts is dependent in a special way upon the end
- Human acts considered in the abstract can be morally indifferent, but, considered in the concrete, must be morally good or morally evil

ARTICLE I

MORALITY IN GENERAL

860. Notion of morality.— 1° Morality, in general, may be described : *the property in virtue of which human acts are good or evil in a special way.* For, since human acts are destined for an end, they are good or evil in relation to their end ; but, since they are directed to their end in a special way in as much as man freely moves to an end, they are good or evil in a special way.

2° The principle which directs free acts to their end is reason. For a free act is done for an end in as much as reason, apprehending the end and the means of attaining it, directs it to the end in the manner proper to it. If reason is right, i.e., if it apprehends a right end and correctly directs the means to it, the free act is good ; if, however, it directs the act to a wrong end, or does not correctly direct the means to the end, the free act is evil. Hence morality may be defined : *the conformity or disconformity of a human act with right reason, which is its rule.*

NOTE.— Hence, if liberty is taken away, morality is impossible. Therefore there can be no moral acts which are not free ; and untenable is the teaching of those who hold that morality results from *sociability*, not from liberty.

861. Formal constituent of morality. — 1° *Preliminaries.*— *a)* The formal constituent of morality is the first essential constituent of the special goodness or evil of a moral act.

b) Some hold that the formal constituent of morality consists in liberty (an opinion ascribed to Scotus), others in imputability (Pufendorf), others in the *extrinsic* denomination of a human act (Suarez), others in a relation of reason (Vasquez), and others in a predicamental relation. All Thomists teach that morality formally consists in the transcendental relation of a free act to its object as in conformity or disconformity with the rules of morals, i.e., with right reason and the eternal law.

2° *Proof of the Thomistic opinion.*

The formal constituent of morality consists in the transcendental relation of a human act to an object as in conformity or disconformity with the rules of morals.

1) A moral act is formally constituted by its transcendental relation to a moral object. But an object is moral in as much as it is subject to the rules of morals. Therefore the formal constituent of morality consists in the transcendental relation of a human act to an object as in conformity or disconformity with the rules of morals.

Major.— Every act is transcendentally related to its object.

The *minor* is self-evident.

2) Morality formally consists in the order which reason establishes in human acts. But this order is the transcendental order, i.e., relation, which a human act has to its object as subject to the rules of morals. Therefore.

Major.— A special goodness or evil is found in a human act because it is directed in a special way to its end by reason.

Minor.— This order is the intrinsic tendency of a human act to an object as moral, i.e., as in conformity or disconformity with the rules of morals.

862. Division of morality.— Morality is divided essentially, in relation to its subject, in relation to its rule, and in relation to imputability.

a) Essentially, morality is divided into goodness, evil, and indifference(¹).

Moral goodness is the transcendental relation of an act to an object which is in conformity with the rules of morals.

Moral evil is the transcendental relation of an act to an object which is in disconformity with the rules of morals.

Moral indifference is the property in virtue of which an act, as related to an object, is neither morally good nor morally evil because its object has no relation either of conformity or of disconformity to the rules of morals ; v.g., to go into a field is of itself neither good nor evil, but can become such in the moral order according to the end of the agent and the circumstances.

b) In relation to its subject, morality is divided into morality of the act and morality of the object.

Morality of the act is morality which affects a human act.

Morality of the object is morality which affects the object with which a human act is concerned, in as much as this object is considered in relation to the rules of morals.

Morality of the act and morality of the object are called formal morality and objective morality respectively by some Scholastics.

c) In relation to its rule, morality is divided into objective morality and subjective morality.

Objective morality is morality considered in relation to the moral laws, independently of the practical judgment of any agent ; v.g., theft is objectively evil.

Subjective morality is morality considered in relation to the practical judgment of the agent ; v.g., theft is objectively evil, but can be subjectively good in the case of a person who considers that theft, especially in certain circumstances, is lawful.

We must be careful not to confuse objective morality in
_____
(1) *De Malo,* q. 2, a. 5, c.

relation to the rule with morality of the object, which also is called objective morality.

Objective morality may be intrinsic or extrinsic.

Intrinsic morality is morality which derives from nature, i.e., from the natural law; v.g., the morality of any act commanded or prohibited by the natural law.

Extrinsic morality is morality which derives only from the positive law of a superior, i.e., from the command or prohibition of a superior ; v.g., to eat meat on Friday is extrinsically evil.

d) *In relation to imputability,* morality is divided into material morality and formal morality.

Material morality is involuntary, and consequently non-imputable.

Formal morality is voluntary and imputable morality.

Example : a lie told by a child who has not yet reached the use of reason has material morality, but no formal morality.

Formal morality in this sense must not be confused with formal morality as used to signify morality of the act.

POINTS FOR REVIEW

1. Describe morality in general.

2. Define morality, and state the teaching of Thomists in regard to its formal constituent.

3. Show how morality is divided essentially, in relation to its subject, in relation to its rule, and in relation to imputability.

4. Distinguish between intrinsic morality and extrinsic morality.

ARTICLE II

GOODNESS AND EVIL OF HUMAN ACTS

863. Statement of the question.— 1° We are concerned at present with the question of the goodness and evil of human acts in the moral order, i.e., in relation to the rules of morals.

2° The conscience of the individual man and the universal consent of mankind testify that moral goodness is distinct from moral evil.

Nevertheless, there are some, as Sceptics, Atheists, Fatalists, and Deists, who refuse to admit a distinction between good and evil in the moral order, because they do not recognize the existence of this order.

There are others who contend that every human act is good, because it proceeeds from a cause in act.

3° We, on the contrary, teach that human acts not only can be good, but can be evil, and this we can prove from the very nature of human acts.

864. Statement of the thesis.

THESIS.—SOME HUMAN ACTS ARE MORALLY GOOD, AND OTHERS ARE MORALLY EVIL.

Human acts are good or evil in as much as they possess or do not possess the plenitude of being due to them. But, just as in the physical order, so also in the moral order, i.e., in relation to the rules of morals, some human acts possess the plenitude of being due to them, and others do not. Therefore some human acts are morally good, and others are morally evil([1]).

Major.— We must speak of goodness and evil in actions as we speak of them in things, because a thing produces actions which correspond, i.e., are proportionate, to its nature. But things are good in as much as they possess the plenitude of being due to them, and evil in as much as they do not possess the plenitude of being due to them ; for a thing is good when good in every respect, and evil when not good in any respect : *bonum ex integra causa, malum ex quocumque defectu.* Therefore human acts are good or evil in as much as they possess or do not possess the fullness of being due to them.

Minor.— Human acts, like all created things, possess the plenitude of their being from the convergence of several component factors, even considered in their relation to reason, i.e., in the moral order; v.g., a human act must be performed in a proper place, in a measure determined by reason, etc. But human acts can possess or not possess the plenitude of being due to them, even in the moral order. Therefore, not only in the physical order, but also in the moral order, human acts can possess or not possess the plenitude of being due to them, i. e., some acts possess the plenitude of being due to them, and others do not.

---

(1) I-II, q. 18, a. 1, c.

ARTICLE III

INTRINSICALLY GOOD AND INTRINSICALLY EVIL HUMAN ACTS

865. Statement of the question.— 1° We are concerned at present with the *objective* morality of a human act, i.e., with the morality which belongs to a human act independently of the practical judgment (conscience) of the person who is actually performing it.

2° It is certain that some actions are objectively good and others objectively bad *extrinsically*, i.e., because of the positive law of a superior.

Our present problem is this : are some actions intrinsically, i.e., of their very nature, good, and others intrinsically evil, independently of any positive determination of man or of God ?

866. Opinions.— 1° Moral Positivism teaches that no act is essentially good or evil, but that some acts are good or evil solely from the positive determination of man or of God.

a) Certain philosophers of ancient times, as Archelaus, Protagoras, Pyrrho, and Carneades, teach that this positive determination of goodness or evil is made by man. According to certain philosophers of more recent times, it is made by civil law (Hobbes), or by the social contract (Rousseau), or by education (Montaigne), or by the public opinion and customs of peoples (St. Lambert), by the discovery of the wise and powerful (Mandeville), or by the evolution of the moral sense or collective conscience, or of culture (Evolutionists, as Hartmann, Levy-Bruhl, and Durkheim).

MORALITY

b) Nominalists, as Descartes and Pufendorff, teach that the distinction between good and evil derives from the free will of God.

2° According to the *teaching of Catholics*, some actions are intrinsically good, and others are intrinsically evil, independently of any will, human or divine.

867. Statement of the thesis.

THESIS.—SOME ACTIONS ARE INTRINSICALLY GOOD, AND OTHERS ARE INTRINSICALLY EVIL, INDEPENDENTLY OF ANY WILL, HUMAN OR DIVINE.

1° Actions which are of themselves suited to man's nature are intrinsically good, and those which of themselves are not suited to man's nature are intrinsically evil. But some actions are of themselves suited to man's natures, and other are not. Therefore some actions are intrinsically good, and others are intrinsically evil, independently of any will, human or divine.

The *major* is self-evident.

Minor.— Man has a determinate nature. But every nature has its own proper operations, and hence there are some operations which of themselves are suited to it, and others which are not. Therefore(¹).

2° Actions which of their very nature lead man to God are intrinsically good; and actions which of their very nature lead man away from God are intrinsically evil. But some actions of their very nature lead man to God, and others of their very nature lead man away from God, independently of any will, human or divine. Therefore some actions are intrinsically good, and others are intrinsically evil, independently of any will, human or divine.

Major.— Actions by which a thing tends to its natural end are naturally suited to it, i.e., are intrinsically good ; and

---
(1) *Contra Gentes*, l. III, c. 129.

those by which it is turned away from its natural end are naturally unsuited to it, i.e., are intrinsically evil. But man is naturally destined for God : God, as we have seen, is man's ultimate end. Therefore [1].

The *minor* is evident from examples. Man tends, i.e., is led, to God by knowledge and love of God and also by such acts as lead him to the knowledge and love of God ; and he is turned away, i.e., is led away, from God by hatred of God and by anything that destroys his knowledge and love of God.

3° Actions without which man cannot attain what is natural to him are intrinsically good, and their contraries are intrinsically evil. But there are certain actions without which man cannot attain what is natural to him. Therefore some actions are intrinsically good, and others are intrinsically evil, independently of any will, human or divine.

Major. — Actions without which man cannot do what is natural to him are naturally suited to him, because nature never fails to provide for necessities.

Minor. — a) Society is natural to man. But there are certain actions without which society cannot subsist, as the acts of abstaining from injury and rendering to everyone his due.

b) Every man has a natural right to use inferior things for his life's necessities, but only according to a determinate measure. If he does not observe this measure, the use of inferior things becomes harmful to him; v.g., excess in eating or in drinking, which is the inordinate use of food or of drink, is harmful to man.

c) According to the natural order, the body is destined for the good of the soul, and the inferior powers for the good of the rational powers. Therefore human operations by which the good of the rational powers is attained by means of the inferior powers are naturally good, and those by which this good is impeded are naturally evil ; v.g., the act of becoming drunk is naturally evil[2].

---

(1) *Ibidem.*
(2) *Ibidem.*

4° The testimony of conscience and the universal consent of mankind corroborate the teaching enunciated in the thesis.

Conscience apprehends certain actions as good in themselves, and others as evil in themselves, independently of any positive determination.

Likewise, among all peoples, some actions are regarded as good in themselves, and others as evil in themselves, independently of any law or custom.

868. Scholia.— 1° Since knowledge of truth appertains to the intellect, judgment on moral matters appertains to the intellect, because such judgment is judgment which concerns the *true* conformity or disconformity of operations with human nature.

2° In all knowledge, three distinct elements must be considered : the faculty, the habits, and the acts.

In the knowledge of morality :

1) the faculty is reason :

2) the habits are three in number : *a) synderesis*, i.e., the habit of first principles of the practical order, which is natural ; *b) moral science*, i.e., Ethics, which is concerned with general conclusions, and is acquired ; *c) prudence*, which is concerned with operations which are actually operative, i.e., with individual operations in the concrete ;

3) the acts are also three in number : *a) speculative judgment*, as, for example, theft is evil ; *b) practical judgment* in the universal, as, for example, theft must be avoided ; *c) practical judgment* in the individual case, as, for example, this act must be avoided ; it is called conscience, and is an act of prudence.

869. Difficulty.— If some actions were intrinsically good, and others intrinsically evil, there would be unanimity of judgment on them among all men. But there is not unanimity of judgment on them among all men; v. g., polygamy, human sacrifices, and robbery are, in the judgment of some men, evil actions, and, in the judgment of others, not intrinsically evil actions, but good actions. Therefore no actions are intrinsically good or intrinsically evil.

Major.— Among all men of right judgment, *I concede*; among men of false judgment, *I deny*.

Minor.— Among men of false judgment, *I concede*; among men of right judgment, *I deny*.

There is nothing to prevent men whose judgment is vitiated by their education (so-called), ignorance, or passions from the possibility of error concerning what is naturally good or evil.

ARTICLE IV

RULE OF MORALITY

870. Statement of the question.— 1° We have already learned that human acts can be morally good or morally evil, and that some human actions are intrinsically good and others intrinsically evil, independently of any will, human or divine. Now we shall deal with the question of the rule by which we can know that some actions are good, and others evil. This question is evidently of fundamental importance in Ethics.

2° We are dealing now with the morality of human acts, not with the obligation of doing or avoiding certain acts. Morality may be described as the *special goodness of a human act*.

3° Our problem concerns not subjective morality, but objective morality, i.e., the morality which belongs to a human act independently of the variable judgment of the person who actually performs it.

4° The rule of morality is *the norm, the measure*, i.e., *something determinate and fixed, which is the exemplar cause to which a human act must be conformed, in order that it be good;* or it is *the rule which enables us to recognize some human acts as good, and others as evil, according to their conformity or disconformity with it.*

The *supreme* rule of morality is the rule which is the first exemplar cause from which all morality of human acts derives.

The *proximate* rule of morality is the rule by which human acts are immediately regulated, and which is itself subordinate to the supreme rule of morality.

871. Opinions.— There is great diversity of opinion in regard to the rule of morality. A brief statement of the principal opinions follows.

1° There are some philosophers who make no distinction between the supreme and proximate rule of morality.

According to some, there is only one rule of morality, and it is merely *subjective*. This rule, according to Thomas Reid, Hutcheson, A. Smith, Jouffroy, etc., is a certain moral sense; according to Herbart, a certain moral taste; according to Kant, practical reason, which is *pure* because of its complete independence of experience, and *autonomous* because of its complete independence of law.

According to others, there is only one rule of morality, and it is *objective*. This rule, according to Hobbes, is the civil law; according to the Positivists, human custom; according to the negative utilitarianism of Schopenhauer and Eduard von Hartmann, utility in lessening pain and sorrow; according to the moral sensualism or hedonism of Aristippus, Epicurus, Democritus, Spinoza, Diderot, Helvetius, etc., utility in the acquisition of the sensible joys of this life; according to the private utilitarianism of Christian von Wolff, utility in the advancement of private perfection; according to the social utilitarianism or altruism of Auguste Comte and Stuart Mill, utility in the cause of public happiness; according to the evolutionism of Herbert Spencer, etc., utility in fostering the indefinite progress of humanity.

2° Others, including all Catholics, make a distinction between the proximate and supreme rule of morality, but do not agree on what these two rules are.

The proximate rule, according to Suarez and Cathrein, is human nature; and according to Liberatore, the essential order of things.

The remote rule, according to Scotus, Suarez, Vasquez, and Cathrein, is the divine essence which, according to our mode of conceiving it, is anterior to the divine reason and will;

and according to Ockam, Descartes, and Pufendorf, the divine will, i.e., the positive law of God.

According to the common opinion of Thomists, the proximate rule of morality is right reason, and its supreme rule is the eternal law.

a) Right reason is reason which judges rightly of the end of a human act and of the means of attaining this end.

Therefore in right reason there is a judgment of each of two orders :

a judgment in the order of ends : a judgment ascribed to synderesis, which proposes to the will the end which it should pursue ;

a judgment in the order of means : a judgment attributed to prudence, the practical truth of which consists in conformity to the rectified desires of the end. For the truth of prudential judgment is practical truth which consists in conformity to directive rules. Moreover, the directive rule of prudential judgment is the right desire of the end, i.e., the desire of a due end [1].

b) The eternal law is divine reason which, in virtue of its knowledge of the divine essence, orders all acts to their due ends [2].

872. Statement of the thesis.

THESIS.— THE PROXIMATE RULE OF MORALITY IS RIGHT REASON, AND ITS SUPREME RULE IS THE ETERNAL LAW.

First part.— *The proximate rule of morality is right reason.* 1° The principle by which man acts in the manner proper to man for a due end is right reason. But the proximate rule of morality is the principle by which man acts in the manner proper to man for a due end. Therefore the proximate rule of morality is right reason.

---
(1) I-II, q. 19, a. 3, ad 2.
(2) *Ibid.*, q. 93, a. 1.

Major.— Man acts in the manner proper to man for a due end, i.e., directs and moves himself to this end, because reason apprehends an end as an end, and directs, as means to the end, whatever are related to the end.

Minor.— The principle by which man acts in the manner proper to man for an end regulates this special manner of acting, and consequently is the proximate rule of the special goodness which results from it, i.e., of morality(1).

2° Human acts are good in as much as they proximately conform to right reason. But the proximate rule of morality is the rule to which human acts, in order to be good, must proximately conform. Therefore the proximate rule of morality is right reason.

Major.— A thing is good in as much as its operation is in conformity with its form. But man's proper form is that form by which he is constituted a rational animal. Hence it follows that man's operation is good in as much as it is in conformity with right reason(2).

The *minor* is evident from the definition of the proximate rule of morality.

Second part. — *The supreme rule of morality is the eternal law.* — 1° The principle to which the proximate rule of morality is primarily subordinate is the supreme rule of morality. But the eternal law is the principle to which the proximate rule of morality is primarily subordinate. Therefore the eternal law is the supreme rule of morality.

The *major* is evident from its very terms.

Minor.— It is as a second cause that right reason is the proximate rule of morality. Hence it is subordinate to the first cause, which is divine reason as directing all things to their end, i.e., to the eternal law (3).

---

(1) *Ibid.*, q. 90, a. 1, and q. 97, a. 2.
(2) *In Ethic.*, l. II, l. 2, n. 257.
(3) I-II, q. 19, a. 4.

2° The supreme rule of morality is the principle which first directs human acts to their ultimate end. But the principle which first directs human acts to their ultimate end is the eternal law. Therefore the supreme rule of morality is the eternal law.

Major.— A human act is good or evil in as much as it is directed or is not directed by reason to its ultimate end.

Minor.— God, in virtue of the universality of His causality, is the cause which first directs all things to their end by His divine reason, i.e., by the eternal law : for the act of directing things to their end is an act proper to the intellect.

The supreme rule of morality cannot be something created, as utility, civil law, custom, or autonomous human reason, because God is the ultimate end to which human acts of their very nature are directed. Similarly, the supreme rule of morality cannot be the divine essence in as much as it is anterior to the divine reason and will, nor can it be the divine will: for the supreme rule of morality orders human acts to their end; but the act of ordering things to an end is an act proper to the intellect. Therefore...

873. The essential order of things, human nature, and the ultimate end may be called the fundamental rules of morality.— *a)* The essential order of things and human nature, as we are speaking of them at present, mean the same thing : for human nature is accepted in its adequate meaning, with all the relations which it has to other beings[1]; and the essential order of things comprehends the relations between human nature and other beings.

b) The fundamental rule of morality is that which reason considers, in order to discern what is good and what is evil. But the essential order of things, human nature, and the ultimate end are the things which reason considers, in order to discern what is good and what is bad, for these things are the goods by which man tends to his end, and they are also the goods which reason apprehends as resulting from human nature and the essential order of things ; v.g., suicide is an evil act because it is contrary to the inclination of man's nature for self-preservation. Therefore.

---

(1) BOYER, *Cursus Phil.*, t. 2, p. 465.

874. Difficulty.— A human act should conform to reason, because man has a rational nature. Therefore the rule of morality is human nature, not reason.

Antecedent.— Because man has a rational nature, reason should be the formal rule of the morality of human acts, *I concede*; nature itself is the rule of morality of human acts, *I distinguish:* the fundamental rule, *I concede*; the formal rule, *I deny.*

Consequent.— Human nature is a fundamental rule of morality, *I concede*; the formal and proximate rule, *I deny.*

POINTS FOR REVIEW

1. Define: the rule of morality in general, the supreme rule of morality, the proximate rule of morality.

2. What, according to Thomists, is the proximate rule of morality? Define right reason.

3. Are there judgments of several orders in right reason? Explain.

4. State the habit to which the judgment of right reason in the order of ends is ascribed, and the virtue to which its judgment in the order of means is attributed, and also the constituent of the truth of the judgment of right reason in the order of means.

5. Under what aspect may the essential order of things, human nature, and the ultimate end be called the fundamental rules of morality?

6. Explain why the proximate rule of morality is the principle by which man acts in the manner proper to man for an end, and why human acts are good in as much as they proximately conform to right reason.

ARTICLE V

SOURCES OF MORALITY

875. Notion and division of the sources of morality.
1° The sources of morality are the elements of a human act in virtue of which it is in conformity or in disconformity with the rules of morals.

2° The sources of morality are *a)* *the object* (primary source), *b)* *the circumstances* (secondary source), the most important of which is the end, because it exercises the greatest influence on the act.

876. The primary goodness or malice of a human act is derived from its object.— 1° *Preliminaries.*— *a)* The object has a wide meaning and a strict meaning.

The object, *in the wide sense*, is anything which is in any way the object of the will. In this sense, the object includes the circumstances of a human act.

The object, *in the strict sense*, is that which is primarily and directly attained by the will; in other words, it is the first and immediate term to which an act of its very nature tends. Thus the object is the opposite of the circumstances, which, as such, are attained only secondarily; it is the *end of the work*, i.e., the matter with which human acts are concerned; v.g., when a person commits an act of theft, the thing stolen is the object of the theft, whereas the quantity of the thing stolen and the relief of his friend are circumstances.

It is with the object in its strict meaning that we are concerned at present.

b) The object may be considered either in its physical aspect, i.e., as regards its physical entity, or in its moral aspect, i.e., in relation to the rule of morals.

It is with the object in its moral aspect that we are dealing at present.

c) We shall refute the error of Kant, who, denying that the morality of an act derives from the end of the work, teaches that it derives only from the subjective form of *practical* reason, in as much as a moral act proceeds solely from motives of reverence for universal law.

2° *Proof.*— The object specifies a human act in the moral order. But the primary goodness or malice of a human act is derived from its principle of specification. Therefore the primary goodness or malice of a human act is derived from its object[1].

Major.— Every act is specified by its object.

Minor.— The goodness or malice of a human act, as of other things, is dependent on its plenitude of being or its lack of this plenitude. But it is from the principle of the specification of a thing that its plenitude of being is primarily derived; v.g., the primordial evil of an engendered natural thing is derived from the thing's failure to attain its specific form, as, for example, when a monster is engendered instead of a man. Therefore...

877. Human acts derive a certain morality from their circumstances.— 1° *Preliminaries.*— a) Circumstances may be defined: *the accidental elements of a human act which can morally affect it in its moral aspect*, i.e., which can modify its morality.

Accidental elements, i.e., elements which are not of the essence of the act, but which are in some way related to it.

Which can affect it in its moral aspect: if it gave an act its primary and essential moral species, it would no longer be a circumstance, but would pass into the condition of object and essential differentia.

Which can morally affect it, i.e., which can modify it in relation to the rules of morals.

---
[1] I-II, a. 2.

b) The circumstances of a human act, which are seven in number, may be enumerated in the following verse:

Who, what, where, by what means, why, how, when.

c) Circumstances are not essential elements of an act, but rather accidental elements, i.e., elements which affect a human act already constituted in its nature (¹). Hence:

Who does not signify the substance or nature, but rather a quality of the agent; v.g., it may signify that the agent is a priest, a religious or a layman, a rich man or a poor man, etc.

What denotes not the substance or nature of the act, but some accident, as quality or quantity, annexed to it; v.g., in an act of theft, it does not denote that the object belongs to another, but that it is sacred or profane, large or small in quantity.

Where does not give information about the place as such, but about the quality of the place; v.g., it may indicate that it is public, sacred, etc.

By what means has reference to the accidental means or instruments used by the principal agent; v.g., sinful means.

Why denotes not the end of the work, i.e., the intrinsic end proper to the nature of the work, but the end of the agent, i.e., the extrinsic end; v.g., a person may steal *for the purpose of becoming drunk.*

How signifies the accidental mode in which the act was performed; v.g., passionately or calmly, out of contempt or levity, ignorance or fear, malice or passion.

When signifies an accidental condition of time, namely, quality, as on a holy day or on a week day; or quantity, as of long or of short duration.

2° *Proof.*—1) What is true of the derivation of the goodness or malice of natural things is in a proportionate manner true also of the derivation of the goodness or malice of human acts. But the whole of the goodness and perfection of natural things is not derived solely from the form which specifies it, but is dependent

---
(1) BILLUART, *De Actibus Humanis*, Diss. IV, a. 3.

also on supervening accidents; v.g., the whole of man's goodness and perfection depends both on his substantial form and on various accidents, as color, figure, and the like. Therefore the whole of the goodness and perfection of human acts is not derived solely from the objects which specify them, but is dependent also on circumstances, which are accidents of human acts ([1]).

2) Human acts derive their morality from any element of a human act which connotes a relation of conformity or disconformity to the rules of morals. But circumstances are elements of a human act which can connote a relation of conformity or disconformity to the rules of morals; v.g., theft in itself is at variance with right reason, and so also is its commission *in a sacred place*. Therefore.

878. Moral circumstances sometimes merely increase or lessen the goodness or malice of an act without changing the species of its morality. — 1° A moral circumstance merely increases or lessens the goodness of an act when, as a result of it, a good act becomes better or worse in its species of goodness; or it merely increases or lessens the malice of an act when, as a result of it, a sinful act becomes more sinful or less sinful in its species of malice; v.g., theft can be light or grave; fortitude admits of degrees.

2° A circumstance increases or lessens the goodness or malice of an act without changing the specific morality of the act when the circumstance itself has no special relation to right reason and the eternal law. Though this circumstance does not constitute a species of morality distinct from that of the act, it increases or lessens the goodness or malice of the act in its own species of morality, not because it has of itself any relation to right reason and the eternal law, but because it has such a relation in virtue of something of which it is a circumstance; v.g., the quantity of the thing stolen does not constitute a malice distinct from that of the act of theft, but merely increases or lessens the malice of the act : for the

---

(1) I-II, q. 18, a. 3.

quantity of the thing has of itself no relation to reason ; but, on the supposition that the thing belongs to another, the quantity has a relation to reason(¹).

879. Moral circumstances sometimes give an act an essential or accidental species in the genus of morality.
1° A circumstance gives a human act a specific morality not when it increases or lessens the goodness or malice of the act in its own order of morality, but when it gives it a goodness or malice distinct from that which it already has.

2° A circumstance gives a human act an essential species of morality when this act derives its primary goodness or malice from the circumstance.

3° A circumstance gives a human act an accidental species of morality when this act derives from the circumstance a goodness or malice distinct from that which it has from its object; v.g., almsgiving in expiation for sin has a twofold goodness : the goodness of an act of mercy and the goodness of an act of penance ; murder committed for the purpose of theft has the malice of both homicide and theft.

4° A moral circumstance gives a human act a species in the genus of morality when it does not remain purely a circumstance, but passes into the condition of object, i.e., assumes the aspect of object (²).

A circumstance assumes the aspect of object when of itself, and independently of anything else, it has a relation of conformity or disconformity to the rules of morals. Thus theft in a sacred place is a sacrilege because the circumstance of place in this case has a special relation of disconformity to the rules of morals : it is the profanation of a sacred place.

5° A moral circumstance gives an essential species of morality to a human act when it passes into the condition of

---
(1) JOANNES A SANCTO THOMA, *Cursus Theol.*, t. V, XXI, disp. X, art. 2, pp. 864-865 (Vivès).
(2) I-II, q. 18, a. 10.

primary object, i.e., becomes the primary object of the act. In this case, the human act derives its primary goodness or malice from the circumstance : every act is specified by its object.

There are two cases in which this may occur:

a) when an act which of itself is good becomes evil from a circumstance ; v.g., almsgiving from vainglory ;

b) when a morally indifferent act becomes good or evil from a circumstance ; v.g., walking for the purpose of theft or of almsgiving.

In other cases, a circumstance does not give an act its primary goodness or malice, i.e., its essential species in the genus of morality. For either a good circumstance is added to an act which is evil from its object; or an evil circumstance is supervenient to an act which is evil from its object, and, in this case, the primary malice of the act is derived from its object, not from the circumstance; or a good circumstance is annexed to an act which is good from its object, and, in this case, the primary goodness of the act is derived from its object.

6° A moral circumstance gives a human act an accidental species of morality when it passes into the condition of object, but does not give the act its primary goodness or malice.

In this case, the circumstance becomes a secondary object of the act.

In order that a moral circumstance give a human act an accidental species in the genus of morality, three conditions must be fulfilled :

a) the act must be morally good or evil in virtue of its object, not indifferent ;

b) the circumstance must of itself have a relation of conformity or disconformity to the rules of morals ;

c) the circumstance must not change the goodness of the act into malice (¹); v.g., theft committed for the purpose of adultery which is intended from a motive of vengeance has three distinct species of evil : an essential species of evil, which

---

(1) JOANNES A SANCTO THOMA, *Cursus Theol.*, t. V, q. XXI, disp. X, a. 1 (Vivès).

is theft; and two accidental species of evil, namely, of adu'tery and of vengeance.

880. The morality of human acts is dependent in a special way upon the end.— 1° We must make a distinction between the end of the work and the end of the agent.

The *end of the work* is the object to which an act of its very nature tends.

The *end of the agent* is the end which the agent intends.

2° A distinction must be made too between the internal act and the external act, in as much as both are considered as voluntary acts.

The *internal act* is the act of willing and intending the end.

The *external act* is the act which results from the internal act, and is related to it as the act commanded to the act commanding ; v.g., the choice of means.

3° The end of the agent may be considered under three aspects.

First, the end may be considered in relation to the internal act, in which case it is not a circumstance, but the object which properly and directly specifies the act.

Secondly, the end may be considered in relation to the external act as concerned with means essentially related and conducive to the end, and hence intended only because of the end. In this case, the end of the agent is not a circumstance in relation to the external act, but rather appertains indirectly to the first specification of this act : for the means, which constitute the proper object of the exterior act, are sought only as related to and because of the end.

Thirdly, the end may be considered in relation to the external act as concerned with means which are accidentally related to the end. In this case, the end of the agent is a circumstance, which gives the external act an accidental goodness or malice[1].

---

(1) JOANNES A SANCTO THOMA, *Cursus Theol.*, t. V, q. 1, disp. 1, a. 3, n. XXXIX (Vivès).

Thus theft committed for the purpose of vengeance has the malice of theft, which is its primary malice derived from the object, and also the accidental malice of vengeance, which is specifically distinct from the malice of theft. In other words, the end of the agent as a circumstance in this case gives the external act an accidental species in the genus of morality.

4° Nevertheless, under the aspect of a voluntary act, a human act whose component parts are an internal act and an external act is formally specified by the end of the agent. For the *formal element* of such an act is the internal act, which is the commanding act, and its *material element* is the external act, which is commanded. But the internal act is specified by the end of the agent in the role of object, whereas the external act is specified by its proper object. Hence it follows that the formal element in a voluntary act is specified by the end of the agent. In other words, the species of a human act is considered formally in relation to the end, and materially in relation to the object of the external act ([1]). Therefore *a man who steals for the purpose of committing adultery is, strictly speaking, more adulterer than thief.*

881. Human acts considered in the abstract can be morally indifferent, but, considered in the concrete, must be morally good or morally evil. — 1° *Preliminaries.*— a) It is with human, i.e., deliberate, acts that we are dealing at present, not with acts of man, i.e., indeliberate acts, such as the rubbing of the hands because of the influence of the imagination.

b) Moral indifference is the lack of both conformity and disconformity with the rules of morality.

c) A human act may be considered *in the abstract* (*in specie*), i. e., in relation only to the object which specifies it, and hence without reference to its circumstances; and *in the concrete* (*in individuo*), i.e., in relation to all the circumstances which give it determination.

---

(1) I-II, q. 18, a. 6.— CAJETANUS, *supra eumdem articulum.*

d) Scotus teaches that no human act, considered in the abstract, can be morally indifferent, but, considered in the concrete, some human acts are morally indifferent.

According to Vasquez, human acts, considered both in the abstract and in the concrete, can be morally indifferent.

St. Thomas holds that some human acts, considered in the abstract, can be morally indifferent; but, considered in the concrete, every human act must be morally good or morally evil.

2° *Proof.* — 1) *Human acts, considered in the abstract, can be morally indifferent.* — Every human act is specified morally by its object. But there are some objects which of themselves have no relation of conformity or disconformity to the rules of morality ; v.g., the objects of walking, eating, talking, etc. Therefore.

2) *Considered in the concrete, human acts must be morally good or morally evil.* — A human act which is done for an end cannot be morally indifferent. But every human act, considered in the concrete, is done for an end. Therefore, considered in the concrete, human acts cannot be morally indifferent, i.e., must be morally good or morally evil.

Major. — A human act which is done for an end either is directed to its due end, and thus conforms to the order of reason, and is morally good ; or it is not directed to its due end, in which case it is at variance with reason, and is morally evil. Hence a human act which is done for an end cannot be morally indifferent.

Minor.— A human act, considered in the concrete, i.e., as related to all its circumstances, is always done for an end, at least for the end of the agent.

POINTS FOR REVIEW

1. What is meant by the sources of morality ?

2.. Define the object of a human act in its wide and strict acceptation, state what is meant by the object of a human act in its moral aspect; and explain why the primary goodness or malice of a human act derives from the object which specifies it.

3. Define circumstances of a human act, and name them; explain when a circumstance increases or lessens the goodness or malice of an act without changing its specific morality; state what is required that a circumstance give a human act a species in the genus of morality, when it passes into the condition of object, in what cases it gives a human act its primary goodness or malice, and what is required that it give a human act an accidental species in the genus of morality.

4. Distinguish between: internal act and external act, end of the work and end of the agent; explain whether the end of the agent is a circumstance in relation to the internal act, how the end of the agent specifies the external act concerned with means essentially related and conducive to this end, when the end of the agent gives the external act an accidental goodness or malice, and under what aspect the species of a human act is considered formally in relation to the end.

5. What is moral indifference? Can human acts be morally indifferent? Explain.

CHAPTER II

CONSEQUENCES OF MORALITY

Prologue.— A human act is righteous or sinful in relation to its end, praiseworthy or blameworthy in as much as it is in the power of the will, and meritorious or demeritorious in relation to retribution rendered according to justice (¹). Hence there will be three articles in this chapter.

Sin
- Definition of sin
- Divisions of sin
- Specific and numerical distinction of sins
- Philosophical sin

Imputability and responsibility
- Statement of the question
- Thesis: Moral acts are imputable; and man, as a moral agent, is responsible for his moral acts
- Corollaries

Merit and demerit
- Statement of the question
- Thesis: By his human acts, man can merit or demerit before individual men, before society, and before God
- Difficulties

---

(1) I-II, q. 21, a. 3.

ARTICLE I

SIN

882. Definition of sin.— The terms evil, sin, and fault (*culpa*), though used synonomously, differ in comprehension. *Evil* is the privation of good in a thing or in an act. *Sin* is the privation of good in an act. Thus sin is found in the order of nature, v.g., when a monster is engendered; in the order of art, when an artifact does not conform to the rules of art; and in the order of morality, when an act is at variance with the rules of morals. A sin is a *fault* when it is the evil of a human act. Thus sin has greater extension than fault, but lesser extension than evil. Moralists usually consider sin and fault as one and the same thing. Therefore sin, under the aspect of fault, may be defined: *an evil human act* ([1]).

883. Divisions of sin.— 1° Theologians distinguish between *original* sin, committed by Adam and transmitted to all his posterity, and *personal* sin, which a person contracts by his own action.

2° Personal sin may be actual or habitual. *Actual* sin is an act, or the omission of an act, which is in disconformity with the rules of morality; and *habitual* sin is the moral disorder which remains in the soul after the commission of actual sin, and is called the state of sin.

3° Actual sin is *grave* in as much as man absolutely and efficaciously turns away from his ultimate end and finds delight in a created good; and *light* in as much as man relatively and inefficaciously turns away from his ultimate end and finds delight in a created good, i.e., only as regards a determinate act.

---

(1) I-II, q. 71, a. 6.

and without ceasing to be habitually turned to God as his ultimate end.

4° There are many other divisions of sin; v.g., sins of omission, sins of commission, sins of the flesh, spiritual sins, etc.

884. Specific and numerical distinction of sins.— 1° Since a sin is an evil human act, sins are *specifically* distinct which have distinct formal objects in the order of morality.

2° Sins are also *numerically* distinct in virtue of their objects. Hence there are as many sins as there are total objects in the order of morality: if there is only one total object, there is one sin; if there are many total objects, there are many sins; v.g., completed external sins are multiplied according to the multiplication of their total object. Thus a man who murders three persons is guilty of three sins of murder.

885. Philosophical sin.— In the seventeenth century, there was much heated discussion on the possibility of philosophical sin, i.e., of the possibility of sin which would be at variance with reason, but would not be offensive to God; v.g., sin in a person ignorant of the existence of God.

On 24 August, 1690, Alexander VIII put an end to the controversy by declaring and condemning the following proposition as scandalous, temerarious, erroneous, and offensive to pious ears [1]: « Philosophical or moral sin is a human act in disconformity with rational nature and right reason; and theological and mortal sin is a free transgression of the Divine law. However grievous it may be, philosophical sin in one who is either ignorant of God or does not actually think of God is indeed a grave sin, but not an offense to God, nor a mortal sin dissolving friendship with God, nor deserving eternal punishment. »

---

(1) DENZINGER-BANNWART, 1290.

ARTICLE II

IMPUTABILITY AND RESPONSIBILITY

886. Statement of the question.— 1° To impute, in its etymology, has the same meaning as to compute, and is used to signify the act of computing what is due to man in virtue of his morals acts.

2° Imputation may be briefly described: *the attribution of a moral act;* and defined: *the judgment by which a moral act, or its omission, is attributed to its author in as much as its author is a moral agent.*

Hence imputability may be defined: *the property of a moral act in virtue of which it is attributed to its author in as much as he has dominion over this act, i.e., is a free agent.*

3° The concept of responsibility is correlative to the concept of imputability. But imputability has reference to the act, whereas responsibility has reference to the agent: an act is imputable, whereas man is responsible for his act.

Responsibility may be defined: *the property of man as a free being in virtue of which he must render an account of his acts.*

Responsibility is *moral*, as concerned with the obligation of rendering an account in conscience, in the internal forum, and before God; and *juridical*, as concerned with the obligation of rendering an account in a court, in the external forum, or before a judge.

Juridical responsibility may be *penal*, i.e., concerned with the inflicting of punishment for crime, or *civil*, i.e., concerned with redress for harm done even inculpably.

4° Determinists generally, and the school of anthropology or criminal sociology of Lombroso, Ferri, and others, which attribute the crimes of men to abnormal physico-organic states, deny the imputability of human acts, and consequently man's responsibility. However, the arguments for the existence of liberty are a valid refutation of this teaching.

887. Statement of the thesis.

THESIS.— MORAL ACTS ARE IMPUTABLE; AND MAN, AS A MORAL AGENT, IS RESPONSIBLE FOR HIS MORAL ACTS.

First part.—*Moral acts are imputable.*—All acts are attributable to agents : actions belong to supposits. But a moral act has morality in addition to its physical entity. Therefore, besides the physical attribution which appertains to all acts, a moral act as such has a special attribution, called imputability ; in other words, moral acts are imputable.

Second part.— *Man, as a moral agent, is responsible for his moral acts.*— A free agent is responsible for his moral acts. But man, as a moral agent, is a free agent. Therefore man, as a moral agent, is responsible for his moral acts.

Major.— A free agent is under obligation to render an account of his acts in as much as he has dominion over them.

888. Corollaries.— 1° Imputability is always associated with morality, because moral acts are imputable ; but morality is distinct from imputability. Morality is the relation of an act to right reason, which is the rule or measure of goodness or evil ; imputability is the relation of an act to the will, by which man has dominion over his acts.

2° The foundation of imputability and responsibility is liberty. Hence, if liberty is lessened, imputability and responsibility are lessened ; and, if liberty is taken away, imputability and responsibility are taken away.

3° The concept of responsibility must be carefully distinguished from the concept of solidarity as interpreted by many moderns. Solidarity is derived from the *solid* or whole, and signifies the mutual dependence of parts in a whole, and, according to Comte(¹), Leon Bourgeois, and others, it means the dependence which exists between successive generations in a society. Hence, according to this teaching, responsibility does not properly belong to the individual men who perform human acts, but to society and preceding generations. Moreover, individual man would not be responsible only for his own acts, but for the acts of others.

This concept of solidarity is untenable because it implies that man is a part of society, not as a person who has dominion over his acts, but in the same way, for example, as an organ is a part of a living being.

The foundation of responsibility is liberty ; and liberty belongs essentially to individual man. Provided that these two truths are safeguarded, we admit that a certain solidarity does obtain among men ; and of it we shall speak later.

POINTS FOR REVIEW

1. Define: imputation, imputability, responsibility, moral responsibility, and juridical responsibility.

2. Prove that moral acts are imputable, and also that man, as a moral agent, is responsible for his moral acts.

3. Distinguish between imputability and morality.

---

(1) Dans chaque phénomène social, surtout moderne, les prédécesseurs participent plus que les contemporains.— *Polit. Positive, Dist. prél.*, I, 364.

ARTICLE III

MERIT AND DEMERIT

889. Statement of the question.— 1° Merit may be defined in a general way as a relation in justice to retribution.

2° The requisites of merit are four in number :

a) The person who merits must be free ; for a person who merits cannot give his act in exchange for a reward except in as much as he has dominion over his acts[1].

b) Merit, which may be considered *in the concrete* and *in the abstract*. In the concrete, merit is the meritorious action. In the abstract, merit is the property of an action in virtue of which this action implies a relation to retribution, because of its author's having acted to the benefit or injury of another.

c) Reward (in the case of merit) or punishment (in the case of demerit).

d) A person who rewards or punishes.

3° Merit must be measured according to justice (commutative) ; for there must be an equality between the reward (or punishment) received by the person who merits and the service (or injury) done by his act to another. Hence a person properly merits because by his act he destroys his equality with another, which equality should be restored by the reward he receives for the service rendered by his act. In this sense, merit may be defined in relation to retribution made according to justice ; in other words, it is the right in justice to retribution.

---

(1) *De Veritate*, q. 29, a. 6.

4° Merit is divided into *condign merit* (*meritum de condigno*), which is merit *in the strict sense*, and *congruous merit* (*meritum de congruo*), which is *quasi-merit* or *merit of fitness*.

Condign merit is *the relation of the work to the reward due to the work, and therefore is a claim to reward in justice.*

Condign merit is of two kinds:

a) condign merit *of rigorous justice* (*ex rigore justitiae*), if the relation of the work to the reward excludes all favor previously done to the person meriting by the person making the retribution ;

b) condign merit *of condignity* (*ex condignitate*), if the relation of the work to reward presupposes some element of favor previously accorded to the person meriting by the person making the retribution; v.g., the merit of a creature in relation to God presupposes existence and movement to act received from God.

Congruous merit is the relation of the work to the reward not in virtue of the work, but rather because of fitness, liberality, or friendship, all of which are allied to justice; v.g., honors are due in virtue of a certain fitness (de congruo) to a soldier who has distinguished himself by bravery in the defense of his country.

890. Statement of the thesis.

THESIS. — BY HIS HUMAN ACTS, MAN CAN MERIT OR DEMERIT BEFORE INDIVIDUAL MEN, BEFORE SOCIETY, AND BEFORE GOD.

First part. — *By his human acts, man can merit or demerit before individual men.* — He who by his free acts can cause a relation to retribution in accordance with justice before individual men can merit or demerit with individual men by his human acts. But man can cause this relation by his free acts. Therefore, by his human acts, man can merit or demerit before individual men.

The *major* is evident from the statement of the question.

Minor.— By his free acts, man can destroy the equality of justice between himself and other men; and this equality of justice can be restored by reward or punishment.

Second part.—*By his human acts, man can merit or demerit before society.*— There are three cases in which this is possible. *a)* If a man does a service or injury to another individual man, he merits or demerits directly before that individual man, and indirectly before society: individual man is a part of society. *b)* If the does a service or an injury directly to society, he merits or demerits directly before society, and indirectly before individual men, who are parts of society. *c)* If he does good or evil to himself, he does not merit or demerit before himself, for, in this case, the person who merits and the person who makes retribution are not distinct; but he merits indirectly before society, for every man is naturally a part of society.

Third part.— *By his human acts, man can merit or demerit before God.* — *Note:* we are dealing with merit of *condignity*, which presupposes a favor received from God.

1° He who can render due honor to God and can also dishonor Him can merit or demerit before God. But man by his human acts can render due honor to God and can also dishonor Him. Therefore man by his human acts can merit or demerit before God.

Major.— God is the ultimate end. But he who renders due honor to God performs an act for the ultimate end, and therefore merits the ultimate end; and he who dishonors God acts at variance with the ultimate end, and hence demerits this end. Therefore.

Minor.— If man performs acts which are referable to God, he renders due honor to God; and, if he performs acts which cannot be referred to God, he dishonors Him.

2° In every community, the ruler of the community is concerned chiefly with the care of the common good; hence it appertains to him to make retribution for the good or evil done in the community. But God is the governor and ruler of the whole universe. Therefore it is evident that human acts are meritorious or demeritorious in as much as they are referable or not referable to God; for otherwise God would not be concerned with human acts (¹).

.**891. Difficulties.**— 1° Merit or demerit implies a relation to retribution for the benefit or injury done to another. But a good or evil human act cannot benefit or injure God. Therefore a good or evil human act cannot be meritorious before God.

Major.— Implies a relation to retribution for the benefit or injury done to another or to the honor due to him, *I concede*; solely for the personal benefit or injury done to another, *I deny*;

Minor.— Does no benefit or injury to the honor due to God, *I deny*; does no personal benefit or injury to God, *I concede*.

2° An instrument neither merits or demerits before the person who uses it. But man is the instrument of God. Therefore man neither merits or demerits before God.

Major.— An instrument which is not free, *I concede*; a free agent, *I deny*.

Minor.— An instrument which is not free, *I deny*; a free agent, *I concede*.

POINTS FOR REVIEW

Explain each of the following terms: merit in general, merit in the concrete, merit in the abstract, condign merit, condign merit of rigorous justice, condign merit of condignity, congruous merit.

---

(1) I-II, q. 21, a. 4.

BOOK IV

Principles of moral acts

Prologue.— The principles of moral acts are of two kinds: extrinsic and intrinsic. The extrinsic principles are laws; and the intrinsic principles are virtues. First, we shall deal with laws, and, secondly, with virtues. Hence there will be two chapters in this book.

Chapter I. Laws.
Chapter II. Virtues.

CHAPTER I

LAWS

Prologue.— In this chapter, first, we shall treat of law in general; afterwards, we shall discuss the eternal law, the natural law, and positive laws; and, finally, we shall deal with conscience, which is the act by which laws are applied to particular acts. Hence there will be five articles in this chapter.

Law in general
- Notion of law
- Real definition of law
- Law and precept
- Effect and acts of law
- Moral obligation
- Moral obligation, morality, and liberty
- Division of law

Eternal law
- Statement of the question
- Thesis: The eternal law exists in God
- Corollaries

Natural law
- Statement of the question
- Thesis: The natural law exists in rational creatures
- Distinction of the precepts of the natural law
- Immutability of the natural law
- Difficulties
- Dispensation from the natural law
- Obligation of the natural law
- Sanction of the natural law

Positive law
- Notion of positive law
- Difference between positive law and natural law
- Divine positive law
- Derivation of human laws from the natural law
- Necessity of human law
- Extension of human law
- Change of human law
- Custom can have the force of law
- Obligation imposed by human law
- Penal law

Conscience
$\begin{cases} \text{Notion of moral conscience} \\ \text{Three functions of conscience} \\ \text{Conscience is the proximate rule of subjective} \\ \quad \text{morality and obligation} \\ \text{Division of conscience} \\ \text{Rules of conscience} \end{cases}$

ARTICLE I

LAW IN GENERAL

892. Notion of law. — The term *law* has various significations.

a) In a very wide sense of the term, law is a rule by which a being *is moved to action or withheld from it*. In this sense, we speak of law even in reference to *irrational* beings ; v.g., the laws of physics.

b) In a wide sense, law is a rule of actions which are dependent on reason ; v.g., the laws of art.

c) In a more restricted sense, law is the remote and extrinsic norm of the *morality* of human acts. Thus any precept is a law ; v.g., the precept of a father, of a master, etc.

d) Law, in its strict and proper sense, is a rule of human acts given to a *community* which commands what accords with right reason.

893. Real definition of law. — Law, in its strict and proper sense, is defined : *an ordinance of reason designed for the common good, and promulgated by one who has charge of the community.*

a) Ordinance, in its modern acceptation, sometimes signifies the act of commanding, and sometimes the act of *establishing order.* As used in the definition, it means a dictate which establishes an order or disposition : *a)* for the attainment of a due end, *b)* by means which are proportionate to the end[1].

---

(1) I-II, q. 102, a. 1.

b) Ordinance of reason: for only reason, which alone is competent to devise means for the attainment of an end(²), can establish the relation of one thing to another (³).

This may be proved briefly. Law is a rule of human acts. But the rule of human acts is reason : for reason is the first principle of human acts ; and that which is the first principle in any genus is the rule and measure of that genus ; v.g., unity in the genus of numbers. Therefore it follows that law is something which pertains to reason(³).

Hence, although law presupposes an act of the will, it formally derives from reason. For law is a *motive ordinance* of reason, an ordinance given only in as much as the will tends to an end, i.e., wills an end.

c) Designed for good: if it were an ordinance for evil, it would not truly be a law.

d) For the common good: for reason, in its direction of human acts, is concerned with the ultimate end, i.e., with happiness, which is the first principle of human acts. Therefore, since law is an ordinance of reason, it is concerned chiefly with the direction of human acts to happiness, and, indeed, to the happiness of the community: for the happiness of the community exceeds the good of one man, who is only a part of the community(⁴).

e) By one who has charge of the community: law is an ordinance designed for the common good. Now the establishing of an order or disposition for the attainment of the common good is the function of the community, or of a public person charged with the care of the community, for, in all matters, the directing of anything to the end is the concern of him who is charged with the care of the end(⁵).

f) Promulgated: promulgation, which is a condition that is absolutely required for the validity, i.e., the binding force,

---
(1) I-II, q. 90, a. 1.
(2) In II *Sent.*, d. 38, q. 1, a. 3.
(3) I-II, q. 90, a. 1.
(4) I-II, q. 90, a. 2.
(5) I-II, q. 90, a. 3.

of a law, is the public notice or intimation of the law, not the knowledge of it. For it is the promulgation of a law, not the knowledge of it, which makes a law binding on those subject to it.

894. Law and precept. — Precept may be considered in its genus and in its species.

Precept in the generic sense is used to signify law and also precept in the specific sense.

Precept in the specific sense, i.e., mere precept, signifies an ordinance which has not the perfection of law. It may be distinguished from law:

in its *end*: the end of a law is the common good, whereas the end of a precept is a private good;

in its *author*: a legislator is a public person charged with a political community; the author of a precept may be a private person possessed only of private power; v.g., the father of a family;

in its *subject*: a law is applicable to the community as such; a precept can be imposed on individual persons;

in its *extension*: a law is not binding outside the territory of the community for which it was made; a precept may be imposed on a person, and in this case is binding on him everywhere;

in its *stability*: a law is of itself perpetual, and does not disappear at the death of the legislator; a precept may of its nature be transitory, i.e., given for a definite time or for a definite act, and, unless otherwise stipulated, terminates when its author dies or loses his authority.

895. Effect and acts of law. — 1° The effect of law consists in its *making men good*. This it does in two ways:

first, it induces subjects to be duly obedient to those governing them, and thus leads them to their proper virtue: for the proper virtue of a subject consists in due submission to superiors;

secondly, it directs men to good actions, for the end of every law is the common good (¹).

2° The acts of law are four in number: it *commands, prohibits, permits,* and *punishes.*

Law commands, or at least may command, acts which are generically good, i.e., acts in virtue.

Law prohibits acts which are generically evil, i.e., acts of vice.

Law permits acts which are generically indifferent. All acts which are not totally evil or totally good may be called indifferent.

Finally, law punishes in as much as it induces its subjects, because of fear of punishment, to obey it (²).

896. Moral obligation. — Whether law commands, prohibits, permits, or punishes, it is always obligatory. For, even when law permits certain acts, it imposes the obligation of not preventing these acts. Therefore we may say that obligation is a general effect of law. And, since this obligation is imposed in relation to human acts, it is called moral.

The concept of obligation connotes necessity. But the first principle in the order of human action is the end. Hence we may say that moral obligation is a certain necessity which derives from the end.

Moral obligation may be defined: *the absolute necessity of doing or omitting certain acts in view of an end.*

a) Necessity: that is necessary which cannot not be.

b) Absolute necessity: thus the doing and omitting of human acts are not only useful for the attainment of the end, but are so related to it that its attainment is impossible without them.

c) Absolute necessity in view of an end: thus is excluded conditional, i.e., hypothetical, necessity.

---
(1) I-II, q. 92, a. 1.
(2) I-II, q. 92, a. 2.

Necessity which derives from an end, i.e., final necessity, is *absolute* when it concerns means without which the end *intended* cannot be attained; it is *hypothetical* when it concerns means without which an end which is not intended, but could be intended, could not be attained; v.g., a ship or an airplane is of absolute necessity for a person who makes a crossing of the Atlantic ocean. On the supposition that a person wishes to cross the Atlantic ocean, a ship or an airplane is of hypothetical necessity (¹).

Since the common good is the end of law, the obligation which results from law is of absolute necessity in relation to the end.

Considered in reference to human acts, moral obligation may be defined: *the property of a human act in virtue of which this act must be performed or omitted in view of the ultimate end.*

897. Moral obligation, morality, and liberty. — 1°
Moral obligation is distinct from morality.

Morality is the transcendental relation of a human act to its object as conformed or not conformed to right reason and the eternal law.

Moral obligation is the transcendental relation of necessity which a human act has to the ultimate end.

2° Moral obligation is a kind of bond, but does not destroy liberty.

Liberty is the physical power of doing or not doing an act.

Moral obligation is necessity deriving from the end, and therefore is not destructive of the physical power of acting or not acting.

For, even though the doing or omitting of an act be necessary for the attainment of the end, the will always has the physical power of not tending to the end in particular circumstances, i.e., has the physical power of acting or not acting, even though it does not tend to the end.

---

(1) *Contra Gentes*, l. II, c. 30.

898. Division of law. — 1° Law is divided into the eternal law, the natural law, and positive law.

The *eternal law* is the law which resides in the supreme intellect which governs all things, i.e., in God.

The *natural law* is the law which is imprinted in us by nature; in other words, it is the law which natural reason knows in the light of the first principles of the practical order.

Positive law is law established by the free determination of the legislator.

2° Positive law may be essentially (per se) positive or accidentally positive.

An *essentially positive law* is a law which contains determinations of the natural law not found in the natural law; v.g., the punishment of murderers is prescribed by the natural law, but the particular kind of punishment is determined by positive law[1].

An *accidentally positive law* is a law which promulgates precepts contained in the natural law ; v.g., the law by which a legislator forbids theft or murder.

3° Positive law, essentially or accidentally such, is divided into divine law and human law.

Divine law is law freely promulgated by God. Sometimes the natural law is called divine because it derives from God as the immediate author of nature.

Human law is established by human authority.

4° Human law is *civil* or *ecclesiastical* as it derives from civil authority or from ecclesiastical authority.

POINTS FOR REVIEW

1. Give and explain: the definition of law; the effect and acts of law.
2. Define and distinguish between moral obligation and morality.
3. Is moral obligation destructive of liberty ? Explain.

---

(1) I-II, q. 95, a. 2.

ARTICLE II

ETERNAL LAW

899. Statement of the question. — 1° The eternal law is defined : *the ordinance of God's wisdom which directs all acts and movements*(1), i.e., all beings, *to the end proper to them.*

We shall arrive at a clearer understanding of this definition if we compare the eternal law with the divine ideas and with divine Providence.

a) The divine ideas are the exemplars of the things of creation, i.e., of all things created by God ; and therefore they are many in number. The eternal law is the exemplar of order, i.e., of the order which should exist in all the actions by which created things should tend to their end; and therefore there is only one eternal law.

b) Divine Providence is the plan of the order, i.e., of the manuduction or direction, of things to their end. The eternal law is the ordinance containing the rules which ought to direct all things to the common good, and according to which Providence disposes the acts and movements of creatures.

Therefore divine Providence is related to the eternal law as conclusion to principle : because of the ordinance which sets forth the rules for the direction of things to their end, God formulates, as it were, a plan by which all creatures are directed to the end proper to them.

2° All who deny God's existence and Providence, as Atheists, Materialists, Pantheists, Fatalists, and Evolutionists, in doing so, deny the existence of the eternal law.

---

(1) I-II, q. 93, a. 1.

900. Statement of the thesis.

THESIS.— THE ETERNAL LAW EXISTS IN GOD.

If all created things are ruled by God's Providence, the eternal law exists in God. But all created things are ruled by God's Providence. Therefore the eternal law exists in God(1).

Major.— God rules all created things by His Providence in as much as He directs them to their end. But God directs all created things to the end predetermined for them by a divine ordinance. Therefore, if all creation is ruled by God's Providence, the rules for the direction of all things to their end are contained in an ordinance of God's wisdom, i.e., there exists in God a law which is eternal, because God conceives nothing in time, but everything from eternity.

The *minor* is evident from what was said in Metaphysics (n. 806).

901. Corollaries.
— 1° The eternal law is a law in the strict sense, for, although it was not promulgated passively in creatures from eternity, it was promulgated actively in the Word from all eternity.

2° All created beings are subject to the eternal law, but all are not subject in the same way : rational creatures are subject to it in the sense that they move and direct themselves to their end, whereas irrational creatures are subject to it in as much as they are moved to their end ; in other words, rational creatures are subject to the eternal law through their intellectual knowledge of God's commandments, and irrational creatures are subject to it by means of simple movement, i.e., because directed to their end by instinct and natural inclination.

---

(1) *Ibid.*

ARTICLE III

NATURAL LAW

902. Statement of the question. — 1° Law is a product of reason. Hence a law may not be called natural in the sense that it is constituted of the essential principles of things, independently of reason. A law is called natural in as much as it is constituted by natural reason, i.e., in as much as reason, in constituting it, acts under the impulse of nature.

Reason is called natural in the strict sense when it judges without discourse, i.e., without recourse to reasoning. In a wider sense, reason is called natural when it judges by means of a very easy process of reasoning, of which all men are capable. When reason judges without an act of reasoning, or with a very simple act of reasoning, it is called *natural*, because, in making its judgment, it acts under the impulse of its nature.

2° Therefore the natural law may be defined: *an ordinance of natural reason designed for the common good*. In relation to its exemplar cause, which is the eternal law, natural law is defined by St. Thomas: *a participation of the eternal law by which rational creatures are naturally inclined to the mode of acting and end proper to them*(¹).

3° Atheists, Materialists, and Positivists directly or indirectly deny the existence of the natural law.

903. Statement of the thesis.

THESIS.— THE NATURAL LAW EXISTS IN RATIONAL CREATURES.

1° *By the way of descent.*— The participation of the eternal law by which rational creatures are naturally inclined to the

---
(1) I-II, q. 91, a. 2.

mode of acting and end proper to them is the natural law. But this participation of the eternal law exists in rational creatures. Therefore the natural law exists in rational creatures [1].

Major.— The participation of the eternal law by which rational creatures are naturally inclined to the mode of acting and end proper to them is a direction to an end which natural reason knows and makes known, because, in rational creatures, inclination follows intellectual knowledge. Therefore this direction is a moral law in the strict sense, and it is the *natural law*, because by it rational creatures are naturally inclined to action.

Minor.— Since law is a measure and a rule, it can exist in a person in two ways: first, in the person considered as the one who rules and measures; secondly, in the person considered as the one who is ruled and measured, for a thing is ruled or measured in as much as it has a participation of the rule and measure. And, since all things which are subject to God's Providence are ruled and measured by the eternal law, it is evident that all things have a certain participation of the eternal law, in as much, indeed, as they are inclined, in consequence of its being imprinted in them, to the acts or mode of acting and ends proper to them. Hence there is found in rational creatures a participation of the eternal law whereby they are naturally inclined to the manner of acting and end proper to them.

2° *By the way of ascent.*— The natural knowledge (conceptio) in virtue of which rational creatures can perform their proper operations and render them conformable to their end is the natural law. But such natural knowledge exists in rational creatures. Therefore the natural law exists in rational creatures.

The *major* is evident from the notion of the natural law.

Minor.— It is in virtue of principles which naturally exist in them that all things are able to perform their proper opera-

---

(1) I-II, q. 91, a. 2, c.

tions and to render them conformable to their end. But, in rational creatures, this principle is natural knowledge, for the intellect is the principle of the acts proper to rational creatures. Therefore.

3° *From experience.*— Experience clearly shows that human reason has knowledge of the inclinations of human nature to its proper acts and proper ends. But natural inclination known by reason, i.e., the knowledge of natural inclination, is the natural law. Therefore.

Minor.— Since natural inclination derives from the eternal law, knowledge of natural inclination is a participation of the eternal law as known by reason under the impulse of its nature, i.e., is the natural law.

904. Distinction of the precepts of the natural law.— The precepts of the natural law may be distinguished *materially*, i.e., in relation to their matter, and *formally*, i.e., with reference to the mode in which they are contained in the natural law.

1° The first question which we must answer in regard to the material distinction of the precepts of the natural law is this: what is the first principle of the natural law? Just as there is an indemonstrable first principle of speculative reason on which all other principles of the speculative order are founded, so too there is a first principle of practical reason, i.e., of reason as directive of human acts, on which all principles of the practical order are founded.

That which primarily falls under the apprehension of practical reason whose end is operation, is good. Therefore the first principle of practical reason, i.e., the first principle of the natural law, is founded on the notion of good, and may be enunciated thus: *good, i.e., good of reason, must be done and pursued, and evil avoided.*

Since a good is an end, and an evil is the contrary of an end, practical reason apprehends all things to which man is naturally inclined as good, and consequently as objects to be pursued, and their opposite as evil and as objects to be avoided. Hence, under this aspect, the order of the precepts of the natural law corresponds to the order of natural inclinations.

In man, we can distinguish the aspects of substance, animal, and rational being.

As a *substance*, man has a natural inclination to self-preservation. From this point of view, everything which protects life, and also everything which prevents the contrary of life, i.e., death, is subject to the natural law.

As an *animal*, man has a natural inclination in a more special way to those things which are in accordance with the nature which he shares in common with other animals. In virtue of this inclination, everything which nature has taught all animals, as the union of male and female, the rearing of offspring, etc., is subject to the natural law.

As a *rational being*, man has a natural inclination to those goods which are proper to him in as much as they accord with his rational nature; v.g., man has a natural inclination to know truths concerning God, to live in society; and, in this respect, whatever pertains to this inclination, as the eschewing of ignorance, the avoidance of harm to his neighbor, etc., comes under the natural law (¹).

2° The precepts of the natural law are divided formally, i.e., in relation to the mode in which they are contained in this law, into primary and secondary precepts.

The *primary precepts of the natural law* are those precepts which concern the primary ends of natural inclinations, the things required for the attainment of these ends, and the avoidance of whatever is at variance with them; v.g., the preservation of life and the use of food and drink are commanded by the primary precepts of the natural law, because the preservation of life is the end of a natural inclination, and its attainment is certainly impossible without the use of food and drink.

The *secondary precepts of the natural law* are those precepts concerned either with the secondary ends of natural inclinations or with those things by which the primary ends can be attained

---

(1) I-II, q. 94, a. 2.

easily and in a becoming manner; v.g., the use of suitable food and drink pertains to the secondary precepts of the natural law, because this is designed for the *better* preservation of life.

It is to be observed that the primary precepts of the natural law are self-evident at least *in themselves*, for they are concerned with things to which nature is immediately inclined. The secondary precepts, however, are not self-evident in themselves, but are conclusions deduced from the primary precepts, for they concern things to which nature is inclined not immediately, but in virtue of its primary ends.

905. Immutability of the natural law. — 1° *Preliminaries.*—*a)* Change in the natural law may be conceived as taking place in two ways: by way of addition and by way of subtraction. Change by way of addition takes place in the natural law when precepts are added to it. Change of this kind is possible in the natural law. Indeed, many precepts useful for human life have been added to the natural law by both divine and human law. Change by way of subtraction takes place in the natural law when precepts are removed from it ([1]). It is with the very difficult problem of this kind of change that we are concerned at present.

b) The modern doctrine of *absolute immobilism* holds that the natural law is absolutely immutable, whereas *absolute relativism* holds that it is essentially mutable([2]). The latter doctrine was proposed in ancient time by Aristippus, a Socratic philosopher ([3]), and, in modern times, has been supported by the Positivists, as Comte, Durkheim, Levy-Bruhl, and others, who argue from the mutability of laws and institutions among many peoples.

c) Before attempting to give the Thomistic solution of the problem, we must make certain distinctions.

---
(1) I-II, q. 94, a. 5.
(2) Deux tendances se sont toujours partagé les esprits relativement à la fixité ou à la variabilité du droit. Hyptonisés par l'abstrait, les uns immobilisent les notions, oublieux de la relativité qu'imposent les contingences. D'autres frappés de cet excès courent à l'excès opposé, versant dans un relativisme absolu, destructeur des notions premières.— SERTILLANGES, *La Phil. morale de S. Th. d'Aquin*, p. 148, 2e édit.
(3) *In Eth.*, l. V, l. 12.

The precepts of the natural law are primary or secondary.

First, the primary precepts are concerned with the primary and immutable end of every natural inclination, an end which is absolutely possible of attainment, and therefore they are self-evident.

The secondary precepts are concerned with the primary end of natural inclinations as attainable in a fitting manner, and with their secondary end, and therefore these precepts may be called conclusions deduced from the primary precepts.

Secondly, the primary precepts of the natural law are of two kinds: most common precepts and first precepts in each order of inclination.

The most common principles are those which are convertible with the supreme first rule of practical reason: *good must be done, and evil avoided.*

The first precepts in each order of inclination are reducible to the most common precepts, are dependent on them and protected by them, and are self-evident in themselves, even though to us they can be conclusions. Therefore these precepts are sometimes called conclusions or quasi-conclusions, and secondary precepts in relation to the most common principles, which are self-evident in themselves and to us ([1]).

Thirdly, according to St. Thomas, a change in the natural law by way of subtraction may be considered under two aspects: *subjectively*, i.e., in regard to our knowledge of the law; and *objectively*, i.e., in regard to their rectitude ([2]).

2° *In the light of the foregoing remarks*, we may now set forth the propositions which follow.

a) *As regards our knowledge of them, the most common precepts of the natural law are the same for all men, i.e., are immutable.*

---

(1) CAJETANUS, in I-II, q. 94, a. 1.
(2) I-II, q. 94, a. 4.

These principles are the very first principles of practical reason, just as the principle of contradiction is the first principle of speculative reason (1). Hence a person who is ignorant of these principles does not distinguish between good and evil, and is incapable of thinking of morality, obligation, or law; in other words, such a person has not the use of reason.

b) As regards our knowledge of them, the first principles in each order of inclination and the secondary principles of the natural law are the same for almost all men, i.e., may be unknown to a relatively small number of men, and hence may be said to be mutable in a few exceptional cases.

Examples : Suicide, which is contrary to a primary precept of the natural law, is regarded as a sin by almost all men, but can be considered as lawful by the few, and, indeed, was considered such by certain philosophers. In like manner, theft, though expressly at variance with the natural law, was not considered wrong by certain German tribes of ancient times(2). This is explained by the fact that the first principles in each order of inclination and the secondary principles of the natural law are not always self-evident to us, but are quasi-conclusions or proximate conclusions deduced from the most common principles. Therefore knowledge of them requires a certain intellectual effort. Hence, though knowledge of them is easily accessible to all men, they remain unknown to a certain few in whom reason is perverted by the passions, evil habits, or evil dispositions of nature, as feeble-mindedness.

c) As regards their rectitude, the most common precepts of the natural law and the first precepts in each order of inclination are the same for all men, i.e., are absolutely immutable.

The most common precepts of the natural law and the first precepts in each order of inclination concern ends which immediately pertain to different aspects of human nature. These aspects are immutable(3) : for man is immutably a being,

---

(1) I-II, q. 94, a. 2.
(2) I-II, q. 94, a. 4.
(3) *In Ethic.*, l. V, l. 12, n. 1029.

a substance, an animal, and a rational being. Hence all the first precepts of the natural law, i.e., the most common precepts and the first precepts in each order of inclination, are absolutely immutable as regards their rectitude.

d) As regards their rectitude, the secondary precepts of the natural law, though mutable for the few, are the same for almost all men. In its process of reasoning, reason deals with human acts, which are contingent and mutable in consequence of the mutable nature (^{1}) from which they result, and because of different circumstances of time, place, etc. But the secondary precepts are proximate conclusions which practical reason deduces from the primary precepts. Therefore, as *proximate* conclusions, they have for almost all men the same immutability as regards their rectitude as have the primary precepts; but, as *conclusions*, they may be mutable in particular cases of rare occurrence in which they are opposed, because of circumstances, to the primary precepts of the natural law(^{2}). Example : Material things are destined, according to the primary intention of nature, for the conservation of human life ; and private ownership is required by the secondary precepts of the natural law. Nevertheless, if a material thing possessed by another is required to save the life of a person in extreme need, the right of private ownership in this case becomes null and void, in order that the primary intention of nature may be realized.

The Thomistic teaching on the immutability of the natural law may be summarized schematically as follows :

Precepts of the natural law	Primary	*Most common:* immutable as regards our knowledge of them and as regards their rectitude.
		First in each order of inclination: immutable as regards their rectitude, but mutable as regards our knowledge of them in particular cases of rare occurrence.
	Secondary:	mutable as regards their rectitude and as regards our knowledge of them in particular cases of rare occurrence.

---

(1) I-II, q. 57, a. 2, ad 1.
(2) I-II, q. 94, aa. 4 and 5.

906. Difficulties.— 1° Whatsoever appertains to nature is absolutely immutable. But the natural law appertains to nature. Therefore the natural law is absolutely immutable (Absolute immobilism or determination).

Major.— What appertains to an immutable nature, v.g., to the divine nature, *I concede*; to a mutable nature, v.g., to human nature, *I deny*.

Minor.— The natural law appertains to an immutable nature, *I deny*; to human nature, which is mutable, *I concede*.

The primary precepts which appertain to the immutable aspects of human nature are, as we have already seen, absolutely immutable; but, because men are immersed in corruptible things, human nature in the concrete is not immutable; and therefore the secondary precepts of the natural law admit of some exceptions in their application.

2° If the natural law were immutable, moral institutions would not be changeable. But moral institutions are changeable. Therefore the natural law is not immutable.

Major.— Immutable as regards its most common precepts, *I deny*; immutable as regards its secondary precepts and as regards precepts of positive law, *I concede*.

Minor.— Changeable in their relation to the most common precepts of the natural law, *I deny*; changeable in their relation to the secondary precepts of the natural law and to the precepts of positive law, *I concede*.

The advocates of absolute relativism admit that there are certain fundamental rules in the moral and juridical institutions of peoples which are the same for all men (1); and thus they confirm the scholastic teaching.

907. Dispensation from the natural law.— Dispensation may be *improper* or *material*, and *proper* or *formal*.

Improper dispensation from a law consists in a change made by a superior authority in the matter of the law.

Proper dispensation consists in the relaxation of the law in certain special cases.

It is certain that no human power, civil or ecclesiastical, can, *on its own authority*, grant a dispensation from the natural law : for a dispensation from a law can be granted only by its founder or by his lawful successor. But can God, Who, as the first efficient cause of all nature, is the founder of the natural law, grant a dispensation from this law ?

It is the common teaching of all authors that God can grant a dispensation from the precepts of the natural law.

---

(1) En dépit des variations, dans le temps et l'espace, la morale est toujours composée d'un petit nombre de principes essentiels, conditions essentielles de vie sociale, qui forment en quelque sorte le thème fondamental de la moralité et qui se développent selon les milieux, les circonstances, et les prescriptions particulières.— Espinas, *Les Sociétés Animales*, p. 147, 2e édit.

Some, as Ockam and Gerson, hold that God can grant a dispensation, in the proper sense of the term, from all the precepts of the natural law. Others, as Billuart, teach that God can dispense only *improperly* or materially from certain precepts of the natural law. This opinion, which commends itself to us because of its clarity, is the opinion we follow.

1° *God cannot grant a dispensation, in the proper sense of the term, from the precepts of the natural law.*— God cannot render good an act which is essentially evil. But, if God properly dispensed from the precepts of the natural law, He would render good an act which is essentially evil. Therefore God cannot grant a dispensation, in the proper sense of the term, from the precepts of the natural law(¹).

Major — The essential malice of human acts, like their essential goodness, does not depend on the divine will (n.867).

Minor.— All acts forbidden by the natural law are essentially, i.e., intrinsically, evil. Hence, if God properly dispensed from the precepts of the natural law, He would render good an act which is essentially evil.

2° *God cannot grant a dispensation, in the improper sense of the term, from certain precepts of the natural law.*— This statement has reference to precepts of the natural law which concern immutable matters ; v.g., God cannot dispense from the precepts which forbid blasphemy and lying.

3° *God can grant a dispensation, in the improper sense of the term, from certain precepts of the natural law.*— This statement has reference to precepts of the natural law which concern mutable matters. Man is forbidden by the natural law, for example, to put another person to death on his own private authority. But Abraham could have been permitted, in virtue of God's command, to put his son to death. Again, in order to increase the number of the chosen people, God granted a dispensation, in the improper sense of the term, from the precept of the natural law which forbids polygamy, and thus the right

---

(1) I-II, q. 100, a. 8, c. et ad 2.

over the body of her husband which belongs to one wife was divided among several wives.

908. Obligation of the natural law.— 1° *Preliminaries.*
— 1) Moral obligation, as we have seen, is the transcendental relation of necessity which a human act has to the ultimate end.

2) The Positivists, as Guyau, Durkheim, and Levy-Bruhl, deny the objective obligation of the natural law, and attempt to reduce it to illusion and prejudice.

Kant and the Idealists admit the existence of moral obligation, but maintain that it derives solely from autonomous human reason.

Others recognize moral obligation only in as much as it is a condition of public or private utility.

Descartes, Ockam, and Pufendorf hold that moral obligation is derived from the positive will of God, and, when once established, is immutable.

3) Since obligation is a relation, the solution of our present problem depends on our finding the foundation, proximate and remote, of moral obligation. In doing this, we shall sufficiently refute the arguments of those who deny that the natural law is of moral obligation.

The foundation of a relation is twofold : proximate, i.e., that from which the relation immediately derives ; and ultimate, i.e., that from which the relation first, i.e., ultimately, derives.

2° *In the light of the foregoing observations*, we shall now give the solution of the problem in the proofs of the propositions which follow.

First proposition.—*The proximate foundation of the obligation of the natural law is the essential order of things.*— The proximate cause whence derives the relation of necessity which an act commanded by the natural law has to its ultimate end is the essential order of things. But the proximate foundation of the obligation of the natural law is the proximate cause whence derives the relation of necessity which an act commanded by the natural law has to its ultimate end. Therefore the proximate foundation of the obligation of the natural law is the essential order of things.

Major.— The proximate cause of the obligation of an act commanded by the natural law is the necessary and essential connexion of the act with its ultimate end. But the essential connexion of an object with its ultimate end is the essential order of things : it is a relation of necessity imposed by the very nature of things. Therefore.

Minor.— Obligation is defined : the relation of necessity of a human act to the ultimate end.

Second proposition.— *The u timate foundation of the obligation of the natural law is not human reason, but the eternal law.*— The first or ultimate cause of the relation of necessity of a human act to its ultimate end is the ultimate foundation of moral obligation. But this first cause is not human reason, but the eternal law. Therefore the ultimate foundation of the obligation of the natural law is not human reason, but the eternal law.

The *major* is evident.

Minor.— The essential order of things is a created order whose first cause is the ordinance of God's wisdom which directs all creatures to their proper end, i.e., is the eternal law.

NOTES.— 1° The third proposition condemned by the Syllabus is as follows : *Human reason, in absolute independence of God, is the one and only arbiter of truth and falsity, of good and evil, and is a law unto itself.*

2° Ontologically speaking, the eternal law, i.e., God, is the ultimate foundation of obligations which derive from the natural law. But can man, without explicit knowledge of God, know the obligation of the natural law ? In answer to this question, we may reply : in order that man perceive the obligation of the natural law, it is sufficient that he know that the natural law is destined for good in general, i.e., for happiness. To know this is to know God not explicitly, but implicitly, i.e., in an obscure manner.

909. Sanction of the natural law. — 1° *Preliminaries.* — 1) A law is sanctioned when it is made holy, i.e., inviolable. A law should be made inviolable against transgressors bound to its observance. Transgressors can be forced to the observance of a law not by the mere manifestation of the good or end of the law to them, — for as transgressors they have an aversion for the good of the law, — but by the *fear of punishment*, which is a movement or change of the sensitive appetite. The fear of punishment engenders in man a disposition which makes him see that the observance of the law is destined for his good, not for his harm, as he had thought before he became possessed of this disposition. Thus it is by coaction that man is led to the observance of the law.

Hence sanction may be defined : *the penalty attached to a law to which transgressors of the law are liable, and which efficaciously leads men, out of fear of punishment, to be law-abiding,* i.e., to observance of the law.

Hence the sanction of a law is incorrectly defined as a reward or recompense attached to a law. For, if the reward is a good, i.e., an end, to which the direction of the law leads, it does not move the human will *in a coactive manner,* and hence is not a sanction of the law. If the reward is a counter-promise or a recompense by which the legislator can win over men, and thus lead them to act in conformity with the law, we may say that such men are led to the observance of the law because of fear of separation from this good, i.e., because of fear of punishment([1]). Example : in the injunction of St. Paul, *honor thy father and thy mother, that thou mayest be long-lived upon earth* (Eph. VI, 2-3), is implied the threat of an early death for all who dishonor their father and mother.

2) Sanction may be sufficient or insufficient, and perfect or imperfect.

---

(1) I-II, q. 92, a. 2, c.

Sanction is *sufficient* or *insufficient* as it does or does not lead efficaciously to the observance of the law; and *perfect* or *imperfect* as it deprives or does not deprive man of all the goods which his will can desire. Perfect sanction in this life is capital punishment; and, in the next life, eternal damnation.

2° *In the light of foregoing remarks, we shall give the solution to the problem of the sanctions of the natural law in the propositions which follow.*

1) *The natural law has sanctions even in this life.*— In a certain sense, remorse of conscience, dishonor, and sickness which are consequences of the violation of the natural law may be called sanctions of the natural law.

Moreover, in consideration of the obligation which the natural law imposes on man of living in society under constituted authority, we may say that the natural law has sanctions in as much as its violation is liable to punishment from human authority; v.g., a person who commits murder or attempts suicide is liable to punishment from human authority.

2) *The natural law has not always sufficient sanctions in this life.*— *a)* Remorse, sickness, and dishonor do not always lead men to the observance of the natural law. Indeed, some sinners are so morally corrupt that they do not experience remorse of conscience. Moreover, some transgressors of the natural law abound in riches and honors.

b) The penalties imposed by human authority are not always sufficient sanctions. Indeed, human authority punishes only external and serious acts of transgression of the natural law, namely, transgressions which are directly or indirectly detrimental to the common good of society. Hence there are many transgressions of the natural law which escape the sanctions of human legislators.

3) *The natural law has a perfect sanction in the next life.*— The natural law must have a perfect sanction which deprives man of every good which the human will can desire. But such a sanction cannot exist in this life. Therefore the natural law has a perfect sanction in the next life.

Major.— The sanction of a law must be proportionate to the end of the law. But the end of the natural law is not only the common good, but also the infinite good, i.e., God. Hence the sanction of the law must be the privation of every good which the human will can desire.

Minor.— Even capital punishment does not deprive man of every good which the human will can desire, for it does not deprive man of the goods of the next life.

4) *The perfect sanction of the natural law in the next life does not consist solely in the privation of the infinite good, which is God, but also in the infliction of punishment.*— Every sanction must be proportionate to the violation of the law. But there are two elements in the violation of the natural law: *a)* the abandonment of the true ultimate end, which is God, and *b)* an unlawful attachment to creatures as ultimate ends. Therefore, just as the abandonment of the true ultimate demands the privation of God, so the unlawful attachment to creatures demands the infliction of punishments which have their source in creatures. In other words, the perfect sanction which the natural law has in the next life does not consist solely in the privation of the infinite good, but also in the infliction of punishments.

POINTS FOR REVIEW

1. Define: natural reason, the natural law, proper dispensation from law, improper dispensation from law, sanction of law, sufficient sanction, and perfect sanction.

2. Enunciate the first principle of the natural law, and state the matter of the primary and secondary precepts of the natural law.

3. Discuss the mutability of the primary and secondary precepts of the natural law as regards *a)* our knowledge of them, *b)* their objective rectitude.

4. Explain why God can properly dispense from none of the precepts of the natural, and improperly dispense from only some of them.

5. What is *a)* the proximate foundation, *b)* the ultimate foundation of the obligation of the natural law? Prove your answer.

Article IV

POSITIVE LAW

910. Notion of positive law.— Positive law is a participation of the eternal law, which takes place by means of a special, i.e., positive, promulgation. Positive law, as we have seen (n. 898), may be essentially positive or accidentally positive, and divine, ecclesiastical, or civil. Sometimes civil law is simply called human law.

911. Difference between the natural law and positive law.— The natural law differs from positive law in the following ways:

1° *in its matter:* the object of the natural law is intrinsically good or evil acts, whereas the object of positive law may be acts which are not intrinsically good or evil;

2° *in its author:* God alone is the author of the natural law, whereas the author of positive law may be God or man;

3° *in its subject:* the natural law is binding on all men, whereas positive law may be binding only on the members of a community;

4° *in its mutability:* the natural law cannot be abrogated and is intrinsically immutable, whereas positive law admits of abrogation and is not intrinsically immutable;

5° *in its promulgation:* the natural law is promulgated by the natural light of reason, whereas positive law requires a special act of promulgation.

912. Divine positive law. — 1° *In the state of elevation to the supernatural order, divine positive law was absolutely nec-*

essary for precepts concerned with the supernatural life. — Divine positive law was absolutely necessary for these precepts because precepts concerned with the supernatural life have reference to an end whose attainment surpasses the powers of nature, and to which the natural law and human laws are not proportionate.

2° *Divine positive law was morally necessary for precepts concerned with the natural order.*— Human judgment on human acts which are particular and contingent does not attain certitude. Therefore, in order that man might not remain in doubt as regards what he was bound to do and what he was bound to avoid, it was necessary that he be directed in his proper acts by an infallible law given by God (¹).

913. Derivation of human laws from the natural law.
— 1° *Every human law is derived from the natural law.*—A human law has the force of law in as much as it is just. But a law is just in as much as it accords with the rule of reason, which is the natural law. Therefore a human law is truly a law only in as much as it is derived from the natural law; and, if it is at variance with the natural law, it is not a true law, but a perversion of law.

2° *Human laws are derived from the natural law in different ways.*— Some human laws are derived from the natural law as conclusions from principles, i.e., they are conclusions deduced from the principles of the natural law; v.g., the human law (accidentally positive), *thou shall not kill*, is a conclusion deduced from the principle of the natural law, *thou shalt not do evil to any person*. Others are derived from the natural law as determinations of certain precepts contained in an indeterminate manner in the natural law; v.g., the natural law makes preceptive the punishment of evil-doers, but leaves to human law (essentially positive) the determination of the particular punishments that should be inflicted.

The force of human laws of the first kind derives in part from the natural law, whereas the force of the latter derives immediately and solely from human authority (²).

---

(1) I-II, q. 91, a. 4.
(2) I-II, q. 95, a. 2.

Nevertheless, all human laws are of mediate obligation in virtue of the precept of the natural law which requires inferiors to obey their superior.

914. Necessity of human law. — Human laws are necessary for two reasons:

first, human laws make determinate the indeterminate precepts of the natural law, or they manifest conclusions deduced from principles of the natural law (1);

secondly, they institute sanctions against the wicked and prone to vice, who are not easily amenable to words, but who, because of fear, turn away from evil, and thus become virtuous and leave others in peace (2).

915. Extension of human law. — 1° *Human law directly commands only external acts.*— The end of human law is the pursuit of the common good in society. But only external acts are directly destined for the pursuit of the common good in society. Therefore human law can directly command only external acts.

Nevertheless, it is probable that human law can also command internal acts which are the immediate causes of external acts.

2° *Human law does not repress all vices.*— Law is a measure, and therefore it must be applied to men in accordance with their conditions, because a measure should be homogeneous to the thing measured. But human law is applied to the mass of the people, the majority of whom are not perfect in virtue. Hence human laws do not forbid all the vices from which the virtuous abstain, but only the more grievous vices, from which it is possible for the majority of people to abstain, and especially those vices which are harmful to others, without the prohibition of which life in human society would be impossible. Thus, for example, human law forbids murder, theft, and similar crimes (3).

---

(1) I-II, q. 91, a. 3.
(2) I-II, q. 95, a. 1.
(3) I-II, q. 96, a. 2.

3° *Human law commands acts of all the virtues, but not all the acts of all the virtues.*— The end of human law is the pursuit of the common good in society. Now there are acts of every virtue which are destined, immediately or mediately, for the common good of society, and hence which can be commanded by human law. But there are certain acts of the virtues which are not destined for the common good, v.g., certain internal acts; and hence such acts are not commanded by human law (¹).

916. Change of human law.— 1° Human law is a dictate of reason by which human acts are directed. Hence there are two reasons which can justify changes in human laws: 1) the changeableness and imperfection of human reason; 2) the exigencies of new human conditions.

a) The changeableness and imperfection of human reason can justify changes in human laws.— It is natural to human reason to advance gradually from the imperfect to the perfect. Hence we find that the teaching of the early philosophers in the field of the speculative sciences was imperfect, and that it was perfected by their successors. Moreover, we find a parallel case in the field of the practical sciences; the early lawgivers instituted laws which were defective in many ways; and these laws were changed and perfected by legislators of a later day.

b) The exigencies of new human conditions can justify changes in human laws. — Laws are measures which must be adapted to the measured, i.e., to the community, for which they were made. But circumstances arise which bring about a change in the conditions of human society, and hence which make it expedient to change old laws and make new ones, for different things are expedient for man according to the differences of his condition (²).

2° A change in human law is justified in as much as such change is conducive to the common good. But the change of a law is of itself always somewhat prejudicial to the common

---
(1) I-II, q. 96, a. 3.
(2) I-II, q. 97, a. 1.

good, simply because custom plays an efficacious role in the observance of laws. Consequently, when a law is changed, the observance of law is lessened because of the abolition of custom. Hence every change in law, in as much as it is a change, is detrimental to the common good because the binding force of the law is diminished. Therefore human laws should never be changed unless compensation be made for the harm done by the changing of them. Such compensation is realized: *a)* when some great and evident benefit results from the new enactment; *b)* when the change was necessitated because the existing law was clearly unjust, or its observance extremely harmful (¹).

917. Custom can have the force of law.— 1° Law is an ordinance of reason. But the inward movement of the will and the concepts of reason are most effectually manifested by the repetition of external acts. Hence custom, which results from the repetition of external acts, manifests the ordinance of reason, and thus can have the force of law (²).

2° The legal force of a custom which is introduced among a people is dependent in two ways on the social condition of the people:

a) if the people are free and able to make their own laws, the consent of the people expressed by a custom is a much more effectual means of ensuring the observance of a law than is the authority of a ruler who has power to make laws only in as much as he is the representative of the people;

b) if the people are not free and able to make their own laws or to abolish a law made by a superior power, a prevailing custom among them has the force of law in as much as it is tolerated by the superior power; for, in this case, the toleration of what custom introduced is tantamount to its approbation (²).

---

(1) I-II, q. 97, a. 2.
(2) I-II, q. 97, a. 3.
(2) *Ibidem*, ad 3.

918. Obligation imposed by human law.— 1° The problem of the binding force of human laws may be expressed in the question: are human laws binding in conscience?

2° There are four ways in which a human law can be unjust:

a) in its matter: when it commands acts which are intrinsically evil;

b) in its end: when it is conducive not to the common good, but to the cupidity and vainglory of its author;

c) in its author: when the legislator has no authority to make laws;

d) in its form: when, for example, its burdens are imposed unequally on the community, even though they are intended for the common good.

3° The observance of a law which is unjust in its matter is never permissible, for such a law is a variance with divine law: *we ought to obey God rather than men* (*Acts* V, 29).

The observance of other unjust laws is not forbidden, and, indeed, is sometimes necessary, namely, when it is required for the avoidance of scandal or the disturbance of the peace of society, or for the common good. In these cases, it is, properly speaking, the natural law, not the unjust law, which makes obedience obligatory.

4° Every just human law ultimately derives from the eternal law. But the eternal law is binding in conscience. Therefore every just human law is binding in conscience.

919. Penal law.— 1° Laws may be purely preceptive or prohibitive, mixed, or penal.

a) A purely preceptive or prohibitive law is a law which commands or prohibits an act, but imposes no penalty on transgressors of the law; v.g., the ecclesiastical law of hearing Mass.

b) A mixed law is a law which commands or prohibits an act, and also imposes a penalty on transgressors of the law.

A mixed law may be such copulatively or disjunctively.

A copulatively mixed law is a law which is binding in conscience as regards the performance or omission of acts, and also as regards the undergoing of penalties.

A disjunctively mixed law is a law which is not binding in conscience in a determinate manner as regards the performance or omission of acts, or as regards the undergoing of penalties, but as regards one or other of these. In other words, no one is bound under pain of guilt by a disjunctively mixed law to do or omit an act, but is bound under pain of guilt to undergo the penalties when the act is performed or omitted.

c) A purely penal law is a law which does not explicitly command or prohibit acts, but only states the penalties for violations of the law; v.g., *anyone guilty of this determinate act or omission shall pay this determinate penalty.*

A purely penal law is reducible to a disjunctively mixed law (1).

2° The question with which we are concerned at the moment is this: do disjunctively mixed laws exist?

The majority of modern moralists answer this question in the affirmative.

Others, however, do not agree with this answer, because, according to them, a penalty, in the proper sense of the term, presupposes a fault. Hence a person who is guilty of no fault in the doing or omitting of an act is not bound to pay the penalty.

3° In any case, a law should not be considered disjunctively mixed unless the intention of the legislator is known with certainty.

POINTS FOR REVIEW

1. Explain why all human laws derive from the eternal law, how they derive from the natural law, why they are necessary, why they can directly command only external acts, and why they cannot repress all vices.

---

(1) BILLUART, *Summa Sancti Thomae*, vol. II, p. 621 (Palmé).

2. Can human law command all the acts of all the virtues? Explain.
3. Discuss briefly the advisability of changing human laws.
4. When has custom the force of law? Explain.
5. Are all human laws binding in conscience? Explain.

ARTICLE V

CONSCIENCE

920. Notion of moral conscience.— Conscience, in its etymology, signifies the application of knowledge to something (*cum alio scientia*, i.e., knowledge applied to an individual case), i.e., the act by which we apply knowledge to a particular fact.

Conscience is divided into *psychological* conscience, which deals with internal facts in their entitative aspect, and *moral* conscience, which is the application of knowledge to human acts in their moral aspect.

Hence moral conscience is an act of the intellect, and may be defined: *the judgment of practical reason which regulates our human acts in their concrete individuality*. By this act of practical reason, we judge that certain things are good and ought to be done, and that others are evil and to be avoided.

921. Three functions of conscience.— 1° Conscience *testifies:* by it we recognize that we have done or have not done something.

2° It *binds* or *incites:* by it we judge that that something should be done or should not be done.

3° It *excuses* or *accuses*, i.e., *rebukes*: by it we judge that we have acted well or ill in something we have done.

Hence the act of conscience may be considered as taking place before the action, and is called *antecedent* conscience, which binds or incites; or as taking place after the action, and is called *consequent* conscience, which testifies, excuses, or accuses.

922. Conscience is the proximate rule of subjective morality and obligation.— Law, which is the rule by which objective morality and obligation are measured, proximately directs the act of the will and makes it binding only if it is known by the agent and is applied to the act of the will. But the application of law to acts of the will in the concrete is conscience. Therefore conscience is the proximate rule of the morality of acts in the concrete, i.e., of subjective morality and obligation (¹).

923. Division of conscience.— 1° In relation to its object, conscience may be true or erroneous.

A *true conscience* is one which declares the truth, i.e., what is truly good and truly evil.

An *erroneous conscience* is one which declares to be good something which is evil, or vice versa.

An erroneous conscience is vincibly or invincibly erroneous in as much as the error can or cannot be overcome by the exercise of moral diligence.

2° In relation to its assent, conscience may be certain, dubious, or probable.

A *certain conscience* is one whose judgment on the goodness or malice of an act is free from all fear of erring.

A *dubious conscience* is one whose assent in regard to the goodness of an action is suspended because of the fear of erring.

A *probable conscience* is one whose judgment on the goodness or malice of an act is made with fear of the other part of the contradiction, i.e., with fear that the opposite may be true.

924. Rules of conscience. — 1° *It is never lawful to act with a practically dubious conscience.*— A practically dubious conscience is a conscience by which a person doubts the lawfulness of an act considered in the concrete. A person who acts with such a conscience is disposed to perform an unlawful act

---

(1) *De Veritate,* q. 17, a. 3.

i.e., is disposed to commit sin. Hence a morally certain conscience is required for the performance of good acts.

2° *It is always lawful to act with a morally certain conscience.* — Moral certitude is certitude regarding human acts which is generally true, and is the certitude proper to matters of morality.

3° *It is never lawful to act contrary to a morally certain conscience.* — To act contrary to a morally certain conscience is to will what is judged with moral certitude to be evil. Hence it is never lawful to act at variance with an invincibly erroneous conscience. A person who acts with a vincibly erroneous conscience is culpable of his action in the degree that his error is culpable.

4° *When there is a question only of the lawfulness or unlawfulness of an act, it is lawful to follow a solidly probable opinion which denies the existence or application of the law.* — A dubious law is not binding. But a law whose existence or application is doubted with well-founded probability is a dubious law. Therefore.

A person who follows a solidly probable opinion does not act with a practically dubious conscience, but rather with a practically certain conscience, for he is certain of the lawfulness of following a solidly probable opinion.

When there is question not solely of the lawfulness or unlawfulness of an act, but of the avoidance of some evil, the safer opinion, i.e., the opinion which favors the existence and application of the law, must be followed. Thus, in the administration of the Sacraments, the greatest care must be taken to use only such matter as it certainly valid.

CHAPTER II

THE VIRTUES

Prologue.— In the preceding chapter, we dealt with laws, which are the extrinsic principles of human acts. Now we shall study the virtues, which are the intrinsic principles of human acts. First, we shall discuss the virtues in general, and, afterwards, the cardinal virtues and their parts. The cardinal virtues are prudence, justice, whose object is right, fortitude, and temperance. Finally, we shall treat of friendship, which results from the other virtues. Hence there will be seven articles in this chapter.

The virtues in general
- Necessity of virtue
- Definition of virtue
- Subject of the virtues
- Division of the virtues
- Comparison between the intellectual and moral virtues
- Parts of the cardinal virtues
- Moral virtue consists in a mean
- Connexion between the moral virtues
- Equality and inequality of the moral virtues
- Vice

Prudence
- Notion of prudence
- Acts of prudence
- Prudence, synderesis, and moral virtue
- Prudence and art
- Art and morality
- Integrant parts of prudence
- Subjective parts of prudence
- Potential parts of prudence
- Vices opposed to prudence by deficiency
- Vices opposed to prudence by excess

Right
- Right is the object of justice
- Meanings of right
- Notion of subjective right
- Relation between objective right and subjective right

VIRTUES 151

Right (Cont.)
- Division of objective right
- Division of subjective right
- Subject of dominion in general
- God's dominion
- Man's dominion over himself and others
- Immanent duties
- Man's dominion over external things
- Scholia
- Right and coaction
- Scholia

Justice
- Definition of justice
- Acts of justice
- Subjective parts of justice
- General justice
- Particular justice
- Sins against commutative justice
- Integrant parts of justice
- Potential parts of justice
- Homicide
- Suicide
- Religion
- Lying
- Adulation, quarreling, avarice, and prodigality
- Epiky or equity

Fortitude
- Two meanings of fortitude
- Definition of fortitude
- Vices opposed to fortitude
- Integrant and potential parts of fortitude
- Magnanimity
- Characteristics of magnanimous persons
- Vices opposed to magnanimity
- Magnificence
- Vices opposed to magnificence
- Patience
- Vices opposed to patience
- Considerations for acquirement of patience
- Perseverance
- Vices opposed to perseverance

Temperance
- Definition of temperance
- The rule of temperance is dependent on the necessities of this life
- Vices opposed to temperance
- Integrant parts of temperance
- Subjective parts of temperance
- Abstinence
- Sobriety
- Drunkenness
- Alcoholism
- Chastity
- Notion of virginity
- Virginity is lawful
- Difficulties
- Virginity is more excellent than matrimony
- Difficulties

Temperance (*Cont.*)
: Lust
  Species of lust
  Potential parts of temperance
  Continence and incontinence
  Clemency
  Meekness and vices opposed to it
  Modesty and its species
  Humility
  Vices opposed to humility
  Gravity of pride
  Studiousness
  Vices opposed to studiousness
  Eutrapelia (good cheer), modesty of external movements and of dress

Friendship
: Love, friendship, love of preference (dilectio), charity
  Definition of friendship
  Division of friendship
  Causes of friendship
  Love of neighbor
  Order of love of neighbor
  Internal effects of friendship
  External effects of friendship
  Domestic friendship
  Political friendship
  Justice, friendship, and charity
  Vices opposed to friendship

ARTICLE I

VIRTUES IN GENERAL

925. Necessity of virtue.— In order to attain his end, man must perform good acts. But man's faculties are not of themselves determined to tend towards good acts, for they may tend to evil acts. Hence, in order that man may easily and with stability perform good acts, virtues, i.e., certain dispositions of the powers of the soul, are required.

Therefore virtues are necessary for three reasons:

a) to overcome the indetermination of the powers;

b) to enable man to act easily for an end;

c) to enable man to act in a stable manner for an end.([1]).

926. Definition of virtue.— Virtue may be defined: *a good operative habit*([2]).

a) Habit, i.e., a stable disposition.

b) Operative, i.e., it is a habit which is destined for operation, and is the complement of the power or faculty.

c) Good, in as much as virtue is destined for the performance of good acts, and from it result only good acts.

927. Subject of the virtues.— 1° The subject of the virtues is that which the virtues immediately determine, i.e., that in which the virtues are immediately inherent as accidents.

2° Since virtues are operative habits, powers or faculties are their subject, for the operative power, not the essence, is the immediate principle of operation in creatures.

---

(1) *De Veritate*, q. 20, a. 2.— I-II, q. 49, q. 4.
(2) I-II, q. 55, aa. 1-3.

3° The external members, vegetative powers, and external senses cannot be the subject of habits or virtues([1]), for they have a determinate mode of acting, and, given the due disposition of their nature, have no difficulty in their acts. Any facility which they may seem to acquire from use or exercise does not result from habit, but solely from the removal of impediments, just as, for example, material instruments become polished and improved from use.

4° The sensitive powers (senses) of apprehension may be considered in two ways: *first*, in relation to nature, and thus they receive their determination from nature, not from virtue or disposition; *secondly*, as they are subject to reason in man, and thus we may admit of certain habits whereby man has facility of memory, thought, or imagination.

The sensitive powers of apprehension as subject to reason are merely preparatory to knowledge of the intellect, whose perfect act is the knowledge of truth. Therefore habits which can be in the sensitive powers of apprehension are not virtues, because they cannot complete the perfect act: for the knowledge of truth is completed only in the intellect. Hence the virtues by which we know truth are not found in the sensitive powers of apprehension, but rather in the intellect or reason([2]).

5° The intellect may be considered either in itself or as moved by the will.

Considered in itself, the intellect can be the subject of virtue, because of itself it has a certain indifference of perfectibility in relation to its object, which is truth, in as much as it may succeed or fail in attaining it, i.e., it may attain truth, or falsity under the appearance of truth.

As moved by the will, both the practical and the speculative intellect can be the subject of virtue, for as such it can be moved by the will in different ways. Under this aspect, the speculative intellect is the subject of faith, and the practical intellect is the subject of prudence ([3]).

---

(1) I-II, q. 50, q. 3, ad 3.
(2) I-II, q. 50, a. 3, ad 3.— Q. 56, a. 5— *De Virtutibus*, q. I, a. 4, ad 6.
(3) I-II, q. 56, a. 3.— *De Virtutibus*, q. 1, a. 7.

6° The will may be considered in relation to the good of reason proportionate to the will, or in relation to a good which exceeds its capacity.

The good of reason proportionate to the will is the private or proper good of the person willing.

A good exceeds the capacity of the person willing either as regards the whole human species, such as Divine good, which transcends the limits of human nature, or as regards the individual, such as the good of one's neighbor.

In regard to the good of reason proportionate to the will, the will, *as regards itself*, does not need virtue to perfect it, because the will is of itself perfectly proportionate to this good: the will is a natural inclination to the good of reason.

In regard to a good which exceeds the capacity of the person willing, the will needs to be perfected by virtues, for it is not of itself perfectly proportionate to this good. Therefore the will is the subject of such virtues as direct man's affections to God or to his neighbor, as charity, justice, and the like.(¹)

NOTE.— In the pursuit of a good of reason which is the private and proper good of the person willing, the will can meet with extrinsic and accidental difficulties caused by the passions of the sensitive appetite. For the removal of these difficulties, virtue in the will is not required, for they can be overcome by the virtues of the sensitive appetite which moderate the passions.

7° The sensitive appetite, concupiscible or irascible, may also be considered under two aspects: in itself, in as much as it is common to man and the brute; or as having a certain participation in reason, in as much as it is naturally designed to obey reason.

In itself, the sensitive appetite, concupiscible or irascible, is not the subject of virtues.

---

(1) I-II, q. 56, a. 6.

In as much as it has a participation in reason, it can be the subject of virtue. For, under this aspect, the sensitive appetite is a principle of human acts, and is in a certain way indeterminate in as much as it can be well or ill disposed to obey reason. Hence, in order to operate well, there is required in the sensitive appetite a certain habitual conformity to reason, which is nothing other than virtue(1).

928.— Division of the virtues.— 1° In their origin or cause, virtues are infused or acquired.

Infused virtues are virtues which are immediately produced by God, and are destined for a supernatural end; v.g., *faith, hope, charity, infused justice, infused temperance, etc.*

Acquired virtues are virtues which are caused by our own acts, and are destined for a natural end; v.g., *natural justice, natural temperance, etc.*

2° Acquired virtues are divided, according to their subject, into intellectual and moral virtues.

Intellectual virtues are virtues whose subject is the intellect; v.g., *science*.

Moral virtues are virtues whose subject is the appetite; v.g., *justice*.

3° Intellectual virtues are divided into virtues of the speculative intellect and virtues of the practical intellect.

The virtues of the speculative intellect are *intelligence (intellectus), wisdom,* and *science*.

The *virtues of the practical intellect* are *art* and *prudence*.

4° The moral virtues are divided into virtues which are the complement of the will, the complement of the concupiscible appetite, and the complement of the irascible appetite.

The *virtues which are the complement of the will* are justice and its annexed virtues.

---

(1) I-II, q. 56, a. 4.

The *virtues which are the complement of the concupiscible appetite* are temperance and its annexed virtues.

The *virtues which are the complement of the irascible appetite* are fortitude and its annexed virtues.

929. Comparison between the intellectual and moral virtues.— 1° The intellectual virtues are: science, wisdom, intelligence or understanding (intellectus), and art. Though prudence is an intellectual virtue as regards its subject, it is a moral virtue in its matter, because it is concerned with operations (agibilia).

The moral virtues are virtues which perfect the appetite; v.g., justice, fortitude, and temperance.

2° A thing can be more or less perfect in an absolute manner or in a relative manner; v.g., learning is, absolutely speaking, better than riches, but riches can be, relatively speaking, better than learning, as in the case of a person in extreme poverty.

3° Virtue is considered in an absolute manner when considered in relation to its object, for virtue, as an operative habit, is specified by its object: a thing is considered in an absolute manner when it is considered under the formal aspect of its species, i.e., in its proper specific nature.

Virtue is considered in a relative manner, when considered in relation to act; for, since virtue perfects the power, it is a principle of action.

4° The answer to the question of whether the moral virtues are more perfect than the intellectual virtues may be stated in the propositions which follow[1].

a) *The intellectual virtues are, absolutely speaking, more perfect habits than the moral virtues.*— A habit is considered in an absolute manner in relation to its object. But the object of the intellectual virtues, which is truth, is more excellent than the object of the moral virtues, which is goodness:

---
(1) I-II, q. 66, a. 2.

truth is more abstract and universal than goodness. Hence the intellectual virtues are, absolutely speaking, more perfect habits than the moral virtues.

b) The nature of virtue is more perfectly realized in the moral virtues than in the intellectual virtues.— The nature of virtue is more perfectly realized in virtues which make man good in an absolute sense than in virtues which make him good in a relative sense. But the moral virtues make man good in an absolute sense, whereas the intellectual virtues make him good in a relative sense. Therefore the nature of virtue is more perfectly realized in the moral virtues than in the intellectual virtues.

The *major* is evident, for a thing is good when good in every respect — bonum ex integra causa. Hence the nature of virtue is best realized in virtues which make man good in an absolute sense.

Minor.— The intellectual virtues give man the power of performing good acts, but do not give him the right use of this power, i.e., do not make him use this power in a right manner. Hence they render good the operation of a particular faculty, but do not make man good in an absolute sense; v.g., as a result of intellectual virtue, a person can be a good philosopher, but yet not a man who is good in every respect, for he can *knowingly*, and without sinning against intellectual virtue, be the author of sophistries.

The moral virtues not only give man the power of performing good act, but make him use this power rightly, for the moral virtues perfect the appetite, whose function consists in moving the other powers to act. Hence the moral virtues make man good in an absolute sense[1].

930. Cardinal virtues.— 1° The cardinal or principal virtues are the virtues which sustain all virtuous life[2]. Only the moral virtues, it is evident, may be called cardinal virtues[3].

---

(1) I-II, q. 56, a. 3, et q. 66, a. 3.
(2) Cajetanus, in I-II, q. 61, ar. 1.
(3) I-II, q. 61, a. 1.

2° Certain moral virtues may be called cardinal or principal virtues under two aspects:

first, in relation to their common formal principles, in as much as they are general, as it were, in comparison with the other virtues; v.g., any virtue which renders good reason's act of consideration is called prudence;

secondly, in as much as they are concerned with what is most important in the matter of the moral virtues; v.g., the virtue which gives strength against the greatest dangers, i.e., the dangers of death, is called fortitude [4].

Under the first aspect, the cardinal virtues are general conditions found in all the virtues. Under the second aspect, the cardinal virtues are special virtues which are distinct from the other virtues[5].

3° The number of the cardinal virtues can be derived either from their formal principles or from their subjects.

a) From their formal principles. — The formal principle of virtue is the good of reason, i.e., good in conformity with reason.

The good or perfection of reason may be considered:

as consisting in the very act of reason; and thus we have one principal virtue, called *prudence;*

as consisting in putting the order of reason into something else, namely, into operations, and we have *justice;* into the passions of the concupiscible appetite, and we have *temperance;* into the passions of the irascible appetite, and we have *fortitude.*

b) From their subjects. — The subjects of the moral virtues are rational in essence or by participation.

There is one subject which is essentially rational, namely, reason, which is perfected by *prudence.*

---

(4) I-II, q. 61, a. 3.
(5) I-II, q. 61, a. 4.

There are three subjects which are rational by participation:

the will, which is perfected by *justice;*

the concupiscible appetite, which is perfected by *temperance;*

the irascible appetite, which is perfected by *fortitude*(1).

Hence there are four cardinal virtues: *prudence, justice, temperance,* and *fortitude.*

931. Parts of the cardinal virtues.— 1° Each of the cardinal virtues has integrant, subjective, and potential parts.

2° The integrant parts of a cardinal virtue are the conditions required for a perfect act of the virtue; v.g., memory is required for a perfect act of prudence, and hence it is an integrant part of this virtue.

3° The subjective parts of a cardinal virtue are the species into which the virtue is divided; v.g., prudence is divided into two distinct kinds of prudence: personal prudence and governing prudence.

4° The potential parts of a cardinal virtue are virtues annexed to the principal virtue in which the essence of this principal virtue is not perfectly realized; v.g., filial piety is a virtue annexed to justice, for it renders *to another,* i. e., to the father, what is his due; but the essence of justice is not perfectly realized in it, for the father, from the point of view of the son, is not perfectly another: the son is something of the father, a certain participation of the father.

932.— Moral virtue consists in a mean.— 1° Moral virtue is designed to direct man to good. But the goodness of human acts consists in their conformity with the rule of reason. This conformity is a mean between excess and deficiency. Hence moral virtue consists in a mean(2).

---
(1) I-II, q. 61, a. 2.
(2) I-II, q. 64, a. 1.

2° The mean in which moral virtue consists is a mean of reason, not in as much as this mean exists in the act of reason, as though the act of reason were reduced to a mean, but in as much as this mean is established by reason in some particular matter.

3° In justice, the mean of reason is also the mean of reality, for justice gives each one his due, neither more nor less. In other words, what is right in the case of justice must be established absolutely and in itself (simpliciter et secundum se).

4° In the other moral virtues, the mean of reason is not the mean of reality, for these virtues are concerned with internal passions, in which what is right cannot be established in the same way for all persons, since men stand in different relations to their passions. Hence the rectitude of reason must be established in the passions in relation to us, who are moved in accordance with our passions(1).

933.— Connexion between the moral virtues. — 1° The moral virtues are connected in as much as one cannot exist without the others.

2° The moral virtues may be perfect or imperfect.

An imperfect moral virtue is an *inclination existing in us for the performance of certain good deeds*. This inclination may be produced in us by nature or acquired by repeated acts

A perfect moral virtue is *a habit, i.e., a stable disposition, which inclines us to do a good work well*, i.e., in accordance with the exigencies of the virtue.

3° The imperfect moral virtues are not connected, i.e., one can exist without another, for a man may be inclined from natural temperament or from custom to acts of liberality, but not to acts of chastity.

4° The perfect moral virtues are connected. We may prove this either by considering the cardinal virtues as general conditions of all the virtues, or by considering them as distinct virtues.

---

(1) I-II, q. 64, a. 2.

a) The connexion between the perfect moral virtues is manifested from a consideration of the cardinal virtues as general conditions of all the virtues, for discretion pertains to prudence, rectitude to justice, moderation to temperance, and strength of mind to fortitude. But strength of mind cannot be virtuous without moderation, rectitude, or discretion; and the same may be said of the other virtues.

b) The connexion between the perfect moral virtues may be proved from a consideration of the cardinal virtues as distinct virtues, i.e., in as much as each has its own proper matter.

No moral virtue can be possessed without prudence; and, in like manner, prudence cannot be possessed without the other moral virtues. Hence all the moral virtues are connected.

Antecedent.— *a*) *No moral virtue can be possessed without prudence.*— A moral virtue is an elective habit, and therefore it makes a right choice. Now right choice requires not only the inclination to a due end, which inclination is the direct result of moral virtue, but also correct choice of means to the end, which choice is made by prudence. Hence no moral virtue can be possessed without prudence.

b) *Prudence cannot be possessed without the other moral virtues.*— Prudence is a habit which chooses the means to the end. Hence ends are the principles from which prudence proceeds. But man is rightly disposed for ends by the other moral virtues: man is disposed by justice to render to everyone his due, etc. Therefore prudence cannot be possessed without the other moral virtues[1].

934.—Equality and inequality of the moral virtues.—

The question of the equality and inequality of the moral virtues may be considered under various aspects.

1° *First*, the question may be considered as concerned with specifically distinct virtues, i.e., as referring to the specific nature of different virtues. From this point of view, it is evident that one virtue can be greater than another.

---

(1) I-II, q. 65, a. 1.— VI *Ethic.*, c. 13.

The cause is always greater than the effect; and the effect is greater as it approximates more closely to the cause. But reason is the cause and root of all human goodness. Hence *prudence*, which perfects reason, is superior in goodness to the virtues which perfect the appetitive powers, in as much as it participates in reason. Next to prudence comes *justice*, which perfects the will, for the will has a greater participation in reason than has the sensitive appetite. Next to justice comes *fortitude;* and after fortitude comes *temperance.* For the irascible appetite, which is perfected by fortitude, has a greater participation in reason than has the concupiscible appetite, which is perfected by temperance.

2° *Secondly*, the question of the equality and inequality of the moral virtues may be considered as concerned with virtues of the same species.

Virtues of the same species may be considered under two aspects: in themselves and in relation to the subjects which partake of them.

In itself, one virtue could be greater than another only as regards extension. But one moral virtue cannot be greater in this regard than another, for a person who has a moral virtue has it in the whole of its extension; v.g., no person has the virtue of justice unless he renders to everyone his due.

In relation to the subjects which partake of them, one virtue can be greater than another either in relation to different times in the same man, or in relation to different men. This is so because one man can be better disposed than another to attain the mean of virtue, which is determined by right reason. The cause of these differences may be a greater habituation, a better natural disposition, a more discerning judgment of reason, or even a greater gift of grace([1]), for, according to St. Paul, *to every one of us is given grace according to the measure of the giving of Christ* (Eph. IV, 7).

3° *Thirdly*, the question may be asked: does equality obtain among all the virtues which exist in the same subject at

---

(1) I-II, q. 66. a. I.

the same time? Under this aspect, the quality of virtues may be understood in two ways: *first*, as referring to their specific nature; and, in this way, undoubtedly one virtue can be greater than another in a man: justice, for example, can be greater than fortitude; *secondly*, as referring to the degree of participation by the subject, in as much as a virtue becomes intensified or lessened in a subject. In this sense, all the virtues in a man are equal according to an equality of proportion, in as much as their growth in a man is equal, just as the fingers of the hand are unequal in size or quantity, but equal according to an equality of proportion, since they grow in proportion to one another. The reason of this equality of proportion is the connexion of the virtues.

Considered under their material aspect, i.e., as regards inclination to acts of virtue, a man may be better disposed by nature, by custom, or even by God's grace to perform acts of one virtue than acts of another([1]).

935.— Vice.— 1° Vice is the opposite of virtue. Hence vice may be defined: *an evil operative habit.*

2° *The vices are more numerous than the virtues.—* Virtue consists in a mean. Hence a man may be wanting in virtue either by excess or by deficiency. Therefore the vices are more numerous than the virtues.

3° *The vices are not connected as are the virtues.—* One vice can be in opposition to another vice; v.g., avarice is an obstacle to intemperance.

4° *The vices are not equal to one another.—* Evil acts, which result from vices, are not equal.

The evil of vices derives either from their objects, or from their participation in their subject.

POINTS FOR REVIEW

1. Define: virtue, integral, subjective, and potential parts of a cardinal virtue, and vice.

---

(1) I-II, q. 66. a. 2.

2. State three reasons why virtues are necessary, and explain why faculties are their subject, and whether virtue is in the will as regards a private and proper good.

3. Explain under what aspect: *a)* the sensitive powers of apprehension are subjects of habits; *b)* the sensitive appetite is the subject of virtues; *c)* the intellectual virtues are more perfect than the moral virtues.

4. Explain why the nature of virtue is more perfectly realized in the moral virtues than in the intellectual virtues, under what aspects moral virtues may be called cardinal, and how the number of the cardinal virtues is derived from their formal principles.

5. Explain why moral virtue consists in a mean, and whether this mean is a mean of reason or a mean of reality.

6. State what is meant by the connexion of the virtues; and show why prudence cannot be possessed without the moral virtues.

ARTICLE II

PRUDENCE

936.— Notion of prudence.— Prudence is defined: *right reason applied to practice,* i.e., to operations; or, the *virtue which rightly directs reason in regard to operations.*

a) Virtue which rightly directs reason: prudence resides in the intellect, for the prudent man obtains knowledge of the future from the past and present, and this is properly the work of reason(¹). Moreover, it is to practical reason, not to speculative reason, that prudence gives direction. For prudence is concerned with things to be done for an end. But it is practical reason which knows and judges things to be done for an end(²).

b) In regard to operations: operations (*agibilia*) are distinguished from products (*factibilia*).

Operations are those things which pertain to *acting* (agere), in as much as *to act* is distinguished from *to make.*

To act (agere) is used here in the strict sense, and signifies: to perform a human act which is free and measurable by the rules of morals.

To make (facere) means to perform either an external work, v.g., in the servile arts, or an internal work, v.g., in the liberal arts.

Prudence is a virtue of practical reason. But practical reason is concerned with things which are singular and concrete. Hence prudence is concerned with operations, i.e., with human acts, considered as singular and in the concrete(³).

(1) II-II, q. 47, a. 1.
(2) II-II, q. 47, a. 2.
(3) II-II, q. 47, a. 3.— *In Ethic.*, l. VI, l. 6 and l. 7.

937.— Acts of prudence.— 1° The acts of prudence are three in number: *to take counsel, to judge rightly,* and *to command.*

First, prudence takes counsel, i.e., inquires what means and circumstances are necessary, in order that a work be performed honestly and in accordance with virtue.

Secondly, prudence judges that the means sought and found are good and suitable.

Thirdly, prudence commands in as much as it applies to operation the things counseled and judged.

2° Command is the principal act of prudence. We may prove this from reason and from a sign.

From reason.— Prudence is a virtue of practical reason. But command is the principal act of practical reason, in as much as command is the application of things discovered and judged to operation. Hence command is the principal act of prudence.

From a sign.— A man who sins voluntarily against his craft is a better craftsman than he who does so involuntarily, because the former seems to do so from right judgment, and the latter from defective judgment. In the case of prudence, however, a man who sins voluntarily is more imprudent than he who sins involuntarily, because he who sins voluntarily fails in the principal act of prudence, which is the act of command(¹).

938.— Prudence, synderesis, and moral virtue.— 1° Since prudence is directed to an end, it presupposes a right desire of the end in the order of morality. But the appetite or desire is made right by the moral virtues. Hence prudence presupposes the moral virtues.

2° Since the appetite follows knowledge, the moral virtues presuppose right knowledge of the end. This knowledge is derived from synderesis.

---

(1) II-II, q. 47, a. 8.

Synderesis is defined: *the habit in virtue of which the intellect naturally knows the ends of the moral virtues, i.e., the first precepts of the natural law.*

3° Thus we can understand the relation between synderesis, the moral virtues, and prudence.

Synderesis makes known to us the general ends of moral life, as temperance in living, justice in acting, fortitude in suffering.

The *moral virtues* incline the will in a firm and stable manner to these ends.

Prudence, presupposing this firm and stable inclination, i.e., presupposing right desire, prescribes how man ought to act in particular and determinate cases in order to live temperately, to act justly, and to suffer with fortitude.

Hence prudence not only prescribes the means to the end but is concerned with particular ends in determinate cases, in as much as it dictates and orders that the end be sought and attained by determinate means([1]).

939.— Prudence and art.— 1° Prudence and art are intellectual virtues of practical reason.

2° Prudence and art, nevertheless, are distinct from each other in their matter, form, and mode of procedure.

a) In matter.— The matter of prudence is operation (agibile), i.e., human acts as voluntary and free. Prudence is *right reason applied to operations.*

The matter of art is a product (factibile), i.e., an external work in a servile art, or an internal work in a liberal art. Art is *right reason applied to products.*

b) In form.— The form of prudence is moral regulation in relation to due ends. This regulation is not a quality introduced into moral acts, but is only the transcendental relation of the act to objects conformed to the rules of morals.

---

(1) JOANNES A SANCTO THOMA, *Cursus Theol.*, t. VI, pp. 469-471 (Vivès).

Therefore moral regulation is first applied to objects, and through these objects it is applied to acts.

The form of art is regulation in accordance with the idea of the artist, i.e., conformity to the idea of the artist.

In the servile arts, this regulation or conformity is a quality introduced into products, as, for example, a certain shape in a house or in a ship, or a certain posture or order.

In the liberal arts, this regulation is first applied to objects, to which man's acts are directed, as, for example, in Logic.

But the regulation of art differs from the regulation of prudence.

The regulation of prudence is dependent upon the rectitude and intention of the will, whereas the regulation of art is entirely independent of the rectitude and intention of the will.

c) *In mode of procedure.*— The mode of procedure of art and of prudence may be considered in relation to the intellect and in relation to the will.

In relation to the intellect, art proceeds according to fixed and determinate rules, whereas prudence proceeds according to rules which are arbitrary and which vary according to diversity of occasions and circumstances, for rectitude of judgment in art does not derive from occasions and circumstances, as it does in prudence.

In relation to the will and the executive powers, art does not require that the artist act with a right intention, but only that he act with knowledge, whereas prudence requires a right intention[1]. Hence, in the moral order, a man who sins voluntarily is imprudent; but, in art, a man who sins voluntarily is not an evil artist.

940.— Art and morality.— 1° According to some writers, an artist, because of the superiority of his art, is independent of the moral law in the use of his art.

---

[1] JOANNES A SANCTO THOMA, *Cursus Theol.*, t. VI, pp. 469-471 (Vivès)

According to others, art in itself is subject to the moral virtues.

2° The solution to the problem is set forth in the propositions which follow.

a) Art in itself is independent of morality.—Moral virtue is not necessary for the production of a work of art. Hence art in itself is independent of morality.

Antecedent.— The production of a work of art does not require rectitude of will: a great sinner may be an accomplished artist.

b) The use of art is regulated by the moral law.— The use of art, i.e., the application of a power to operation, is an act which proceeds from the will, and therefore it is a free act which must be regulated by the moral law.

NOTE.— The subordination of art, as regards its use, to the moral law is binding on the artist who produces a work of art, and also on him who contemplates or uses it. Hence an artist must exercise prudence in the use of his art, and hence may not produce works of art which are occasions of sin.

For the same reason, the artist may not place his ultimate end in his art.

941.— Integrant parts of prudence.— The integrant parts of prudence are those qualities of mind which concur in the production of a perfect act of prudence. The integrant parts of prudence are eight in number. Five of these, namely, *memory, reasoning, understanding, docility,* and *personal sagacity,* belong to prudence in as much as it is cognitive; and three, namely, *foresight, circumspection,* and *caution,* belong to prudence in as much as it is preceptive, i.e., as it applies knowledge to action[1].

a) Memory is defined: *the remembrance of past events.* Memory is a part of prudence, because prudence is concerned with contingent operables, in which man must be directed in

---

(1) II-II, q. 48, a unicus.

accordance with what happens in the majority of cases. But experience, which is required for knowledge of what happens in the majority of cases, is constituted from the remembrance of past events(¹).

b) Reasoning is an *act of knowledge in virtue of which a man uses his knowledge of certain things, in order to know and judge other things*. The necessity of reasoning in prudence is evident, for prudence takes counsel, and therefore passes from knowledge of certain things to knowledge of other things.

c) Understanding, as a part of memory, is not a faculty, nor a habit of speculative first principles, but a *right appreciation of a particular end*(²).

Understanding, in this sense, is a part of prudence, because prudence is terminated in particular operables. Hence by reasoning it proceeds not only from a universal principle (universal major), but also from a singular principle (singular minor), by which a universal principle is applied to a singular conclusion.

But the principle in action is the end. Hence a right appreciation of a particular end, i.e., *understanding*, is required for an act of prudence.

d) Docility is an *aptitude for the reception of discipline*, i.e., an aptitude for the acceptance of counsel, warning, and suggestion from another. Docility is a part of prudence, for prudence is concerned with particular operables, which are of almost infinite diversity. Hence, in matters of prudence, man needs to be taught by others, especially by the old, who have a sane understanding of the ends of operables or practical matters(³).

e) Personal sagacity (shrewdness) is *facility and promptness in finding suitable means*. Hence, just as docility consists in a man's being well disposed to acquire a right opinion from another, so personal sagacity consists in a man's being well disposed to acquire a right appreciation by himself(⁴).

---

(1) II-II, q. 49, a. 1.
(2) *Ibidem*, a. 2, ad 1.
(3) *Ibidem*, a. 3.
(4) *Ibidem*, a 4.

f) **Foresight** is the *right direction of means to an end*. It is the principal integrant part of prudence, for all else required for prudence is necessary in order that some particular thing may be rightly directed to an end([1]).

g) **Circumspection** is the *right consideration of circumstances in whatever is directed to an end*. Circumspection is necessary because it happens in the case of singular operables, which contain many combinations of circumstances, that a thing which is good in itself and conformed to the end may, because of certain circumstances, become evil, or unsuitable for the end([2]).

h) **Caution** *is a disposition by which are avoided extrinsic expedients which can impede good or render an act evil.*

To pursue good and to avoid the opposite evil appertain to the same act; but the avoidance of extrinsic impediments pertains to another act, and hence caution is said to be concerned with extrinsic impediments([3]).

942. Subjective parts of prudence. — 1° The subjective parts of prudence are the different species of this virtue.

2° Prudence is first divided into *personal prudence* (*prudentia communiter dicta*) and *political prudence* in a generic sense (*prudentia regitiva multitudinis*).

Personal prudence is *prudence by which a person rules himself in relation to his own good* ([4]).

Political prudence in the generic sense is *prudence by which a person rules or is ruled in relation to the common good.*

3° Political prudence in the generic sense is divided into *economic prudence, governmental prudence, political prudence in a specific sense,* and *military prudence.*

Economic prudence is *prudence by which the home or family is ruled.*

---

(1) *Ibidem*, a 6, ad 1.
(2) *Ibidem*, a. 7.
(3) *Ibidem*, a. 8, ad 2.
(4) II-II, q. 48, a. unicus, c., and q. 50, a. 2, ad 3.

Governmental prudence is *prudence by which the ruler governs civil society.*

Political prudence in a specific sense is *prudence by which subjects rule themselves by obedience to their rulers in anything related to the common good.*

Military prudence is *prudence by which military matters are directed to the protection of the entire common good*([1]).

943.— Potential parts of prudence.— 1° The potential parts of prudence are annexed virtues related to certain secondary acts or matters which have not the whole power of prudence, i.e., in which are not realized the complete essence of prudence.

2° The principal act of prudence is the act of command. Its secondary acts are the acts of taking counsel and of judging. Hence the potential parts of prudence are concerned with counsel and judgment.

The virtue concerned with counsel is *eubulia;* and the virtues concerned with judgment are *synesis* and *gnome.*

3° *a) Eubulia* is the virtue whose object is *good counsel.*

b) Synesis is the *virtue which enables a man to judge well concerning things to be done according to ordinary laws.*

c) Gnome is the *virtue which enables a man to judge well concerning things to be done to which the ordinary laws of human activity are not applicable;* v.g., when a man, in order to safeguard justice, must perform an action to which the words of the law do not apply.

4° Eubulia, synesis, and gnome are distinct from prudence, for the proper act of prudence is the act of command, whereas the proper act of eubulia is the act of taking counsel, and the proper act of synesis and gnome is the act of judgment.

Eubulia and synesis are distinct virtues, for they are destined for distinct acts.

---

(1) II-II, q. 50, a. 4, ad 2.

Synesis and gnome are distinct from each other, because judgment beyond the ordinary rules of acting, which is the proper act of gnome, offers special difficulties not encountered in judgment according to the ordinary rules of action, which is the proper act of synesis. Gnome is to synesis as wisdom is to science([1]).

944. — Vices opposed to prudence by deficiency. — 1° Imprudence is the vice opposed to prudence by deficiency.

Imprudence may be understood in three ways:

a) negatively, as signifying solely the lack of prudence; and, under this aspect, it is possible for it not to be a principle of sin; v.g., the imprudence of children.

b) privately, as signifying the lack of that prudence which a man should possess. Under this aspect, it has a share in all vices, for just as prudence, which directs the acts of all the virtues, is found by participation in all the virtues and in all acts of the virtues, so imprudence is found by participation in all vices and sins;

c) contrarily, in so far as reason moves and acts directly contrary to prudence, by spurning and refusing counsel or divine prescription; and, under this aspect, imprudence is a special vice and sin.

2° Under imprudence, as contrarily opposed to prudence, are included *precipitation, thoughtlessness (want of consideration), inconstancy,* and *negligence*([2]).

a) Precipitation is the vice opposed to eubulia. Precipitation causes a person to omit acts required for the taking of counsel, as remembrance of the past, understanding of the present, shrewdness in considering future events, reasoning which compares one thing with another, docility in accepting the opinion of others([3]).

---

(1) II-II, q. 51, aa. 1-4.
(2) II-II, q. 53, aa. 1-2.
(3) II-II, q. 53, a. 3.

b) Thoughtlessness (lack of consideration) is *the vice which causes a person to fail to judge rightly, because of contempt or negligence of those things on which a right judgment depends*(¹).

c) Inconstancy is the *vice which causes reason to fail in commanding what has been counseled and judged.* Hence, just as precipitation results from a defect in the act of counsel, and thoughtlessness from a defect in the act of judgment, so inconstancy arises from a defect in the act of command.

Inconstancy implies the abandonment of a good purpose. The origin of this abandonment is found in the appetite, for it is only because of something which gives him inordinate pleasure that a person abandons his good purpose; this abandonment, nevertheless, is completed only because of a defect of reason, which is deceived in as much at it repudiates what earlier it had rightly accepted. Therefore inconstancy is opposed to prudence, which is an intellectual virtue(²).

Lust is the chief source of thoughtlessness and inconstancy, for the perfection of prudence, like the perfection of every intellectual virtue, consists in withdrawal from sensible objects; moreover, pleasure, and especially venereal pleasure, wholly engrosses the mind and draws it to pleasures of the senses, and therefore is most ruinous of the estimate proper to prudence(³).

d) Negligence has two meanings.

First, it is used in a general way to signify the omission of any due act, and thus is not in a special way opposed to the virtue of prudence, but to the virtue requiring the performing of the act; v.g., negligence in making restitution is opposed to the virtue of justice.

Secondly, it signifies the lack of the care required in an internal act of the intellect to arouse and direct the will in the execution of a good work demanded by counsel and judgment, and thus it is opposed in a special way to the virtue of prudence.

---

(1) II-II, q. 53, a. 4.
(2) II-II, q. 53, a. 5.
(3) II-II, q. 53, a. 6.

Negligence differs from inconstancy: the inconstant person, as if prevented by something, fails in the act of command, whereas the negligent person fails because of the deficiency of his will.

In like manner, negligence is distinct from omission, laziness, and torpor.

Negligence, as we said, consists in a deficiency of the internal act of the will which fails to command what it ought to command, or in the manner in which it ought to command; omission concerns the external act; laziness and torpor concern the execution of the act: laziness has reference to slowness in undertaking the execution of the act, and torpor to a certain remissness in the execution itself (¹).

945.— Vices opposed to prudence by excess.— 1° The following are the vices opposed to prudence by excess: *prudence of the flesh, astuteness, guile, fraud,* and *excessive solicitude concerning temporal goods and the future.*

2° *a)* Prudence of the flesh is *the vice which moves a person to use unsuitable means to perform works of the flesh;* it is a sin: mortal, if works of the flesh are made one's ultimate end; venial, if there is inordinate attachment to works of the flesh, but without their being made one's ultimate end.

b) Astuteness is *the vice which inclines a person to use feigned and apparently true means to attain an end, good or evil.*

c) Guile and fraud are vices which are destined for *the execution of astuteness.* Guile has recourse to *deeds,* whereas fraud depends chiefly on *words,* in the execution of astuteness.

d) Excessive solicitude concerning temporal goods and the future is *unlawful concern for temporal goods and the future.*

Solicitude concerning temporal goods and the future may be unlawful in three ways:

first, if temporal things are sought as ends in preference to spiritual goods;

---

(1) II-II, q. 54, aa. 1-3.

secondly, if too much effort is used to acquire or preserve them;

thirdly, if a person has fear and anxiety that the fulfilment of his duties will result in his not having what is necessary for his needs.

A certain solicitude concerning temporal goods and the future is permissible; only excessive solicitude is condemnable.

3° Avarice (covetousness) is the chief source of prudence of the flesh, guile, fraud, and excessive solicitude concerning temporal goods, because in these vices there is some use of reason, albeit inordinate. But, among all the virtues, the right use of reason appears chiefly in justice, which is in the rational appetite. Therefore the inordinate use of reason appears chiefly in the vices opposed to justice. Since avarice is the vice most opposed to justice, it is chiefly in avarice that the foregoing vices originate.[1]

POINTS FOR REVIEW

1. Define prudence, name its acts, and prove that the act of command is its principal act.

2. Distinguish between: to act and to do; prudence, synderesis, and the moral virtues; prudence and art in relation to their form; personal sagacity and circumspection; eubulia, synesis, and gnome; negligence and inconstancy; astuteness, guile, and fraud.

3. Do prudence and art presuppose rectitude of desire? Explain.

4. Is art in any way dependent on the moral law? Explain.

5. Name the integrant parts of prudence.

6. Under what aspect is imprudence a special vice?

---

(1) II-II, q. 55, aa. 1-8.

ARTICLE III

RIGHT

946.— Right is the object of justice.— According to its nominal definition, right signifies that which is just. That which is just, as the term implies, signifies a certain equality; and equality has reference to another. Of all the moral virtues, it is justice which properly directs man in his relations with others. What is right in the works of the other virtues depends on its relation to the agent only, as, v.g., in temperance. Therefore justice has its own special object, and this object is called the just, which is the same as *right*(1).

947.— Meanings of right.— 1° In its primary meaning, right signifies the just, i.e., a just thing. Right, as signifying a just thing, is *objective right*.

2° In a secondary meaning, right signifies the lawful power of doing, omitting, acquiring, possessing, or alienating something. In this meaning, right is *subjective right*, i.e., right as a power.

3° In derived meanings, right signifies the art by which we know what is just — the study of law; the place where justice is administered, as when a man is said to appear *in jure;* and the passing of legal sentence — to administer justice(2).

948.— Notion of objective right.— Objective right is that which is due to another. That which is due to another

---

(1) II-II, q. 57, a. 1.
(2) The second and third of the derived meanings are scarcely intelligible in English translation. We speak, for example, of a man's appearing in court, and of a barrister at law; but we do not speak of a man's appearing *in jure.*—*Translator's note.*

makes for him a certain adjustment in conformity with law, which is the rule of human acts.

Hence we can know the elements of objective right.

Right has reference to another, and hence it puts two or more persons in relation to each other.

But, since persons communicate with one another by means of external operations and things, right implies the existence of an intermediary between persons. This intermediary is the just thing, i.e., external operation or the thing with which external operation is concerned.

This external operation or thing has reference, i.e., is due, to another, because it implies the making of a certain adjustment for him.

Hence there are three elements in objective right:

a) an external operation or thing, or rather two external things; v.g., service rendered and the recompense of due reward;

b) a relation of equality between these two things, and consequently a relation of equality between two persons;

c) a relation of necessity or due, in virtue of which *another* may claim a thing as his own.

The just thing is objective right in its material aspect; and the relation of equality is the formal constituent of objective right. The relation of necessity or due is a consequence of the relation of equality, for a person may claim a thing as his own because it is due to him by law.

Hence objective right may be defined: *that which is adjusted and due to another.*

949.— Notion of subjective right.— Subjective right may be defined: *the lawful and inviolable power of doing, omitting, acquiring, possessing, or alienating something.*

a) Lawful power, i.e., a power conformed to law. Therefore subjective right is a moral power, not a mere physical power.

b) Inviolable: subjective right imposes on another the obligation of avoiding injury, i.e., of not impeding the power of acting or of not acting.

c) Of doing . . . something: these words determine the threefold object of subjective right, namely, one's own action, the action of another, and external things.

950.— Relation between objective right and subjective right.—1° Some Scholastics, as Suarez and Billuart, claim that subjective right is right in the strict sense, that objective is dependent on it, and hence that subjective right is the foundation of objective right. For, according to them, a just thing is due to another primarily because he has the inviolable power of demanding it. Moreover, since they conceive subjective right as an inviolable power, they add that to this subjective right corresponds a duty in another of not violating it.

This teaching, which has been adopted by moderns, especially by jurists, is untenable, and contrary to the principles bequeathed to us by Aristotle and St. Thomas.

2° Right, in the strict and formal meaning of the term, is objective right. The moral power is called right only as it is concerned with objective right, i.e., with a just thing. A person has this power, i.e., subjective right, only because first the thing is due to him in accordance with law, i.e., only because objective right first exists. Hence this inviolable power is called right only by *extrinsic denomination*, i.e., only by *analogy of attribution*.

3° If objective right is understood as right in the strict sense, it follows that subjective right, i.e., right as a power, is measured by the just thing, according to conformity to law. Moreover, since law is an ordinance for the common good, it follows that the whole juridical order is directed to the common good.

But, if subjective right is understood as right in the primary, strict, and formal meaning of the term, it follows that the juridical order consists in a certain autonomy, independence, and liberty. For subjective right is not measured by the just thing, but the just thing is measured by the inviolable faculty, which is a certain liberty.

Therefore, according to moderns, the jurical order is directed to liberty rather than to the common good. This gives rise to errors among moderns, who speak of liberty of speech, liberty of worship, economic liberty, — economic liberalism, — without any consideration of their relation to the common good.

951.— Division of objective right.— 1° From the point of view of its origin, objective right is divided into *natural right* and *positive* or *legal right*.

a) Natural right is *that which of its very nature is due to another*.

Positive or legal right is *that which is due to another in virtue of the authority of the people or ruler*, i.e., in virtue of positive law(¹).

b) Natural right is divided into *immediate natural right* and *mediate natural right*.

Immediate natural right is *a thing whose commensuration to another is established by nature without relation to another thing;* v.g., the male of its very nature has commensuration to the female for the engendering of offspring, the parent to the child for the latter's nutrition.

Mediate natural right is *a thing whose natural commensuration is established in relation to another thing;* v.g., private ownership(²). For, if a particular piece of land be considered absolutely, there is no reason why it should belong to one man rather than to another; but, if it be considered in relation to its adaptibility for cultivation, and in relation to the unmolested use of the land, it has a certain commensuration to be the property of one man rather than of another(³).

---

(1) *In Ethic.*, 1. V, 1. 12.— II-II, q. 57, a. 2, c.
(2) II-II, q. 57, a. 3, c.
(3) *Politic.*, L. II, c. 3.

The old Scholastics called mediate natural right the *right of nations;* today, the right of nations is understood as signifying *international law.*

c) Positive right is divine or human as it is determined by *divine* or *human* law.

2° From the point of view of its nature, objective right is divided into *right in the proper sense* (jus simpliciter) and *right in the restricted sense* (jus secundum quid).

This distinction derives from the fact that right connotes a relation to *another.* When this other is perfectly *other,* i.e., distinct, the nature of right is perfectly realized. When the other is, so to speak, a part or the thing of him who is bound to render the right, the notion of right is not perfectly realized; and, in this case, we have right in the restricted sense.

Right in the proper sense, i.e., political right, is *that which unites persons within a political group;* v.g., such right is found in the case of two men, neither of whom is subject to the other, but both of whom are subject to the civil ruler.

Right in the restricted sense is *that which is established within domestic society;* v.g., a son belongs to his father, for he is in a certain sense a part of his father([1]).

The right which binds father to son is called *paternal right;* the right which obtains between husband and wife is called *economic right,* and the right which obtains between master and servant in the proper sense (cf. n. 1078) is called *dominative right.* i.e., *right of master*([2]).

952.— Division of subjective right.— 1° By reason of its origin, subjective right, like objective right, is divided into *natural* right and *positive* right.

2° By reason of its term, subjective right is divided into *real right* (*jus in re*) and *personal right* (*jus ad rem*).

A real right is *the right a person possesses over a thing already his own.* It gives a hold on the thing itself.

---

(1) *In Ethic.*, 1, V, I. II.— II-II, q. 57, a. 4.
(2) II-II, q. 57, a. 4.

Three conditions are required for a real right:

a) the existence of the thing;

b) a lawful title, as buying, gift, etc;

c) the transfer of the thing.

A personal right is *the right a person has that a thing he made his own.* It gives power over the person bound to give the thing demanded.

A legitimate title, i.e., donation, purchase, election to office, is the only condition required for a personal right.

3° *Dominion* is the principal species of subjective right.

a) Dominion is derived from the Latin word *dominus.* A master, i.e., a person who has dominion (dominus), is a man who possesses as his own something of which he may dispose, or over which he may exercise authority.

Hence dominion implies, *on the one hand,* authority and power over a thing or a person; and, *on the other hand,* such subjection of this person or thing that it may be called the possession of another.

b) Dominion is of two kinds: *dominion of jurisdiction* and *dominion of ownership.*

Dominion of jurisdiction is *the power of governing subjects in relation to the common good.*

Dominion of ownership is *the power of disposing of something as one's own for one's personal advantage.*

c) Dominion of ownership may be *perfect and complete* or *imperfect and incomplete.*

Complete dominion, called *direct dominion,* is *the right to the ownership and fruits of a thing.*

Incomplete ownership, called *useful dominion,* is *the right to the ownership of a thing without its fruits,* or *the right to the fruits of a thing without the ownership of it.*

d) Useful dominion is divided into *usufruct* and *use.*

Usufruct is defined: *the right of using and enjoying things belonging to another, without impairing their substance.*

Right, i.e., the moral power of performing an act.

Of using, i.e., of taking the fruits of the thing and of using it for one's own daily needs.

Of enjoying, in as much as the usufruct includes not only the taking the fruits of a thing for one's own daily needs, but also the right of renting them, selling them, or gratuitously surrendering them.

Without impairing their substance: the person who has the usufruct of a thing must keep the thing intact for its owner, for his right is over what belongs to another[1].

953.— Subject of dominion in general.— 1° Dominion is authority and power over a person or thing.

2° The subject of dominion is a being which has this authority and power.

3° Pythagoras, Empedocles, Gerson, and Arhens taught that irrational animals, as well as beings endowed with an intellect, are subjects of rights and dominion.

Damiron taught that every creature is a subject of dominion.

In ancient times, certain philosophers held that the slave was not a subject of rights.

4° We, on the contrary, teach that all intellectual beings, and only intellectual beings, are capable of dominion. Hence all beings endowed with an intellect, as God, the angels, and man, are subjects of dominion.

Even the demented and children who have not attained the use of reason are capable of dominion, for the use of reason, though required for the actual use of dominion, is not required for habitual dominion, which is immediately founded in in-

---

[1] BILLUART, *Summa Sancti Thomas*, t. IV, diss. II, a. 1, pp. 8-10 (Palmé, editio nova).

tellectual nature and its powers, as is evident from the proof which follows; otherwise a person who was drunk or asleep would lose his dominion.

5° We shall use two arguments to prove our teaching.

a) All beings which can dispose of their acts, and only these, can be subjects of dominion. But all beings endowed with an intellect, and only these, can dispose of their acts. Therefore all beings endowed with an intellect, and only these, can be subjects of dominion(1).

Major.— Every being which can dispose of its own acts, and only such a being, is capable of dominion over external things and persons, for it is by their own acts that beings dispose of external things and persons.

Minor.— A being disposes of its acts when it has dominion over them. But only a being endowed with an intellect and will has dominion over its acts. Therefore.

b) Only beings which can immediately attain the common end of the whole universe can be subjects of dominion. But all beings endowed with an intellect, and only these, can immediately attain the common end of the whole universe. Therefore all beings endowed with an intellect, and only these, can be subjects of dominion.

Major.— When many beings tend to a common end, the being which immediately attains the common end disposes of the beings which do not attain this end in the same manner, and directs them to it(2). In other words, beings which do not immediately attain the end are for the *use* of the being which does immediately attain it. The latter, therefore, has a power of superiority, i.e., of dominion, over the former.

Minor.— God is the common end of the whole universe. But all beings endowed with an intellect, and only these beings, have the power of immediately attaining God by knowledge and love. Therefore.

---
(1) II-II, q. 66, a. 1, c.
(2) *Contra Gentes*, l. III, c. 112.

954. — God's dominion.— 1° God, because of His creation and conservation of them, has independent, absolute, and universal dominion (¹) over all created things.

2° This dominion over creation God can neither renounce nor communicate to any creature; and from this dominion no creature can be freed. This is so because the title of God's dominion, namely, His creation and continual conservation of creatures, cannot be communicated to any creature, just as no creature can destroy this title.

3° Just as God, notwithstanding His first and universal causality, communicates second and particular causality to created things, so, although He is the universal master of all things, He communicates particular dominion subordinate to His universal dominion. Hence it follows that all dominion of creatures is subject to God's dominion, just as the creature's causality is subordinate to God's causality. Therefore God's dominion is infinitely greater and of a higher order than the dominion of creatures.

955. — Man's dominion over himself and others.— 1° Man, as endowed with liberty, moves himself to his end. Hence, under this aspect, he is active in relation to himself, and therefore has a certain dominion over himself.

2° Man has perfect dominion over all operations which he exercises by his intellect and will, by his external senses, and by his power of locomotion, for these operations are subject to his free will.

Man, however, is not perfectly the master of actions which he naturally exercises by his internal senses and by his sensitive appetite, because these actions sometimes depend on the disposition of his bodily organs, which is not in man's power.

Man has no dominion over the actions of his vegetative faculties, for these powers are not subject to the command of reason.

---
(1) II-II, q. 66, a. 1, ad 1.

3° Man has not direct and absolute dominion over his own life and members, but only the guardianship and use of them. For life and body are prerequisites of man's dominion, and are its foundation. Hence they are not subject to man's dominion.

4° Neither rulers nor the State have direct dominion over the life and members of citizens, and hence they may not at will mutilate citizens, or even put them to death. This is so because the private citizen has the same relation to the State as the member has to the body. But no one is master of his own members. Therefore.

5° Man can acquire dominion over the activity of other men. Man is naturally a social being. Moreover, nature makes men unequal. Therefore it follows that some men are superiors and rulers, and others are inferiors and subjects. Hence certain men may acquire dominion over the activity of other men.

6° All dominion of rational creatures is subject to God's sovereign dominion, as we have seen.

956.— Immanent duties.— 1° *Preliminaries.—* a) By immanent duties we understand the obligations by which man is bound in actions related not to the good of others, but to his own good.

b) Two difficulties are proposed which make it necessary for us to deal with the question of the existence of immanent duties: *first*, if an action is directed to the proper good of a man, this man can always decline this good, and hence is not bound to perform the action; *secondly*, since no one can impose an obligation on himself, it would seem that man cannot have duties towards himself.

c) In the time of St. Thomas, there were some who taught that only actions which scandalized others or did harm to them were sins[1].

---

(1) *Contra Gentes*, 1. III, c. 121.

All philosophers, like Pufendorf and others of the same school, who hold that all human rights and duties have their origin in man's social nature deny at least implicitly the existence of immanent duties.

Thomasius, Fleischer, Schopenhauer, Herbart, Lipps, and many moderns directly deny that man has duties towards himself.

Sound moral philosophy, nevertheless, teaches that man has duties towards himself. This, indeed, is a fundamental doctrine of Christian ethics.

2° *In the light of what has been said*, we shall now prove the proposition which follows.

Man is bound by the natural law to perform certain immanent duties. — 1) A free being which is naturally subject to God's perfect dominion is bound by the natural law to perform certain immanent duties. But man is a free being which is naturally subject to God's perfect dominion. Therefore man is bound by the natural law to perform certain immanent duties.

Major. — Such a free being has over himself only imperfect dominion, i.e., dominion by which he may govern himself only in accordance with the ordinance established by God through the eternal law. Therefore, in ruling himself, man is bound to perform certain immanent duties.

The *minor* is evident from the fact that God is the first and most universal cause of all being, as we have already said.

2) According to the natural law, just as man's reason is subject to God, so the body is destined for the perfection of the soul, and the inferior powers should be developed in conformity with the dictates of reason. Therefore, in all his acts, man is bound to observe this order by which he is subject to God, the body to the soul, and the inferior powers to reason; or, in other words, man is bound to perform certain immanent duties.

VIRTUES 189

NOTE.— Man does not impose upon himself obligations towards himself, for all immanent duties derive from the sovereign dominion of God as first cause. Moreover, man may not decline goods intended for him by the eternal law, which is naturally participated in the light of natural reason.

957.— Man's dominion over external things.— 1° We are dealing now not with this or that man, nor with men taken collectively, but with any individual man, i.e., with any rational animal.

2° By external things we mean material things, which are less perfect than man, as irrational animals, plants, and inorganic beings.

3° Dominion over external things is physical and moral power over these things. This dominion is called *possession* by St. Thomas, and is understood in a generic sense. Therefore our present problem does not concern private ownership, nor the common ownership of possessions.

4° According to St. Thomas, man has no power over the nature of things, in as much as he cannot change the nature of things. For God alone is the author of nature, and therefore the nature of things is not subject to the power of man, but only to the power of God, Whose mere will things obey. Nevertheless, man has dominion over external things, in as much as he may use them for his own benefit, for this is the purpose for which they were made(1).

5° The use of a thing implies the application of that thing to some operation. Hence the operation to which we apply a thing is its use; v.g., horseback riding is the use of a horse, striking is the use of a club. Moreover, since the will is the faculty which moves all the powers of the soul to their acts, it is to the will as first mover that *use* primarily and chiefly belongs. Nevertheless, it belongs to reason as the power which directs, for reason alone knows how to refer one thing to

---
(1) II-II, q. 66, a. 1.

another, and therefore how to direct the application of operation to a thing(¹). In other words, use properly belongs only to a being endowed with free will; and the dominion which man has over external things is nothing more than the extension of the dominion which he has over his acts by means of free will.

6° Finally, man is said to have *natural* dominion over external things, for this dominion has its origin in the *natural* law.

7° We shall now prove that *man has natural dominion over external things, as regards their use.*

Man has natural dominion over external things, as regards their use, if he may use them for his own benefit as the purpose for which they were made. But man may use external things for his own benefit as the purpose for which they were made. Therefore man has natural dominion over external things, as regards their use(²).

Minor.— Man may use for his own benefit things which were made for him. But external things were made for man. Therefore.

The *latter major* is evident from the fact that man has a reason and a will, and therefore use properly belongs to him.

Latter minor.— External things are less perfect than man. But, in the order of nature, the less perfect exists for the perfect. Hence external things were made for man. This conclusion becomes very evident if we consider that first matter tends to the human soul as its ultimate form. Therefore first matter, as it exists under the forms of external things, tends to man. In other words, man is the end of external things.

958.— Scholia.— 1° The order or relation (ordinatio) of external things to man is immediately dependent on the nature of external things. Therefore man's dominion over external things, which we have established, is in accordance with a primary precept of the natural law.

---
(1) I-II, q. 16, a. 2.
(2) II-II, q. 66, a. 1.

2° Since man's dominion over external things belongs to him in virtue of his nature, it belongs to every man, even to children and the demented. Similarly, this dominion is inalienable, for it is inherent in human nature.

3° Man's natural dominion over external things is given to him, in order that he may satisfy the exigencies of his nature. Hence, as an individual, he has this dominion for the preservation of his life and for the acquirement of his physical, moral, and intellectual perfection; as a member of the human species and of society, he has it for the living of his domestic and married life, by which the human species is preserved and propagated, and also for the attainment of happiness. Hence society in which man cannot live his domestic life without great difficulty is not well ordered.

4° Man's natural dominion over external things is given to him, in order that he may satisfy the exigencies of his nature. Therefore this dominion naturally results from human nature, and is the means naturally destined for the preservation and perfection of life as its end.

Nevertheless, in ordinary circumstances, this dominion imposes the duty of labor on man, for, generally speaking, man acquires external things by means of labor. In extraordinary cases, however, without in any way losing his dominion over external things, man is not bound by the duty of labor; v.g., if he is sick, or is a child, or if, because of social circumstances, he cannot or does not need to labor.

Untenable, therefore, is the opinion of Marx and his disciples, who teach that labor is the first title of the use of external things. The first title by which man has dominion over external things is human nature.

959.— Right and coaction. — 1° Coaction is of two kinds:

a) improper or moral, which is the obligation in justice by which a person is morally bound to give to everyone his due;

b) proper or physical, which is the moral power of using physical force to protect the inviolability of one's rights.

2° Coaction is a property, not an essential element, of right. Coaction, nevertheless, is not a consequence of rights which belong to citizens in virtue of distributive justice: for citizens are not allowed to use violence against the civil authority to obtain a just distribution of burdens and honors, because this would lead to serious disturbance of public order.

3° Since all rights are ultimately intended for the good of the community, the exercise of physical force is reserved to the authority charged with the common good, i.e., to the public authority. Nevertheless, private persons may have recourse to violence to defend their rights in two cases: when civil society is not yet constituted, i.e., is in a primitive state, and when recourse to the public authority is impossible. In these cases, a private person may, *under certain conditions*, or, as we say, *provided that the moderation of a blameless defense be observed*, defend his rights by recourse to violence: by wounding, or even by killing an unjust aggressor.

These conditions are as follows:

a) only the defense of one's rights may be intended, for this is the sole purpose of coaction; therefore it is not lawful to do violence to an adversary from a motive of hatred;

b) one's rights cannot be defended in any other way, for otherwise violence would be done to an aggressor, who, except in the circumstance mentioned, has a right to his life and to the integrity of his members;

c) coaction may be used only during the act of aggression, for otherwise there would not actually be an aggressor;

d) the rights defended must be of great importance, as are life, the members of the body, liberty, chastity, and material goods of great value: for there must be due proportion between the violence used and the rights defended.

4° The adversaries of this teaching are Kant and many modern jurists, who teach that coaction is an essential element of right, and not its property.

a) Coaction is not an essential element of right.— That which presupposes the existence of right is not an essential element of right. But coaction presupposes the existence of right. Therefore.

Minor.— Coaction exists for the defense of right.

b) Coaction is a property of right.— That which, according to the natural law, is a consequence of right is a property of right. But, according to the natural law, coaction is a consequence of right. Therefore coaction is a property of right.

The *major* is self-evident.

Minor.— The natural law constitutes rights as certain goods destined for the community or for its parts. Therefore, in order that rights may not, as a result of the depravity of those who refuse to give the community and its parts their due, become illusory, the natural law also intends that coaction be a consequence of rights.

c) In a well-ordered society, coaction is of its nature reserved to the public authority.— Coaction is of its nature reserved to the authority entrusted with the care of the common good. But, in a well-ordered society, it is to the public authority that the care of the common good is entrusted. Therefore, in a well-ordered society, coaction is of its nature reserved to the public authority.

Major.— Since rights are ultimately intended for the good of the community, coaction which is a consequence of rights is properly reserved to the authority entrusted with the care of the common good.

d) When recourse to the public authority is impossible, a private person may use coaction to defend his rights.— If this were not so, the rights of private persons would become illusory because of the wickedness of those whose impunity would endanger public safety.

960.— Scholia.— 1° Honor may not be defended by the wounding or the taking of the life of another, for these means are not sufficient to prevent harm to it. Honor is harmed by injury; but injury cannot be prevented by the wounding or killing of the person who inflicts the injury.

2° A duel is a prearranged single combat with deadly weapons between two persons for the purpose of settling some private grievance. As *prearranged*, a duel differs from a quarrel which has a sudden beginning; as intended *to settle a private grievance*, a duel is private, and is distinct from a public duel, i.e., from a duel undertaken on public authority, for the common good; v g., the duel between the Horatii and the Curiatii.

Private duels are unlawful because they are entirely insufficient for the attainment of the end for which they are usually intended, namely, the repairing of injury to honor, and also because in a duel private persons, without the fulfilment of the required conditions, arrogate to themselves the coaction of right which of its nature is reserved to the public authority.

POINTS FOR REVIEW

1. Explain why right is the object of justice.
2. Define: objective right, subjective right, natural right, positive right, immediate natural right, mediate natural right, real right, personal right, immanent duties, and proper coaction.
3. Explain why every intellectual being, ond only such a being, is the subject of dominion, and why man has no dominion over his life and members. What is the foundation of man's dominion over external things?
4. What is implied in the use of a thing?
5. Explain why coaction is not an essential element of right, and why in a well-ordered society, it is of its nature reserved to the public authority.

ARTICLE IV

JUSTICE

961.— Definition of justice.— 1° Justice has two principal meanings.

First, justice is used in a general way to signify Christian sanctity, i.e., acts of all the virtues. For acts of all the virtues render the will conformed to its rule, which is the divine law. But that is just which is conformed to its rule; and justice effects this conformity. Hence all the virtues taken together may be rightly called justice, and each virtue a part of justice. But justice thus understood is justice in a metaphorical sense(1).

Secondly, justice, in its special meaning, is that cardinal virtue which inclines a person to give to everyone his due.

It is with justice in this sense that we are at present concerned.

2° Justice, as a cardinal virtue, is defined by Ulpian: *the constant and perpetual will of giving to each one his due*. It may also be defined: *a virtue which constantly inclines the will always to give to each one his due*.

Explanation of Ulpian's definition(2):

a) Will: will is used here to signify not the faculty, but the act of willing. Since justice is an operative habit, it is correctly defined in relation to act, for every operative habit is essentially destined for act.

b) Constant, in as much as the will firmly perseveres in its perpetual purpose of preserving justice. Hence constancy signifies firmness on the part of the will. Therefore, in the definition, constant will has not the same signification as

---
(1) II-II, q. 58, a. 2, ad 1.
(2) II-II, q. 58, a. 1.

perpetual will. For justice is called perpetual will not with reference to the will, but to the object.

c) Perpetual, not in the sense that the act is of perpetual duration, but with reference to the object, in as much as a just man always and in all circumstances wills to give to each one his due. A man who does not always render to each one his due is not just.

d) Of giving to each one his due: the right of another is the proper object of justice. Justice is thus distinguished from the other moral virtues, whose proper object is the good of their subject.

To give to each one his due may also be understood *negatively*, as signifying: *to injure no one.* For a person who does not injure another is regarded as giving him his due.

962. Acts of justice. — Justice has, in a certain sense, two acts:

a) the act of giving to each one his due; this act has reference to the execution of justice;

b) the act of determining, i.e., of judging, the equality and proportion between persons and things. Justice is thus distinguished from the moral virtues, which are concerned with the regulation of acts as they proceed from the will. In other words, justice consists in a mean of reality, — which is at the same time a mean of reason, — whereas the other moral virtues consist solely in a mean of reason.

The act of judging equality and proportion is an act of knowledge. Therefore it is not the proper act of justice itself, but of synesis, which is the part of prudence which pronounces correct judgment. This judgment, nevertheless, pertains to justice in as much as justice disposes the will to move the intellect to judge correctly(¹).

963.— Subjective parts of justice.— 1° The subjective parts of justice are the different species into which justice is divided.

---
(1) II-II, q. 60, a. 1, ad 1.

2° Justice is a virtue which directs man in his relations with other men; and this may happen in two ways:

first, as regards his relations with individual men;

secondly, as regards his relations with other men in general, in as much as a man who serves a community serves all men who are in this community.

Justice which directs man in his relations with the political community is called *general, legal*, or *social justice*.

Justice which directs man in his relations with other individual men is called *particular* justice(¹).

3° Justice which directs man in his relations with another either directs one private person in his relations with another private person, as one part of the political community with another part, or it directs the political community in its relations with the private person, as the whole with the part.

Justice which directs one private person in his relation with another private person is called *commutative* justice, because it regulates mutual dealings of private persons, as buying, selling, and other *commutations*.

Justice which directs the community in its relations with the private person is called *distributive* justice, because it regulates the *distribution* of common goods, as honors and rewards, in accordance with the dignity and merits of the persons concerned(²).

Therefore the subjective parts, i.e., the species, of justice are three in number: *general justice, commutative justice*, and *distributive justice*.

964.— General justice.— 1° A thing may be general in two ways:

first, by predication, as animal is general in relation to man and horse; such a general thing is essentially the same as the things of which it is predicated;

---

(1) II-II, q. 58, a. 5.— *In Ethic.*, 1. V, 11. 1-3.
(2) II-II, q. 58, a. 7, and q. 61, a. 1.— *In Ethic.*, 1, V. 11. 3-4.

secondly, as a universal cause is general in relation to all its effects; such a general thing need not be essentially the same as the things in relation to which it is general, just as a cause is not essentially the same as its effects.

General justice directs individual man in his relations with society, as the part with the whole. In other words, the proper and immediate object of general justice is the common good of political society. Moreover, since the acts of all the virtues can be directed to the common good, justice is general not as a predicate, but as a universal cause, in as much as it directs the acts of all the virtues to its own end, i.e., in as much as it moves all the acts of the other virtues by its command.

Hence general justice, as a special virtue, is distinguished from the other virtues(¹).

Since it is the function of law to direct to the common good, general justice is also called *legal* justice, because by it man conforms with the law which directs the acts of all the virtues to the common good(²).

General justice is also called *social* justice, because by it man is directed to the whole of society, i.e., to the end of society as a whole.

2° General justice is a virtue which perfects the will, because it is justice. Moreover, since its proper object is the common good, it is in the ruler principally and architectonically, whereas it is in his subjects secondarily and administratively(³).

3° General justice is distinguished from obedience and piety towards one's country.

Obedience proceeds from reverence towards superiors(⁴), and its proper object is an implied or expressed precept, i.e., the will of a superior made known in any way(⁵).

---

(1) II-II, q. 58, a. 6.
(2) II-II, q. 58, a. 5.
(3) II-II, q. 58, a. 6, c.
(4) II-II, q. 104, a. 3, ad 1.
(5) II-II, q. 2, a. 5, ad 3.

Piety extends to our country in as much as it is for us a principle of being, and pays duty and homage to our country.

Legal justice extends to our country, i.e., to civil society, not in as much as it is for us a principle of being, but in as much as it is a whole of which the private person is a part. Therefore it is related to the good of our country under the formal aspect of the common good[1].

965.— Particular justice.— 1° As we have seen, particular justice is divided into two species: commutative justice and distributive justice.

2° Commutative justice and distributive justice are distinguished from each other, *first*, in equality, i.e., in mean, and, *secondly*, in matter.

a) In mean.— In distributive justice, something is given to a private person, in as much as what belongs to the whole is due to the part, and in a quantity that is proportionate to the importance of the position of the part in relation to the whole. Therefore, in distributive justice, the mean is observed not according to equality between thing and thing, but directly according to proportion between things and persons, in such manner that as one person surpasses another, so the thing which is given to the former surpasses that which is given to the latter. Hence, in distributive justice, the real mean is observed according to geometric proportion, in which equality depends not on quantity, but on proportion; thus we say, according to geometric proportion, that six is to four as three is to two.

In commutative justice, the real mean is observed according to equality of thing to thing, i.e., according to arithmetic proportion: if one hundred dollars are owed, one hundred dollars must be paid. This is seen chiefly in buying and selling, in which the notion of commutation is primarily found[2].

---

(1) II-II: q. 101, a. 3, ad 3.
(2) II-II, q. 61, a. 2.— *In Ethic.*, l. V, ll. 5-7.

b) In matter.— The matter of justice is of two kinds: proximate and remote.

The proximate matter of justice is external operation, i.e., the use of external things, as when one man takes from or restores to another that which is his; or of persons, as when a man does an injury to the person of another, or when he shows him respect; or of works, as when a man justly exacts a work from another, or does a work for him.

The remote matter of justice consists in things, persons, and works, whose external operation is use.

Distributive justice and commutative justice have, it is evident, the same remote matter.

Distributive justice and commutative justice have not the same proximate matter, i.e., the same principal actions by which we make use of persons, things, and works. For distributive justice directs *distributions* which are made between society and the individual person, as between the whole and the part, whereas commutative justice directs *commutations* which can take place between two persons(1).

Nevertheless, it should be observed that the remote matter of distributive justice is not so much quantitative goods for distribution as burdens, honors, and social conditions in general, which must be given to all according to due proportion.

3° Distributive justice exists principally in the ruler (government), and secondarily in subjects, in as much as they are satisfied with the just distribution of the common good.

NOTE.— 1° In distributive justice, a person's condition or station is taken into account directly and in itself; in commutative justice, it is taken into account indirectly as it causes a diversity of things; v.g., the striking of a public official is a greater offense than the striking of a private person, and therefore deserves a greater penalty than the latter. But punishment is meted out in proportion to the injury done, and therefore the condition of the injured official is considered only to estimate the injury, i.e., the seriousness of the offense,

---

(1) II-II, q. 61, a. 3.

not directly to establish equality between the penalty and the injury done. Hence penalties are meted out according to equality of thing to thing, and according to commutative justice(¹).

2° The sin opposed to distributive justice is respect of persons. Respect of person exists when consideration is given not to the conditions which render a person worthy of receiving something, but to other conditions of his person; v.g., if a person is given a professorship not because he has sufficient knowledge for the position, but because he is rich, or because he is a relative of him who promotes him to the position(²).

966. Sins against commutative justice. — 1° Commutative justice directs commutations; and these may be voluntary or involuntary.

An involuntary commutation consists in a person's using another person's chattel, person, or work against his will.

A voluntary commutation consists in a person's voluntary transferring his chattel to another person(³).

Sins against commutative justice are first divided into sins committed *in involuntary commutations* and sins committed *in voluntary commutations*.

2° *Sins of injustice in involuntary commutations.*— Injustice in involuntary commutations may be committed by deed and by word.

1) *If injustice is committed by deed,*

a) one's neighbor is injured in *his own person;* and thus we have the sin of *homicide, mutilation of members,* and *unjust imprisonment;*

b) or one's neighbor is injured in *a person related to him:* if this person is a husband or wife, we have the sin of *adultery;* if this person is a virgin under her parents' care, we have the

---
(1) II-II, q. 61, a. 2, ad 3.
(2) II-II, q. 63, a. 1.
(3) II-II, q. 61, a. 3.

sin of *seduction*. Adultery and seduction are sins of lust, and also sins against justice;

c) or one's neighbor is injured in *his possessions;* and thus we have the sin of *theft*, which is the taking of what belongs to another by stealth, i.e., secretly; or *robbery*, which is the taking of what belongs to another openly and with violence.

2) If injustice committed in involuntary commutations is committed by *word*, it is committed in lawsuit or outside of lawsuit.

a) If injustice is committed in lawsuit, we have

the *injustice of a judge* who fails in his duty;

the *injustice of the prosecutor* who knowingly makes false accusation;

the *injustice of the defendant* who defends himself by withholding the truth when he is not allowed to do so, or by accusing others by the use of calumny, or by refusing trial by the use of appeal, without a just cause, or by defending oneself by the use of violence when justly condemned;

the *injustice of the witness* who gives false testimony;

the *injustice of the counsel* who knowingly defends an unjust case, or uses unlawful means in defending a case.

b) If unjustice is committed outside of lawsuit, we have
contumely;
detraction;
talebearing;
derision;
cursing.

Contumely consists in words by which a person brings something against his neighbor's honor to the knowledge of the latter or of others.

Detraction consists in blackening the good name of one's neighbor by the utterance of words in his absence.

Contumely and detraction are distinguished from each other in two ways.

First, contumely is directly against one's neighbor's *honor*, whereas detraction is directly against his *good name*. Honor presupposes superiority of virtues in the person honored, and consists chiefly in the *external testimony* of those who honor him; good name presupposes the existence of virtues, without any special superiority, in him who enjoys the good name, and consists chiefly in the general *internal* opinion of the virtuous life of a person.

Secondly, the contumelious person differs from the detractor in the manner of his utterance: the former speaks openly, whereas the latter speaks secretly, against his neighbor (1).

Talebearing (whispering) consists in secretly speaking evil of one's neighbor, in order to destroy true friendship. Talebearing and detraction differ not in matter, but in end: the former intends the severance of the ties of *friendship*, whereas the latter is directed against the *good name* of a person(2).

Derision is the vice by which a person, intending to cause shame to his neighbor, makes known in jest the latter's vices.

Cursing consists in wishing one's neighbor evil, i.e., by imprecating evil upon him. That cursing be unlawful, a person must imprecate evil as such upon his neighbor, being intent upon the evil. If a person desires another's evil under the aspect of good, cursing in this case is lawful. It is thus that the Church curses by pronouncing anathema(3).

3° *Sins of injustice in voluntary commutations.*— The two chief sins of injustice committed in voluntary commutations are *fraudulence* (cheating) and *usury*.

Fraudulence takes place in buying, selling, trading, and other similar business transactions. According to Aristotle and St. Thomas, *buying* or *selling* is a commutation of thing for thing for the purpose of providing the necessities of life.

---
(1) II-II, q. 73, a. 1, c.
(2) II-II, q. 75, a. 1, c.
(3) II-II, q. 76, a. 1, c.

Trading, i.e., business, is the commutation of thing for thing for the sake of profit([1]).

Usury is a sin of injustice committed in loans.

967. Integrant parts of justice. — 1° The integrant parts of justice are those dispositions or perfections required for a perfect act of justice.

2° The integrant parts of justice are the doing of good and the avoiding of evil.

Good and evil may be understood in a general sense, and thus the doing of good and the avoiding of evil belong to every virtue.

Good may also be considered as that which is due to one's neighbor, and evil as that which is hurtful to one's neighbor. It is under this aspect that the doing of good and the avoiding of evil are the integrant parts of justice. For it pertains to justice to do good under the aspect of what is due one's neighbor, and to avoid the opposite evil.

These two acts are the integrant parts of justice, for it belongs to justice to establish equality in our relations with others. Moreover, the preserving of a thing appertains to the cause which established that thing. Now a person constitutes the equality of justice by doing good, i.e., by rendering to another his due, and he preserves the equality of justice already established by declining from evil, i.e., by doing no injury to his neighbor([2]).

968. Potential parts of justice. — 1° The potential parts of justice are the virtues annexed to justice which are deficient in the perfection of that virtue, i.e., which do not completely satisfy the conditions which define it.

Hence two points must be observed in regard to the potential parts of justice:

---

(1) II-II, q. 77, a. 4, c.
(2) II-II, q. 79, a. 1.

a) that they have something in common with justice, in virtue of which they are virtues annexed to justice;

b) that in some respect they lack the complete perfection of justice.

2° Justice expresses a relation of one man to another, and therefore all virtues which express this relation may, in virtue of this common aspect, be annexed to justice.

Justice consists essentially in the rendering to another his due according to equality.

Therefore there are two ways in which a virtue may be deficient in the complete perfection of justice:

a) first, in as much it renders to another his due, but not according to equality, i.e., by being deficient in the aspect of equality;

b) secondly, in as much as its object is deficient in the aspect of debt.

3° The virtues annexed to justice which render another his due, but not according to equality, are the following:

religion towards God;

piety towards parents;

observance or veneration, the virtue by which we show honor and respect to persons constituted in dignity and authority.

4° The virtues annexed to justice whose objects are deficient in the aspect of debt are those virtues which are concerned with *moral debt* (due), not with *legal debt.*

A legal debt is a *debt which one is bound to render in virtue of legal obligation:* it is the proper object of justice.

A moral debt is a *debt to which one is bound in accordance with the rectitude of virtue.*

There are two kinds of moral debt:

a) first, debt without which moral rectitude cannot be preserved;

b) secondly, debt which is conducive to greater moral rectitude, but without which moral rectitude can be preserved. Therefore the virtues annexed to justice which are deficient in the aspect of debt may be divided according to the two degrees or kinds of moral debt.

5° A virtue annexed to justice which is concerned with moral debt without which moral rectitude cannot be preserved may be considered either in relation to the one who owes the debt; and thus we have *truthfulness* or veracity, the virtue by which a man in his words and deeds shows himself to his neighbor to be such as he really is;

or in relation to whom the debt is due, either in good things, and thus we have *thankfulness* or *gratitude;* or in evil things, and thus we have *vengeance.*

Thankfulness or *gratitude* is the virtue which renders benefit to benefactors, i.e., which recompenses benefactors for favors done by them.

Vengeance is the virtue by which a man, in accordance with all the circumstances of the case, observes due measure in avenging, i.e., in meting out punishment for injuries inflicted.

6° The virtues annexed to justice which are concerned with moral debt which is conducive to greater moral rectitude, but without which moral rectitude can be preserved, are *liberality* and *affability.*

Liberality is the virtue which moderates man's love for riches and makes him part with them easily when right reason so dictates.

Affability (politeness, civility, honesty) is the virtue which establishes, in accordance with the conditions of persons and other circumstances, agreeable relations in social life.

Affability, though sometimes called friendship, is not friendship, but only bears a certain likeness to it. As a result of affability, a person lives in cordial relations with others not because he wishes them well, i.e., from benevolence, but only because this is suited to social life(¹).

969. Homicide.— 1° Homicide is the unjust killing of an innocent person.

The killing of an innocent person is unjust when it is *willed;* when it is done on *private authority,* or on *public authority* without sufficient reason, for civil society, as we shall see, may put a private citizen to death, in punishment for a very grave crime; and when it is *outside the case of the unjust aggressor,* i.e., when, as we said, *the moderation of a blameless defense is not observed.*

2° Homicide is gravely illicit, *a)* because it is an arrogation of the perfect dominion over man which belongs to God alone; *b)* because it is an injury to society, which is deprived of a member; *c)* because it is an injury to the person who is killed, for he has a right to the preservation of his life.

Abortion, which consists in the ejection of the immature fetus from the mother's womb, is homicide in the proper sense of the term, and therefore is gravely illicit.

970. Suicide.— 1° Suicide is the direct and voluntary killing of oneself on one's own private authority. *Voluntary:* positively, or negatively as when a person refuses to take any food whatsoever; *direct,* i.e., willed in itself, and thus is excluded indirect killing, which takes place when a person, for a sufficiently grave reason, places a cause from which death results, but was not intended, as, for example, when a soldier exposes himself to death in defense of his country; *on one's own authority,* for, on God's authority, a person is allowed to put himself to death.

2° Seneca, Epictetus, and Marcus Aurelius in ancient times, and, in modern times, Montaigne, Montesquieu, Rousseau, Hume, Bentham, Schopenhauer, Nietzsche, Haeckel, Renan, and others hold that suicide is sometimes lawful.

---
(1) II-II, q. 80, a. *unicus.*

3° But it is evident that suicide is unlawful, for it is, *a*) contrary to the rights of God, in as much as man is immediately destined for the divine good, and therefore has not perfect dominion over himself; *b*) contrary to the rights of society, in as much as man is destined for the good of society, and therefore may not deprive society of one of its parts by putting himself to death; *c*) contrary to the ordinance of the natural law which requires man's self-preservation.

Therefore the public authority is not allowed to command a man to inflict death upon himself, nor may a man obey such a command, for the public authority is not allowed to command an act which is contrary to a primary precept of the natural law.

Nevertheless, God may command suicide, because the act of suicide in this case is destined for the divine good, and hence for the good of the person who inflicts death upon himself.

The direct mutilation of one's own body has the malice of suicide in proportion to the gravity of the mutilation.

971. Religion.— 1° Religion may be understood as consisting in the truths and duties which bind man to God. It may also be understood as a moral virtue.

It is with religion as a virtue that we are at present concerned.

2° Religion, as a virtue, is defined: *the virtue by which men give to God the reverence and worship due to Him.*

Worship is a testimony of submission in recognition of the excellence of another. *Divine worship* is the testimony and mark of submission in recognition of God"s excellence, or it is the sign which signifies submission to God as the supreme Lord.

3° Religion is not a theological virtue, but a moral virtue. The proper object of the theological virtues of faith, hope, and charity is God Himself, whereas the proper object of religion is not God Himself, but the worship due to God. Therefore religion is a moral virtue annexed to justice, whose object is that which is due another.

4° Religion is the most excellent of the moral virtues, because it has a more immediate relation to God than any other moral virtue, in as much as it gives to God the worship due to Him.

Nevertheless, under a certain aspect, legal justice is more excellent than religion.

Legal justice may be considered in the subjects or in the ruler.

As it exists in the subjects, legal justice directs man to the common good, and thus it is not superior to religion, which directs man to divine good.

As it exists in the ruler, legal justice not only directs man to the common good, but directs the common good to divine good. Thus it is more excellent than religion, because it commands the acts of religion and regulates divine worship.

5° Acts of religion are distinguished in virtue of their matter, i.e., in virtue of the things consecrated to the worship of God.

A thing consecrated to God may be either a spiritual thing or an external thing. The spiritual thing submitted to God and to the worship of Him may be either the will or the intellect. If it is the will, we have *devotion*, which is a certain actual readiness to do what pertains to divine worship; if it is the intellect, we have *prayer*, which is petition made to God for becoming things.

If the thing consecrated to God is an external thing, we have:

adoration, which consists in the external humiliation of the body in token of God's excellence and of our submission to Him;

sacrifice, which is the offering of a sensible thing through a real immolation by a lawful minister to God in testimony of His supreme dominion and of our subjection to Him.

6° The vices opposed to religion either have something in common with religion in as much as they give worship to God, or they are, by defect, manifestly contrary to religion.

a) The vice which gives worship to God is *superstition*.

Superstition is opposed to religion by excess, and is defined: *the vice by which a person offers divine worship to someone to whom it is not due, or to God in an improper manner*.

b) The vice opposed to religion by defect is *irreligion*, which includes *tempting of God, perjury, sacrilege*, and *simony*.

972. Lying.— 1° *Preliminaries.*— a) A lie may be defined in relation to moral truth, i.e., to veracity, of whose concept it is the negation. Moral truth is the *conformity of speech with judgment*. Therefore a lie implies a disconformity of speech with judgment. But this disconformity can be involuntary; and, in this case, there is no lie, but an error in speech, i.e., a false statement. In order that a false statement be a lie, it must be *voluntary*. Therefore a lie may be defined: a *statement made with the intention of saying what is false*.

Statement made, i.e., the enunciation of a concept made by words, deeds, or any sign, is the genus of this definition; and *with the intention of saying what is false* is the differentia which formally constitutes a lie.

b) Lies are *essentially* divided into lies which greatly transcend the truth, and these pertain to *boasting;* and into lies which are slightly deficient in truth, and these pertain to *irony*.

Lies are accidentally divided in relation to the end intended, as it increases or lessens the guilt of a lie. Guilt is increased when harm to another is intended — *pernicious lie;* is lessened when some good or amusement is intended — *jocose lie;* or is useful — *officious lie*.

c) Closely allied to lying are *simulation*, by which we deceive our neighbor by an external sign or deed, and *hypocrisy*, by which a person pretends to be other than he is, as when a sinner pretends to be a holy person.

d) According to traditional Catholic teaching, all lies are intrinsically evil, i.e., essentially at variance with the order of nature, and of their nature evil.

In ancient times, Plato[1], Origen, and Cassian taught that a lie is sometimes lawful; in modern times, Grotius[2] teaches that a lie is lawful under the following conditions: if the person addressed has no right to demand the truth, if harm is done to no one, and if grave evil can be averted.

Many Protestants, and some Catholics, as Dubois[3] and Fonsegrive[4], follow the opinion of Grotius.

2° We may now prove the proposition which follows.

Lies are intrinsically evil.

Whatsoever is at variance with the order of nature is intrinsically evil. But lies are at variance with the order of nature. Therefore lies are intrinsically evil.

The *major* is self-evident.

Minor.— To put a thing to a use which is contrary to the end intended by nature is a variance with the order of nature. But this is done in lying. For a lie is a statement at variance with the mind; and the end of a statement (speech) is the expression of the mind in manifesting its concepts to others: for words are the signs of concepts. Therefore.

NOTE.— 1° The concealing of the truth is not the same as lying. Lying is intrinsically evil, whereas the concealing of the truth is lawful if *a)* there is a sufficiently grave reason, *b)* and the hearer has no right to the knowledge of the truth concealed.

---

(1) *De Rep.*, I, c. 3.
(2) *De jure belli et pacis*, 1, III, c. 1.
(3) *Une théorie du mensonge.*
(4) *Eléments de philosophie*, t. II, p. 175.

2° Although a lie is always intrinsically evil, it is permissible sometimes to use *equivocation, amphibology,* and *mental restriction in the wide sense* to hide what is in one's mind, provided that this is done with prudence and for a sufficient reason.

Equivocation is the *use of a word or sign which, according to common usage, can have two or more different meanings.*

Amphibology is an *ambiguous statement.*

Mental restriction is the *act by which a word, statement, or deed is given, because of the intention of the speaker, a meaning other than its natural and obvious meaning.* If the meaning of the statement cannot be determined from the context or circumstances, it is called *pure mental restriction;* if, however, the speaker's meaning can be known from circumstances, signs, or deeds, it is called *mental restriction in a wide sense.*

Pure mental restriction is a lie, and therefore is never permissible.

973. Adulation, quarreling, avarice, and prodigality.
— 1° *Adulation* (flattery) is opposed to affability by excess, and *quarreling* is opposed to it by deficiency.

Adulation is the *vice by which a person is disposed to please others in everything, even in sin.*

Quarreling is the *vice by which a person intends to contradict another, not from lack of that love which unites minds* (thus it pertains to discord and is opposed to friendship), *but for the purpose of being disagreeable to him in conversation and of causing him sadness* (thus it destroys what is due in human relations, and is opposed to affability).

2° *Prodigality* is opposed to liberality by excess, and *avarice* is opposed to it by deficiency.

Prodigality is *an inordinate passion for giving which causes a person to make expenditures without taking into account circumstances of time, place, persons, etc.*

Avarice (covetousness) is *an inordinate love of possessions or money which prevents a person from giving when required by his human relations to do so.*

Man is strongly attracted to the possession of worldly goods because he greatly desires self-sufficiency, which is a condition of happiness. Hence avarice is a capital vice, and engenders the vices of *treachery, fraudulence, falsehood, perjury, restlessness, violence,* and *insensibility to mercy*(1).

974. Epiky or equity.— 1° Epiky (epicheia) or equity is defined: *that virtue whose object is the common good to be attained not in any way whatsoever, but by disregarding the common rules and letter of the law in particular cases in which the observance of the law would be evil.*

Epiky is necessary because human acts, with which laws are concerned, consist of contingent singular acts, which are innumerable in their diversity, and make impossible the institution of rules of law which are applicable to all particular cases. Therefore, when the observance of the law is contrary to the equality of justice and at variance with the common good, man is bound to disregard the letter of the law and to do what is required by justice and the common good.

The object of epiky or equity is the quest of the common good not according to the letter of the law, but, in disregard of the letter of the law, in conformity with higher principles.

2° Epiky, as is evident from its proper object, is a subjective part, i.e., a species, of legal justice.

Hence legal justice in the generic sense has two divisions:

a) *legal justice in the strict or specific sense,* whose object is the attainment of the common good by the observance of the letter of the law;

b) *epiky* or equity, whose object is the attainment of the common good by disregarding the letter of the law. Since epiky seeks the common good by complying with principles

---

(1) II-II, q. 118, a. 8.

which are superior to the common principles of the law, it is the more important part of legal justice in the generic sense([1]).

POINTS FOR REVIEW

1. Define justice, name its two acts, and describe its subjective parts.
2. State the proper object of legal justice, and explain why general justice is called legal justice.
3. Distinguish between the mean of distributive justice and the mean of commutative justice.
4. Under what aspect are the doing of good and the avoiding of evil integrant parts of justice?
5. Distinguish between legal debt and moral debt.
6. Define a lie; and prove that lying is intrinsically evil.
7. Define: mental restriction in the wide sense, and epiky or equity.
8. Distinguish between epiky and legal justice in the specific sense.

([1]) II-II, q. 120, aa. 1-2.— *In Ethic.*, 1. V. 1. 16.

ARTICLE V

FORTITUDE

975. Two meanings of fortitude. — 1° Fortitude has two meanings:

a) first, it signifies a certain firmness of mind, and thus understood is a general virtue, or rather a condition of any virtue, because, as the Philosopher says([1]), firmness and immobility in operation are requisites of every virtue;

b) secondly, it denotes firmness of mind in bearing and warding off things in which it is very difficult to be firm, namely, in certain serious dangers. Fortitude in this sense is a special virtue, for it has determinate matter([2]).

2° It may be objected that every virtue implies firmness of mind, and therefore that fortitude is not a special virtue; v.g., a person possessed of the virtue of chastity in a heroic degree cannot be induced by the fear of any evil to act in violation of this virtue.

In reply to this objection, we may state that firmness of mind is found in virtues distinct from fortitude because they seek their own proper good, whereas firmness of mind is found in fortitude because it seeks its own special proper good, which is the moderation of fear and audacity. Hence, when great dangers hinder the exercise of a virtue, v.g., chastity, this virtue commands the moderation of fear and audacity, for this is necessary for the attainment of its end; but the moderation of fear and audacity, though commanded by another virtue, is an act elicited by fortitude([3]).

(1) *Ethic.*, 1. II, c. 4.
(2) II-II, q. 123, a. 2. c.
(3) II-II, q. 123, a. 7, c.

976. Definition of fortitude.— Fortitude, as a special virtue, is defined: *a virtue which moderates the movements of the soul in difficulties and dangers, and especially in bearing and warding off dangers of death.*

a) Virtue, because fortitude makes a man be and act in conformity with reason, in as much as it prevents him from turning away from the good of reason because of difficulties and dangers.

b) Which moderates the movements of the soul in difficulties and dangers: these words indicate the subject, the proximate matter, and the remote matter of fortitude.

The subject of fortitude is the irascible appetite, because fortitude moderates the movements of the soul in difficulties and dangers, i.e., it regulates fear and audacity, which are the passions of the irascible appetite.

The proximate matter of fortitude is fear to be curbed and audacity to be moderated in accordance with right reason[1].

The remote matter of fortitude is anything terrible, i.e., any difficulty or danger.

c) Especially in bearing and warding off dangers of death: these words indicate the acts of fortitude, which are *sufferance* and *aggression*[2].

Sufferance is the act of repressing fear.

Aggression is the act of moderating audacity.

But, since it is more difficult to repress fear than to moderate audacity, the principal act of fortitude is sufferance, i.e., the act of standing immovable in the midst of dangers[3].

NOTE.— 1° Fortitude is chiefly concerned with dangers occurring in a just private or general war[4]. This is so because, in a just general war, dangers are undergone for the common good; and, in a just private war, dangers are undergone because of some virtue, as justice, chastity, or faith; v.g., when a judge,

---
(1) II-II, q. 123, a. 3.
(2) II-II, q. 123, a. 4, c.
(3) II-II, q. 103, a. 6, c. and ad 1.
(4) II-II, q. 103, a. 5.

or even a private person, does not refrain from giving a just judgment because of fear of impending death; when a virgin exposes herself to the danger of death for the preservation of her virginity; when a Christian suffers martyrdom for the sake of his faith.

2° Other dangers of death, such as those arising from sickness, storms at sea, attacks from robbers, and the like, are not directly and of themselves the matter of fortitude, for they do not come upon a man because of his pursuit of some good. Nevertheless, they can become the matter of fortitude, — and thus they pertain in a secondary way to fortitude, — from the end of the agent, that is, when the agent accepts or suffers them for the sake of some virtue; v.g., when a person attends a friend suffering from an infectious disease, or undertakes a dangerous voyage in the interest of religion[1].

3° Martyrdom, by which a person remains firm in truth and justice against the attacks of his persecutors, is the greatest act of fortitude[2].

977. Vices opposed to fortitude.— 1° Since fortitude is concerned with acts of fear and audacity, it is possible to sin against fortitude by fear and by audacity.

2° From the point of view of fear, *immoderate fear* is opposed to fortitude by deficiency, and *fearlessness* is opposed to it by excess.

Immoderate fear is the *vice which causes a person to refuse to expose himself to danger, even for a reasonable cause*.

Fearlessness is the *vice which causes a person not to fear, even when there is a reasonable cause for fear*.

3° From the point of view of audacity, *immoderate audacity* is opposed to fortitude by excess, and *lack of audacity* is opposed to it by deficiency.

---

(1) *Ibidem*.
(2) II-II, q. 124.

Immoderate audacity is the *vice which causes a person to thrust himself into danger without taking counsel and without reason.*

Lack of audacity is the *vice which prevents a person who has taken counsel from facing danger and from steadfastness in execution.*

A person usually lacks audacity because of fear which militates against his steadfastness in purpose. Therefore lack of audacity is not a vice distinct from fear. Nevertheless, when a person is lacking in audacity, not in consequence of fear, but because of a lack of hope, i.e., because he has no hope of success, it is probable that in this case there is a special vice opposed to audacity by deficiency. This vice is called cowardice.

978. Integrant and potential parts of fortitude.— 1° Fortitude has no subjective parts, i.e., is not divided into specifically distinct virtues. For fortitude is concerned with very special matter, namely, dangers of death, all of which, though differing in degree, are formally the same.

It has, however, integrant and potential parts.

2° The integrant parts of fortitude are those dispositions which concur in the production of a perfect act of fortitude.

The acts of fortitude are two in number: sufferance and aggression.

1) There are two requirements for an act of aggression:

a) readiness to undergo dangers; and this is provided by *confidence* or *magnanimity;*

b) vigorousness in the execution of what one has confidently begun; and this is provided by *magnificence.*

2) There are also two requirements for an act of sufferance:

a) that a person's courage (animus) be not weakened and lessened by the stress of impending evil; and this is provided by *patience;*

b) that a person become not wearied to the point of yielding as a result of prolonged bearing of hardship; and this is provided by *perseverance*.

Hence there are four integrant parts of fortitude: *magnanimity, magnificence, patience,* and *perseverance*.

3° The potential parts of fortitude are virtues annexed to fortitude, but which have not the full perfection of fortitude.

Magnanimity, magnificence, patience, and perseverance, when concerned with dangers of death, concur, as it is evident, in the production of a perfect act of fortitude, and therefore are the integrant parts of fortitude. When these virtues are concerned with lesser dangers, they have not the full perfection of fortitude, but have a certain likeness to it. Therefore, under this aspect, they are the potential parts of fortitude[1].

979. Magnanimity.— Magnanimity, in its etymology, signifies greatness of mind. But a mind is great only when it aspires to great things, plans great things, has esteem for great things, and neglects little things and regards them as worthless.

Hence magnanimity may be defined: *a virtue which tends, in every genus of the virtues, to great deeds worthy of great honor.*

a) *Tends to great deeds:* this is indicated by the term magnanimity.

b) *In every genus of the virtues:* because there is nothing truly great in human things except virtue, which makes man absolutely good. The works of virtue are not all equal: some are ordinary and trifling, and others are great and lofty.

Every virtue, as perfect, tends to what is great in its own order under the aspect of the particular worthiness which it has from its nature; v.g., the virtue of abstinence, as perfect, tends to great fasting because of the worthiness proper to abstinence. Magnanimity tends to what is great under the aspect of what is great and difficult, and therefore it is dis-

---

(1) II-II, q. 128, a. unicus.

tinguished, in virtue of its formal object, from the other virtues(¹).

c) *Worthy of great honor:* for great deeds of virtue deserve great honor from both God and men. Hence great honor is the remote matter of magnanimity; and the desire for honor is its proximate matter(²). Indeed, magnanimity modifies the appetite in a special way, so that no person may desire honors which are greater or less than are becoming to him.

NOTE. — Magnanimity engenders two things: credulity in regard to the conquest of evil and to the attainment of good, and hope of accomplishment. For magnanimity makes a man believe that he can do what is difficult, and therefore it produces in him a desire for difficult goods. Hence *confidence*, which is strength of hope resulting from a consideration which gives a person a strong opinion that he will obtain a certain good, pertains to magnanimity(³).

980. Characteristics of magnanimous persons. — 1° The characteristics of magnanimous persons may be considered in relation to the matter of the virtues, to human acts, to the dispositions of the magnanimous, and to external things.

2° *In relation to the matter of the virtues.* — External dangers, favors, and honors constitute the matter of the virtues.

1) As regards dangers, which are the matter of fortitude, the magnanimous person has two characteristics.

a) *The magnanimous person does not expose himself to dangers for trivial reasons, nor is he a lover of danger.* The magnanimous person, however, will expose himself to any dangers whatsoever when something great is involved, as the common safety, justice, divine worship, and the like.

b) *The magnanimous person, in exposing himself to dangers, does so with vehemence, and hence makes no effort to spare his*

---

(1) II-II, q. 129, a. 4, ad 1.
(2) II-II, q. 129, aa. 1 and 2.
(3) II-II, q. 129, a. 6.

life. He considers that it is more worthy to obtain great goods by his death than to wish to live.

2) In relation to favors, the magnanimous person has five characteristics.

a) The magnanimous person is ever ready to bestow favors on others, but is slow to accept them from others. He who gives is greater then he who receives.

b) If the magnanimous person receives favors, he ever strives to return greater favors. This, indeed, pertains to greatness of mind.

c) The magnanimous person is of such disposition that he takes delight in doing favors, but with reluctance receives favors. A person who receives favors is not so great as he who bestows them.

d) The magnanimous person finds delight in hearing of favors which he has bestowed on others, but not in hearing of favors of which he is the recipient. He prefers to give than to receive.

e) The magnanimous person does not easily allow his neede to be known, for he has no desire to ask for anything or to receivs anything from anybody. He is ever ready to do favors for others.

3) In relation to honors, the magnánimous person has one characteristic.

The magnanimous person shows himself to be great to those who are possessed of high office and the goods of fortune, but shows a certain moderation towards ordinary persons by not displaying his greatness to them. There are two reasons for this.

First, the magnanimous person tends to what is difficult and arduous. To surpass great men in goodness is difficult and noble, whereas to surpass ordinary persons in this respect is easy.

Secondly, to be esteemed by great men is a sign of manliness of mind, whereas to be esteemed by persons of low station is a characteristic of persons who are troublesome to others.

3° *In relation to human acts.*— A person's human acts may have relation to himself or to others.

1) As human acts have relation to oneself, the magnanimous person has one characteristic.

The magnanimous person is quiet, i.e., does not engage in many enterprises, *and is slow,* i.e., does not easily become involved in new enterprises. This is so because the magnanimous person confines himself to acts which are destined for the attainment of great honor and for the accomplishment of great deeds. And acts of this kind are few in number.

2) As human acts have relation to others, the characteristics of the magnanimous person pertain either to truth or to delight found in the company of others.

As regards truth, the magnanimous person has four characteristics.

a) The magnanimous person plainly shows himself to be a friend or an enemy. It is as a consequence of fear, which is incompatible with magnanimity, that a person hides his love or hatred.

b) The magnanimous person places greater value on truth than on the opinions of men. The opinions of men cannot induce him to neglect virtuous acts.

c) The magnanimous person speaks and acts openly. This is so because he does not esteem others beyond their due. Hence he is not influenced by fear of others to hide his words or deeds.

d) The magnanimous person is ever truthful in his words. It may happen, however, that he will speak ironically in the company of others; but he will do so only for their amusement.

As regards delight found in the company of others, the magnanimous person has one characteristic.

The magnanimous person shows no readiness to live in the company of persons other than friends. A person who is familiar with everybody is a person of servile mind.

4° *In relation to the dispositions of the magnanimous.* — Under this aspect, the characteristics of the magnanimous person are properties of heart and properties of speech.

1) The magnanimous person is characterized by two qualities of heart.

a) *The magnanimous person shows no readiness to admire.* Only great things are worthy of admiration. But any external event whatsoever does not appear great to the magnanimous person, for his whole life is concerned with internal goods, which are truly great.

b) *The magnanimous person gives little thought to evils he has suffered.* For, *first*, the magnanimous person is not much inclined to admiration. Moreover, we usually remember only those things which we admire for their greatness. *Secondly*, it is especially characteristic of the magnanimous person to forget injuries he has suffered, in as much as he regards them as evils which cannot lessen his greatness.

2) The magnanimous person is also characterized by two qualities of speech.

a) *The magnanimous person does not speak much of himself or of others.*

The magnanimous person does not place much value on particular human goods, but is wholly concerned with divine and common goods.

b) *The magnanimous person neither complains nor murmurs when he lacks life's necessities, nor does he ask that he be supplied with them.* Complaint and entreaty of this kind manifest smallness of soul such as characterizes persons who regard life's necessities as great things.

5° *In relation to external things.*— Under this aspect, the characteristics of the magnanimous person are two in number: one in regard to external possessions, and the other in regard to movements of the body.

a) *The magnanimous person is more interested in the possession of unproductive goods which can bring him honor than in the possession of useful goods which can bring him riches.* A magnanimous person is self-sufficient, and hence does not need to be enriched by goods which are productive of wealth.

b) The magnanimous person acts slowly, and is demure in his words and speech. The magnanimous person is intent on doing only a few things, and is not contentious. Sharpness of words and rapidity of speech pertain to persons prone to contention[1].

981. Vices opposed to magnanimity.— 1° The vices opposed to magnanimity are four in number, of which three are opposed to it by excess, and one by deficiency.

The following vices are opposed to magnanimity by excess:
presumption, which has relation to works;
ambition, which has relation to honor;
vainglory, which has relation to fame and opinion.

The vice opposed to magnanimity by deficiency is *pusillanimity.*

2° *a)* Presumption is *the vice which causes a person to undertake to do what is beyond his powers*[2].

b) Ambition is *an inordinate desire for honor.* Honor denotes reverence shown to a person in testimony of his excellence, as the offering of titles of office or rank.

c) Vainglory is *an inordinate desire for fame and praise.*

Fame consists in opinion and praise, and is distinguished from honor, of which it is an effect and the end. Therefore ambition and vainglory are distinguished by their objects.

d) Pusillanimity is *the vice which causes a person to fail to attempt deeds which are commensurate with his natural powers.*

A person is pusillanimous because he does not regard himself worthy of things of which he is worthy. This happens because he is ignorant of his condition or qualifications. This

---
(1) *In Ethic,* 1. IV, 1. 10.
(2) II-II, q. 130, a. 1.

ignorance is not a consequence of stupidity, because the stupid are not worthier than he, but is a result of laziness: pusillanimous persons refuse to engage in great undertakings which are compatible with their station(1).

982. Magnificence.— 1° Magnificence, as the etymology of the term indicates, consists in *doing great things*. Hence the doing of great things pertains to magnificence.

The act of doing (facere) may be understood in two senses:

a) in its general and wide sense, it signifies any action, transitive or immanent.

b) in its proper sense, it signifies transitive action exercised upon external matter, as the building of a house and other works of servile art, which are properly called products (factibilia).

2° Magnificence, considered as concerned with the act of doing in the wide sense of the term, is not a special virtue, but rather a condition of every virtue; for every virtue, as perfect, tends to what is great in its own order.

Magnificence, considered as concerned with doing in the proper sense of the term, is a special virtue, for it is concerned with special matter, i.e., with great products (magnum factibile); in other words, it is destined for the production of great works.

3° Magnificence, as a special virtue, may be defined: *the virtue which inclines a man to do great works at great and proportionate cost, as demanded by right reason.*

There are two points to be noted in regard to this definition.

a) Since the doing of great works is not possible without great expenditures, abundance of money and love of abundance of money constitute the matter with which magnificence is concerned.

b) Magnificence is not the same as liberality.

---
(1) *In Ethic,.* 1. IV, 1. 11, n. 786.

In virtue of liberality, a man spends money in gift-giving; in virtue of magnificence, a man spends large sums of money on external works, but not under the aspect of gift, but rather under the aspect of what is great and difficult. Hence liberality, as a virtue annexed to justice, resides in the will, whereas magnificence, as a virtue annexed to fortitude, resides in the irascible appetite.

983. Vices opposed to magnificence.— There are two vices opposed to magnificence: one by defect, called *parsimony;* and one by excess, called *wastefulness*.

Parsimony is *the vice which causes a person to intend to spend less than his work is worth, and thus to fail to observe due proportion between his expenditure and his work*(¹).

Hence the parsimonious person is principally concerned with smallness of expenses, and consequently intends to produce what is small, that is to say, he does not shrink from producing a little work, provided that the cost of it is small. The magnificent man, on the contrary, is primarily concerned with the greatness of his work, and only secondarily with the greatness of the expense, which he does not shirk, in order that he may produce a great work(²). Thus it is evident that parsimony is opposed to magnificence by deficiency.

Wastefulness is *the vice which causes a person to spend more than is proportionate to his work*(³).

984. Patience.— Patience is defined: *the virtue which moderates sadness resulting from ordinary evils by strengthening the soul against succumbing to it.*

Patience strengthens against ordinary evils, but not against dangers of death, for dangers of death constitute the proper matter of fortitude.

The *primary* act of patience is the act of moderating the sadness and affliction of soul which result from present evils;

---

(1) II-II, q. 135, a. 2.
(2) II-II, q. 135, a. 1.
(3) II-II, q. 135, a. 2.

and its *secondary* act is the act of so moderating external actions that they may manifest internal moderation.

985. Vices opposed to patience.— There are two vices opposed to patience: one by deficiency, called *insensibility* (lack of feeling); and the other by excess, called *impatience*.

Insensibility is *the vice which prevents a person from being in any way moved by personal evils or by evils suffered by others*.

This vice is not consentaneous with human nature or with social life. It resembles brute stolidity and inhuman hardness.

Impatience is *the vice which causes a person to be unduly sad because of evils, or to give up doing good as a result of sadness or sorrow*.

986. Considerations for acquirement of patience.— Both natural and supernatural patience are very necessary in the life of a Christian. In our efforts to acquire this virtue, it will be helpful to us to consider:

a) the patience of God in tolerating sinners;

b) the patience of Christ in dying for us;

c) the patience of the Saints;

d) the rewards of patience in this life and in the next: satisfaction for our sins in this life, and eternal glory in the life to come;

e) deliverance from the punishments of Hell and of Purgatory;

f) the evils of impatience: loss of the merits of patience; increase rather than decrease of evil; torture which is a greater evil than the evil which causes it; lapse into other sins([1]).

987. Perseverance.— Perseverance is defined: *the virtus which moves a person to choose and to resolve to persist in doing*

---

(1) BILLUART, *Summa Sancti Thomae*, t. V, Dissert. II, a. V, p. 149, (Palmé).

good works to the end of life, in conformity with the dictates of right reason, and notwithstanding the annoyance attendant upon the long duration of these works.

Perseverance differs from patience and constancy.

Patience strengthens the soul against sadness arising from present evils.

Constancy gives the soul strength to firmly persist in doing good in the face of the special difficulty which arises from external obstacles.

Perseverance gives the soul strength to persist in doing good in the face of the special difficulty which results from the long duration of this work.

988. Vices opposed to perseverance.— There are two vices opposed to perseverance: one by deficiency, called *mollities* (softness); and the other by excess, called *pertinacity*.

Mollities is *the vice which causes a person to give up easily, contrary to the dictates of conscience, a good work because of the difficulties which occur in his continuing in it.*

Pertinacity is *the vice which causes a person to persevere in a good work undertaken by him for a longer time than the dictates of reason permit.*

POINTS FOR REVIEW

1. Under what aspect is firmness of mind given by (a) any virtue, (b) fortitude?

2. Define fortitude, name its chief act and its integrant parts, and state when its integrant parts are also its potential parts.

3. Define: magnanimity, ambition, presumption, vainglory, magnificence as a special virtue, patience, and perseverance.

4. When is magnificence a condition of every virtue?

ARTICLE VI

TEMPERANCE

989. Definition of temperance.— Temperance, in its etymology, signifies a certain suitable proportion, i.e., moderation, and has a twofold acceptation:

a) in its wide meaning, it signifies that moderation required by reason in any moral matter; and this is common to every moral virtue;

b) in its strict meaning, it signifies moderation in any matter which greatly attracts the appetite.

Under the second aspect, temperance is a special virtue and also a cardinal virtue, and is defined: *the virtue which moderates the appetite in regard to the pleasures of touch.*

The following observations regarding this definition should be noted.

a) The subject of temperance is the concupiscible appetite, not the irascible appetite, which is the subject of fortitude: for temperance is concerned with concupiscences and pleasures[1].

b) Bodily and sensible goods are not of themselves repugnant to reason, but rather are instruments for good. They are repugnant to reason in as much as they are desired immoderately and contrary to the order of reason. Because temperance moderates the appetite in regard to goods of the senses, it is chiefly concerned with the passions which tend towards sensible goods, and consequently with the sorrows which result from the absence of these goods.

---

[1] II-II, q. 141, aa. 1-3.

c) Temperance is *primarily* concerned with pleasures of touch, and *secondarily* and *in consequence* with pleasures of the other senses, especially of the sense of taste[1].

Temperance is chiefly concerned with pleasures towards which it is most inclined by nature, just as fortitude is chiefly concerned with fear and audacity in regard to the greatest of dangers, which are dangers of death. Now the pleasures towards which nature has the greatest tendency are pleasures which result from the most natural operations, namely, from those operations which preserve the nature of the individual by means of food and drink, and the nature of the species by the union of the sexes. But the pleasures which are essentially annexed to the use of food and to sexual acts result from the sense of touch; and the pleasures of the other senses, viz., of sight, hearing, smell, and especially taste, are annexed in a secondary way to the use of food and to sexual acts in as much as they increase the pleasure of touch in the use of food and in the acts of sexual relations. Hence temperance is chiefly concerned with the pleasures of touch, and only as a consequence with the pleasures of the other senses; and of the latter it is most concerned with the pleasure of taste.

990. The rule of temperance is dependent on the necessities of this life.— 1° The end is the rule of whatever is directed to the end.

2° The necessities of the present life are the rule of temperance, not in as much as the necessities of the present life are the end of *temperance*, — this end is happiness, — but in as much as the necessities of this life are the end *of those things of which temperance makes use*. Hence, when we say that the necessities of this life are the rule of temperance, we mean not that they are the rule of temperance itself, but rather that they are the rule of these things of which temperance makes use.

3° The necessities of this life may be understood in two ways:

---

(1) II-II, q. 141, aa. 2-4.

a) first, they may be understood in the sense in which we apply the term *necessary* to that without which a thing cannot exist; v.g., thus food is necessary for an animal;

b) secondly, they may signify those things without which life cannot be lived in a becoming manner.

The term *necessities* is understood at present in the two meanings we have given to it.

Some things are a hindrance to health and to the sound condition of the body; and of such things the temperate man makes no use whatsoever, for to do so would be a sin against temperance.

Other things are not a hindrance to health and to the sound condition of the body; and these things the temperate person uses in moderation, in accordance with circumstances of place and time, and of the persons among whom he lives.

4° In the light of the foregoing observations, we may easily prove that the rule of temperance is dependent on the necessities of this life. For the rule of things which are directed to an end is derived from that end. But all pleasurable objects which are available for man, and with which temperance is concerned, have the necessities of this life as their end. Therefore temperance takes the necessities of this life as the rule of the pleasurable objects which it uses, and uses them only in so far as they are required for the necessities of this life(¹).

991. Vices opposed to temperance.— There are two vices opposed to temperance: one by deficiency, called *insensibility* or stupor; and the other by excess, called *intemperance*.

Insensibility or stupor is *the vice which causes a person so to shun pleasures of the senses, and especially of taste and touch, that he is unwilling to make the use of them when they are dictated by right reason.*

---

(1) II-II, q. 141, a. 6.

Intemperance is *the vice which causes a person to desire pleasures of the senses when, where, or in a manner forbidden by right reason, or in excess of what right reason dictates.*

992. Integrant parts of temperance.— The integrant parts of temperance are certain conditions required for the exercise of an integral and perfect act of temperance. The integral function of temperance consists in two things:

 a) avoidance of the disgrace contrary to temperance;
 b) love of the beauty of temperance.

Hence there are two integrant parts of temperance:

 a) shame (verecundia), which aids in avoiding disgrace;
 b) honesty (sense of propriety), which aids in loving beauty(¹).

Shame is defined: *the fear of disgrace, and consequently of acts from which disgrace results.*

Shame, properly speaking, is not a virtue, but rather a praiseworthy passion. For shame shuns base acts because of the disgrace to which they lead, and therefore it is not a habit of a perfect man, because a perfect man does not apprehend a base or disgraceful act as difficult for him to avoid(²).

Honesty has two meanings: *in its general meaning,* it signifies the conformity of an act with the judgment of right reason, and is common to all the virtues; *in its special meaning,* it signifies that which is opposed to what is base or disgraceful, and hence is an integrant part of temperance.

Honesty, as an integrant part of temperance, may be defined: *the love of honesty or beauty, as the honest is opposed to what is most disgraceful, namely, animal lusts*(³).

993. Subjective parts of temperance.— The subjective parts of temperance are the different species of that virtue.

---
(1) II-II, q. 143, a. unicus.
(2) II-II, q. 144, a. 1.
(3) II-II, q. 145, a. 4.

But the species of the virtues are first diversified in accordance with the diversity of their matter or object. Moreover, temperance is chiefly concerned with the pleasures of touch, which are divided into two genera.

Some of the pleasures of touch are concerned with nutriment, i.e., with food and drink. The pleasures of touch related to food are moderated by *abstinence;* and the pleasures of touch related to drink are regulated by *sobriety.*

Other pleasures of touch are concerned with the power of procreation. The chief of these pleasures, which is the pleasures of coition, is moderated by *chastity;* and the attendant pleasures of this act, as the pleasures resulting from kisses, touches, and embraces, are regulated by *reserve (pudicitia)* (1). Hence there are four species of temperance: *abstinence, sobriety, chastity,* and *reserve.* These, however, are not the lowest species of temperance, for they are subdivided into other species of this virtue.

994. Abstinence.— 1° Abstinence, as the very term indicates, means retrenchment of food.

The term abstinence may be understood in two ways:

first, as signifying retrenchement of food in an absolute manner, and in this sense it signifies neither a virtue nor an act of virtue, but something indifferent;

secondly, as signifying use and retrenchment of food as regulated by reason, and in this sense it is either a virtue or an act of virtue(2).

2° Abstinence, as a virtue and a subjective part of temperance, may be defined: *the virtue which moderates the desires for food and the pleasures thereof in accordance with the dictates of reason, in order that they may not be impediments to the good of reason.*

Abstinence is proximately concerned with the pleasures which derive from the use of food, and remotely with food

---

(1) II-II, q. 143, a. unicus.
(2) II-II, q. 146, a. 1.

itself. Food, as the matter of abstinence, includes any drink that is not intoxicating. Intoxicating drink is the matter of a special virtue, i.e., of sobriety.

3° The principal act of abstinence is fasting, which is practised for the purpose of bridling the lusts of the flesh, of elevating the mind to God, and of making expiation for sin.

4° The vice opposed to abstinence is *gluttony.*

Gluttony is defined: *an inordinate desire for food solely as pleasing to the palate,* i.e., sought solely for the pleasure it affords.

Gluttony is not of its nature a mortal sin. Nevertheless, it can become a mortal sin, if a man, because of gluttony, is prepared to trangress precepts which bind under the pain of mortal sin.

995. Sobriety.— 1° *In a very wide sense,* sobriety signifies all moderation of the soul in not deviating from the rule in any matter whatsoever.

In a wide sense, it signifies temperance which observes the rule of moderation in pleasures of the senses.

In a strict sense, it is the virtue of abstinence: persons who are moderate in their use of food and drink are sober.

In a very strict sense, is it the special virtue concerned with the use of intoxicating drink.

Sobriety, as a special virtue, is defined: *the virtue which moderates the desire for and use of intoxicating drink.*

Sobriety is a special virtue, because the use of intoxicating drink presents a special hindrance to the good of reason, i.e., a special obstacle to rational life. The moderate use of intoxicating drink may serve a good purpose; but its immoderate use is very harmful, for it is a hindrance to the use of reason[1].

2° Sobriety is necessary for all men, because all must avoid disorder of mind and the sins which are born of this mental condition.

---

(1) II-II, q. 149, a. 1.

Moreover, there are reasons why adolescents, women, spiritual leaders, political leaders, and elderly persons should be possessed of this virtue(1).

Adolescents should be sober, for they are very strongly attracted, because of their youth, to pleasures of the senses, which must be bridled by the practice of virtue.

Women should practise sobriety, because they easily become victims of mental agitation and have not the strength of mind sufficient for the resistance of concupiscence.

Spiritual leaders, such as bishops and other ministers of the Church, should live sober lives, in order that they may be able to devote their best efforts to their spiritual duties.

Political leaders should be adorned with the virtue of sobriety, in order that they may govern their subjects with wisdom.

Elderly persons should be sober, in order that they may have that vigor of reason required for the instruction of others, and also that they may exercise a salutary influence on others by their example.

996. Drunkenness. — 1° Drunkenness has two meanings:

a) it signifies the deficiency of reason, i.e., the loss of the use of reason, which results from the use of intoxicating drink; and, under this aspect, it is not a fault, but a penal defect resulting from a fault;

b) it signifies the act by which a person loses the use of reason as a result of the use of intoxicating drink. When this act is voluntary, it is a sin against sobriety.

2° Drunkeness, as a sin, may be defined: *voluntary excess in the use of intoxicating drink to the point of loss of the use of reason*.

a) *Voluntary excess:* in order that drunkeness be a sin, not only must the act of drinking be voluntary, but the loss of the use of reason must also be voluntary, i.e., voluntary in

---

(1) II-II, q. 149, a. 4.

its cause, in as much as it was foreseen, or could have been and ought to have been foreseen, that loss of the use of reason would result from the act of drinking.

b) *In the use of intoxicating drink:* thus drunkenness is distinguished from gluttony in the strict sense, which is excess in the use of food and non-intoxicating drink.

997. Alcoholism.— 1° Alcoholism is defined: *the habit of the frequent drinking of intoxicating beverages.*

Alcoholism neither includes nor excludes drunkenness. A man who has the habit of the frequent drinking of intoxicating beverages may or may not drink to the point of drunkenness.

Alcoholism is a vice opposed to the virtue of sobriety, and is a habit which, when once contracted, is difficult to conquer.

2° Alcoholism engenders innumerable evils for the individual person, for the family, and for society.

a) *For the individual person.*— Alcoholism weakens the individual person *physically, intellectually,* and *morally.*

It weakens him *physically:* alcohol is not assimilated, and therefore it weakens the powers of the body and does serious harm to the vital organs. It is for this reason that the victim of alcoholism has difficulty in resisting sickness and easily contracts serious diseases.

It weakens him *intellectually:* it weakens the sensitive faculties, as the memory and the phantasy, on which the intellect is objectively dependent.

It weakens him *morally:* the passion of drinking intoxicating beverages is concerned with pleasures common to men and brutes, and hence it degrades men and is offensive to human dignity. Moreover, this passion is essentially selfish: it is the cause of an inordinate self-love, and hence is entirely incompatible with human generosity.

b) *For the family.*— Alcoholism, the sign and cause of inordinate self-love, looses all the ties of affection and intimacy necessary for the life of the home.

Parents who are slaves to alcoholism waste on intoxicating drink money needed for the support of their family and the education of their children. Therefore alcoholism is the cause of discord in the family, poverty, and the neglect of the education of children.

c) For society.— The evils which alcoholism produces in the individual person and in the family do harm to civil society.

Parents who are victims of alcoholism beget children who are weak, predisposed to alcoholism, and sometimes feebleminded or insane.

Hence alcoholism, of its very nature, and in its evil consequences, is contrary to the natural law.

3° Alcoholism should be avoided; and, when it exists, it should be conquered.

In order to save their children from alcoholism, parents should teach them the evil consequences of this vice, and should lead them by word and example to the cultivation of the virtue of temperance.

As a remedy for alcoholism, *temperance associations* should be established and supported; and the victims of alcoholism should do penance, pray, and avoid the occasions of this evil.

Finally, the State should make laws which encourage the practice of the virtue of temperance.

998. Chastity.— 1° Chastity has two meanings:

in its improper and metaphorical sense, it is a virtue which moderates pleasure arising from the union of the mind to certain objects; and, thus understood, it is a general virtue, because every virtue withholds the mind from taking pleasure from union with things which are unlawful;

in its proper sense, it is a virtue which moderates venereal pleasures; in this sense, it is a special virtue and a subjective part of temperance.

Chastity, as a special virtue, is defined: *the virtue which moderates venereal pleasures in accordance with the dictates of reason.*

The passions related to veneral pleasures are the proximate matter of chastity, and such external acts, as coition, touches, kisses, etc., are its remote matter. Chastity represses and regulates these internal and external acts in accordance with the norm of reason.

Chastity is distinguished from abstinence, for sexual pleasures, with which chastity is concerned, are formally distinguished from the pleasures of food and drink, with which abstinence is concerned. Pleasures are proportionate to the operations of which they are the perfections. But operations related to the use of food are different generically from operations related to the use of venereal things: the former are destined for the preservation of the individual person, whereas the latter are destined for the preservation of the species. Hence chastity and abstinence are distinct virtues.

2° There are three kinds of chastity: *conjugal chastity, vidual chastity,* and *virginal chastity.*

Conjugal chastity is *the chastity of a person who abstains from unlawful pleasures of the flesh and is moderate in the use of the lawful pleasures of the married state.*

Vidual chastity is *the chastity of a person who, after the dissolution of the matrimonial bond, abstains ever afterwards from unlawful pleasures of the flesh and from the lawful pleasures of the flesh of the married state.*

Virginal chastity, i.e., virginity, is *the chastity of a person who, never having known unlawful pleasures of the flesh, wholly abstains forever from all lawful and unlawful pleasures of the flesh.*

999. Notion of virginity.— 1° Virginity is of two kinds: *a) natural virginity,* which consists in integrity of the flesh, in as much as the person possessed of virginity is unseared by the heat of concupiscence, which, it would seem, reaches its greatest intensity in the greatest of bodily pleasures, which is the pleasure of coition;

b) *moral virginity,* which is of two kinds: a *special state of chastity* and a *special virtue distinct from chastity.*

2° Virginity, considered as a special state of chastity, implies two things:

a) that the person has not been voluntarily defiled, i.e., has preserved natural virginity;

b) that the person intends to preserve natural virginity if there is no subsequent matrimonial contract.

Virginity, as a special state of chastity, is called virtuous celibacy.

3° Virginity, as a special virtue distinct from chastity, has already been defined. It is *the virtue of a person who, having preserved the integrity of the flesh, has the resolve to abstain forever from all carnal pleasures.*

Three elements are contained in this definition:

integrity of the flesh;

abstinence from carnal pleasure;

the resolve to abstain forever from carnal pleasure.

a) The integrity of the flesh is accidental to virginity. For, if the integrity of the flesh is involuntarily lost, by chance or in some other way, this is no more prejudicial to the virtue of virginity than the loss of a hand or a foot.

b) Abstinence from carnal pleasure is the matter of virginity in its moral aspect.

c) The resolve to abstain forever from carnal pleasure is the formal element of virginity. But, in order that the resolve to abstain forever from carnal pleasure be stable and virtuous in a special way, it must make the experience of carnal pleasure illicit even in the married state. But this can be done only by vow. Therefore virginity is not a special virtue distinct from chastity except when consecrated to God by vow.

1000. Virginity is lawful. — 1° That is unlawful which is not in conformity with right reason and law, especially the natural law.

2° We are considering virginity at present as a special virtue, i.e., as consecrated to God by vow.

3° According to Luther and his followers, virginity is **unlawful.**

4° In the order of human acts, that is lawful which is in conformity with right reason. But virginity is in conformity with right reason. Therefore virginity is lawful.

The *major* is evident, for right reason is the proximate rule of morality.

Minor.— To abstain from carnal pleasure for the good of the soul is in conformity with right reason. But this is what is done by virginity. Therefore virginity is in conformity with right reason.

1001. Difficulties. — 1° What is contrary to a precept of the natural law is unlawful. But virginity is contrary to the precept of the natural law which imposes matrimony on men for the preservation of the human species. Therefore virginity is unlawful.

Major.— What is contrary to a precept of the natural law given to men as individuals, *I concede;* what is contrary to a precept of the natural law given to men not as individuals, but only as a multitude, i.e., as mankind, *I deny.*

Minor.— The natural precept of matrimony is imposed on individual men, *I deny;* on mankind, *I concede.*

2° If everyone remained a virgin, the world would perish. Therefore virginity is unlawful.

I deny the consequent. a) The precept of matrimony is given to the human race. It binds individuals only in cases of necessity, that is to say, when an individual person would have to marry, in order to preserve the human species, as would happen if only one man and one woman were in the world.

b) Even if all men married, the world, nevertheless, would have to perish. Hence we may not say that virginity is the cause of the extinction of the human species.

c) The world was created to complete the number of the elect. If all remained virgins, the number of the elect would be complete. The world in this case could perish, because it would have attained its end.

d) Moreover, St. Jerome wrote the following words to Jovinianus: «Fear not that all will remain virgins; virginity is difficult, and therefore rare.»

3° A person who does not know that he has the gift of virginity may not make virginity the matter of a vow. But no one can know that he has the gift of virginity. Therefore no one may make virginity the matter of a vow, i.e., virginity is unlawful (Luther's argument).

Major.— A person who depends upon his own strength for the gift of virginity, *I concede*; a person who knows that he can preserve virginity with the help of grace, *I deny.*

Minor.— On his own strength, *I concede;* no one knows that he can depend on divine grace for this gift, *I deny.*

1002. Virginity is more excellent than matrimony.—
1° We are not concerned with the question of whether the integrity of the flesh is more excellent than the use of matrimony. This kind of integrity is physical rather than moral.

Is the state of virginity more excellent in the moral order than the state of matrimony? This is the question we must answer.

By the state of virginity, we mean both virginity as a special virtue and virtuous celibacy.

2° According to Jovinianus, who, because of the annoyances of married life, neither married nor wished to marry, the preservation of chastity is no more meritorious than the use of matrimony.

According to Luther and his followers, virginity is not only not more excellent than matrimony, but is an impious superstition if practised for the honor and worship of God. They maintain that virginity practised for its utility in life and to facilitate the work of spreading the Gospel is not evil. Nevertheless, they add that it is foolish and unlawful for a person to bind himself to virginity if he is not certain that he has the gift of continence.

The Council of Trent declared and defined that the state of virginity and celibacy is preferable to the state of matrimony(¹).

3° We shall now prove that virginity is more excellent than matrimony.

a) The good of the soul is preferable to the good of the body, and the good of the contemplative life is preferable to

---

(1) *Conc. Trident.*, sess. 24, can. 10.

the good of the active life. But virginity is directed to the good of the soul in regard to the contemplative life, which consists in thinking of the things of God; and matrimony is directed to the good of the body, which is the bodily multiplication of the human race, and pertains to the active life, because men and women living in the matrimonial state have to think on the things of the world. Therefore(1).

b) That which directly perfects the rational part of man is superior to a good which befits man in as much as he is an animal. But virginity directly perfects the rational part of man, whereas matrimony befits man in as much as he is an animal. Therefore.

Major.— By his reason man resembles the angels, and by his animal nature he resembles inferior beings.

Minor.— Virginity is destined for man's spiritual good, whereas marriage is directed to the multiplication of the human race by means of the functions of generation. Consequently matrimony corresponds to man's generic tendencies, i.e., to the tendencies of man in as much as he is an animal.

1003. Difficulties.— 1° That which is directed to the common good is better than that which is directed to private good. But matrimony is directed to the common good, whereas virginity is directed to private good. Therefore matrimony is better than virginity.

Major.—If the common good and private good belong to the same order *I concede;* if private good belongs to a different and superior order, *I deny.*

Minor.— Virginity is directed to private good which belongs to the same order as the common good to which matrimony is directed, *I deny;* which belongs to a different and superior order, *I concede.*

The good sought in matrimony is human and temporal good, whereas the good sought in virginity is divine and spiritual good. Moreover, virginity is also directed to the common good: for divine good is the greatest common good.

2° The person who has the greater merit practises the greater virtue. But the person who preserves conjugal chastity can have greater merit than the virgin. Therefore conjugal chastity is more excellent than virginity.

Major.— When other things are equal, *I concede;* when other things are not equal, *I deny.*

Minor.— Because he can have greater charity, *I concede;* because chastity is a more excellent virtue than virginity, *I deny.*

Merit results from charity. Hence the married person who has greater charity than the virgin, in as much as he would be willing to practice virginity if this were proper to his state, can have greater merit than the virgin.

---

(1) II-II, q. 152, a. 4.

1004. Lust.— 1° Lust is the vice which is opposed to chastity. It is divided into several species, as we shall see later. Lust is defined: *an inordinate desire for venereal pleasures.*

2° Lust is of its nature a mortal sin. Therefore all venereal pleasure voluntarily sought outside the state of matrimony constitutes the matter of mortal sin.

3° Lust is a capital vice because it has a most desirable end, namely, venereal pleasure, for the sake of which men are led to commit many other sins[1].

4° Lust engenders eight internal daughters, and they are the following:
blindness of mind;
inconsiderateness;
precipitation;
inconstancy;
self-love;
hatred of God;
inordinate love of this world;
abhorrence of the next world[2].

5° Lust engenders four external daughters:
obscenity, which causes the lustful man readily to use lewd words;
scurrility, which causes the lustful man to say or do unbecoming things, in order to excite laughter;
wanton words, i.e., words intended for venereal pleasure;
foolish talking, when by his words he expresses a preference for his own proper pleasures to anything else[3].

1005. Species of lust. — To distinguish the species of lust, we must consider the act of generation *in relation to the*

---
(1) II-II, q. 153, a. 4.
(2) II-II, q. 153, a. 5.
(3) *Ibidem,* ad 4.

begetting of children, which is its natural end, and *in relation to the person with whom this act is consummated*(¹).

1) In relation to the begetting of children, the abuse committed, by the very nature of the act, totally impedes the begetting of children; or it merely hinders the due education, i.e., the rearing, of the child.

If the abuse committed in the matter of lust totally impedes the begetting of children, in as much as a physical impediment is placed in the way of procreation by the wasting of the semen, there is a *sin against nature*.

The sin against nature is divided into four species:

a) *bestiality*, which is carnal intercourse with a being of a different species;

b) *sodomy*, which is carnal intercourse with a person of the same sex: man with man; woman with woman;

c) *uncleanness* or *effeminacy*, which is the procuring of pollution without carnal intercourse, for the sake of venereal pleasure (solitary sin);

d) *onanism*, which is carnal intercourse with a person of different sex in an unnatural manner at variance with the end of the act of generation(²).

If the abuse committed hinders the education of children, there is *simple fornication*, which is sexual intercourse between an unmarried man and an unmarried woman.

2) In relation to the person with whom the carnal act is performed, there are different species of lust.

If the person concerned is owed special respect in virtue of a tie of consanguinity, there is *incest;*

if the person is under the authority of another as regards matrimony, there is *adultery*, which is an act of injustice against the other spouse;

if the person is under the authority of parents as regards the custody of virginity, there is *seduction*, if no violence is employed; and *rape*, if violence is used;

---

(1) II-II, 2. 154, a. 1.
(2) II, q. 154, a. 11.

if the person is under the power of another in virtue of consecration to God by vow, there is *sacrilege*.

1006. Potential parts of temperance. — The potential parts of temperance are virtues annexed to temperance, i.e., secondary virtues, which observe in certain less difficult matters the measure observed by temperance in regard to its own proper matter.

Temperance moderates the pleasures of touch.

Hence every virtue which represses the disorders of the appetite as tending towards pleasure other than the pleasure of touch may be called a potential part of temperance.

Apart from the movement of concupiscence, three kinds of movements are found in man:

a) movements of the will aroused by the impulse of passion, which are moderated by *continence;*

b) movements of anger which tend to do harm to others, which are moderated by *clemency* or *meekness.*

c) bodily movements and acts, which are moderated by *modesty.* Hence there are three potential parts of temperance: *continence, clemency,* and *modesty.*

1007. Continence and incontinence. — 1° Two meanings may be assigned to continence:

a) it may signify abstention from all carnal pleasures: and thus it is the same as chastity;

b) it may signify resistance of reason to vehement passions; and thus it is a potential part of temperance. It is defined: *a disposition of the will by which a person resists evil desires in regard to touch, i.e., in regard to food, and especially in regard to venereal acts.*

Continence is called a disposition for, properly speaking, it is not a virtue, because the appetite is not completely subdued and made subject to reason by continence, but the will is merely strengthened by it against succumbing to the passions.

The subject of continence is the will, not the concupiscible appetite.

Therefore continence is distinguished from temperance. By temperance the good of reason reaches the concupiscible appetite; by continence it resides in the will. The temperate man conquers, whereas the continent man continues to fight[1]. Therefore a person cannot at the same time and under the same respect perform an act of continence and an act of temperance.

2° Incontinence, the vice opposed to continence, is defined: *that disposition of the will which abandons the will to the passions and leaves it without strength to conquer them.*

The will is the subject of incontinence. Nevertheless, incontinence does not habituate the will to choosing evil, but merely leaves it disposed to succumb to passion.

Hence incontinence is distinguished from intemperance, for the latter strongly attracts the will to evil objects. The continent man repents after the performing of a bad act and the passing away of passion, whereas the intemperate man rather rejoices in having sinned.

1008. Clemency.— Clemency is defined: *the virtue which, from motives of leniency and kindness, mitigates punishment in the measure permitted by justice.*

a) Mitigates punishment: complete remission of punishment would be pardon, not clemency.

b) From motives of leniency and kindness: a person who remits punishment not from a motive of love of his neighbor, but from some other motive, does not perform an act of clemency.

c) In the measure permitted by justice: if the remission of punishment were contrary to justice, clemency would not be a virtue.

---
(1) II-II, q. 155, a. 4.

It is evident that the virtue of clemency belongs chiefly to superiors, i.e., to persons who exercise authority over others.

1009. Vices opposed to clemency.— They are two vices opposed to clemency: *cruelty* and *excessive leniency*.

Cruelty is *atrocity of soul in exacting punishment*. Excess in punishing, as regards the external action, pertains to injustice; but, as regards hardness of heart, which disposes a person to increase punishment, it pertains to cruelty.

Excessive leniency is *a vice by which a person, contrary to the dictates of reason, lessens or remits punishments which, according to law, a guilty person ought to undergo*.

Excessive leniency is the vice of a superior, and is very harmful to civil society, for it shows favor to the wicked.

1010. Meekness and vices opposed to it.— 1° Meekness is defined: *the virtue which moderates anger as concerned with doing harm to one's neighbor*.

Meekness is a virtue distinct from clemency: for the matter of clemency is the mitigation of punishments, especially of legal punishments, within the bounds of justice, and therefore clemency is a virtue proper to superiors in relation to their subjects, and especially to rulers, whereas the matter of meekness is the moderation of anger as concerned with doing harm to another, but not with the imposing of legal penalties, and therefore meekness is practised between equals.

2° There are two vices opposed to meekness: one by excess, which is *anger*; and the other by deficiency, which is *the lack of anger*.

Anger is defined: *an inordinate desire for revenge*.

Revenge may be desired in conformity with right reason; such revenge is good. If it is inordinately desired, it is evil.

Lack of anger is *the vice of a person incapable of anger, even when he has just cause for anger*.

1011. Modesty and its species.— 1° Modesty is the virtue which moderates matters in which moderation is relatively easy[1]. Such matters are movements of the soul other than those concerned with the pleasures of touch, which are moderated by temperance, and also passions which incite a person to inflict punishment and to anger, which are moderated by clemency and meekness; v.g., movements of the soul towards high things, desire for knowledge, external movements and carriage of body, external display in dress.

Hence modesty may be defined: *the virtue of a person who, in his external and internal movements and in his apparel, observes the measure which conforms to his station in life, to his talents, and to his fortune.*

2° Modesty is divided into four species, for there are four matters, i.e., movements of the soul, in which moderation is relatively easy.

a) The first is the desire for personal excellence, by which a person wishes to excel others, and not to remain in the station that belongs to him. This movement of the soul is moderated by *humility*.

b) The second is the desire for knowledge, especially knowledge of sensible things. This movement is moderated by *studiousness*, which is opposed to curiosity.

c) The third regards external actions, which may be serious or sportive. The former are moderated by *good bearing* (bona ordinatio), whereas the latter are regulated by *eutrapelia*.

d) The fourth has relation to external display and dress. This matter is regulated by *modesty in dress*.

1012. Humility.— Humility is defined : *the virtue of a person who, in consideration of his own deficiencies, takes the lowest place, according to his mode*, i.e., according to his station.

a) The matter of humility is the desire for personal excellence and for honors greater than one deserves.

---

(1). II-II, q. 160, a. 1.

b) The motive of humility is reverence for God and one's neighbor and submission to them.

The humble person considers in himself:

gifts received from God;

deficiencies which are proper to himself.

Because of the deficiencies which are properly his own, the humble man regards himself as unworthy of the honors which he has, and submits himself to God and to his neighbor; but, in consideration of the gifts received from God, he does not regard himself as unworthy of these honors. Therefore humility does not cause dejection of soul([1]).

1013. Vices opposed to humility. — There are two vices opposed to humility: one by deficiency, which is *excessive abjectness (nimia abjectio);* the other by excess, which is *pride.*

1° Excessive abjectness is *the vice of a person who applies himself more to vile things than becomes a virtuous man in accordance with his God-given gifts.*

2° Pride is defined: *an inordinate desire for one's own excellence.*

a) Desire: pride presupposes an act of the intellect whence it derives, i.e., the consideration of the deficiencies of others and the false and exaggerated esteem of one's own merits. Nevertheless, pride formally resides in the irascible appetite, because its matter is something difficult, namely, one's own excellence([2]).

The irascible appetite, as it is the subject of pride, is not merely the irascible appetite in the strict sense, i.e., the sensitive appetite which is distinguished from the concupiscible appetite, but the will as it tends to what is difficult. Hence pride is found in the devils, who have no sensitive appetite.

b) Inordinate desire: the proud man tends beyond reality, and consequently is borne towards things which are greater than become him.

---
(1) II-II, q. 161, a. 3.
(2) II-II, q. 161, a. 6, ad 2.

c) *Desire for excellence:* not only for relative excellence but also for absolute excellence. The proud man wishes not only to be above others, but to surpass his own condition, whether he thinks of others or not.

d) *For one's own excellence,* i.e., for personal excellence, because the object of pride is the excellence of the person.

Thus pride is distinguished from *ambition, presumption,* and *vainglory.*

The object of ambition is excellence in honors and dignities.

The object of presumption is excellence in enterprises.

The object of vainglory is excellence in fame and glory.

Since the proud man inordinately desires his own excellence, he seeks excellence in honors and dignities, in enterprises, and in fame and glory. Hence ambition, presumption, and vainglory have their origin in pride and are at its service.

1014. Gravity of pride.— 1° In pride, as in every sin, there are two movements which we must consider:

a) *conversion to a mutable good;*

b) *aversion,* i.e., turning away, *from God.*

Under the aspect of conversion to a mutable good, pride is not the most grievous of all sins, for personal excellence, which the proud man inordinately desires, is not essentially incompatible with the good of virtue.

Under the aspect of aversion from God, pride, when it is complete, is one of the most grievous of sins. In other sins, man turns away from God through ignorance, weakness, desire for some other good, whereas, in pride that is complete, he directly turns away from God, because unwillingness to submit to God and His laws is of the very nature of pride[1].

It must be observed, however, that the object of pride is not aversion from God, but personal excellence, which the proud man so inordinately desires that he is unwilling to sub-

---

(1) II-II, q. 162, a. 6.

mit to God, and turns away from Him. Therefore sins which directly have aversion from God as their object, as hatred, are more grievous than pride.

2° Pride is a capital vice, for many other sins have their origin in it. Some theologians, as St. Gregory, in consideration of the general influence of pride on all vices, not only consider it a capital vice, but regard it as the queen and mother of all capital vices.

1015. Studiousness.— Studiousness is defined: *the virtue which moderates desire and pursuit for the knowledge of truth according to the rules of right reason.*

The proximate matter of studiousness is not knowledge of truth, which is good in itself and needs not to be regulated by moral virtue, but the desire for knowledge, i.e., the inclination to knowledge.

In man, there is a twofold inclination in regard to knowledge:

a) man, as possessed of a soul, naturally desires knowledge:

b) man, as possessed of a bodily nature, is inclined to avoid the labor required for the pursuit of knowledge.

Studiousness moderates these two inclinations([1]).

In as much as it moderates man's desire for knowledge studiousness is a potential part of prudence.

In as much as it moderates the inclination to avoid the labor required for the pursuit of knowledge, studiousness is annexed rather to fortitude.

The first function of studiousness is more essential than the second, because desire for knowledge is directly related to knowledge, which is the end of studiousness, whereas the labor of learning is an obstacle to knowledge. Hence studiousness is accidentally, i.e., indirectly, concerned with the labor of learning, in as much as it removes obstacles to knowledge.

---

(1) II-II, q. 166, a. 2, c. and ad 3.

1016. Vices opposed to studiousness.— There are two vices opposed to studiousness: one by deficiency, which is *negligence;* and the other by excess, which is *curiosity.*

1° Negligence is *the voluntary failure to acquire the knowledge required for one's condition and state of life.*

Negligence is mortal or venial, as the obligation to acquire knowledge is grave or light.

2° Curiosity, in the general sense of the term, means superfluous care in regard to useless things.

In its proper sense, it is a vice opposed to studiousness. It is defined: *an inordinate desire for knowledge.*

Curiosity, in the proper sense, implies superfluous care in acquiring knowledge of things which do not concern us, or which are beyond the capacity of our intelligence, simply for the sake of knowing them and passing judgment on them; for, if a person uses superfluous care, not from a desire for knowledge, but for operation, in order, for example, to find pleasure in the use of things, not in the knowledge of them, he is not formally curious, but only materially curious. Thus a person who desires to hear music for the enjoyment of its harmony, not for the purpose of distinguishing voices and passing judgment on them, is not formally curious[1].

1017. Eutrapelia, modesty of external movements and of dress.— 1° Modesty of external movements, in a generic sense, is a virtue which moderates external movements, not under the aspect of what is due and becoming, as does affability, which is a part of justice, but according to moderation, so that a person may not go to excess or fail in matters related to external bearing and reserve.

Modesty of external movements in the general sense is divided into two species: *eutrapelia* and *good bearing,* i.e., modesty of external movements in the specific sense.

---

(1) II-II, q. 167, aa. 1 and 2.

Eutrapelia is *the virtue of a person who gives his words and deeds a cheerful turn, and refrains from immoderation in play.*

Good bearing is *modesty in external movements and behavior.*

2° Modesty of dress is *the virtue which uses reasonable moderation in external display,* as in clothing, ornaments, banquets, etc.

Virtue does not exist in external things, but in man who makes good use of them.

A person can fail in two ways to make good use of things:

first, in relation to his own condition and to the customs of the persons among whom he lives;

secondly, because of an inordinate desire to use them.

His desire can be inordinate in three ways by excess, and in two ways by deficiency.

By excess, *a)* when a person seeks human glory, or some other evil end, by paying excessive attention to dress;

b) when a person seeks sensuous pleasure by excessive attention to dress;

c) when a person is too solicitous in his attention to external apparel.

By deficiency, *a)* when a person through negligence fails in attention or care in regard to his external apparel;

b) when a person seeks glory from his lack of attention and care in his dress: this is hypocrisy.

Modesty of dress corrects all these disorders in accordance with right reason.

POINTS FOR REVIEW

1. Define temperance, name the pleasures with which it is chiefly concerned, and explain whether or not the necessities of this life are its end.

2. Define: abstinence as a subjective part of temperance, sobriety as a special virtue, drunkenness, alcoholism, chastity as a special virtue, lust, continence, humility, pride, studiousness, and eutrapelia.

3. Explain why virginity is not unlawful, why continence is not properly a virtue, and whether pride is the greatest of all sins.

4. Distinguish between *a)* continence and temperance, *b)* clemency and meekness.

ARTICLE VII

FRIENDSHIP

1018. Love, friendship, love of preference, charity.—
1° Love, friendship, love of preference (dilectio), and charity bear a certain likeness to one another, but, nevertheless, are distinct from one another.

2° Love, friendship, love of preference, and charity are concerned with good, and pertain to it. Hence we must first consider what good is.

Good, as we have said, is *that which is desirable*, and formally consists in perfection, not as the constituent of being, but as it is related to the appetite and perfects it as the term and object in which the appetite attains its perfection (n. 529).

Therefore good proposed to the appetite moves, attracts, and inclines the appetite to itself. Thus we have love.

3° Hence love may be defined: *the inclination or propensity of the appetite to good.*

Love may be *natural*, *sensitive*, or *rational*, i.e., intellective.

Natural love is *love by which any thing, even a thing which cannot have knowledge, desires a good suitable to itself, not in virtue of its own knowledge, but in virtue of the knowledge of the Author of nature.*

Sensitive love is *love which results from sensitive knowledge.*

Intellective love is *love which results from intellective knowledge.*

4° Intellective love is divided into *love of concupiscence* and *love of benevolence*.

Love of concupiscence is *inclination to an object which is loved*.

Love of benevolence is *inclination to a person for whom a good is loved*, i.e., it is an act of the will by which good is wished to another.

5° Friendship is *mutual love of benevolence between two or more persons*.

Love of preference (dilectio) is *love of one good in preference to another*.

Charity is *a divinely infused virtue by which we love God for His own sake, and our neighbor for the love of God*.

1019. Definition of friendship.— Friendship is defined: *mutual love of benevolence, which consists in a certain sharing of life*.

a) Love, i.e., an inclination towards good.

b) Love of benevolence, i.e., love by which a person is inclined not to the good which is loved, but to the person for whom he wishes and seeks it, in so far as he can.

c) Mutual love: friendship implies reciprocity. Friendship does not exist when a person loves, but is not loved in return(¹).

d) Which consists in a certain sharing of life: the mutual benevolence which friendship implies ought not to be hidden; and friends share their goods in common, which is impossible without a certain sharing of life among friends(²).

1020. Division of friendship.— 1° Friendship may be divided in relation to the object sought in friendship, and in relation to the sharing of life in which friendship consists.

---

(1) *In Ethic.*, 1. VIII, 1. 2, nn. 1559-1560.
(2) *In Ethic.*, 1. VIII, 1. 9, nn. 1657-1660.

2° The object sought in friendship is goodness (the good). But goodness is formally divided into *goodness of utility, goodness of pleasure,* and *goodness of rectitude.* Hence, under this aspect, there are three species of friendship: *friendship of utility, friendship of pleasure,* and *friendship of rectitude,* i. e., *perfect friendship.*

Friendship of utility is *friendship whose object is the good of utility.*

Friendship of pleasure is *friendship whose object is the good of pleasure.*

Friendship of rectitude is *friendship whose object is the good of rectitude,* which is absolute good(¹).

3° *In relation to the sharing of life,* friendship is divided into *natural friendship towards one's neighbor, domestic friendship, political friendship,* and *divine friendship*(²).

Natural friendship towards one's neighbor is *the friendship which exists among all men, in as much as they have the same specific nature.*

Domestic friendship is *the friendship which exists among the members of the same domestic society, i.e., of the same family.*

Political friendship is *the friendship which exists among the members of the same civil society.*

Divine friendship is *the friendship which exists between creatures and God, in as much as God is loved in Himself and for Himself.* Divine friendship surpasses the powers of nature, and therefore can exist only as a gift of God.

1021. Cause of friendship.— Since friendship has different species, its causes are not always the same.

a) Ambition and desire are sufficient causes of *friendship of utility.*

b) Natural inclination is a sufficient cause of *friendship of pleasure.*

---
(1) *In Ethic.*, 1. VIII, 1.3.
(2) *In Ethic.*, 1. VIII, 1. 12.— II-II, q. 23, a. 5.

c) *Friendship of rectitude*, i.e., true friendship, has two causes: first, the natural inclination by which persons love one another; secondly, the virtues(¹).

It is evident that natural inclination is required for friendship. In addition to natural inclination, virtues are required for two reasons.

First, friendship is a firm and stable sharing of life. But only a virtuous life is stable. Therefore virtues are required for friendship.

Secondly, true friendship has the aspect of what is worthy and praiseworthy. But it can have this only from its object, as founded upon the rectitude of the virtues.

Therefore true friendship, even though it may be called a moral virtue annexed to justice, in as much as it is concerned with something morally due among friends, may be said to be a consequence of all the virtues, rather than a special virtue(²).

1022. Love of neighbor.— 1° Supernatural friendship, i.e., charity, should extend to all men, according to the divine precept, *Thou shalt love thy neighbor as thyself* (Matt. XXII, 39).

But, in the natural order, is every man bound to love his neighbor as himself? To this question we must reply in the affirmative: *in the natural order, every man is bound to love his neighbor as himself.*

a) *Every man*, i.e., every being endowed with rational nature.

b) *Is bound to love*, i.e., is bound to love with love of benevolence.

c) *His neighbor*, i.e., others, all men.

d) *As himself:* this does not mean that a person is bound to love his neighbor as much as he loves himself, but that

---

(1) In III Sent., 27, q. 2, a. 2, ad 1.
(2) II-II, q. 23, a. 4, ad 1.— q. 114, a. 1, ad 1.— *De Virtutibus*, q. 1, a. 5, and q. 2, a. 2, ad 8.

man's love for himself should be the pattern of the love which he should have for his neighbor(¹).

Hence, just as we do not wish evil to ourselves, so we should not wish evil to our neighbor, but should wish him good.

And, just as we wish good to ourselves, so we should wish good to our neighbor, i.e., should love him with love of benevolence.

2° We shall now prove the proposition already enunciated.

All men are possessed of rational nature. But union in rational nature imposes on every man the obligation of loving his neighbor as himself. Therefore, in the natural order, every man is bound to love his neighbor as himself.

Minor.— Every man tends to his own nature as to a great good. Hence he ought to tend to that same nature when found in others, for otherwise he would not love that nature. In other words, union in the same nature founds mutual love. And this love, as founded in union of rational nature, is true friendship.

For, *first*, this union connotes a sharing in the same life.

Secondly, since this union connotes a sharing in rational good, it is founded on rectitude, i.e., has its foundation in the virtues.

1023. Order of love of neighbor.— 1° Man is bound to love all men as himself. It does not follow, however, that man should not love himself more than his neighbor, or that he should have the same degree of love for all his neighbors.

Thus man is not bound to love his enemies as enemies, and sinners as sinners, for, if he did, he would be inclined to evil for himself or for his neighbor. But man is bound to love his enemies and sinners in as much as they are possessed of rational nature.

2° In friendship, we must distinguish between:

---

(1) II-II, q. 26, a. 4, *Sed contra*.

a) *the object*, which is the good the friend wishes his neighbor;

b) *the intensity of friendship*, which arises from the dispositions of the person who loves([1]).

In consideration of the object, our love for others should be proportionate to their virtue, i.e., our love for neighbor should be greater as his virtue is greater, in as much as we should wish others good in proportion to their virtue.

In consideration of the intensity of friendship, our love for others should be proportionate to their nearness to us.

Thus a child does not wish his father a great good, such as the office of ruler, of which he knows his father is incapable. This good he wishes another who is capable of it. Nevertheless, the lesser good which he wishes his father is wished with more ardor and intensity than is the greater good he wishes another.

In other words, the child's friendship, from the point of view of the object, is greater for another than for his father; but, from the point of view of the intensity of friendship, it is greater for his father than for another.

1024. Internal effects of friendship.— The internal effects of friendship are *joy, concord,* and *mercy.*

a) Joy is delight either because of the presence of the good loved or *because the proper good exists and is conserved in the one lov'd.* Under the second aspect, joy is an effect of friendship, for the friend wishes good to the person loved.

b) Concord *denotes union of appetites among various persons,* in as much as the wills of various hearts accord in consenting to the same thing([2]).

Friendship is love which is virtuous and mutual, and, as such, it produces concord of wills in the pursuit of good of rectitude.

---

(1) II-II, q. 26, a. 7.
(2) II-II, q. 29, a. 1.

VIRTUES 261

c) Mercy is defined: *a virtue which inclines a person to be compassionate towards and to give relief to another who is in misery.*

Mercy springs from the viscera of friendship, for the friend considers his friend's misery as his own and wishes to relieve it.

1025. External effects of friendship.— There are three acts or external effects of friendship: *beneficence, almsgiving,* and *fraternal correction.*

a) Beneficence is *the act of doing good to another when this is possible and the occasion presents itself.*

The formal motive of beneficence is not the right of one's neighbor, nor his misery, nor any special aspect of good, but merely good, as good wished and desired for another. Thus it is evident that beneficence is the external fruit of friendship. For by friendship a person wishes good to another, and does this good to him when he can do so and the occasion for doing so arises.

b) Almsgiving is *the act of giving something to a person in need from a motive of compassion.*

This is the definition of natural almsgiving. Christian almsgiving is the act of giving to the needy from a motive of compassion and *for God's sake.*

The motive of almsgiving is the necessity or misery of the needy; and an almsdeed is an act of mercy. But since mercy is an internal effect of friendship, almsgiving is an effect of friendship by means of mercy. In other words, almsgiving is an act *elicited* by mercy and *commanded* by friendship.

c) Correction, in general, is reproof with a view to amendment.

Correction may be *judicial* or *fraternal.*

Judicial correction *is given in a court, and is an act of justice.*

Fraternal correction is defined: *an act of friendship and mercy by which we try, by the use of suitable words of admoni-*

tion, or by something equivalent, to turn our neighbor from evil to the good of virtue, i.e., to the practice of virtue.

Fraternal correction is an act elicited by mercy and commanded by friendship — by charity in the supernatural order: it is spiritual almsgiving.

1026. Domestic friendship. — 1° Domestic friendship is the friendship which exists among the members of the same domestic society, i.e., family.

This kind of friendship is essentially distinguished from the natural friendship every man should have towards his neighbor.

For, *first*, the sharing of life in domestic society is different from the sharing of life common to all men.

Secondly, the motive of friendship is not the same in domestic society as it is in human society as a whole.

In human society as a whole, the motive of friendship is likeness in the same rational nature.

In domestic society, the motive of friendship is a special union, namely, consanguinity or affinity.

2° Domestic friendship is divided into the following specifically distinct species of friendship:

paternal friendship;

maternal friendship;

filial friendship;

conjugal friendship (between spouses);

friendship towards relatives by blood or affinity.

3° The love of parents for their children should be greater than the love of children for their parents, for parents love their children as a part of themselves, whereas children love their parents not as a part of themselves, but as the principle of their being. The first aspect is a greater cause of love than the second, for man loves himself more than he loves his neighbor.

On the other hand, children are more indebted to their parents than their parents are to them.

Therefore a father may abandon a wicked son, but a son may not abandon a wicked father.

4° In relation to the object of friendship, the filial friendship of married persons towards their parents should be greater than the conjugal friendship between themselves, for the married persons are more indebted to their parents than they are to each other.

In relation to the intensity of friendship, conjugal friendship should be greater than filial friendship, for the married persons are *one flesh*, and this union is a better disposition for friendship than is the relation of children to parents.

5° Children should have greater love for their father than for their mother, for the father, as the active principle, is a more excellent principle than the mother, who is a passive principle, in the begetting of children; but they should have greater love for their mother as the one who has the greater love for them([1]).

Children should love each other as companions who have an equal share in domestic life.

6° This order in domestic friendship is based on abstract considerations. In the concrete, the order may be changed because of certain circumstances; v.g., if the father is a man of vicious life, whereas the mother is a virtuous person, the children of such parents should love their mother more than they love their father.

1027. Political friendship.— 1° Political friendship is defined: *the friendship which exists between the members of the same political or civil society.*

a) This kind of friendship is natural, for nature inclines men to establish civil society and to pursue the common good in this society.

---

(1) II-II, q. 26, a. 10.

b) This kind of friendship is, under a certain aspect, superior to domestic friendship, and to other kinds of friendship of a more restricted order.

The end of domestic friendship and of other kinds of friendship of a limited order consists in certain particular benefits, i.e., goods, whereas the end of political friendship is the common utility, i.e., the common good of all men living in the same civil society. Therefore domestic friendship and other kinds of friendship of a limited order are contained in political friendship as parts in the whole(¹).

2° In political friendship, there are three things to be considered:

the relations of subjects to their ruler;
the relations of the ruler to his subjects;
the relations of subjects, i.e., of citizens, to one another.

a) Subjects are under obligations to their leader in three things:

fidelity, in as much as they are not allowed to show to another the honor which they owe to their ruler;

reverence, in as much as they ought to do no injury to their ruler;

service, i.e., *quasi-filial friendship,* in as much as subjects owe a debt of gratitude to their ruler in return for the benefits they receive from him(²). Citizens, indeed, are directed by their civil leader to the common good, and hence they receive a very important benefit from him.

b) The ruler is constituted such, in order that he may govern his subjects not according to human will and passions, but in accordance with law, which is a dictate of reason. In other words, a ruler is a man who rules in accordance with reason.

Hence a ruler should enforce justice in dealing with his subjects.

---

(1) *In Ethic.*, 1. VIII, 1.9, nn. 1669-1671.
(2) I-II, q. 100, a. 5.

He should not work for his own utility, but for the utility of others. Hence he should not become possessed of greater goods than his subjects, except perhaps in accordance with the due proportion of distributive justice.

But, since a ruler spends himself for society, he has a right to reward from society, namely, to honor and glory, which are the greatest goods which can be given by men[1].

Finally, in dealing with his subjects, the ruler should use clemency in as much as justice allows it, whereas he should employ severe and strict justice in protecting them against foreign enemies.

c) Political friendship among citizens is the same as concord [2], which exists when there is unity of choice in regard to practical activities of considerable importance, such as matters pertaining to political society.

Therefore concord does not require unity of opinion in speculative matters, or unity of choice in principal matters of minor importance.

1028. Justice, friendship, and charity.— 1° In order to understand the relations between justice and charity, we must first consider equality, which pertains to both, although in different ways.

It pertains to justice to reduce unequal things to equality, that is, justice is concerned with the reestablishment of equality. Hence, when equality once more exists, the work of justice is finished, and when equality has been established, it pertains to friendship to take advantage of it. Friendship, indeed, does not exist among persons separated from each other by great inequality, but among those who are in a certain way equals. Therefore equality is the term in justice, whereas it is the principle in friendship[3].

From the foregoing conclusions, we can deduce the four propositions which follow.

---

(1) *In Ethic.*, 1 V. 1. 11, nn. 1009-1011.
(2) *In Ethic.*, 1. IX, 1. 6.
(3) *In Ethic.*, 1 VIII, 1. 7, n. 1632.

a) *There can be no friendship without justice.*— Equality is the principle in justice. But where justice does not exist, there can be no equality. Therefore.

b) *Injustice is directly opposed to friendship — and to charity.* — Injustice destroys equality, which is the principle in friendship.

This proposition may also be proved from a sign. Injustice towards a person to whom we owe great friendship is greater than injustice towards a person to whom we owe lesser friendship; v.g., a person who murders his father sins more grievously than a person who murders a stranger.

c) *Friendship disposes a person for justice and preserves it.* — Friendship is the love of benevolence by which a person wishes good to another. But he who wishes good to another gives him his due, and does no injury to him. Therefore.

This is evident: for no one is unjust towards friends whom he truly loves.

d) *Justice is insufficient without friendship.* — Justice reduces unequal things to equality, but does not produce beneficence, mercy, peace, and joy, all of which are necessary for life in society. Therefore friendship must be added to justice, not to establish equality, but to complete the political duty already begun by justice.

2° Charity is much more excellent than friendship of the natural order, because its end is the love of God in Himself, and the love of one's neighbor for God's sake, in as much as God is the Father of all men, and gives Himself in a wonderful communication of life as the beatifying object.

Therefore charity, like friendship, but in a manner superior to that of friendship, presupposes justice and preserves it, and perfects the work begun by justice, in as much as it directs all things to God, Who is loved in Himself.

Therefore, for the restoration of the social order, the Church urges the exercise of charity as well as of justice(¹).

---

(1) How completeley deceived are those inconsiderate reformers who, zealous only for commutative justice, proudly disdain the help of charity. Cha-

1029. Vices opposed to friendship.— The following are the vices opposed to friendship:

a) hatred, which is opposed to the love of preference of friendship;

b) envy, which is opposed to the joy concerning one's neighbor's good;

c) discord, which is opposed to the effect of friendship, which is peace;

d) contention, which is opposed to peace, in relation to speech;

e) the spirit of division, sedition, war, and *quarreling*, which are opposed to peace, in relation to work, i.e., actions;

f) scandal, which is opposed to the effect of friendship, which is beneficence.

1) Hatred, in general, is the act or movement of the will by which a person is malevolently disposed towards something.

Hatred is of two kinds: hatred of abomination and hatred of enmity.

Hatred of abomination is the hatred of a person who has an aversion for something as unsuitable and evil to him. This kind of hatred is opposed to the love of concupiscence, by which we wish ourselves good. Hatred of abomination of one's neighbor is of two kinds: hatred of abomination of the person, by which we have an aversion for the person himself, his nature,

---

rity cannot take the place of justice unfairly withheld, but, even though a state of things can be pictured in which every man receives at last all that is his due, a wide field will nevertheless remain open for charity. For justice alone, even though most faithfully observed, can remove indeed the cause of social strife, but can never bring about a union of hearts and minds. Yet this union, binding men together, is the main principle of stability in all institutions, no matter how perfect they may seem, which aim at establishing social peace and promoting mutual aid. In its absence, as repeated experience proves, the wisest regulations come to nothing. Then only will it be possible to unite all in harmonious striving for the common good, when all sections of society have the intimate conviction that they are members of a single family and children of the same Heavenly Father, and further, that they are « one body in Christ and everyone members one of another » (Rom., XII, 5), and hence that « if one member suffer anything, all the members suffer with it ». (I Cor., XII, 26).— *Quadragesimo Anno.*

and his grace as evils displeasing to us, and this is always evil; *or* hatred of abomination of one's neighbor's quality; and this kind of hatred is evil if it concerns good qualities, and is good if concerned with evil qualities.

Hatred of enmity is *hatred by which we wish evil as such to a person.* This kind of hatred is opposed to the love of friendship, by which we wish good as such to another. Hatred of enmity is of its nature evil, and, indeed, gravely so.

2) Envy is *sadness concerning another's good apprehended as evil to oneself, in as much as it lessens one's own glory and excellence.* The envious person experiences sorrow concerning something which should make him rejoice, namely, the good of another.

3) Discord, in general, is disagreement of wills or judgments.

Discord, as opposed to friendship, is defined: *disagreement of wills in regard to good which, in virtue of friendship, should be desired and pursued.*

If the good should be pursued because of another virtue, discord is opposed to this virtue, not formally to friendship. A person who does not pursue legal good, i.e., what is legally due, sins against justice; and a person who does not agree to the will of his superior sins against obedience.

4) Contention, in general, is a verbal battle.

As opposed to friendship, it has a special meaning. It is defined: *an assault which a person makes on truth, without observing in his words the moderation required by circumstances of the matter and persons concerned.*

The principal element in contention is the attack on truth, not the lack of moderation in words.

5) Spirit of division or schism is *the voluntary and unlawful scission of the unity of civil society.*

Quarreling, which is a kind of private war, is defined: *contradiction in deeds by which one man intends harm to another, or a few men intend harm to a few others.*

Hence, just as contention implies contradiction in words, so quarreling implies contradiction in deeds.

Sedition is *the tumult of the parts of the same social whole preparing themselves for battle.*

Sedition is distinguished from quarreling in two ways:

a) quarreling implies actual aggression on each side, whereas sedition implies either actual aggression or only preparation for it;

b) quarreling exists between one individual person and another, or between a few persons on one side and a few on the other, whereas sedition exists between large parts of a multitude, i.e., between social factions.

We shall deal with war later.

6) Scandal is defined: *a word or deed somewhat lacking in rectitude which is an occasion of spiritual ruin to another.*

a) Word or *deed*, i.e., any external action, or omission of external action, and not simply a thought or desire.

b) Somewhat lacking in rectitude, i.e., in some way deficient in rectitude, either because it is evil in itself or from its circumstances, or because, even though it is good, it has an appearance of evil through circumstances of persons or matters concerned.

c) Occasion of spiritual ruin, in as much as it can lead others into sin.

Therefore not every sin committed in the presence of others has the malice of scandal, but only such sins as are foreseen, or can and ought to be foreseen, as capable of leading others into sin. Thus neither persons of very vicious life nor persons of great virtue can be easily influenced, i.e., scandalized, by the bad example of a sinner.

Nevertheless, in the matter of lust, it is very difficult to avoid scandal.

POINTS FOR REVIEW

1. Define friendship, give its divisions in relation to its object, and state the causes of true friendship.

2. What is the significance of the word *as* in the proposition: every man is bound to love his neighbor *as* himself?

3. Under what aspect should a child love his father more than his mother, and vice versa?

4. Explain why injustice is directly opposed to friendship and charity.

5. Define envy.

END OF MONASTICS

ECONOMICS

INTRODUCTION

1030.— Notion of Economics.— 1° Man is destined by his nature to live in society. But society, as we have seen, is a whole which has not absolute unity, but only unity of order. Therefore the part of a society has operations distinct from the operations which are common to the society as a whole. Hence the science which deals with society, i.e., with man living in society, is a practical science specifically distinct from the science which deals with individual or solitary man.

Therefore, having dealt in Monastics with individual man, we now turn our attention to the study of man living in society.

2° The first natural society in which man must live is the home or family, i.e., domestic society.

The home is defined: *a community constituted in accordance with nature for the acts of daily life* (¹).

a) Community constituted in accordance with nature: nature inclines man to the home, i.e., to domestic society, which is constituted in accordance with nature. Hence something more is required for domestic society than the sharing in a common life: this sharing or communication must be in accordance with nature. Thus a community of the aged in a home for the old is not a domestic society.

b) For the acts of daily life, i.e., for such acts as eating, gathering about the same fireplace, etc. Thus domestic life is distinct from life concerned with acts other than daily acts, as are the acts of commercial life, of war, etc.

3° We may now define Economics: *the practical science which deals with man living in domestic society;* or, *the practical*

---
(1) *In Politic,* l. 1, l. 1.

science which deals with the daily acts of man in a community constituted in accordance with nature, i.e., in domestic society.

Economics is a practical science because it is concerned with human acts performed for an end.

1031. Division of Economics.— Economics is a practical science which deals with man living in domestic society. But, before we discuss domestic society, we must know what is meant by society in general. Hence we divide Economics into two books. In the first book, we shall deal with society in general; and, in the second, with domestic society.

> Book I : Society in general.
> Book II: Domestic society.

BOOK I

THE ONLY CHAPTER

SOCIETY IN GENERAL

Prologue.— There will be only one chapter in this book; and in it, in two distinct articles, we shall deal with society and with authority.

Society
- Statement of the question
- Opinions of adversaries
- Thesis: Man is destined by his nature to live in society
- Scholia
- Division of society

Authority
- Statement of the question
- Opinions
- Thesis: Authority is necessary in a heterogeneous society, but not in a homogeneous society
- Scholia
- All authority as such derives from God
- Difficulties

ARTICLE I

SOCIETY

1032. Statement of the question. — 1° Society, according to its etymology, is a union or association of two or more persons. Hence two elements are found in the concept of society: union and plurality.

1) The kind of union proper to society is not union in being. Hence the union of first matter and substantial form, or of substance and accidents, may not be called a society.

In like manner, the union of two or more subsisting things in being, according to relations of identity, likeness, or equality, does not constitute a society. Thus, for example, when parents and children abandon their common life, they no longer form a single society. Similarly, it is possible for members of the same nationality to live in distinct civil societies. Hence we must conclude that society is the union of two or more persons in operation.

But it is not any kind of union of several persons in operation which is the constituent of society. There is a certain union in operation among statuaries in as much as they act for a common end; but, if they work, each for himself, they do not form a society. Moreover, it is possible for them to work in opposition to each other. Similarly, persons who are engaged in the same work, but who are not united by a social bond, do not form a society. Among such persons quarrels, which are a sign of dissociation, frequently arise (¹).

Hence the kind of union proper to society comprises two elements:

a) an end, i.e., a common good, to which its actions tend;

---
(1) II-II, q. 66, a. 2.

b) a community, i.e., a union, of its operations of such kind that the operations of its individual members are the component *parts* of a *whole* or *total* operation which, as a single operation, is directed to the common good.

Hence two kinds of unity characterize the operation of a society: an *objective* unity of operations, arising from the unity of the end, i.e., of the common good, of society ; a *subjective* unity of agents as such arising from the unity of their common operation.

2) The second element found in the concept of society is plurality, as we have already observed. The members of a society pursue a common end. But only a being endowed with intelligence can pursue an end in a strict and proper manner, for only the intellect can have knowledge of an end as such and as the reason for the existence of the means. Therefore society is composed of a plurality of beings endowed with intelligence.

Therefore it is improper and ill befits the philosopher to speak of a swarm of bees or a herd of gregarious animals as consitituting a society.

Society may be defined : *a stable union of a plurality of persons in pursuit of a common good*[1].

2° In the thesis, we state that man is destined by his nature to live in society in as much as he is, according to the natural law, necessarily a part of some society. In other words, we state that man is naturally a social animal.

1033. Opinions of adversaries.— Hobbes and Rousseau, in consequence of their teaching that man's natural and primitive state is the savage and solitary state, deny that man is by his nature a social animal.

1034. Statement of the thesis.

THESIS.— MAN IS DESTINED BY HIS NATURE TO LIVE IN SOCIETY.

---

(1) *Contra Impugnantes Dei cultum ac religionem*, c. 3.

1° Society is necessary for the preservation of human life and for the development of rational life. But man is destined by his nature to do that which is necessary for the preservation of his human life and for the development of his rational life. Therefore man is destined by his nature to live in society.

The *major* may be established in various way.

a) All men are engendered by their parents, and receive nurture and education from them, all of which are necessary for life. Moreover, the individual members of the family mutually assist one another in providing life's necessities([1]).

b) Nature supplies irrational animals with food, covering for the body, and means of self-defence, as teeth, horns, claws, or at least swiftness of flight. It has supplied men with none of these things, but instead has endowed them with reason, by which they can provide themselves with all these things *by the use of their hands*. But an individual man is unable without the help of other men to provide himself with these things. Therefore life in society is necessary for man([2]).

c) Irrational animals are endowed with a natural instinct which inclines them to seek what is useful, and to flee from what is harmful to them; v.g., the lamb instinctively recognizes the lion as an enemy. Some animals, in virtue of natural instinct, know that certain herbs have medicinal properties, and that other things are necessary for life. But man has only a general natural knowledge of what is necessary for life : from his knowledge of general principles he comes to a knowledge of the particular needs of human life. Without the aid of other men, however, an individual man cannot arrive at this knowledge. Therefore society is necessary for men, in order that they may render mutual help to one another, and may share life's tasks by contributing different kinds of labor ; v.g., one is a farmer, another is a medical doctor, etc.([3]).

d) Again, without the aid of his followmen, it is impossible for a man to arrive at a sufficient knowledge or love of

---
(1) *In Ethic.*, l. I, l. 1, n. 4.
(2) *De Reg. Princ.*, l. 1, c. 1.
(3) *Ibid.*

God or to lead a virtuous life, for, to do so, he requires spiritual formation, instruction, admonition, and correction. Hence society is necessary for man, in order that he may know and love God, and lead a virtuous life, i.e., in order that he may attain the imperfect happiness of this life.

The *minor* is evident, for just as man is naturally inclined to preserve his human life and to develop his rational life, so also has he a natural inclination to what is necessary for the attainment of these ends.

2° A being endowed with the faculty of speech is destined by its nature to live in society. But man is a being endowed with the faculty of speech. Therefore man is destined by his nature to live in society.

Major. — Irrational animals are capable of giving only general expression of their passions; v.g., a dog expresses its anger by barking, and other animals express other passions in other ways. Man, who can completely express his concepts to other men, has a greater capacity of communication with others, i.e., is more social, than any gregarious animal whatsoever, as the crane, the ant, or the bee([1]).

Minor. — Man can communicate his concepts to other men by vocal sounds he: is a *rational animal*.

3° The thesis is confirmed from the fact that everywhere men live in society. The invariableness and universality of this fact derive from man's natural inclination to live in society; in other words, this fact remains invariable and universal because man is destined by his nature to live in society.

More briefly, man's natural inclination to life in society may be proved from the following considerations: *a)* at his birth, he requires the assistance of others for the preservation of his life; *b)* as a solitary man, i.e., a man left to himself, he is incapable of protecting and defending himself against injuries; *c)* as a solitary man, he would lack many sciences, arts, and perfections; *d)* man is endowed with the faculties of speech and hearing, and, in consequence, has a natural inclination to live in society; *e)* man's living in society is a fact proper to all peoples, places, and times.

---

(1) *Ibid.*

1035. Scholia.— 1° Society is necessary not only for mankind as a whole, but also for individual men. But it can happen that man does not live in society: *a)* because of an accident of fortune; v.g., Robinson Crusoe on his lonely island; *b)* because of the corruption of nature, which impels man to shun the society of his fellowmen, as happens in the case of the insane; *c)* because of a high degree of perfection, a perfection which elevates a man above human conditions and enables him, without the society of other men, to be self-sufficient, as happened in the case of John the Baptist and of St. Anthony the Hermit [1]. Hence « a man, » says St. Thomas, « may lead a solitary life for two motives. One is because he is unable, as it were, to bear with human fellowship on account of his uncouthness of mind; and this is beast-like. The other is with a view to adhering wholly to divine things; and this is superhuman. Hence the Philosopher says (*Polit.* 1.2) that he who associates not with others is either a beast or a god, i.e., a godly man » [2].

2° Society is formally a stable union in operation, i.e., is formally a dynamic entity. But since action follows being, society may be said to be fundamentally a stable union in being, i.e., a static entity.

3° Since society is a stable union of men in pursuit of a common good, its formal constituent is a real predicamental relation.

There are three requisites of a predicamental relation:

a real subject;

a real term, really distinct from the subject;

a real foundation.

These three elements are found in society.

Its real subject is man, i.e., a being endowed with an intellect.

Its real term is another man, or other men.

---
(1) *In Politic.*, l. I, l. 1.
(2) II-II, q. 188, a. 8, ad 5 (Literally translated by Fathers of The English Dominican Province).

Its real foundation is a common good which must be pursued.

Society, under its material aspect, is a plurality of beings endowed with intelligence.

Society, in its complete entity, is an ordered plurality, i.e., a plurality to which is added a relation. Hence it is not a mere plurality, as certain jurists contend, but a plurality to which order, i.e., a predicamental relation, is added. It is a being which has unity of order.

4° Society is called a *moral person*.

It is only in an equivocal sense that society is a person in the metaphysical meaning of the term, i.e., person considered as a subsisting, individual, complete susbtance, for society has only unity of order, and is not a substance, but an accidental being.

But society is properly called a person in the juridical meaning of the term (n. 633), i.e., a being which is a subject of rights and capable of presenting a case before a judge.

Society is called a *moral person*, to distinguish it from a *physical person*, such as is a man.

5° Society is a whole, of which men are the constituent parts. Since the part has the same relation to whole as the imperfect to the perfect, it follows that men, *as the parts of society, have the same relation to society, as has the imperfect to the* perfect.

An individual man is a part of a society in virtue of those actions in which he communicates with other men in that society.

Moreover, actions are commensurate to their end. Hence, if a society has a particular end, a man's relation to it is determined by the actions by which he tends to that particular end; v.g., it is in virtue of actions proper to carpenters that a carpenter is a part of a society of carpenters, and that his relation to this society is determined.

But if the end of a society is the good of the whole of human life, i.e., the perfect sufficiency of life, it is evident that a man as a part of it is related to it by all his operations.

1036. Division of society.— In every society, there are two elements: a *common end* and the *subjective union of operations*.

The end, moreover, may be considered in *its nature* and in *its perfection*.

Hence society may be divided under three headings: *according to the nature of its end, according to the perfection of its end,* and *according to the union of its operations*.

1° *According to the nature of its end.*

a) Under this aspect, society is first divided into *prudential society* and *artificial society*.

A prudential society is a *society whose end is the perfection of the members as such,* i.e., a society instituted and destined for life; v.g., domestic society, civil society.

An artificial society is a *society which is destined for the performance of work;* v.g., a society for house-building.

b) Again, society is divided into *necessary society* and *free society*.

A necessary society is a *society in which man must live, in order to attain an end imposed either by nature or by the positive will of a superior;* v.g., the family, civil society, the Church.

A free society is a *society in which man is not bound of necessity to live, in order to attain an end imposed either by nature or by the positive will of a superior;* v.g., labor unions, associations of employers.

c) Again, society is divided into *natural society*, and *supernatural society*, as its end is natural or supernatural.

2° *According to the perfection of its end.*

Under this aspect, society is divided into *perfect society*, and *imperfect society*.

A |perfect society| is a *society whose end is a perfect good*, i.e., happiness.

An imperfect society is a *society whose end is an imperfect good*.

Observations in regard to the foregoing definitions :

a) Since the imperfect is always destined for the perfect, it follows that an imperfect society, whose end is an imperfect good, is always destined for a perfect society, as the part for the whole.

Hence an imperfect society is not *independent*, i.e., *autonomous*, but is always dependent on a perfect society, as the part on the whole.

b) Two elements are found in a perfect society :

a perfect good as its end ;

independence in its own order.

Moderns conceive independence as the principal and essential end of a perfect society, whereas Aristotle and St. Thomas hold that a perfect good, i.e., a perfect end, is its principal element.

Therefore the former define a perfect society : *a society which is perfectly self-sufficient, i.e., which is autonomous.*

Moderns thus define a perfect society, because they conceive subjective right as a right in the strict and proper sense of the term. Aristotle and St. Thomas, according to whom a perfect society is a society whose end is a perfect good, hold that it is objective right which is a right in the strict and proper sense of the term.

A particular civil society, according to the modern definition of a perfect society, cannot be dependent on a superior society, v.g., on an international society, whereas, according to the definition of Aristotle and St. Thomas, it can be dependent on a superior society. For such a particular civil society, as pursuing the perfect sufficiency of life, may be conceived as an independent and perfect society in its own order, even though it is not completely autonomous.

c) Human happiness is of two kinds, natural and supernatural.

If natural happiness were the only kind of happiness, there would be only one perfect society, namely, civil society; and it would also be a religious society, as is evident from the history of the kingdoms of pagan antiquity, in which the king was also the pontiff.

But, with the founding of the Church, "The Almighty has given the charge of the human race to two powers, the ecclesiastical and the civil, the one being set over divine, and the other over human things"(¹).

Hence there are now two perfect societies : *the Church*, whose end is man's supernatural happiness, and *civil* or *political* society, whose end is man's natural happiness, i.e., the perfect sufficiency of this life.

3° *According to the union of its operations.*

a) Under this aspect, society is first divided into *juridical society* and *amicable society*.

A juridical society is a *society composed of members juridically bound, i.e., under obligations in justice, to it ;* v.g., civil society, the Church, conjugal society.

An amicable society is a *society composed of members united for some worthy end, but free from juridical obligations ;* v.g. a literary society.

b) Again, society is divided into *heterogeneous society* and *homogeneous socie'y*.

This division is derived from the fact that the individual actions of the members of a society constitute a single social action of a whole, just as parts constitute a whole.

But wholes may be of two kinds : *homogeneous*, which is a whole whose constituent parts have the form of the whole ; v.g., a drop of water has the same form or nature as the water of the whole of which it is a part; *heterogeneous*, which is a whole

---

(1) *Immortale Dei*, n. 13.

of which each part has a form different from that of the whole ; v.g., no part of a house is a house ; no part of man is man([1]).

Human acts are specified by, i.e., have their form from, the end for which they are performed. Moreover, a human act can have two subordinate forms from two subordinate ends for which it is performed ; v.g., a person who does an act of kindness to win good will has two subordinate ends ; for, in addition to the end of the act of kindness, there is a relation to another end: to win good will. This is the root of the division of society, according to the union of its operations, into heterogeneous society and homogeneous society.

A heterogeneous society is a *society in which the common action and the actions of the individual members are specified by distinct ends :* v.g., in an association of builders, the action of the carpenter it not of itself destined for the building of houses, but for the sawing of lumber, etc.; but, because of its subordination to the end of a superior artificer, it has also another end, which is the building of houses : lumber is sawed with a view to the building of a house.

A homogeneous society is a *society in which the common action and the actions of the individual members are specified by the same end ;* v.g., when a number of persons unite to land a ship, the actions of the individual persons and the total action are specified by the same end, namely, the landing of the ship.

The properties of a heterogeneous society are not the same as those of a homogeneous society:

a) In a heterogeneous society, the total action is the result of the subordination of the individual actions of the members; in a homogeneous society, it is the result of the coordination of their operations.

b) In a heterogeneous society, the action of the society is specifically distinct from the individual actions of the members, because the latter are not specified by the common end of the former; in a homogeneous society, the action of the society and the individual actions of the members are not specifically dis-

---

(1) 1, q. II, a. 2, ad 2.

tinct, but only quantitatively distinct, for the former is merely the sum of the latter.

c) In a heterogeneous society, the common good is specifically distinct from the good of the individual members; in a homogeneous society, they differ only quantitatively.

d) Finally, a heterogeneous society, by analogy to a physical organism, which has heterogeneous parts, may be called a kind of organism; and a homogeneous society may be spoken of as being a kind of mechanichal whole.

POINTS FOR REVIEW

1. Define: society, prudential society, necessary society, perfect society, juridical society, heterogeneous society.
2. Name the two elements found in the kind of union proper to society.
3. What is the formal constituent of society? What is society in its complete entity?

ARTICLE II

AUTHORITY

1037. Statement of the question.— 1° Authority, in the general acceptation of the term, signifies a relation. This relation may obtain between a person and a thing; v.g., we speak of the authority of a book. But this is a wide meaning of authority.

In a stricter sense, authority signifies a relation between persons; v.g., paternal authority expresses a relation between parents and their children.

Moreover, the relation signified by authority is connected with the idea of *principle*. It is for this reason that a person who is vested with authority in civil society is called a *prince*. Therefore we may say that authority, according to its nominal definition, is a relation of superiority and inferiority between two or more persons, i.e., a *relation between a superior and an inferior*.

A relation of this kind is possible: *a)* because one person can be the efficient cause of another as a being, as God is the efficient cause of man; and thus we have *physical authority;* *b)* because one person leads the intellect of another to the knowledge of truth; and thus we have *intellectual authority;* *c)* because one person, by his command, moves the will of another to act for an end; and thus we have *moral authority.*

Hence moral authority, with which we are concerned at present, is a relation according to which one person directs, and another (or others) is directed to an end; and it may be formally defined: *the relation between one person as ruler and another person as subject* (¹).

---

(1) *In* II *Sent., dist.* 44, q. 1, a. 1.

2° Authority in its formal signification and authority considered as power are distinct. The latter is the consequence of the former. For a person has power to command another because, as regards an end, he is anterior or superior to the other.

Authority as power is defined: *the power of coercing subjects by physical and moral means to act for the end of society.*

We may say that authority as power is practical reason endowed with a certain superiority. It is practical reason: it is the power of commanding a subject to act for an end; and the act of commanding is the act of practical reason. It is practical reason with a certain superiority: it moves the subject to an end; and, moreover, a mover as such is superior to that which is moved.

Authority is sometimes used in the concrete as signifying the subject of authority, and, in this case, is the *ruler*, i.e., the part of society which directs society to its end.

3° In the thesis, we state that authority is necessary in a heterogeneous society, but not in a homogeneous society.

A heterogeneous society is a society in which the common action and the actions of the individual members are specified by distinct ends.

A homogeneous society is a society in which the common action and the actions of the individual members are specified by the same end.

1038. Opinions.— 1° All philosophers, and, indeed, all men, generally admit that authority is necessary in society.

2° Anarchism, on the contrary, holds that authority in society is neither necessary nor lawful. Anarchists do not conceive authority as a moral power, but rather as a mere physical and coercive force, a brutal fact. Anarchism is of three kinds: religious anarchism, philosophical anarchism, and political anarchism.

a) *Religious anarchism*, whose chief protagonists are Tolstoï, Ibsen, etc., *first*, presents the abuses which accidentally result from the exercise of authority as essential to it; *secondly,* it attempts to establish its claims by recourse to the theory of the universal brotherhood of all Christians. Mankind, according to Tolstoï, is a Christian community of love, and authority is an obstacle to the communication of love among men. In other words, authority, like all other rights, deprives human relations of love.

b) Philosophical anarchism teaches that the only reality which exists is the *to "ego"*, the thinking subject. Consequently, it holds that all authority and all States should be abolished, and that there should be established some kind of association of egoists in which there would be neither authority, government, nor contracts, and whose sole principle of union would be the interest of the members. Such is the teaching of Max Stirner.

c) Political anarchism, whose chief representatives are Proudhon, Bakounine, Kropotkine, Elisée Reclus, Jean Gravé, etc., reject all authority in the name of full human freedom. For if, as Kant holds([1]), the human will is completely autonomous, obedience would be an abdication of personality([2]).

1039. Statement of the thesis.

THESIS.— AUTHORITY IS NECESSARY IN A HETEROGENEOUS SOCIETY, BUT NOT IN A HOMOGENEOUS SOCIETY.

First part.— *Authority is necessary in a heterogeneous society.—* A heterogeneous society is a society in which the action of the society is composed of the many distinct actions of the members, which actions are subordinate to a single end. But, in order that the many distinct actions of the members of a society be subordinate to a single end, authority, i.e., the relation between one person as ruler and another as subject, is

---

(1) Hence political anarchists are directly dependent on Kant.
(2) Toute obéissance est une abdication.— Elisée RECLUS, *L'Evolution, la Révolution et l'Idéal anarchique*, 1898, p. 88.
Ma liberté, ou ce qui revient au même, ma dignité... d'homme... consiste à n'obéir à aucun autre homme, et ne déterminer mes actes que conformément à mes convictions propres.— BAKOUNINE, *Oeuvres*, t. I, p. 281.

necessary. Therefore authority is necessary in a heterogeneous society(¹).

The *major* is evident from the definition of heterogeneous society.

Minor.— The many distinct actions of the members of a society are subordinate to a single end, either because each member tends of his own accord to the one common end, or because he is directed to it by a member in whom is vested authority over the other members. But, in a heterogeneous society, it is impossible that the members tend of their own accord to one common end : for of themselves many agents act for many ends(²), i.e., each agent acts for his own particular end. Therefore the subordination of the actions of the members to the one common end of society requires the direction of a member in whom is vested authority over the other members, i.e., authority is necessary.

Second part.—*Authority is not necessary in a homogeneous society.*— Authority is necessary in a society in which the common end is specifically distinct from the particular ends proper to the individual members. But, in a homogeneous society, the common end is not specifically distinct from the particular ends of the members, but is merely their sum, and only quantitatively distinct from them. Therefore, in a homogeneous society, authority is not necessary, even though certain administrative bodies may be necessary, as in the case of commercial societies.

1040. Scholia.— 1° Authority as power is practical reason endowed with a certain superiority. Nevertheless, not every superiority of practical reason is sufficient to constitute authority ; v.g., superiority in counsel and prudence etc.; but there is strictly required a superiority of extrinsic derivation which is received by the person who is constituted a superior.

---

(1) I, q. 96, a. 4.
(2) *De Reg. Princ.*, l. i, c. 1.

This superiority a person naturally receives from facts which naturally make other persons subject to him in regard to an end. For a person who is subject to another as regards an end is also subject to him in his activity. There are three cases of this kind of subjection:

a) *When one person is the efficient cause of another.* Thus God has authority over all men, and parents have authority over their children.

b) *When one person is the agent, and the other is the patient or instrument.* It is for this reason that a husband has authority over his wife in regard to the end of the family, and that the master has authority over the servant.

c) *When one is a whole of which the other is a part.* As the imperfect is destined for the perfect, so the part is destined for the whole. This is the source whence derives the authority of civil society over its members.

In addition to these primary sources of authority, there are different modes of the transmission of authority from one person to another ; v.g., *division* of power, by which all the authority which is vested in one person may be delegated to others, as happens in the case of a king and his ministers ; or *translation*, i.e., transfer of power, by which a person who is possessed of authority transfers the whole or a part of his authority to another.

2° Some authors teach that authority is the formal element of society ; others hold that it is a property of society.

The solution to the problem may be reached by making a distinction between the metaphysical essence and the physical essence of society.

The metaphysical essence of a thing is the essence of the thing in the abstract, the essence signified by its definition. It is evident that authority is not the formal element of society (heterogeneous) considered in its metaphysical essence, because authority is not found in the definition of society. From this point of view, authority is a property of society.

The physical essence of a thing is the essence of the thing as it is found in the concrete in nature, not as subject to the abstraction of the intellect. Therefore we may say that authority is the form or formal element of society (heterogeneous) considered in its physical essence, because authority is the relation or order between one person as ruler and other persons as subjects, i.e., the order or relation by which heterogeneous society is formally constituted in the concrete.

1041. All authority as such derives from God.— 1° *Preliminaries.*— *a*) In authority, there are three distinct elements: the *principle, use,* and *form* or mode of authority (¹).

The principle of authority is the manner in which a person acquires authority.

The use of authority is the exercise of authority.

The form or mode of authority is the relation of ruler to subjects, i.e., it is authority in the formal sense.

b) There are two cases in which God is not the principle of authority: *in the case of the unworthiness of the person who receives authority.* Though this unworthiness does not derive from God, it does not, nevertheless, render unlawful the acquisition of the authority, nor does it dispense subjects from obedience to it; *in the case in which authority is acquired in an unlawful manner;* v.g., if a person acquires authority by the use of violence or by any other unlawful means. In this case, subjects may overthrow the superior, unless it chances that he has been subsequently recognized as a lawful superior, either by the consent of the people, or by a superior authority.

There are two cases in which the use or exercise of authority does not come from God: *when a superior gives a command which is contrary to the end of authority;* v.g., a command to sin; in this case, subjects may not obey, but should follow the example of the holy martyrs, who suffered death rather than obey the impious commands of tyrants; *when a superior gives commands beyond his authority;* v.g., imposes unjust taxes; in this

---

(1) *In* II *Sent.,* dist. 44, q. 1, a. 2.

case, subjects have no obligation to obey, but are not forbidden to do so (¹).

Authority in its formal signification, i.e., authority as such, which is the relation between ruler and subjects, always derives from God: *There is no power but from God* (²).

2° *Proofs of the proposition.*— 1) All good derives from God. But authority as such is always a good. Therefore authority as such derives from God. (³)

Major.— God is of His very essence the goodness whence all good derives (Fourth Way).

Minor.— Goodness consists formally in mode, species, and order. But authority as such is order. Therefore authority as such is always a good.

2) Whatever is predicated of both God and creatures comes to creatures from God. But authority is predicated of both God and creatures, i.e., men. Therefore authority comes to creatures from God, i.e., all authority derives from God (⁴).

Major.— Whatever is predicated of both God and creatures is predicated of God as the cause of the creature, and of the creature as the effect of God.

The *minor* is evident.

3) Authority by its commands imposes obligations which bind in conscience. But, if authority did not derive from God, it could not impose obligations which are binding in conscience. Therefore authority as such derives from God.

Minor.— To impose an obligation which binds in conscience is to so place the will of a subject under obligation to do or to omit an action that he becomes reprehensible before God if he fails to obey. This presupposes that authority derives from God.

---

(1) *In II Sent.*, dist. 44, q. 2, a. 2.
(2) *Rom.*, XIII, 1.
(3) *In II Sent.*, dist. 44, q. 1, a. 2.— II-II, q. 104, a. 2.
(4) *Com. in Epist. ad Rom.*, c. 13.

1042. Difficulties.— 1° That which is destructive of love among men is neither necessary nor lawful. But authority destroys love among men. Therefore authority is neither necessary nor lawful.

Major.— That which of its nature is destructive of love among men' *I concede*; which accidentally is destructive of love among men, *I deny*.

Minor.— Authority of its nature destroys love among men, *I deny*; accidentally destroys love among men, *I concede*.

Authority can, because of its abuse, accidentally destroy love among men. But of itself authority does not destroy, but rather fosters, love among men, for it unites them in the knowledge and love of the same common end, and, in the pursuit of this good, it safeguards order among them. Moreover, sometimes authority commands internal acts of love among men; v.g., in the Church.

2° That which is opposed to man's liberty is neither necessary nor lawful. But authority is opposed to man's liberty. Therefore authority is neither necessary nor lawful.

Major.— That which is opposed to human freedom, i.e., to the liberty by which man has dominion over the acts of his will, or to the liberty of perfecting himself, *I concede*; that which is opposed to the liberty by which man is allowed to turn away from good and to do evil, *I deny*.

Minor.— Authority is opposed to human freedom, i. e., to the liberty by which man has dominion over the acts of his will, or to the liberty of perfecting himself, *I deny*; is opposed to the liberty by which man is allowed to turn away from good and to do evil, *I concede*.

The objection has its origin in the Kantian conception of liberty according to which liberty consists in the absolute autonomy of the will, i.e., in its absolute independence. But, as we saw in Philosophy of Nature, freedom of the will consists essentially in the dominion which the will has over its acts, a dominion which comes from the indifferent judgment of reason. Authority is not opposed to free will in this sense, because it does not exercise violence on the will of a subject, but uses moral force on it by proposing to his intellect the means necessary for the attainment of an end.

Moreover, authority is not opposed to man's liberty of perfecting himself; on the contrary, it is destined for man's perfection, for it directs men united in society in the pursuit of the common good. Therefore man has a natural love of authority, and his perfection is proportionate to his love of it. This explains why the Saints so ardently embraced obedience.

Nevertheless, authority limits the liberty of turning away from good and of doing evil; but this liberty or power is not a perfection of free will, but rather a serious imperfection.

3° That which is opposed to equality among men is neither necessary nor lawful. But authority is opposed to equality among men. Therefore authority is neither necessary nor lawful.

Major.— In as much as it destroys equality among men who are of themselves equal, *let it go*; in as much as it directs to a common good men who are of themselves unequal, *I deny*.

Minor.— In as much as it destroys inequality among men who are of themselves unequal, *I deny*; in as much as it directs to a common good men who are of themselves unequal, *I concede*.

Men, considered in their specific nature, are equal, since all have the same nature. But, as individuals, men are unequal, for one is superior to another under various aspects; v.g., a father as such is superior to his son as such, but the son can be superior to his father under other aspects, v.g., in knowledge, in virtue, etc.

Authority establishes order among unequal men in regard to a common end, and therefore is not unlawful, but absolutely necessary.

4° That which is opposed to the pursuit of one's proper good is neither necessary nor lawful. But authority is opposed to the pursuit of one's proper good. Therefore authority is neither necessary nor lawful.

Major.— To the orderly pursuit of one's proper good, *I concede;* to the inordinate pursuit of one's proper good, *I deny.*

Minor.— Authority is opposed to the orderly pursuit of one's proper good, *I deny;* to the inordinate pursuit of one's proper good, *I concede.*

Authority establishes order among the members of society in regard to the common good; therefore it gives order to men's pursuit of their proper good by directing it to the common good.

POINTS FOR REVIEW

1. Give the nominal definition of authority; the formal definition of moral authority; the definition of authority as power.

2. Explain why authority is necessary in a heterogeneous society.

3. Under what aspect does all authority derive from God? Explain.

BOOK II

Domestic society

Prologue.— We find that there are three distinct kinds of union in domestic society: *a)* the union of husband and wife, called matrimonial society; *b)* the union of parents and children, called parental society; *c)* the union of master and slave, called herile society ([1]). We shall deal with matrimonial society and parental society in distinct chapters, and with herile society in an appendix.

Chapter I. Matrimonial society

Chapter II. Parental society.

Appendix. Herile society.

---

(1) *In Polit.*, 1. I, 1. 2.

CHAPTER I

MATRIMONIAL SOCIETY

Prologue.— In this chapter, first, we shall deal with the origin of matrimony; secondly, with its precept; thirdly, with its properties: unity and indissolubility. Therefore there will be four articles in this chapter.

Origin of matrimony
- Statement of the question
- Opinions
- Thesis: Matrimony is natural to man, and is of natural institution.
- Essence of matrimony
- Efficient cause of matrimony
- Ends of matrimony
- Conjugal society is the most natural of all societies
- Matrimony, considered merely as a natural institution, is sacred in character
- Scholia
- Eugenics

Precept of matrimony
- Statement of the question
- Thesis: Matrimony is of natural precept, and is directly obligatory not on individual men, but on the human species as a whole

Unity of matrimony
- Statement of the question
- Opinions
- Thesis: Polyandry is contrary to the primary precepts, and polygyny to the secondary precepts, of the natural law

Indissolubility of matrimony
- Statement of the question
- Opinions
- Thesis: The intrinsic dissolubility of matrimony is contrary to the primary precepts, and its extrinsic dissolubility to the secondary precepts, of the natural law
- Scholion
- Difficulties

ARTICLE I

ORIGIN OF MATRIMONY

1043. Statement of the question.— 1° Matrimony may be described as *the stable union of man and woman for the purpose of propagating the human race.*

a) Stable union: matrimony is thus distinguished from concubinage. Moreover, matrimony is, as we shall prove later, an indissoluble union or society.

b) Of man and woman: these words designate the members of matrimonial society.

c) For the purpose of propagating the human race: these words indicate the primary end of matrimony.

2° Matrimony has its origin in nature, in as much as it is natural to man.

There are two ways in which a thing may be natural: *first*, as necessarily caused by nature; v.g., to ascend is natural to fire; *secondly*, as effected by free will under the impulse of natural inclination [1]. It is in the latter way that matrimony is natural.

3° Moreover, matrimony is of natural institution, i.e., is an *institution of nature*, in as much as its end, the means of attaining its end, and the laws which regulate the activity of its members are determined by nature. Matrimony, nevertheless, remains free, in as much as a person who contracts matrimony does so freely, and also, while observing the laws of matrimony established by nature, freely chooses the person with whom matrimony is contracted.

---

(1) *Suppl.*, q. 41, a. 1.

1044. Opinions.— 1° All Catholics, and also many non-Catholics, hold that matrimony is of natural institution.

2° Many others, however, teach that matrimony is solely of human invention and institution.

a) Some hold that no evidence of the origin or existence of matrimony can be found in nature or in its laws, but only the power and instinct for the procreation of life. Such is the teaching of *communists*, of many socialists, and generally of evolutionists and naturalists, who, in consequence, advocate free unions.

b) Others hold that certain beginnings, or, as it were, seeds of true wedlock, are found in man's nature, because, as they point out, a stable union of man and woman is required for the protection of the dignity of husband and wife, and for the attainment of the end of their matrimonial union, which is the procreation and education of children. Therefore they admit that matrimony is the most perfect of all unions between man and woman. They maintain, nevertheless, that matrimony owes its institution solely to the will of man, and that divorce may be readily admitted. Such is the teaching of the *more moderate* naturalists.

1045. Statement of the thesis.

THESIS.— Matrimony is natural to man, and is of natural institution.

First part.— *Matrimony is natural to man.*— 1) *From the ends of matrimony.*— A union to which nature inclines free man is natural to man. But nature inclines free man to the stable union of man and woman, i.e., to matrimony. Therefore matrimony is natural to man.

The *major* is evident from the statement of the question.

Minor.— *a) From the primary end of matrimony, i.e., from the good of the child.*— Nature intends that the union of man and woman should provide not only for the procreation of children, but also for their rearing and elevation to the status of perfect man, which is the state of virtue: for the imperfect is always destined for the perfect. But the education of children requires the stable union of man and woman. Therefore (¹).

b) *From the secondary end of marriage, which is the mutual assistance of the married persons in their domestic life.* — Nature inclines man to such society as provides for the necessities of human life. But matrimony provides for certain necessities of human life: for human life requires certain activities, as farming, etc., which are proper to man, and others, as housekeeping, for which woman is naturally adapted (²). Therefore.

2) *From a comparison with the union of other animals.* "In the case of certain animals, as dogs, for the rearing of whose offspring the female is alone sufficient, the male and the female do not remain together after coition. But in the case of others, for the rearing of whose offspring the female alone is not sufficient, the male and the female remain together for such time as is necessary for the rearing and training of their young. Evidence of this is found in the case of birds, whose newly-hatched young are incapable of providing themselves with food; since birds, unlike quadrupeds which are supplied with milk by nature, do not suckle their young but must seek food for them abroad, and also keep them warm during the period of feeding, the female cannot do this work alone; hence, in the case of certain animals, divine providence has endued the male with a natural instinct of remaining with the female for the rearing of their brood. Now, in the case of the human species, it is evident that the mother cannot by herself rear her children, for the necessities of human life are such as cannot be provided by only one of the parents. Hence it is in accordance with the exigencies of human nature that the husband cohabit with his wife after coition, and not leave her at once and form a union with any other womam whom he happens to meet, as happens in the case of fornicators "(³).

---

(1) *In Ethic.*, l. VIII, l. 12, n. 1721.
(2) *Contra Gentes*, l. III, c. 122.
(3) *Ibid.*

Second part. — *Matrimony is of natural institution.* — A society whose ends, means of attaining these ends, and laws governing the acts of its members are determined by nature is of natural institution. But matrimony is a society whose ends, means of attaining these ends, and laws governing the acts of its members are determined by nature. Therefore matrimony is of natural institution.

The *major* is clear from the notion of a natural institution.

Minor.— a) The primary end of matrimony, which is the procreation and education of children, i.e., the propagation of the human race, has its origin in nature : for nature, which cannot accomplish the conservation of the human species in a single individual, does so by means of matrimony.

b) The means destined for the attainment of the ends of matrimony are determined by nature : diversity of sex, inclination to the act of generation, different qualities and aptitudes of man and woman adapted for the different kinds of work necessary for human life, etc.

c) Since nature destines matrimony for a common good, which is the propagation of the human race by suitable means, it thereby determines the laws of matrimony : for a law is an ordinance for the common good. The natural laws of matrimony are the laws concerned with its unity and indissolubility, with the authority of the husband, etc.

1046. Essence of matrimony.— 1° The following distinct elements are found in matrimony :

a) mutual consent externally expressed, i.e., the contract;

b) mutual bodily surrender ;

c) the bond between the spouses resulting from the contract ;

d) the mutual right to carnal intercourse ;

e) the use of matrimony, i.e., carnal intercourse.

2° Matrimony may be considered in its cause, according to which it is contracted (matrimonium in fieri). Under this aspect, matrimony is the contract, i.e., consists in mutual consent externally expressed, as we shall prove later.

It may also be considered as a permanent thing or state (matrimonium in facto esse). It is with the problem of the essence of marriage as a state that we are at present concerned.

According to our teaching, matrimony as a state consists essentially in the formal bond, i.e., in the indissoluble tie, which results from the mutual consent of the spouses.

The formal bond is distinct from the bond considered in its cause, i.e., from the contract, which is the thing which unites in the order of efficient causality.

3° It is evident that matrimony as a state or permanent thing consists essentially in the indissoluble tie, i.e., in the formal bond, which unites the spouses. For its essential constituent is not the consent of the spouses, nor the mutual surrender of their bodies, for these are transitory acts, whereas marriage as a state is something permanent. Moreover, neither the right to carnal union, nor the use of matrimony is its formal constituent, for each of these is a consequence of matrimony. Hence matrimony as a state must consist essentially in the formal bond, i.e., in the indissoluble tie, which results from the contract.

1047. Efficient cause of matrimony. — 1° *Preliminaries.*— Matrimony as a state is the stable union of man and woman for the purpose of begetting and educating children. The efficient cause of this union is the mutual consent, i.e., the contract, of the spouses, called matrimony in its cause.

This consent must be : *a) true* and *internal*, i.e., properly an act of the will ; *b) deliberate*, i.e., given with sufficient knowledge and due liberty ; *c) mutual*, because matrimony is an onerous contract, and hence requires the mutual consent of the contracting parties ; *d) concerned with the present* and between persons capable of contracting marriage, because marriage is not a promise, but an act by which a man and a woman actually give to each other power over their bodies for the purpose of engendering children ; *d*) *externally manifested*, either by words, or by signs ; for it is a mutual acceptance.

2° *In the light of the following observations*, we shall now demonstrate the following proposition :

The mutual consent of the spouses is the efficient cause of matrimony.

The determinant of the union of a certain man with a certain woman is the efficient cause of matrimony. But the mutual consent of the spouses is the determinant of the union of a certain man with a certain woman. Therefore.

The *major* is evident.

Minor. — The union of a certain man with a certain woman, and vice versa, is not determined by nature, but depends on the free will of the man and the woman concerned.

1048. Ends of matrimony. — The ends of matrimony are the ends for which matrimony of its nature is destined, and to which it tends, i.e., they are the *ends of the work*. Thus they are distinct from the *end of the agent*, which a person who contracts marriage may join to the ends of matrimony itself.

Matrimony has a primary end and a secondary end.

The primary end is the end for which matrimony is primarily and principally intended; and this end, as we have already seen, is the *procreation and education of children* ([1]), i.e., the propagation of the human species.

The secondary end is an end which is essentially subordinate to the primary end, and a consequence of it. This end is twofold : *a*) the mutual help of the spouses; *b*) the allaying of concupiscence ([2]).

The husband and wife find mutual help in matrimony, for nature has given special endowments to each, in order that each may fulfill his or her special task in the life they lead in common.

---
(1) *Code of Canon Law*, Can. 1013.
(2) *Ibid.*

The allaying of concupiscence and the enjoyment of pleasure are annexed to the use of marriage, in order to ensure the attainment of the primary end of matrimony and to keep concupiscence within the limits of reason.

The mutual inward moulding of husband and wife, the determined effort to perfect each other, can in a very real sense, as the Roman Catechism teaches, be said to be the chief reason and purpose of matrimony, provided that matrimony be regarded not in the restricted sense as instituted for the proper procreation and education of children, but more widely as the blending of life as a whole and the mutual interchange and sharing thereof (1). By this mutual forming and perfecting of themselves in the interior life, husbands and wives should strive to advance daily more and more in virtue, and, especially if they are Christians, to grow in that charity by which God is loved for His own sake, and their neighbor for love of God.

1049.— Conjugal society is the most natural of all societies.— Conjugal society is a natural society not merely in as much as it is effected under the impulse of natural inclination, but in as much as it receives its completion from reason. Under this aspect, conjugal society, and the entire family, is more natural than any other society.

a) First, according to the order of nature, it is more necessary than any other society, for its end is the procreation and education of children, i.e., the propagation of the human species (2).

b) Secondly, it befits man in both his specific and generic nature, for the procreation of offspring, which is the primary end of matrimony, is common to both man and animals (3).

c) Thirdly, it is prior to civil society, because it is its part: the part is prior to the whole (4). Under this aspect, the family is the foundation of civil society, and generally of every social edifice.

---

(1) *Casti Connubii.*
(2) *In Ethic.,* l. VIII, l. 12, n. 1720.
(3) *Ibid.*
(4) *Ibid.*

d) Fourthly, the ends of the family, its constitution, its authority, and the relation between its members are more determinate, because of the natural bond which binds father, mother, and children, than those of any other society [1].

e) Finally, the natural bonds of love, reverence, and benevolence are more helpful to the family in the pursuit of its ends than they are to any other society.

1050.— Matrimony, considered merely as a natural institution, is sacred in character.— The sacredness of marriage is evident from its primary end. In the fulfilment of the duties of their state, parents are in a very special way ministers of God. In begetting children, they dispose first matter for the reception of a spiritual soul immediately created by God and immediately destined for Him. In educating children, parents complete the work begun in generation: they assist their children in the attainment of their natural ends. Thus through matrimony life is transmitted to new worshippers of God, to new creatures destined for Heaven. Therefore matrimony, considered in the purely natural order, is an institution primarily and directly destined for the service of God, and extends to the fundamental relations of men to God [2].

Hence God not only established the sacred institution of marriage, but from the beginning sanctioned it with a positive law and a special blessing, for it is related in the *Book of Genesis* I, 27-28: « Male and female He created them. And God blessed them, saying: Increase and multiply, and fill the earth. »

This is the explanation of the remarkable fact that all the races of mankind, even from the earliest times, have treated matrimony as an act of religion, and surrounded it with sacred rites and ceremonies. Men, moved, it would seem, either by a knowledge of the nature of matrimony, or by the memory of

---

(1) D. LALLEMENT, *Principes Catholiques d'Action Civique*, p. 43 2e édit.
(2) « And Tobias said:... And now, Lord, Thou knowest that not for fleshly lust do I take my sister to wife, but only for the love of posterity in which Thy name may be blessed for ever and ever » — *Tob.*, VIII, 9.— Cf. BELLARMINUS, *De Matrim.*, C. 4.

its origin, have always regarded marriage as a sacred institution (¹).

Christian matrimony is possessed of a special dignity, for it is destined not merely for the propagation and preservation of the human race and for the education of any kind of worshippers of the true God, but rather for the begetting of children who are to become members of the Church of Christ, for the raising up of fellow-citizens of the Saints and members of God's household, that the people of God and the worshippers of our Saviour may daily increase (²). Therefore our Divine Lord, the restorer of human nature, not only restored matrimony to its original sanctity, but sanctified and protected it in a special way by elevating the matrimonial contract among Christians to the dignity of a Sacrament of the New Law.

1051. Scholia.— 1° Any voluntary emission of semen not destined for the lawful begetting of children is a grave sin, for it is contrary not only to the good of the individual, but to the good of nature. For the union of man and woman for the purpose of engendering and educating children is in accordance with the designs of nature; and the human semen is destined for this union and for the begetting of children. Hence St. Thomas teaches that the sin of impeding the engendering of human nature is a close second in gravity to the sin of destroying actually existent human nature (³).

The voluntary effusion of semen is not destined for its lawful end, 1) when it takes place without union with the opposite sex ; 2) when it takes place in such a union, but unlawful means are used to prevent the begetting of children.

Again, every carnal union with the opposite sex outside of wedlock is a mortal sin, and is forbidden not only by the divine positive law but also by the natural law, for it is opposed to the due education of children, which, in the case of the human species, requires the cohabitation of the male and female for a long period of time after coition.

---

(1) LEO XIII, *Arcanum Divinae*.
(2) PIUS XI, *Casti Connubii*.
(3) *Contra Gentes*, l. III, c. 122.

Moreover, all sexual pleasure directly willed or sought outside the ends of matrimony is of its very nature a mortal sin, for it is directly contrary to the ordinance of nature : all sexual pleasure is destined, according to the intention and ordinance of human nature and of its Divine Author, for the engendering of children in lawful marriage.

2° Therefore all persons capable of the conjugal act have a natural and therefore inviolable right to contract marriage : for this right derives from human nature. Hence persons who are naturally fit for matrimony, but who, it is probable, are capable of begetting only defective children, are guilty of no crime in contracting marriage. Often, however, such persons should be dissuaded from entering the state of matrimony.

3° Since the chief reason and purpose of wedlock, considered as a society in which there is the blending of life as a whole and the mutual interchange and sharing thereof, is the mutual interior moulding of husband and wife, and since its primary end is the procreation and the physical, intellectual, and moral education of children, « everywhere and with the greatest strictness the Church forbids marriage between baptized persons, one of whom is a Catholic and the other a member of a schismatical or heretical sect ; and if there is, in addition to this, the danger of the falling away of the Catholic party and the perversion of the children, such a marriage is forbidden also by the divine law(¹) ».

1052. Eugenics.— *Eugenics* is the teaching of those who are concerned with the birth and development of children under the best possible conditions. Eugenics is lawful and most praiseworthy if its purpose is to obtain, without violation of the moral order, the strength and health of the future child, v.g., through the agency of private or social means destined to safeguard the health of the mother and of people in general.

Moreover, the Church, in protecting the unity and indissolubility of matrimony, and in instituting disciplinary laws

---

(1) *Code of Canon Law*, c. 1060.

to govern it, v.g., the law which forbids marriage between blood relatives, etc., does so for the purpose of securing the best possible conditions for the birth and for the physical, moral, and intellectual education of the child ; in other words, it does so for a eugenic end.

But eugenics which puts the *eugenic* end before all other ends, even before those of a higher order, is indefensible and strictly condemned ; and from it flow many pernicious errors.

a) Its adherents advocate that the State forbid marriage between persons who, though naturally fit for marriage, are probably incapable of engendering any but defective children, and that it legislate that by a surgical operation such persons be deprived, even against their will, of the generative power with which nature has endowed them.

The refutation of this erroneous and pernicious teaching will be found in the principles which follow.

First, men are begotten not for the earth and for time, but for Heaven and for eternity. Hence solely the health and physical strength of the child do not constitute the primary end of matrimony.

Secondly, any person who is naturally fit for marriage has a natural and inviolable right, a right anterior to any rights of civil society, to beget children. Hence the State may not deny to any person the exercise of this right.

Thirdly, the State has no direct power over the bodies of its citizens ; therefore, when no crime has been committed and there is no reason for inflicting punishment involving the shedding of blood, it may not, for eugenic or any other reasons, directly harm or tamper with the integrity of the body.

Fourthly, private persons have no power over their bodies other than that which pertains to their natural ends ; and they are not free to destroy or mutilate their members, or in any other way to render themselves unfit for their natural functions, except when no other provision can be made for the good of the whole body.

b) There are other advocates of eugenics who teach that married persons should limit the number of their children, even by the unlawful frustration of the marital act, i.e., by directly preventing the attainment of its natural end, which is the begetting of children. Persons who do this are, as we have seen, guilty of a violation of the order of nature, and commit a crime which is shameful and intrinsically vicious.

c) Finally, there are many who hold that the life of the child still in its mother's womb may be taken if this be necessary for the saving of the life of the mother. But such taking of life is patently the direct murder of the innocent, and, indeed, the heinous crime of homicide.

POINTS FOR REVIEW

1. Give a descriptive definition of matrimony, explain how it is natural to man and of natural institution, and what constitutes its essence as a state.

2. Explain why the mutual consent of the spouses is the efficient cause of matrimony.

3. State the primary and secondary ends of matrimony, and also the chief reason and purpose of it as a society in which the whole of life is intimately shared.

4. What is meant by eugenics? Under what aspect is this teaching unlawful?

ARTICLE II

PRECEPT OF MATRIMONY

1053. Statement of the question.— 1° In the time of St. Thomas, there were some who held that the married state was obligatory on all persons capable of entering it. St. Thomas refutes this teaching in his writings against those who assail perpetual continence.

Luther holds that matrimony is obligatory on all because of physical necessity. Calvin and Melanchton teach that celibacy is contrary to the ordinance of God. Today, certain non-Catholic writers, as Platen, Nystroin, Voivenel, etc., voice disapproval of perpetual continence.

2° Others, as St. Bonaventure (1), and, in more recent times, Palmieri, Gasparri (2), Wernz, Noldin, and Capello, hold that matrimony is preceptive for mankind as a whole and for individuals only accidentally, i.e., in circumstances in which it would be necessary for the preservation of the human species, as was the case at the beginning of the world.

3° It is the common teaching of Scholastics that matrimony is of natural precept, and is directly obligatory on mankind, but only accidentally of obligation for individual men. The individual man could be accidentally bound to fulfil this precept only in extraordinary circumstances; v.g., if he could not live a life of continence, or was unwilling to use the means of doing so; to repair an injury, to legitimize a child, to fulfil a promise, to preserve peace between nations, to prevent civil war, to preserve the Catholic faith in a particular country, in the case in which the lack or decline of population would require it, etc.

---

(1) In 45, d. 26, a. 1, q. 3.
(2) De M itrimonio, n. 14.

1054. Statement of the thesis.

THESIS.— Matrimony is of natural precept, and is directly obligatory not on individual men, but on the human species as a whole.

First part.— *Matrimony is of natural precept.*— A means which is absolutely necessary for the attainment of an end instituted by nature is of natural precept. But matrimony is a means which is absolutely necessary for the attainment of an end of natural institution, i.e., for the preservation of the human species in a due and becoming manner. Therefore matrimony is of natural precept [1].

The case of man is very different from that of animals: the latter are not bound by precept, of which they are incapable, but are sufficiently moved by natural inclination for the preservation of their species, whereas man, though moved by natural inclination, remains free to follow it or to disregard it

Second part.— *The precept of matrimony is directly obligatory not on individual men, but on the human species as a whole.* — A precept which is of necessity required for the perfection of the human species as a whole, but not for the perfection of the individual man, is directly obligatory not on individual men, but on the human species as a whole. But the precept of matrimony is of necessity required for the perfection of the human species as a whole, but not for the perfection of the individual man. Therefore the precept of matrimony is directly obligatory not on individual men, but on the human species as a whole [2].

Major.— If a precept imposed for the perfection of mankind were directly obligatory on individual men, every man would be in duty bound to be a farmer and a tradesman, and to perform all such tasks as are necessary for the human community; moreover, individual men would be under obligation to fulfil incompatible duties, v.g., to lead a contemplative life

---
(1) Billuart, *De Matrimonio*, diss. 1, a. 2, lec. 2.
(2) *Suppl.*, q. 41, a. 2.— *Contra Gentes*, l. III, c. 136.

and also a married life, both of which are necessary for the perfection of mankind. Therefore.

The *minor* is evident: for matrimony is necessary for the propagation of the human species.

ARTICLE III

UNITY OF MATRIMONY

1055. Statement of the question.— 1° The unity of matrimony consists in the conjugal union of one man with one woman. It is called monogamy, which is the opposite of polygamy.

2° Polygamy has a *proper* and an *improper* signification.

Polygamy, in its improper meaning, is *successive*, and exists when one man successively marries two or more wives, or vice versa.

Polygamy, in its proper meaning, is *simultaneous* polygamy, and exists when one man has several wives at the same time, or vice versa.

It is with the latter kind of polygamy that we are at present concerned.

3° Polygamy, in the proper sense, is of two kinds: *polyandry* and *polygyny*.

Polyandry is the marital union of one wife with several husbands at the same time.

Polygyny is the marital union of one husband with several wives at the same time.

4° In the thesis, we state that polyandry is contrary to the primary precepts of the natural law, and polygyny to its secondary precepts.

A thing is contrary to the primary precepts of the natural law when it renders impossible the attainment of the principal end intended by nature in a determinate matter; and to the secondary precepts of the natural law when it stands in the way of the attainment of a secondary end intended by nature in a determinate matter, or is contrary to the principal end in as much as it renders its attainment difficult and imperfect (1)

1056. Opinions. — 1° Luther taught that polygyny was lawful, even under the New Law, and, indeed, he permitted Londgrave Philip of Hesse to have a second wife.

The Anabaptists and Mormons espouse the cause of polygyny.

2° Polygyny was practised among many peoples before the time of Christ, and, indeed, was permitted by a special dispensation of God among the Jews. Today, it exists among certain infidels; v.g., among wealthy Mohammedans, who are capable of supporting more than one wife.

Polyandry was never a common practice, but, in exceptional cases, was practised among certain peoples, especially where women were less numerous than men.

1057. Statement of the thesis.

> **THESIS.** — POLYANDRY IS CONTRARY TO THE PRIMARY, AND POLYGYNY TO THE SECONDARY PRECEPTS, OF THE NATURAL LAW.

First part. — *Polyandry is contrary to the primary precepts of the natural law.*— An institution which directly hinders the attainment of the primary end of matrimony is contrary to the primary precepts of the natural law. But polyandry directly hinders the attainment of the primary end of matrimony. Therefore polyandry is contrary to the primary precepts of the natural law.

Major.— A primary precept of the natural law is concerned with the attainment of the primary end intended by nature in a given matter, or with the means necessary for its attainment.

---

(1) *Suppl.*, q. 65, a. 1.

Minor.— The primary end of matrimony is the procreation and education of children. But polyandry directly hinders the work of educating children because, as a result of it, the child, for whose education the father's care is necessary, cannot know with certainty who is his father([1]) ; moreover, polyandry is a serious obstacle to the begetting of children, because the carnal intercourse of one women with several men greatly reduces her fecundity, and often produces sterility, as happens in the case of prostitutes.

Second part.—*Polygyny is contrary to the secondary precepts of the natural law.*— An institution which renders difficult the attainment of the primary end of matrimony, and is a serious obstacle to the attainment of its secondary end, is contrary to the secondary precepts of the natural law. But polygyny is an institution which renders difficult the attainment of the primary end of matrimony, and is a serious obstacle to the attainment of its secondary end. Therefore polygyny is contrary to the secondary precepts of the natural law.

The *major* is evident from the definition of a secondary precept of the natural law.

Minor.— a) *Polygyny renders difficult the primary end of matrimony.*— Polygyny is a source of dissension in the home and renders cohabitation difficult, and therefore is an obstacle to that complete union of souls necessary for the perfect education of children ; moreover, there is always the danger that the husband will devote almost all his parental attention to the children of the wife whom he loves most, and neglect the others.

b) *Polygyny is a serious obstacle to the attainment of the secondary end of matrimony.*— It hinders the spouses from assisting each other, for the sharing of several persons in one and the same object of their love leads to jealousy, envy, and quarrels ; thus, the husband, in showing equal affection to all his wives, opens avenues to quarrels engendered by the efforts of each to win all his affection for herself ; and, in showing

---

(1) *Suppl.*, q. 65, a. 1, ad 8.

greater love for one than for another, he sows seeds of envy and enmity.

Finally, polygyny stands in the way of the allaying of concupiscence, which is a secondary end of matrimony, for many wives are a stimulus to rather than a remedy for concupiscence, etc.(1).

POINTS FOR REVIEW

1. Define: polygamy in its strict meaning, polyandry, and polygyny.

2. Explain why polyandry is contrary to the primary precepts, and polygyny to the secondary precepts, of the natural law.

---

(1) *Contra Gentes*, l. III, c. 124.

ARTICLE IV

INDISSOLUBILITY OF MATRIMONY

1058. Statement of the question.— 1° Matrimony is essentially a stable union. This stability is called consistency, i.e., firmness of constitution, in as much as it is perpetual from the very nature of matrimony ; and indissolubility, in as much as there is no human power capable of breaking or loosing the marriage bond. Hence the indissolubility of matrimony may be defined : *that property in virtue of which the conjugal bond, because of its inviolable intrinsic consistency, cannot be dissolved by any human power.*

Indissolubility is the opposite of divorce in its strict meaning, which is the loosing of the marital bond together with the right to marry again. Sometimes the term divorce is used in a wide meaning to signify nothing more than separation from bed and board.

2° Indissolubility is of two kinds : intrinsic and extrinsic.

The indissolubility of matrimony is *intrinsic* in as much as the marriage bond cannot be broken by its natural intrinsic cause, i.e., by the mutual consent of the husband and wife ; and *extrinsic* in as much as it cannot be loosed by any extrinsic cause, i.e., by the authority of a superior.

3° The indissolubility of matrimony derives from the natural law. The intrinsic dissolubility of matrimony is contrary to the primary precepts, and its extrinsic dissolubility to the secondary precepts, of the natural law.

1059. Opinions.— 1° According to Luther, Calvin, and almost all Protestants of the present day, there are certain causes, as adultery, heresy, difficulty of cohabitation, etc., which justify the dissolution of the marital bond. Montaigne (¹) and Voltaire support the opinion in favor of the dissolubility of marriage.

Moreover, certain Rationalists and many politicians and civil lawyers have held that divorce, in certain cases, is not only lawful, but useful and praiseworthy, and consequently have obtained its legal sanction in the civil enactments of many countries.

2° Modern naturalists have gone a step farther by preaching free love. They hold that the marriage bond is intrinsically dissoluble, and therefore may be dissolved by the mutual consent of the husband and wife. Hence, instead of defending the perpetual stability of the conjugal bond, such men go so far as to concoct new species of unions, suited, as they say, to the proper temper of men and the times; and these various new forms of matrimony they presume to label « temporary » (v.g., for the period of sojourn in a certain place), « experimental », and « companionate ». These offer all the indulgence of matrimony and its rights without, however, the indissoluble bond, and without offspring, unless the parties alter their cohabitation into a matrimony in the full sense of the law (²).

1060. Statement of the thesis.

THESIS.— THE INTRINSIC DISSOLUBILITY OF MATRIMONY IS CONTRARY TO THE PRIMARY PRECEPTS, AND ITS EXTRINSIC DISSOLUBILITY TO THE SECONDARY PRECEPTS, OF THE NATURAL LAW.

---

(1) Nous avons pensé attacher plus ferme le nœuf de nos mariages pour avoir osté tout moyen de les dissouldre; mais d'autant s'est deprins et relaché le nœud de la volonté et de l'affection que celuy de la contraincte s'est estrecy: et au rebours, ce qui tient les mariages, à Rome, si long temps en honneur et en seureté, feut la liberté de les rompre qui vouldroit; ils gardaient mieulx leurs femmes, d'autant qu'ils les pouvaient perdre; et en pleine licence de divorces, il se passa cinq cents ans, et plus, avant que nul s'en servist.— *Essais*, l. 2, c. 15.

(2) *Casti Connubii*.

First part. — *The intrinsic dissolubility of matrimony is contrary to the primary precepts of the natural law.* — Whatever renders impossible the attainment of the principal end of matrimony is contrary to the primary precepts of the natural law. But the intrinsic dissolubility of matrimony renders impossible the attainment of its principal end. Therefore the intrinsic dissolubility of matrimony is contrary to the primary precepts of the natural law.

The *major* is evident from the definition of a primary precept of the natural law.

Minor.— The principal end of matrimony, which is the begetting of children and their rearing and elevation to the status of perfect man, absolutely requires the stability of the conjugal union. But the intrinsic dissolubility of matrimony would be destructive of the stability of the conjugal union: for the separation of the husband and wife would be possible by mutual consent and at any time. Therefore.

Second part. — *The extrinsic dissolubility of matrimony is contrary to the secondary precepts of the natural law.* — Whatever renders the attainment of the principal end of matrimony very difficult and imperfect and at the same time is a serious obstacle to the attainment of its secondary end and at variance with public morality, is contrary to the secondary precepts of the natural law. But the extrinsic dissolubility of matrimony renders the attainment of the principal end of matrimony very difficult and imperfect, is a serious obstacle to the attainment of its secondary end, and leads to the perversion of public morals. Therefore the extrinsic dissolubility of matrimony is contrary to the secondary precepts of the natural law.

The *major* is evident from the definition of a secondary precept of the natural law.

Minor.— a) *The extrinsic dissolubility of matrimony renders the attainment of its principal end very difficult and imperfect.*— It is detrimental to the begetting of children: for the possibility of the separation of husband and wife by public authority often leads married persons, who regard children as an obstacle to new marriages, to the heinous crimes of voluntary sterility and abortion. The experience of countries in which divorce is practised bears eloquent testimony to this lamentable fact.

Moreover, the extrinsic dissolubility of matrimony renders the rearing and education of children very difficult: when new nuptials are contracted, children are of necessity separated from their father or mother, and are exposed to neglect and abandonment.

b) The extrinsic dissolubility of matrimony is a serious obstacle to the attainment of its secondary end.— It disturbs the stability of the conjugal union, and thus does great harm to the faithfulness, happiness, and peace of the husband and wife. Moreover, it weakens their mutual love, which is destined for a permanent union: as conjugal love is total, it tends to permanence and is irrevocable. Finally, it is deleterious to the dignity of wives, whose place in civil and domestic society is shamefully lowered, and who are exposed to the danger « of being considered outcasts, slaves of the lust of men. »

c) The extrinsic dissolubility of matrimony is at variance with morality.— It disturbs the peace of families, multiplies the occasions for quarrels, and leads to the corruption of morals.

Pope Leo XIII gives the following list of evils which result from divorce : « matrimonial contracts are made mutable; mutual good will is lessened ; pernicious inducements to unfaithfulness are provided ; harm is done to the education and training of children ; occasion is afforded for the breaking up of homes ; the seeds of dissension are sown among families ; the dignity of woman is lessened and brought low, and women, after having been used to satisfy the passions of their husbands, run the risk of being deserted. Therefore, since nothing has such power to ruin families and to destroy the mainstay of kingdoms as the corruption of morals, it is easily seen that divorces are in the highest degree hostile to the prosperity of families and States »(¹).

---

(1) *Arcanum Divinae.*

1061. Scholion.— Since matrimony is extrinsically indissoluble in virtue of the secondary precepts of the natural law, no human power, civil or ecclesiastical, can dissolve it.

Nevertheless, it can be dissolved by divine power, which, as we have seen, can give an improper dispensation from the secondary precepts of the natural law. Such dissolution of marriage takes place when the Church, in virtue of divine power granted t oit, dissolves a non-consummated marriage([1]), or a lawful marriage between unbaptized persons, even though consummated, in favor of the Faith by virtue of the Pauline Privilege([2]).

1062. Difficulties.— 1° Any contract can be dissolved by the free consent of the contracting parties. But matrimony is a contract. Therefore matrimony can be dissolved by the free consent of the contracting parties.

Major.— A contract whose nature and object depend solely on the free consent of the contracting parties, *I concede*; a contract whose nature and object are also determined by the natural law, *I deny.*

Minor.— Matrimony is a contract whose nature and object depend solely on the free consent of the contracting parties, *I deny*; whose nature and object are also determined by the natural law, *I concede.*

2° Matrimony is indissoluble because of the good of the child. But, in certain cases, matrimony is contrary to the good of the child, v. g., when the husband cannot beget a child of one woman, but could of another, and vice versa. Therefore, at least in certain cases, matrimony ought not to be indissoluble.

Major.— Is indissoluble because of the good of the child in an absolute sense, *I concede*; because of the good of this or that child, *I deny.*

Minor.— Is contrary to the good of the child in an absolute sense, *I deny*; to the good of this or that child, *I concede.*

The indissolubility of matrimony is determined by the natural law. But a law is an ordinance for the *common good.* Therefore the laws of matrimony are concerned with what is expedient for all rather than with what may be suitable for one (3).

3° When cohabitation becomes impossible, as in cases of insuperable hatred, of constant discord, etc., divorce is preferable to continual quarreling. But cases of this kind are by no means rare. Therefore sometimes divorce is preferable to the indissolubility of matrimony.

Major.— Imperfect divorce, i.e., separation from bed and board, provided that the necessary precautions are taken, *I concede*; divorce in the strict sense is preferable from the point of view of the good of the husband and wife, *let it go*; from the point of view of the common good, *I deny.*

I concede the minor.

---

(1) *Code of Canon Law,* can. 1119.
(2) *Ibid.,* can. 1120.
(3) *Suppl.,* q. 67; a. 1, ad 4.

The indissolubility of matrimony is because of the common good, and therefore remains firm, even though sometimes beset with inconvenience for individual spouses.

POINTS FOR REVIEW

1. Define: the indissolubility, intrinsic indissolubility, and extrinsic indissolubility of matrimony.

2. Prove that the intrinsic indissolubility of matrimony is contrary to the primary precepts, and its extrinsic indissolubility to the secondary precepts, of the natural law.

CHAPTER II

PARENTAL SOCIETY

Prologue.— In this chapter, we shall deal with parental authority and the education of children. Hence there will be two articles in the chapter.

Parental authority
- Statement of the question
- Erroneous opinions
- Thesis: Parental authority is derived from God, the author of nature
- Authority of husband and wife in parental society
- Emancipation of women
- Duties of children

Education of children
- Statement of the question
- Erroneous opinions
- Thesis: According to the natural law, the education of children belongs properly and directly to the parents
- Rights of the Church in education
- Rights of the State in education
- Scholia
- Monopoly of instruction
- Neutral schools
- Liberty of the school

ARTICLE I

PARENTAL AUTHORITY

1063. Statement of the question.—1° Parental authority is authority proper to parental society. Parental society is defined : *the union of parents and children established by nature for the purpose of education.* This definition contains the material cause of parental society, which is the parents and children ; the efficient cause, which is nature ; and the final cause, which is the education of children : *physical*, which consists in the progressive well-ordered development of these faculties on which bodily health and strength principally depend ; *intellectual*, which consists in the acquirement of truth ; *moral*, which consists in the acquirement of the moral virtues.

2° Parental authority is defined : *the relation of parents to children, in as much as the latter are directed as subjects by the former to the end of parental society.*

3° In the thesis, we state that parental authority is derived from God, the author of nature. By this we mean not only that all authority, considered under its general aspect of authority, is derived from God, but that parental authority as such derives from Him.

1064. Erroneous opinions.— 1° Hobbes teaches that paternal authority is derived from the right of victory, i.e., from the power of possession, in as much as the child, which he considers as a *res nullius*, i.e., as belonging to no one, comes first into the possession of the parents.

2° Pufendorf teaches that parental authority is derived from a pact between parents and children which is implicit on the part of the parents, and tacit or presumed on the part of the children.

3° Arhens maintains that it is derived solely from education.

4° Rousseau holds that parental authority derives from civil authority. This opinion is supported by socialists, who give parents either no jurisdiction whatsoever over their children, or only such power as they derive from the State.

1065. Statement of the thesis.

THESIS.— PARENTAL AUTHORITY IS DERIVED FROM GOD, THE AUTHOR OF NATURE.

Authority derived from nature is authority derived from God, Who is the author of nature. But parental authority is derived from nature. Therefore parental authority is derived from God, the author of nature.

The *major* is evident.

Minor.— Parents are related to their children as efficient cause to its effects. It naturally follows from this that parents are able to conduct children to their end, which is their advance to the state of perfect man. In other words, it naturally follows that parents have authority over their children.

1066. Authority of husband and wife in parental society.— 1° Husband and wife enjoy equality « in those rights which belong to the dignity of the human person, and which are proper to the marriage contract and inseparably bound up with wedlock. In such things, undoubtedly both parties enjoy the same rights and are bound by the same obligations([1]) ».

2° But there cannot be equality of rights of husband and wife in matters which are proper to parental society as such,

---

(1) Pius XI, *Casti connubii*.

for parental authority is vested *principally* in the husband, and *secondarily* in the wife. In order words, for the attainment of the end of parental society, the wife must be subordinate to the husband.

This subordination is not the subordination of a slave to a master : « The husband is the chief of the family and the head of the wife(¹), » and hence « the wife must be subject to her husband and obey him, not, indeed, as a servant, but as a companion(²).» Moreover, this is required for the intimate friendship which should exist between husband and wife.

3° In the light of what we have just said, we may now summarize, in the propositions which follow, our teaching on the authority of husband and wife in parental society.

a) Equal division of authority between husband and wife, in parental society, is contrary to the natural law.— A division of authority which of its very nature is opposed to order is contrary to the natural law. But the equal division of authority between husband and wife, in parental society, is of its very nature opposed to order. Therefore the equal division of authority between husband and wife, in parental society, is contrary to the natural law.

Major. — The natural law is the measure of order.

Minor.— Parental society is a natural society directed to a common end. But, if husband and wife enjoyed equal authority in parental society, paternal society would not tend to a common end: there would be two equal principles of direction to an end, each giving a different direction, for things which are different naturally tend to different ends. Therefore.

b) Parental authority resides principally in the husband.— Parental authority is vested principally in the spouse which is naturally the superior. But the husband is superior to the wife in strength of body, perspicacity of mind, is more prudent, better fitted for achievement, more resolute, and sounder in judgment. Moreover, it is entirely accidental that the wife

---
(1) Leo XIII, *Arcanum.*
(2) *Ibidem.*

sometimes is superior to the husband in qualities of mind and strength of body. But things are superior according to the natural law which are superior of their very nature, not things which are only accidentally superior. Hence parental authority, according to the natural law, resides principally in the husband.

1067. Emancipation of women.— Moderns boldly proclaim the emancipation of woman, i.e., full equality of the rights of husband and wife.

Some proclaim the *physiological* emancipation of women, whereby the wife is free or ought to be freed, at her own good pleasure, from the burdensome duties which properly belong to her as companion and mother. This kind of emancipation is not true emancipation, but a heinous crime.

Others proclaim *economic* emancipation, whereby the wife, even without the knowledge and against the wish of her husband, is free to have, conduct, and administer her own affairs, being chiefly concerned with these rather than with children, husband, and family.

Others proclaim *social* emancipation, whereby the wife, freed from the domestic cares of children and family, may, to the neglect of these, follow her own bent, and devote herself to business and even to public affairs.

In regard to this threefold emancipation of women, the following observations must be made.

a) The so-called emancipation of women proclaimed by moderns constitutes an *unnatural* equality of wife with husband, and therefore is a debasing of the womanly character and the dignity of motherhood, a perversion of the whole family, as a result of which the husband is deprived of his wife, the children of their mother, and the whole family of an ever watchful guardian. Such emancipation, therefore, is detrimental to the wife, for, if woman descends from her truly regal throne in the home, to which the Gospel and nature raised her, she will soon be reduced to her former state of slavery, and become, as among the pagans, the mere instrument of man.

b) Equality of rights of husband and wife must indeed be recognized in matters which pertain to the dignity of the human person, and which are proper to the marriage contract and inseparably bound up with wedlock; in all other matters, however, there must be inequality and due accommodation, such as are demanded for the good of the family and the right ordering, unity, and stability of domestic society, i.e., of home life.

c) The civil authority may, and, indeed, has an obligation to adapt the civil rights of the wife to modern needs and requirements, but always in accordance with the statutes of the natural law (¹).

1068. Duties of children. — The foundation of the duties of children towards their parents is clearly and succinctly explained by St. Thomas in these words: « Man becomes a debtor to others in various ways, in proportion to their various degrees of perfection, and to the various benefits received from them. In both of these ways, God holds first place, because He possesses all perfections, and is the first principle of our being and government; and, in the second place, as principles of our being and government, come our parents and our country, for from our parents and in our country we have received both birth and sustenance. Therefore man is a debtor chiefly to his parents and his country, after God. Hence, just as man, in virtue of religion, owes worship to God, so too, in virtue of piety, he owes reverence to his parents and his country.

Moreover, the reverence man owes his parents extends to reverence owed to his kinsfolk, because the latter receive their name from the fact that they descend from the same parents. The reverence man owes his country extends to reverence owed to all his compatriots and to all friends of his country (¹) ».

POINTS FOR REVIEW

1. Define: parental society, parental authority.

---

(1) Pius XI, *Casti Connubii.*
(1) II-II, q. 101, a. 1.

2. Prove that parental authority is derived from God, the author of nature, and that the equal division of it between husband and wife is at variance with statutes of the natural law.

3. Explain what is meant by the emancipation of women, and show whether or not it is a desideratum of family life.

4. What, according to St. Thomas, is the foundation of children's obligations to their parents?

ARTICLE II

EDUCATION OF CHILDREN

1069. Statement of the question.— 1° St. Thomas defines education as *the rearing and elevation of children to the status of perfect man, which is the state of virtue*(¹).

Education is physical, intellectual, moral, and civic, and consists respectively in the development of the body, the intellect, the will, and the citizen as such. Hence education does not consist merely in instruction, though instruction is an important part of it.

2° In our present study, we are concerned with education from the point of view of the natural order. For, in the supernatural order, the Church has the direct and immediate right of teaching all men, and consequently, in the matter of religious education, parents are only the mandataries of the Church.

3° According to the natural law, the education of children belongs properly and directly to the parents.

Since education belongs to parents according to the natural law, parents have not only the strict duty, but also the inalienable right to educate their children, a right inviolable on the part of any human power.

We say that education belongs *properly* to parents, because, when parents fail in the fulfillment of their duty in this regard, the duty of providing for the education of their children accidentally devolves upon the civil authority.

Moreover, we say that the education of children belongs *directly* to the parents, because, in view of the common good, it belongs *indirectly* to civil society as well.

---

(1) *Suppl.*, q. 41, a. 1.

1070. Erroneous opinions.— 1° Plato in his day, and socialists in our day, hold that the education of children belongs to civil society rather than to the parents.

2° Anarchists, who refuse to recognize the authority of civil society and the indissolubility of the marriage bond, maintain that children born of *free unions* should be educated by those who adopt them.

1071. Statement of the thesis.

> **THESIS.**— ACCORDING TO THE NATURAL LAW, THE EDUCATION OF CHILDREN BELONGS PROPERLY AND DIRECTLY TO THE PARENTS.

1° According to the natural law, the rearing and elevation of children to the status of perfect man properly and directly belong to the parents. But education is the rearing and elevation of children to the status of perfect man. Therefore the education of children, according to the natural law, belongs properly and directly to the parents.

Major.— Since the imperfect always tends to, i.e., is in view of, the perfect, the rearing and elevation of children to the status of perfect man properly and directly belong, according to the law of nature, to those who produce them. But children are produced, i.e., engendered, by their parents. Therefore.

The *minor* is the definition of education.

2° According to the natural law, the education of children belongs properly and directly to those who are naturally possessed of a special inclination and aptitude for the office of educator. But nature has endowed parents with such an inclination and aptitude. Therefore, according to the natural law, the education of children belongs properly and directly to the parents.

Major. — Natural inclination and aptitude correspond to the statutes of the law of nature.

Minor. — Parents are naturally possessed of parental love of their children, patience with them, intimate association with them, lively interest in them, and with all the other qualifications so necessary for the education of children.

3° According to the natural law, the education of children belongs properly and directly either to the parents or to civil society, i.e., to the State. But the education of children does not belong properly and directly to civil society. Therefore.

Minor. — The necessity of education arose with the establishment of conjugal society, i.e., of the family. But conjugal society is anterior to civil society. Therefore.

1072. Rights of the Church in education. — 1° *Existence of the rights of the Church in the education of children.* — *a)* From the point of view merely of the natural law, the Church has as much right as any creditable association, or as any individual, to undertake, with the mandate or consent of the parents, the work of educating children, in order to supply for the insufficiency of families.

For the exercise of this right, two conditions are required :

1) *consent of the parents;*

2) *respect for the order required for the common good of civil society*, i.e., there must be nothing in the children's education which is contrary to the common good.

b) The Church enjoys a special *historical* title to contribute freely to the education of children. For the Church not only always had its own schools, but was, in reality, the founder of popular, i.e., public, schools[1].

c) The right to educate children belongs preeminently to the Church in virtue of a twofold title of the supernatural

---
(1) OTTAVIANI, *Institutiones Juris Publici Ecclesisatici*, t. II, p. 226. (Edit. 1a).

order, which belongs exclusively to the Church and is superior to any title of the natural order.

The *first title* is the supreme authority and teaching office conferred upon the Church by its Divine Founder in these words : « All power is given to me in heaven and in earth. Going therefore teach ye all nations : baptizing them in the name of the Father, and of the Son, and of the Holy Ghost. Teaching them to observe all things whatsoever I have commanded you : and behold I am with you all days, even to the consummation of the world ([1]).»

The *second title* is the supernatural motherhood, in virtue of which the Church, spotless spouse of Christ, engenders, nurtures, and educates souls in the divine life of grace with her Sacraments and doctrine ([2]).

Therefore, just as in the natural order the education of children belongs primarily to the parents, so in the supernatural order it belongs primarily to the Church.

In the natural order, the education of children does not belong exclusively to the parents, because, as we shall see later, the State also enjoys certain rights in regard to the education of children. In the supernatural order, education belongs exclusively to the Church, so that teachers, the State, and even parents act only as the mandataries of the Church in the specifically Christian education of children.

2° *Extent of the rights of the Church in education.*— a) The extent of the rights of the Church in the field of education is such as to embrace all nations.

First, these rights extend over all the Faithful, of whom the Church, as a loving and watchful mother, has the tender care.

Secondly, they extend even to infidels, because all men are called by God to attain eternal salvation.

b) The proper object of the Church's supernatural mission is the specifically Christian formation, i.e., education, of the

---
[1] Matt., XXVIII, 18-20.
[2] *Divini illius Magistri*, 31 Dec., 1929.

child. But, since the Church is a perfect society, it may, independently of any human power, pass judgment on and make use of all the means necessary and useful for the attainment of this end. The rights of the Church in regard to education, therefore, extend to everything which is necessary or useful for Christian education. Hence these rights extend to intellectual, moral, physical, and civic education, in so far as these have relation to faith and morals.

Hence the Church may have its own schools. It has the supreme right of watching over the whole of the education of Catholic children, of taking care that the education provided by parents, teachers, and the State is directed to the supernatural end, and is not opposed to Christian faith and morals.

1073. Rights of the State in education.— 1° Civil society is a *natural and perfect society whose end is the perfect sufficiency of life, i.e., the common good.* Civil society is sometimes called the State. But the State, in a strict sense, is only a part of civil society, namely, the governing body of civil society.

2° We have already learned that the education of children belongs naturally and directly to the parents.

The State, nevertheless, has certain natural and indirect rights in regard to the education of children.

These rights are called *natural*, because they are founded in nature, and *indirect*, because they are not directly concerned with education, but with common good, to which education should be directed.

Hence the rights of the State in the field of education are *primarily* subsidiary, and *secondarily* supplemental.

These rights are primarily *subsidiary*, because the State has an obligation to assist parents and the Church in the education of children; and they are secondarily *supplemental*, because the State may, when necessity arises, complete the education of children by opening schools and institutions of its own.

3° In the light of the foregoing explanation, we may now set forth the rights of the State in regard to the education of children.

a) The State has a natural and indirect right to educate children.— The State has a right to educate children, because it is charged with the care of the common good of the members of civil society. But this right is natural and indirect. Therefore the State has a natural and indirect right to educate children.

Major.— Since the State is charged with the care of the common good, it has received from nature the right to direct to the common good all that is useful and necessary for it. But the education of children is useful and necessary for the common good. Therefore.

Minor.— This right is natural, because the State, as a natural and perfect society, has received from nature the right over all that is useful and necessary for the attainment of its end; and it is indirect, because the State is not directly concerned with education *in itself*, but rather with education *in view of the common good.*

b) Civil society has the right and the duty to protect the anterior educational rights of the family.— Civil society has the right and duty to protect the rights proper to the family. But the family possesses rights of its own in regard to education which are anterior to the rights of civil society. Therefore the State has the right and the duty to protect the anterior educational rights of the family.

Major.— According to the order of nature, the family, just as the individual, has its own proper ends in society, and therefore proper rights, which must be safeguarded in civil society.

Hence civil society has the right and the duty to protect the rights proper to the family, not abolish them.

Minor.— The education of children, which is an end proper to the family, belongs properly and directly to the parents, as we have already seen.

c) Civil society has the right and the duty to promote in various ways the education and instruction of youth.— Civil society has the right and the duty to promote in various ways whatever may be required for the attainment of the ends proper to the family. But the education and instruction of youth are required for the attainment of an end proper to the family. Therefore civil society has the right and the duty to promote in various ways the education and instruction of youth.

Major.— The proper ends of the family, according to the natural law, are directed to the common good, which is the end of civil society. Hence, if civil society did not have the right and the duty to promote in various ways whatever may be required for the attainment of the proper ends of the family, nature would be deficient in necessities.

The *minor* is evident from what has been already said.

1074. Scholia.— 1° The rights of civil society in education are, as we have already said, *subsidiary* and *supplemental*.

a) Hence civil society has an obligation to protect children's rights to education when their parents are found wanting either physically or morally in this regard.

b) In like manner, civil society has the right and the duty to protect, according to the rules of right reason and of faith, the moral and religious education of youth by removing any public impediments that stand in its way.

c) Besides, civil society should promote the education of youth by encouraging and assisting the Church and the family in educational activities undertaken by them. Moreover, if the work of the Church and family falls short of what is necessary, it may supplement it, even by founding its own schools and institutions.

d) Finally, civil society may order and take measures to ensure that all citizens be sufficiently instructed in their civic and political duties, and that they obtain a certain degree of physical, intellectual, and moral culture, which, in consideration of conditions such as obtain in our day, is really necessary for the common good.

2° Civil society may reserve to itself the establishment and direction of schools intended for the training of candidates for civic duties, and especially for military service, provided that it does not violate the rights proper to the Church and to the family.

3° Finally, the State has the right to provide *civic* education not only for its youth, but also for all ages and classes. Civic education consists positively in the practice of presenting publicly a program of almost all the activities related to the end of civil society, and negatively in the suppression of what is opposed to this end[1].

1075. Monopoly of instruction. — 1° *Preliminaries.* — *a)* Monopoly of instruction consists in the exclusive privilege which the State reserves to itself of opening schools, or of binding parents by law to send their children to State schools.

Monopoly of instruction exists also in the case in which the State morally, though not legally, forces parents to send their children to State schools, v.g., by showing favor only to State schools, and by imposing vexatious obligations upon private schools, and by depriving them of their rightful subsides.

b) Monopoly of instruction is advocated by Rationalists and by all who deny that parents have natural and direct rights over the education of their children.

There are some, however, who, making a distinction between *education* and *instruction*, hold that the rights of education belong to the parents, and the rights of instruction to the civil authority. But this contention is false, because instruction *a)* is a part, and not the least important part, of education; *b)* is the principal means of education.

2° *In the light of the foregoing observations,* we may now prove the proposition which follows.

---

(1) *Divini illius M gistri.*

Monopoly of instruction is a direct violation of the natural and direct rights of parents over the education of their children.

1) Parents, according to the natural law, have a direct right and duty to educate their children, and therefore they have the right to determine the means by which their children's education may be completed, and of choosing teachers as mandataries to whom it is entrusted. But monopoly of instruction deprives parents of the right to determine the means by which their children's education may be completed, and also of the right of choosing teachers, for they are denied the right of opening schools. Therefore monopoly of instruction is a direct violation of the natural and direct rights of parents over the education of their children.

Major.— Education is the proper end of the family living in society.

The minor is self-evident.

2) Monopoly of instruction is a violation of the rights of the Church, for the Church received from its Divine Founder the mission of teaching all nations, and therefore it has, by divine ordination, the right to open schools.

1076. Neutral schools.— The neutral or lay school is a school from which is excluded all religious instruction, at least all confessional religious instruction, as it is called.

This kind of school is very dangerous and must be avoided.

In the first place, *neutrality* is impossible. For the silence of the school in regard to God and religious duties is tantamount to a denial of the supreme importance of religion, which is necessarily regarded as something secondary and entirely optional. Moreover, experience has clearly shown that the neutral school either is or will become hostile to religion.

Secondly, the neutral school, in maintaining silence about God, Who is the ultimate end of all education, destroys the very nature of education, interferes with the supreme rights and duties of parents, who are under obligation to provide for the religious education of their children, and with the rights of children, who have a right to religious education. Moreover, it is subversive of the foundations of all morality, since there can be no morality without religion.

We deny that a school can be non-confessional, and that it can teach certain common principles in regard to God and religion. Such a school cannot exist in practice; it is bound to become irreligious. For to teach certain common principles of religion and to be silent about others is tantamount to teaching pupils that the common principles are necessary and that all others are optional. This, of course, is the pernicious error of dogmatic indifferentism.

Again, we may not admit that sufficient provision is made for religious education when religion is taught in school after school hours, or in the home by the parents, or in the church. For, in this case, religion again appears as something of secondary importance and optional, or at least as separable from the other subjects of the school curriculum; and it would appear as if religious truths ought not to illuminate all forms of knowledge and permeate all adolescent training.

Finally, the neutral school is opposed to the rights of the Church, which has the right and the duty to provide for the religious education of baptized children even in the schools; and, as experience everywhere has clearly shown, it leads to spiritual and moral ruin.

1077. Liberty of the school.— 1° Monopoly of instruction, as we have seen, is unjust and unlawful. Hence the State must avoid everything which leads to monopoly of instruction, and must recognize the true liberty of the school.

2° Liberty of the school comprises three elements:

a) the power of parents and of the Church to erect their own schools and institutions, or, as they are called, private (separate) schools and institutions;

b) the suppression of all restrictions on the public effects of instruction given in these schools and institutions;

c) *a proportionate distribution of educational subsidies.*

3° The first element, i.e., the power of erecting private schools, derives from the rights of parents and of the Church in education.

4° The second element consists in giving the same value and public recognition to diplomas and academic degrees obtained in private schools as are given to those obtained in State schools.

If this is not done,

a) the State school becomes, at least in practice, obligatory on all; and this, of course, is a violation of the rights of both parents and the Church;

b) the competence and efficiency of teachers in private schools, who are on a par in ability, training, and academic degrees with teachers in State schools, are not given just recognition, i.e., teachers in private schools are classified as inferior in competence and efficiency to teachers in State schools;

c) the pupils of private schools are, in consequence, deprived of the recognition and advantages accorded pupils of public schools.

The civic authority, however, may require pupils of both public and private schools to pass *State examinations* before admission to universities or institutions of higher learning, or before beginning practice in the professions.

5° The third element is the just distribution of educational subsidies.

This element is necessary, for if the State did not make a just distribution of educational subsidies, it would unjustly discourage private initiative, and would fail in its duty of distributive justice towards *all* its citizens ([1]).

POINTS FOR REVIEW

1. Define education, and prove that the education of children belongs properly and directly to the parents.

---

(1) OTTAVIANI, *op. cit.*, pp. 228-231.

2. Name and explain the titles by which education belongs to the Church.

3. What are the rights of the State in regard to education. Explain why these rights are primarily subsidiary, and secondarily supplemental.

4. State what is meant by monopoly of instruction, and explain why it is a violation of the rights of parents and of the Church.

5. What do you understand by the neutral school? Do you approve of this type of school? Give reasons for your answer.

6. What elements are required for liberty of the school? Explain.

HERILE SOCIETY

1078. Slavery in Aristotle.— 1° Herile society, according to Aristotle, is the union of master and slave in domestic society.

Herile society is regarded by Aristotle as natural, in as much as it naturally befits some to serve, and others to rule. Moreover, he maintains that slavery is necessary for the home.

2° The slave is defined by Aristotle: *a man existing as a separate, active, and animated implement of another man* [1].

a) *Implement*, i.e., a kind of instrument.

b) *Animated:* thus the slave is distinguished from inanimate instruments.

c) *Active*, in as much as the slave's duty is concerned with *actions*, not with *factions*, i.e., the *making* of things. For the slave serves domestic *life*. Thus the slave is distinguished from the artificer, who is a factive animated instrument.

d) *Of another man:* thus the slave is distinguished from the free man, the domestic servant, who, not as the possession of the family, but of his free will, or hired on wages, gives his services in the family.

e) *Separate:* a slave is distinct from a part of another which is not a separate part, as the hand.

f) *Man existing:* the slave is distinct from irrational animals, which are separate possessions.

Hence, according to Aristotle, the slave, though the property of the master, retains his human dignity, and, under a certain aspect, is superior to the artificer. For, whereas the duty of the artificer is concerned with *factions*, i.e., the making of things, the duty of the slave is concerned with *actions*.

Moreover, slavery is a good for the slave, in as much as he is ruled by a superior, i.e., by a master.

Slavery, as conceived by Aristotle, does not exist today.

1079. Domestic servants.— The domestic servant is not a slave, but a person who receives wages for services given in domestic society.

The domestic servant, in serving in domestic society, enjoys a certain participation in the life of the family, and works for the end of domestic society.

Hence, under this aspect, the duty or function of the servant is nobler than that of the artificer, who, as such, is concerned only with the *making* of material things.

Therefore the domestic servant has a special right to protection from the head of the family, and to kindness from the whole family.

End of Economics

POLITICS

INTRODUCTION

1080. Notion of Politics.— Politics is the part of Moral Philosophy which treats of political or civil society.

Politics is defined: *the practical science which considers human acts as directed to the common good of civil society;* or, *the science which deals with man in his life in civil society.*

The *material object* of Politics is human acts.

Its *formal object* « *quod* » is human acts as directed to the end of civil society, i.e., to the common good.

Its *formal object* « *quo* » is the common good, i.e., the end of civil society.

Since the common good, i.e., the perfect sufficiency of life, is specifically distinct from the end of individual man and from the end of domestic society, Politics as a science is specifically distinct from Monastics and from Economics.

Moreover, since the common good is the greatest of all human goods, Politics is the principal part of Moral Philosophy, and is wisdom in the order of the practical sciences, just as Metaphysics is wisdom in the order of the speculative sciences.

1081. Division of Politics.— Politics is specifically and numerically a single science, for it considers human acts as directed to one and the same end, namely, the perfect sufficiency of life, i.e., the natural happiness of this life. We divide it into three books.

In the first book, we shall deal with the causes of civil society, and with civil authority, which is a power which necessarily results from the nature of society.

In the second book, we shall treat of the restoration of society, according to the principles of sound philosophy and the doctrine of the Church.

In the third book, we shall discuss the question of the relations between different societies. In this book, we shall deal with the relations between civil societies as parts of international society, and with the relations between civil society and the Church.

Therefore our division of Politics is as follows:

Book   I: Causes of civil society.
Book II: Restoration of society.
Book III: Relation between societies.

BOOK I

Causes of civil society

Prologue.— Since the end is the principle in practical sciences, our first consideration will concern the end of civil society; and, having determined the end of civil society, we shall study its origin. This will be the work of the first chapter. In the second chapter, we treat of the material cause of civil society. In the third chapter, we shall deal with civil authority. Hence this book will contain the following chapters:

Chapter   I. End and origin of civil society.

Chapter II. Material cause of civil society.

Chapter III. Civil authority.

CHAPTER I

END AND ORIGIN OF CIVIL SOCIETY

Prologue.— There will be two articles in this chapter.

End of civil society
- Statement of the question
- Opinions
- Thesis: Civil society is directed to an end; and this end is the temporal happiness of this life as directed to a divine good
- Scholia

Origin of civil society
- Statement of the question
- Opinions of adversaries
- Thesis: Man is bound by his nature, i.e., by God, the author of nature, to live in society
- Historical causes of civil society

ARTICLE I

END OF CIVIL SOCIETY

1082. Statement of the question.— 1° Civil society, called the State by the ancients, is political society, and may be defined: *the perfect natural society* (¹).

It is called a *natural* society, because it is according to the design of nature, and because it owes its establishment to men acting under the impulse of nature; it is called a *perfect* society, because its end is a perfect good, namely, the perfect sufficiency of life, i.e., happiness.

2° Man's happiness is of two kinds: *natural*, which is the temporal happiness of this life, and *supernatural*, which consists in the beatific vision.

Man cannot attain supernatural happiness unless he lives in, i.e., is a member of, the Church founded by our Savior Jesus Christ. The Church is a perfect society, for its end is a perfect good, the most perfect of all goods.

Hence civil society may be described: *the most perfect of all human societies* (²).

It is described as *most perfect*, because all other human societies, as domestic society, commercial and industrial societies, and the various associations are parts of civil society.

Moreover, it is said to be the most perfect of all *human* societies, because civil society is a society set up according to human reason, and thus is distinct from the Church, which is a society founded and established *by God*.

---

(1) *In Politic.*, l. I, l. 1.
(2) *In Politic.*, Prologus s. Thomae.

3° In the thesis, first, we shall prove that civil society was instituted for an end; and, secondly, we shall prove that this end is the temporal happiness of this life.

The temporal happiness of this life contains two elements: *life*, and a *good life*, i.e., a *life consisting in the practice of the virtues*.

Hence the temporal happiness of this life consists principally in the practice of virtue, and instrumentally in those bodily and external goods, the use of which is necessary for a life of virtue (¹).

4° Although human happiness is the most important of all human goods, it is not, nevertheless, man's absolutely ultimate end, which is the divine good.

The divine good, as we consider it in the thesis, is God, as He is, from the natural point of view only, the ultimate end of all human acts, and also as He is the supernatural end, attainable in Himself, in the beatific vision. We state in the thesis that the end of civil society is the temporal happiness of this life as directed to the divine good considered as the natural and supernatural end.

1083. Opinions.— 1° Some deny that civil society has a natural end, i.e., is directed to an end determined by nature.

a) Agnostics and Positivists teach that civil society has no final cause, or at least no final cause of which we can have certain knowledge.

This opinion is held also by the Evolutionists, as Spencer, who consider the *battle for existence* as the explanation of all social conditions.

b) Haller and Fouillée claim that the end of civil society is the same as the end of the private societies of which it is constituted.

---

(1) Since it is the end of society to make man better, the chief good society can possess is virtue. Nevertheless, in all well-constituted States it is in no wise a matter of small moment to provide those bodily and external commodities, « the use of which is necessary to virtuous action ».— *Rerum Novarum.— Divini Redemptoris*, n. 75.

c) Montesquieu holds that each civil society has a proper and special end of its own choice; v.g., the end of the Spartan State is war; of Athens, culture; of England, political liberty; of the Jewish nation, religion; of the kingdoms of Rome and Carthage, world domination.

2° Others restrict the end of civil society.

a) The adherents of materialism hold that the common good, i.e., the end of civil society, consists in material goods.

b) Kant, considering that liberty, which he confounds with moral independence, is something almost divine to which all else must be subject, restricts the supreme duty of the State to the mere protection of liberty, i.e., to the establishing of conditions under which the liberty of one person is made compatible with the external liberty of all others.

c) The advocates of Liberalism imagine that the liberty of man living in society tends to what is best. Hence they hold that the end of civil society is the protection of private rights from which peace and harmony result. This is the opinion of Quesnay and Adam Smith.

Certain Catholics favor this opinion in some measure. But, in doing so, they are concerned only with the end which is the form of society.

d) Certain Moderns hold that the instinct of the race is the first source and the supreme rule of the whole juridical order. Hence they restrict the end of civil society to the development of the perfection of the race.

3° Others exaggerate the end of civil society, either by considering it as an absolute end not directed to God as to its ultimate end, or, rejecting the natural law, in holding that civil society is the sole source or principle of all individual and domestic rights.

a) Modern Pantheists, as Schelling and Hegel, teach that civil society is the ultimate term of the evolution of the Deity. Durkheim favors this opinion to some degree.

b) According to Plato, the State is a superior man to which the citizens are subordinate as the members to the body, in order that it live a life of virtue.

c) Machiavelli, Hobbes, and the Democrats, as Rousseau, teach that a thing is just or unjust, good or evil, because it is commanded or prohibited either by the ruler or by the State, i.e., by the people.

This opinion is held also by many Moderns, especially in Germany, who teach that the State is the source and the end of man's being.

Later, we shall deal with the relations of individuals and families to the State.

1084. Statement of the thesis.

> **THESIS.**— CIVIL SOCIETY IS DIRECTED TO AND END; AND THIS END IS THE TEMPORAL HAPPINESS OF THIS LIFE AS DIRECTED TO DIVINE GOOD.

First part.— *Civil society is directed to an end.*— Every society instituted by man is directed to an end. But civil society owes its institution to man. Therefore civil society is directed to an end.

Major.— Man performs all his operations in view of something which appears to him as a good, i.e., for some end. But every society instituted by man owes its institution to human operation. Therefore every society instituted by man is directed to an end ([1]).

The *minor* is evident.

Second part.— *The end of civil society is the temporal happiness of this life.*— The end of the most perfect of all human societies is the temporal happiness of this life. But civil society is the most perfect of all human societies.

---

(1) *In Politic.*, l. I, l. 1.

Therefore the end of civil society is the temporal happiness of this life.

Major.— Since the proportion existing between things directed to an end is commensurate to the proportion which obtains between their ends, the end of the most perfect of all human societies is the most perfect of all human goods. But the most perfect of all human goods is the temporal happiness of this life: for happiness is the ultimate end for which man acts; and supernatural happiness, both of this life and of the life to come, is not a human good, but a divine good, i.e., a good which is unattainable by the power proper to man. Therefore.

Minor.— Just as that whole is most perfect of which all other wholes are parts, so too that human society is most perfect of which all other societies are parts. But civil society embraces all other societies, viz., domestic societies, municipalities, associations of various kinds, etc. Therefore.

Third part.— *The temporal happiness of this life is directed to divine good*, i.e., *to the beatific vision.*— Every human good is directed to divine good. But the temporal happiness of this life is a human good. Therefore the temporal happiness of this life is directed to divine good.

The *major* is evident: divine good is the absolutely ultimate end of all human acts.

The *minor* also is evident: the temporal happiness of this life is the most perfect of all human goods.

1085. Scholia.-- 1° The temporal happiness of this life is the common good, in as much as men can attain it only by living in society and by common means (¹), and in as much as private happiness can be only a part of the common happiness (²).

---

(1) *De Regimine Principum*, l. XIV.
(2) II-II, q. 47, a. 10, ad 2.

The end of civil society is called, without qualification, the *common good*, because it is man's most perfect common good. But we may speak of the common good of domestic society, or of any other community, since the end of every society is a common good.

2° The peace and security of all may be called the end of civil society (¹). But peace as signifying the tranquillity of order, i.e., well-ordered harmony among men, which obtains when each one is given his due, is the intrinsic end of civil society, whereas happiness is its extrinsic end.

3° The end of civil society is formally distinct from the good proper to individual men: for the former is the common good which corresponds to human nature, whereas the latter is that good which corresponds to individual man as such. Therefore the end of civil society is not the aggregate of the ends of individual men, and civil society is a heterogeneous society.

4° Civil society must attain its end by external means, for men communicate in society by external actions. Nevertheless, the end of civil society consists chiefly in goods of the soul (²), i.e., in a life of virtue, as we have said.

5° Even though man had not been elevated to the supernatural order, civil society would be a religious society, i.e., it would have the care of religion and of public divine worship. But, because of man's elevation to a supernatural end and the existence of the Church, which is charged by God with all that pertains to the attainment of this end, *a)* the direct care of religion was removed from civil society, and committed to the Church (³); *b)* and civil society is subordinate to the Church,

---

(1) Education cannot pertain to civil society in the same way in which it pertains to the Church and to the family, but in a different way corresponding to its own particular end and object. Now this end and object, the common welfare in the temporal order, consists in that peace and security in which families and individual citizens have the free exercise of their rights and at the same time enjoy the greatest spiritual and temporal prosperity possible in this life, by the mutual union and coordination of the work of all.— *Divini illius Magistri.*
(2) *Divini Redemptoris*, n. 73.
(3) It is the Church, and not the State, that is to be man's guide to heaven. It is to the Church that God has assigned the charge of seeing to,

whose end is the absolutely ultimate end of the whole of human life.

Hence civil society has an obligation to encourage and support the work of the Church, and thus exercise indirect care over religion. In the concrete, civil society is in duty bound to show due reverence to the holy name of God, to rid its territories of the teachings of atheism, and, having embraced the true religion, to protect it by the benevolence and authority of its laws, and to institute or decree nothing which would be a danger to its safety and security ([1]).

POINTS FOR REVIEW

1. Define civil society; explain why it is called a natural society, and why it is the most perfect of all human societies.

2. Distinguish between the temporal happiness of this life and divine good.

3. Prove that civil society is directed to an end, that happiness is its end, and that the temporal happiness of this life is directed to a divine good.

Cf. *In Politic.*, l. I, l. 1.

---

and legislating for, all that concerns religion; of teaching all nations; of spreading the faith as widely as possible; in short, of administering freely and without hindrance, in accordance with its own judgment, all matters that fall within its competence.— LEO XIII, *Immortale Dei*.

(1) *Immortale Dei*.— *Divini Redemptoris*, n. 74.

ORIGIN OF CIVIL SOCIETY

1086. Statement of the question.— 1° The origin of civil society presents two distinct problems. *First*, we are faced with the problem of whether man is inclined by the impulse of his nature to life in civil society, i.e., whether the natural law makes civil society necessary for man. *Secondly*, we must, after having solved the first problem, inquire into the human facts which constitute civil society. For civil society, even though an exigence of human nature, was constituted, as history bears witness, by man's industry: for nature inclines man to act by his reason and his will.

It is with the first problem that we are concerned in the thesis.

2° According to Catholic teaching, man is bound by his nature, i.e., by God, the author of his nature, to live in civil society[1]. These words show that civil society is not merely in accordance with nature, but that it derives from nature, in as much as it is made necessary by the natural law, of which God is the author. Therefore we say that civil society is imposed on man by God as He is the author of nature.

This opinion was held by Aristotle, and it is the opinion commonly held by Scholastics and generally by all Catholic philosophers.

1087. Opinions of adversaries.— The principal opinions opposed to the natural institution of civil society are two in number.

---

(1) LEO XIII, *Diuturnum*.

1° According to the first of these opinions, civil society has not its origin in nature, i.e., does not derive from the natural law, but from the free agreement of men. This opinion, called *the social contract theory*, was known in antiquity, and, in modern times, was systematically presented by Thomas Hobbes (1588-1679) and Jean Jacques Rousseau (1712-1778).

According to Hobbes, man's primitive or natural state was *antisocial*, a condition of natural *warfare*, whereas, according to Rousseau, it was *extrasocial*.

2° According to the second opinion, civil society is the term of the necessary evolution proper either to matter, as Spencer and Darwin hold, or to a unique spiritual being, as Hegel and the Pantheists teach.

Hence, according to the first opinion, civil society did not have its origin in nature, but in a free agreement of men; according to the second opinion, in nature alone, and not in a free agreement of men; and according to the Scholastic opinion, in nature and in human industry, i.e., in reason under the impulse of nature.

1088. Statement of the thesis.

THESIS.— MAN IS BOUND BY HIS NATURE, i.e., BY GOD, THE AUTHOR OF NATURE, TO LIVE IN CIVIL SOCIETY.

1° Nature, i.e., God, the author of nature, requires whatever is necessary for the attainment of the temporal happiness of this life. But the attainment of the temporal happiness of this life necessitates man's living in civil society. Therefore nature, i.e., God, the author of nature, requires that man live in civil society; in other words, man is bound by his nature to live in civil society.

Major.— The temporal happiness of this life is the end to which man is directed by nature, i.e., by God, the author of nature. But nature, i.e., God, the author of nature, requires whatever is necessary for the attainment of a natural end. Therefore.

Minor.— Neither individual persons, nor separate families, but only families working together for the same end, i.e., living in civil society, can acquire all the things necessary for the temporal happiness of this life.

2° The family had its origin in nature. Moreover, one family gave rise to other families, which were held by bonds of love and necessity to remain within the same territorial precincts, for the purpose of pursuing the common good by their united powers and efforts; and these families in turn multiplied and gradually developed into distinct tribal communities (village communities) and political societies. Hence the natural propagation of families shows that civil society is a natural institution, i.e., owes its institution to God, the author of nature.

3° History testifies that some form of political society always existed in all parts of the inhabited world. Moreover, it shows that its perfection has always been proportionate to its respect for and recognition of the dignity of human nature. These facts sufficiently demonstrate that political or civil society necessarily had its origin in human nature, i.e., that it was imposed on man by God, the author of nature.

1089. Historical causes of civil society.— Many theories have been advanced by philosophers on the first historical causes of the establishment of civil society.

1) The theory of *sucessive aggregation*, supported by Alfred Fouillée (¹), holds that civil society is not radically, i.e., in its origin, distinct from private societies, and therefore that it normally resulted from various relations and particular contracts by which men were successively united for the pursuit of particular ends.

This theory is untenable, for it confounds public rights with private rights, and implicity holds that the end of civil society is nothing more than an aggregate of particular ends.

---
(1) *Revue des Deux-Mondes*, XXXII, 759.

2) Rousseau championed the social-contract theory: civil society owes its origin to a social contract, according to which men surrender all their personal rights in favor of the community or society. He denied that man is inclined by his nature to life in civil society.

3) Pufendorf taught that civil society necessarily resulted from a social pact, explicit or implicit. Nevertheless, he held that civil society is consentaneous with human nature; and in this he differs with Rousseau.

This opinion, but with certain modifications, has received the support of some modern Scholastics, as Costa-Rossetti, Vallet, Castelain, Marcellus of the Child Jesus, and Gredt, all of whom claim that they are following the teaching of Bellarmine, Suarez, and certain other Scholastics of an earlier day.

4) But, in our opinion, the older Scholastics and Suarez merely affirmed that civil society, in its historical origin, is the product of *human industry:* for, as we have seen, civil society owes its origin to nature, i.e., *to reason* under the impulse of nature.

In regard to the particular concrete fact to which civil society owes its origin, they assert that civil society owes its origin to the free consent of the people, for this mode of origin, they maintain, is most suited to a multitude composed of free men. Therefore they hold that it was fitting that civil society should, as Adam's posterity became more numerous, be constituted in this way. Moreover, they add that it is probable that many kingdoms, and especially the Roman empire, began in this way.

But, in addition to the free consent of the people, i.e., the social contract, they admit many other possible methods of explaining the historical establishment of a civil society; v.g., a military leader could subjugate men or solitary and uncivilized families, and unite them in a political society. This method of instituting civil society is called a quasi-contract by Suarez, because it has the same effects as a contract or free agreement of the people ([1]).

([1]) SUAREZ, *Defensio Fidei catholicae*, l. III, c. 2, n. 19 et 20.

Hence we may conclude that men are impelled by their nature to set up civil society by means of their reason and will. But it belongs to history to determine the ways in which men first established a concrete civil society, for there are many ways in which this could have been done. However, the manner most consentaneous with man's liberty is the pact, i.e., the voluntary consent of the people.

POINTS FOR REVIEW

1. Explain what is meant by saying that civil society is of natural institution.

2. State the opinions of Rousseau and Hobbes on the origin of civil society, and on the primitive state of men.

3. What is the opinion of Suarez in regard to the historical causes of the constitution of civil society?

Cf. *In Politic.*, l. I, l. 1.

CHAPTER II

MATERIAL CAUSE OF CIVIL SOCIETY

Prologue.— The material cause of civil society is the multitude, of which, as a political union, the proximate elements are families, and the remote elements are individual persons. In this chapter, therefore, the following problems present themselves for our consideration: first, the relation of individual persons and of families to civil society; secondly, private ownership, i. e., the ownership of private property, which is the right of persons and of families living in civil society; thirdly, nationality, from which the multitude and the part of the multitude politically united can receive determination.

Relation of persons and of families to civil society
- Statement of the question
- Opinions
- Thesis: The individual person and the family in civil society have, according to the ordinance of nature, their own proper ends; and these ends are directed to the end of civil society, but not under the aspect of the absolutely ultimate end
- Scholia
- Personalism
- Difficulties offered by personalism

Private ownership
- Lawfulness of private ownership
- Statement of the question
- Opinions
- Thesis: According to the natural law, the private ownership of both productive and consumptible goods is not only lawful, but necessary
- Scholia
- Modes of acquiring ownership
- Social character of private ownership
- Statement of the question
- Opinions
- Thesis: Private property remains in some way common as regards its use
- Scholia

Nationality
{ Description of the nation
Philosophical definition of the nation
Causes of the nation
Definition of nationalism
Principle of nationality
Corollaries

ARTICLE I

RELATION OF THE INDIVIDUAL PERSON AND THE
FAMILY TO CIVIL SOCIETY

1090. Statement of the question.— 1° The problem of the relations which unite individual persons and families to civil society is of utmost importance, for today there are many theories which do not recognize the natural rights of the individual person and of the family, and which regard the State as omnipotent and as possessing all rights over persons and families.

2° The problem has three aspects, which may be stated as follows:

First, admitting that civil society has a proper end which is a good, we may ask: have the individual person and the family, both of which live in society, proper ends distinct from the end of civil society?

Secondly, if they have proper ends, are these ends directed to the end of civil society, or vice versa?

Thirdly, if the ends of the individual person and of the famliy are directed to the end of civil society, is it their absolutely ultimate end?

3° In the thesis, *first*, we state that the individual person and the family have, according to the ordinance of nature, their own proper ends, distinct from the end of civil society. Moreover, since the order, i.e., the ordinance, of nature is the ordinance of God Himself, the author of nature, civil society may not disavow them, nor place any obstacle in the way of their attainment.

Secondly, we state the proper ends of the individual person and of the family are directed to the end of civil society, not vice versa. Moreover, since this order or relation of ends obtains in society, it is directly concerned with external acts by which men work for the common good, although indirectly it can be concerned with internal acts, in as much as the latter can regulate external acts.

Thirdly, we assert that the end of civil society is not the absolutely ultimate end to which the ends of the individual person and of the family are directed.

1091. Opinions.— There are various opinions on the relations of the individual person and the family to civil society.

1° All who conceive civil society as an *organism*, in the strict sense of the term, i.e., as an entity possessing *absolute unity*, not merely *unity of order*, do not admit that the individual person and the family have proper ends which are distinct from the end of civil society. For a part of a whole which is an absolute unit, v.g., a hand, which is a part of man, has no operation which is not the operation of the whole, and therefore has no end which is not the end of the whole.

Such was the teaching of Plato, who conceived society as a superior man.

The same conclusion is reached by the Caesarists, with Machiavelli, who proclaim the omnipotence of the State; by the Democrats, with Rousseau, who conceive the general will as the source of all rights, even of private rights; by the Pantheists, with Fichte, Schelling and Hegel; and by the Socialists, with Bebel, Wagner, and others.

2° All Pantheists and Naturalists hold that the end of civil society is man's absolutely ultimate end.

According to the exponents of these opinions, individual men are dependent on the State for everything, because all their rights are derived solely from the concessions of the State.

A summary of these errors is found in the thirty-ninth sentence of the Syllabus of Pope Pius IX: *Reipublicae status, utpote omnium jurium origo et fons, jure quodam pollet nullis circumscripto limitibus.*

3° Today, some Catholics teach that it is not as a person, i.e., as formally *an individual substance of a rational nature*, but as an individual, i.e., as *multiplied in the same species*, that man is subordinate to the end of civil society; for man, they say, is subordinate to the end of civil society, because he is related to civil society as the part to the whole; but man is not a part of a whole, v.g., of the human species, because of his personality, but because of his individuation by which he is multiplied in the same species.

But this opinion appears untenable, because society is essentially a union of persons, i.e., of intelligible beings. If this were not so, a union of individual horses, or cows, or bears, etc., would be a society.

1092. Statement of the thesis.

THESIS.— THE INDIVIDUAL PERSON AND THE FAMILY IN CIVIL SOCIETY HAVE, ACCORDING TO THE ORDINANCE OF NATURE, THEIR OWN PROPER ENDS; AND THESE ENDS ARE DIRECTED TO THE END OF CIVIL SOCIETY, BUT NOT UNDER THE ASPECT OF THE ABSOLUTELY ULTIMATE END.

First part.— *The individual person and the family have according to the ordinance of nature, their own proper ends.*— The parts of a whole which have operations distinct from the operations of the whole have, according to the ordinance of nature, ends which are not the ends of the whole, i.e., have their own proper ends. But the individual person and the family are in civil society as the parts of a whole, and have operations which are not the operations of the whole. Therefore the individual and the family in civil society have, according to the ordinance of nature, their own proper ends.

Major.— Operation is an end in itself, or tends to a proper end. Therefore, when operations are distinct, ends also are distinct.

Minor.— The parts of a whole which has only unity of order have operations which are not the operations of the whole; v.g., a soldier in an army has operations which are not the operations of the whole army (1). But civil society, of which the individual person and the family are parts, is a whole which has only unity of order: society is a stable union of a plurality of persons in pursuit of a common good. Therefore.

Second part.— *The proper ends of the individual person and of the family are directed to the end of civil society.*— The individual person and the family are to civil society as the parts to the whole: the individual person and the family are the natural parts from which the whole which is civil society results. But the ends of the parts are directed to the end of the whole. Therefore the proper ends of the individual and of the family are directed to the end of civil society.

The *major* is evident, for civil society is composed of individual persons and of families.

The *minor* also is evident: the good of the part, as a part, is necessarily directed the good of the whole (2).

Third part. — *The proper ends of the individual person and of the family are not directed to the end of civil society under the aspect of the absolutely ultimate end.*— The end of civil society is the temporal happiness of this life. But the temporal happiness of this life is not man's absolutely ultimate end. Therefore the end of civil society is not the absolutely ultimate end of the individual person and of the family, i.e., the proper ends of the individual person and of the family are not directed to the end of civil society under the aspect of the absolutely ultimate end.

The *major* is evident from what has been already said.

---

(1) *In Ethic.*, l. I, l. 1, n. 5.
(2) I-II, q. 109, a. 3, c.

Minor. — Man's absolutely ultimate end is the beatific vision, for which man is supernaturally elevated in accordance with the positive ordinance of God(¹).

1093. Scholia. — 1° The civil authority, or the State, as it is called, has no right to refuse recognition to the proper ends determined by nature for the individual person and for the family, nor has it any right to limit them. On the contrary, the civil authority is in duty bound to aid the individual person and the family in the attainment of their proper ends, for these ends, as directed to the common good of society, lead to that temporal happiness which is the end of civil society.

2° The virtue by which the good of the individual person and of the family is directed to the end of civil society is legal justice.

In virtue of legal justice, citizens are mutually dependent on one another in regard to their end. Moderns call this mutual dependence solidarism, which, according to them, is divided into human political, family, and class solidarism.

In dealing with this division, two things must be kept in mind: first, up to the present, humanity is not constituted as a society; secondly, solidarism is not applied univocally to the different kinds of society.

Solidarism, in the strict sense, is found only in civil society, for civil society is the only society whose end is a good which, in the order of nature, is a perfect human good; and therefore only in it is realized, in the strict sense, legal justice by which man is wholly directed to the common good.

In other particular societies, there obtains between the members and the whole a relation only similar to the relation of legal justice, because the good which they pursue is not a perfect good, but rather an imperfect good. Therefore it is only by analogy that solidarism is found in them.

3° Although individual man is destined for civil society,

---

(1) Cf. *In Politic.*, l. VII, l. 2.

society is for man, and not vice versa (¹), because its proper and immediate end is the temporal happiness of this life, which is the good of man. The temporal happiness of this life is directly the common good of the whole multitude, although, as a consequence, it becomes the good of individual men who appropriate it to themselves.

4° Society, under its formal aspect as a union, may be called the *means* by which man attains the temporal happiness of this life (²). Society, however, considered as the union of all the members of the multitude for the pursuit of the common good, is not the means, but the cause by which individual man can attain the temporal happiness of this life: for the united members of the whole multitude are the cause of that happiness which individual men later appropriate to themselves.

5° According to Pius XI (³), the following are the principal goods or rights with which God, the author of nature, has endowed individual man living in society: the right to life, to bodily integrity, and to whatever is necessary for life; the right to pursue his ultimate end in the manner determined for him by God; the rights of association and of the private ownership and use of property.

The proper ends of the family are the procreation and education of offspring, the mutual aid of the spouses, and the allaying of concupiscence. Hence the family, in accordance with the ordinance of nature, has the right to all things necessary for the attainment of these ends, as are the indissolubility and unity of marriage, its own authority and power of determining the means to attain its ends, without violation, however, of its subordination to civil society.

1094. Personalism.— 1° Personalism is the teaching of those who, in order to safeguard the dignity of the human person, hold that the end of man, as a person, is superior to the end of civil society. Hence personalism denies that the proper ends

---
(1) *Divini Redemptoris*, n. 29.
(2) *Ibidem*.
(3) *Ibid*, n. 28.

of individual man are, as we have shown, directed to the end of civil society.

2° All Catholic philosophers hold that the supernatural end of the human person is not subordinate to the end of civil society. The problem with which we are concerned at present is the relation between the ends of the individual person and the end of civil society, in the natural order only.

3° Personalism holds that man may be considered either as an individual or as a person.

Man, considered as an individual, is, according to personalism, a part of civil society, and is related to it as the part to the whole.

But man, considered as a person, is superior to civil society, and is not related to it as the part to the whole. Therefore the ends of the individual man, in as much as the individual man is a person, i.e., has the dignity of a person, are not subordinate to the end of civil society.

Hence personalism may be defined: *the doctrine of those who hold that the ends of the individual man, in as much as the individual man has the dignity of a person, are not subordinate, in the natural order, to the end of civil society, but vice versa.*

4° In refutation of personalism, we may make the following observations.

a) The distinction which the personalists make between the individual and the person is of no value in the present question.

For the individual, considered as distinct from nature, can mean only one of two things:

either a singular nature without subsistence;

or a subsisting supposit in general (¹), not a supposit subsisting in a rational nature.

---

(1) Et dico superfluum non solum respectu sui ipsius, quod est supra id quod est necessarium individuo, sed etiam respectu aliorum quorum cura ei incumbit; respectu quorum dicitur necessarium personae, secundum quod persona dignitatem importat.— II-II, q. 32, a. 5, c.

If the individual signifies a singular nature without subsistence, it is wrong to say that man, as an individual, is a part of civil society. For society is a stable union of men *in the order of operation*, and, moreover, operations are proper to the supposit, i.e., to the subsisting being, not to nature without subsistence.

If the individual means a supposit in general, it is again wrong to say that man, as an individual, is a part of civil society, for otherwise, as we have already pointed out, a union of irrational animals would be a society. The individual man is formally a part of civil society in as much as he is endowed with an intellect, i.e., as he is a person.

b) The end of civil society is the greatest of all human goods. Hence the subordination of the individual person to civil society, as the part to the whole, is not at variance with the dignity of the human person, but is a subordination of the human person to the human person's greatest natural good, i.e., to the temporal happiness of this life.

c) Personalism is a form of *individualism*, because it makes the common good subordinate to the good of the individual person.

1095. Difficulties offered by personalism.— 1° Man is related to civil society as the part to the whole. But man is not a part of a whole as a person, but as an individual: for the principle by which man is multiplied in the same species is not personality, but the principle of individuation. Therefore man is not a part of civil society as a person, but as an individual, i.e., it is as an individual that man is subordinate to society. (So teach the Personalists).

Major.— As the part to the whole in the order of being, *I deny*; in the order of operation, *I concede.*

Minor.— It is not as a person, but as an individual, that man is a part of a whole in the order of being, *I concede*; in that order of operation which constitutes society, *I deny.*

Society, as we have seen, is not a union of a plurality in the order of being, but in the order of operation, for society is a union of men for the pursuit of a common good; and, since operation is proper to the supposit, it is formally as a person that man is a part of society, and therefore it is as a person, not as an individual, than man is subordinate to the end of society.

The principle of individuation, i.e., first matter signed by quantity, is the principle by which man is multiplied in a whole, that is to say, in the same species, in the order of being.

MATERIAL CAUSE OF CIVIL SOCIETY

2° If the person is immediately destined for God, man as a person is not destined for society. But man is immediately destined for God (¹). Therefore man as a person is not destined for society. (So claim the Personalists).

Major.— If the person is immediately destined for God, is as much as he, as living in society, does not attain God, *I concede*; in as much as the person is not destined for another creature, as the irrational animal is destined for man, *I deny*.

Minor.— In as much as he, as living in society, does not attain God, *I deny*; in as much as he is not destined for another creature, as the irrational animal is destined for man, *I concede*.

3° If as a person man were destined for civil society, all that he is and all that he possesses would be destined for civil society. But all that man is and all that he possesses are not destined for civil society (²). Therefore man, as a person, is not destined for civil society.

Major.— All that man is and all he possesses would be destined for society if the end of civil society were the absolutely ultimate end of human acts, *I concede*; if the end of civil society is ultimate only in its own order, in as much as it is the greatest of all human goods, *I deny*.

Minor.— Because the end of civil society is not the absolutely ultimate end of human acts, *I concede*; because man, as an individual person, is not destined for civil society, as the part to the whole, *I deny*.

The absolutely ultimate end of human acts is a divine good, i.e., the beatific vision; and the end of civil society, which is temporal happiness, is the ultimate end of human acts only in the order of human goods. Hence the end of civil society itself must be destined for a divine good. Hence all that man is and all that he possesses are not destined for civil society, but for a higher good.

4° That which has substantial unity is superior to that which has only accidental unity. But the individual person has substantial unity, whereas civil society has only accidental unity, i.e., unity of order. Therefore the individual person is superior to civil society, and is not related to it as the part to the whole.

Major.— As a being, *I concede*; as a good, *I deny*.

Minor.— The private good of the individual person is superior to the common good, *I deny*; is inferior, *I concede*.

Goodness and being, though identical in reality, are logically distinct, i.e., distinct by a distinction of reason; and, moreover, absolute being in not absolute goodness, whereas absolute goodness is relative being (n. 533). Therefore the common good of persons united in society is greater than the private good of the individual person.

POINTS FOR REVIEW

1. Explain why the individual person has his own proper ends in civil society, and why these ends are subordinate to the end of civil society.

2. What is personalism?

3. What distinction may be made between the individual and the person?

---

(1) Sola autem natura rationalis creata habet immediatum ordinem ad Deum; quia caeterae creaturae non attingunt ad aliquid universale, sed solum ad aliquid particulare, participantes divinam bonitatem vel in essendo tantum, sicut inanimata, vel etiam in vivendo et cognoscendo singularia, sicut plantae et animalia. Natura autem rationalis, inquantum cognoscit universalem boni et entis rationem, habet immediatum ordinem ad universale essendi principium.— II-II, q. 2, a. 3.

(2) I-II, q. 21, a. 4, ad 3.

ARTICLE II

PRIVATE OWNERSHIP

I

LAWFULNESS OF PRIVATE OWNERSHIP

1096. Statement of the question.— 1° We know that man has perfect dominion over external things, i.e., over things which are inferior to him, in as much as they are destined for man's use. Such being the finality of external things, we may now ask: may the individual man and the family possess external things? This is the question of private ownership.

2° To understand what ownership is, we must consider the principal acts which man can exercise in regard to external things. These acts, according to St. Thomas (¹), are three in number: *a) management*, i.e., administration, *production*; *b) distribution*, i.e., the disposing of goods; *c) use*, or, in the language of economists, *consumption*, i.e., the immediate application of external goods to their essential end, which is man.

The third of these three acts, *use*, is the end of the other two.

3° Ownership is anterior to and distinct from use or consumption. The thing which a man consumes may be his own, may belong to another, or may be an unclaimed thing which belongs to nobody (res « nullius »). Therefore ownership is conceived as having reference to the acts which antecede use or consumption, i.e., to production or management and to distri-

---

(1) II-II, q. 66, 2.

bution (¹). Therefore ownership may be defined: *the power to administer and to dispose of external things as one's own.*

This power is called common, collective, or public ownership, when it belongs to a community; and private ownership, when it belongs to a private man, i.e., to an individual man or to a private moral person.

4° Private ownership can have various forms; it can be *individual, domestic, patriarchal,* etc. (²).

Again, we may consider private ownership in the abstract, i.e., in relation to external things generally and indiscrimately, or in the concrete, i.e., in relation to particular things.

In our present study, we are not concerned with the various forms of private ownership, but with private ownership in the abstract, i.e., under its general aspect. In other words, the question which at present concerns us is this: has the individual man, i.e., the private person, the right of owning, of administering, and of disposing of external things, or does this right belong solely to civil society?

5° The principal division of external things is their division into *consumptible goods* and *productive goods*. *Consumptible goods* (consumption goods) are goods which are consumed in their use, as food and drink. Productive goods (production goods) are goods which are destined for the production of new goods or products, as a piece of land, etc.

---

(1) The chiefest and most excellent rule for the right use of money is one which the heathen philosophers indicated, but which the Church has traced out clearly, and has not only made known to men's minds, but has impressed upon their lives. It rests on the principle that it is one thing to have a right to the possession of money, and another to have a right to use money as one pleases.— LEO XIII, *Rerum Novarum.*

(2) Leo XIII has wisely taught that « the defining of private possession has been left by God to man's industry and to the laws of individual peoples ». History proves that the right of ownership, like other elements of social life, is not absolutely rigid, and this doctrine We Ourselves have given utterance to on a previous occasion in the following terms: « How varied are the forms which the right of property has assumed ! First, the primitive form used amongst rude and savage peoples, which still exists in certain localities even in our own day; then, that of the patriarchal age; later came various tyrannical types (We use the word in its classical meaning); finally, the feudal and monarchic systems down to the varieties of more recent times. » — *Quadragesimo Anno.*

1097. Opinions.— 1° *Absolute Communism* holds that the ownership of all goods, including consumptible goods, belongs exclusively to the community. Such is the teaching of Plato.

2° *Moderate Communism*, i.e., collectivism, reserves all productive goods to the community ([1]). It teaches that the public authority is bound to distribute the fruits of labor among its citizens, either according to perfect equality, or according to each one's necessity, or according to labor and merit. Such is the teaching of Marx, Engels ([2]), and generally of communists today.

3° Others admit the lawfulness of private ownership, but hold that this lawfulness derives either from the civil law, as teach Montesquieu, Babeuf, Bentham, Robespierre, and the National Socialists in Germany, or from an explicit or an implicit pact, as teach Locke, Grotius, Pufendorf, etc.

4° According to the doctrine commonly accepted among Catholics and sanctioned by the Holy See, the private ownership of both productive and consumptible goods is naturally lawful, i.e., in conformity with the natural law; moreover, it is necessary, i.e., imposed by the natural law. Hence, the right of private ownership may not be abolished by the civil authority, for it has its origin in nature.

1098. Statement of the thesis.

> **THESIS.**— According to the natural law, the private ownership of both productive and consumptible goods is not only lawful, but necessary.

First part.— *According to the natural law, the private ownership of both productive and consumptible goods is lawful.*—Owner-

---

([1]) Nor is the individual granted any property rights over material goods or the means of production, for inasmuch as these are the source of further wealth, their possession would give one man power over another. Precisely on this score, all forms of private property must be eradicated, for they are at the origin of all economic enslavement.— *Divini Redemptoris*, n. 10.

([2]) Engels, in *Anti-Duhring*, teaches that « social ownership extends to lands and to the means of production, and individual ownership to products, i.e., to objects of consumption ».

ship to which man has a strong natural inclination is lawful according to the natural law. But man has a strong natural inclination to the private ownership of both productive and consumptible goods. Therefore, according to the natural law, the private ownership of both productive and consumptible goods is lawful.

The *major* is evident, because the natural law is in accordance with natural inclination.

Minor.— a) Because individual man is a rational being, he has a share in divine Providence, and therefore is destined to provide for his own necessities and his own progress not only in the present, but for the future. But, in order that individual man provide for his necessities and progress, especially in the future, he has a natural inclination to the private ownership of both productive and consumptible goods; indeed, he cannot hope to cope with life's many normal eventualities, as old age, sickness, and accidents, without the private ownership of both productive and consumptible goods. Therefore.

b) Individual man as head of a family must provide for his wife and children, who are naturally dependent on the father for food, clothing, and the other necessities of life. But, to provide for his wife and family, the head of the family has a natural inclination to the acquisition of private ownership of both productive and consumptible goods. Therefore.

c) Individual man has a natural inclination to what is most useful for the protection and safeguarding of his lawful liberty. But the private ownership of both productive and consumptible goods is most useful for the protection and safeguarding of man's lawful liberty: without private ownership, individual man is too dependent on others and on civil society. Therefore.

The whole argument may be stated very briefly as follows: The conservation of life, liberty, etc., are proper ends which individual men and the family are destined by their nature to attain. But the private ownership of both productive and consumptible goods are most useful for the attainment of these ends. Therefore, according to the natural law, the private ownership of these goods is lawful.

Second part.— *According to the natural law, the private ownership of both productive and consumptible goods is necessary.* — Any institution which stimulates production, facilitates the orderly management of human affairs, and fosters peace among men is, according to the natural law, a necessary institution. But the private ownership of both productive and consumptible goods is an institution which stimulates production, facilitates the orderly management of human affairs, and fosters peace among men. Therefore, according to the natural law, the private ownership of both productive and consumptible goods is necessary [1].

Major.— The natural law requires production: according to nature, external things are made useful for man by means of labor and production.

In like manner, the natural law requires order and peace in society.

Minor.— a) *Private ownership...stimulates production.*— Private ownership is a stimulus to labor: a man takes much more care in looking after something which belongs solely to himself than he does in looking after what belongs to everybody, or to a large number of persons: a man will shirk work and leave to another duties which belong to the community, as happens when many are entrusted with the accomplishment of work.

b) *Private ownership...facilitates the orderly management of human affairs.*— The management of human affairs is more orderly in the degree in which individual men are entrusted with affairs of their own; confusion results from the indiscriminate assigning of the management of affairs to a group of individuals, but to no person in particular.

c) *Private ownership...fosters peace among men.*— A man is contented when he possesses goods as his own. On the other hand, we know from experience that quarrels frequently arise among those who possess goods in common.

---

(1) II-II, q. 66, a. 2.

1099. Scholia. — 1° Private ownership is necessary according to the secondary precepts of the natural law. For, in the present state of human nature, it is a *means* which is necessary, in order that the essential end of external things, which is man's utility, may be easily and readily attained.

Many Catholics hold that it is only because of Original sin that private ownership is necessary. For, they say, if our First Parents had not fallen, the common ownership of goods would be sufficient to ensure man's giving his due share of labor, and to maintain order and peace. While we admit that the necessity of private ownership was made greater because of Original sin, we maintain that it would have been necessary even if Original sin had not been committed.

2° The ownership of certain goods may be reserved to civil society when the private possession of them would give individual citizens an economic power which would be harmful to the common good ([1]). But it is a grievous error to hold that the private ownership of productive goods is of its nature unlawful ([2]).

3° The civil authority has an obligation to protect private possessions by the authority of its laws ([3]), but, in doing so, must ever safeguard the common good. Therefore the State must not exhaust the means of individuals by crushing taxes and tributes ([4]).

1100. Modes of acquiring ownership. — 1° *Preliminaries.* — *a)* The modes of acquiring ownership are the ways in which a man can acquire the ownership of determinate things.

b) The modes of acquiring ownership are divided into two main categories: primitive modes and derived modes.

Primitive modes of acquiring ownership are those which do not presuppose the previous ownership of the thing.

---
(1) *Quadragesimo Anno.*
(2) *Ibidem.*
(3) *Rerum Novarum.*
(4) *Rerum Novarum.*

Derived modes of acquiring ownership are those which presuppose the previous ownership of the thing.

c) The primitive modes of acquiring ownership are two in number: first, occupancy of an unclaimed thing which belongs to no one (occupatio rei « nullius »); secondly, labor.

Occupancy of an unclaimed thing which belongs to no one is the appropriation of that thing with the intention of possessing it as one's own. The appropriation of a thing may be *physical*, as the appropriation of a deer or other wild animal by a hunter; or it may be *moral*, which consists in placing on a thing a durable sign indicating that the thing has been appropriated by someone.

Labor is a primitive mode of acquiring ownership in as much as man by his own labor produces something in a material thing, as when he produces a statue from a block of marble. « The only form of labor which gives the workingman a title to its fruits,» writes Pius XI, « is that which a man exercises as his own master, and by which some new form or new value is produced »(1).

The derived modes of acquiring ownership are also of two kinds:

the first consists in transfer from one possessor to another;

the second consists in this: the thing possessed by a man grows (increment) and produces fruit (fructification), as when an animal which a man possesses grows and engenders offspring.

Transfer from one possessor to another can take place in two ways:

1) by *tradition*, i.e., by a positive act of the will extrinsically manifested by which a possessor transfers his property to another, either by donation, or by sale between the living, or by will or testament;

2) by *natural intestate succession*,— natural transfer by an intestate person,— in as much as the possessions of parents naturally, i.e., solely in virtue of the natural law, become the prop-

---

(1) *Quadragesimo Anno.*

erty of their children, even without an express act of the will of the parents.

2° In the light of the foregoing observations, we shall now prove the propositions which follow.

1) *Occupancy of an unclaimed thing which belongs to no one is a primitive mode of acquiring ownership.*— A primitive mode of acquiring ownership is a natural mode of acquiring ownership which presupposes no previous possession. But occupancy of an unclaimed thing which belongs to no one (occupatio rei « nullius ») is a natural mode of acquiring ownership which presupposes no previous possession. Therefore occupancy of an unclaimed thing which belongs to no one is a primitive mode of acquiring ownership.

The *major* is self-evident.

Minor.— An unclaimed thing which belongs to no one is *negatively common*, and therefore lies open for occupancy by anyone: by occupancy a man manifests his will to possess the thing as his own by excluding all others from the possession of it.

2) *Labor is also a primitive mode of acquiring ownership.*— If man has dominion over his own activity, labor is a primitive mode of acquiring ownership. But man has dominion over his own acts. Therefore labor is a primitive mode of acquiring ownership.

Major.— If man has dominion over his own activity, he has dominion also over its term, i.e., over the products of his labor. Hence a man who in his own name expends labor on something which belongs to himself has a right to the ownership of the fruits resulting therefrom. But if a man hires his labor and expends it on what belongs to another, he has a right only to what was determined by a just contract.

The *minor* is evident from what has been already said.

3) *The increment and fructification of a possessed thing constitute a derived mode of acquiring ownership.*— A man who possesses an external thing possesses also its powers and its activity,

and hence also the term of this activity, i.e., whatever it produces from itself.

4) *The transfer of a possessed thing from one possessor to another is a derived mode of acquiring ownership.*— Transfer of this kind is made according to modes which result from the possession of things, and are required by the common good.

a) The modes of acquiring ownership by *tradition,* i.e., by a positive act of the will extrinsically manifested by which a possessor transfers his property to another, either by donation, or by sale between the living, or by will:

result from the possession of things: a man who has perfect possession of a thing may freely dispose of it, and hence transfer it to another, even after his death by means of a will;

are required by the common good: man's social nature, which demands that individual men assist one another by a mutual exchange of goods, requires that *tradition* or exchange of ownership among the living be a derived mode of acquiring ownership.

The common good also requires that transfer of ownership by will be a derived mode of acquiring ownership: the opportunity of choosing his heirs by means of a will provides a man with a great incentive to persevere in his work and to avoid prodigality; on the other hand, if a man were not free to bequeath his property to heirs of his own choosing, especially to his children, he would be inclined, to his own detriment and to that of society, to squander his goods. Finally, the good of the family requires that parents be able to make their children, not strangers, their heirs, and that they be able to distribute their goods among their children according to their deserts and needs.

b) The mode af acquiring ownership by natural intestate succession results from the possession of things as something required by the common good of the family, for the good of the family is the special end of private possession: it is especially as head of the family, as we have seen, that man naturally tends to acquire ownership.

II

SOCIAL CHARACTER OF PRIVATE OWNERSHIP

1101. Statement of the question.— 1° We have already seen that man as a private person may possess as his own both the production and distribution of things. Now we must deal with the question of whether the *use* of things which are possessed privately is wholly private, or whether it remains in some way common. This is the question of the social character of private ownership.

2° Use is the immediate application of an external thing to its essential end, which is man's utility. It is called the *consumption of goods* by modern writers.

1102. Opinions.— 1° Among some peoples, as Aristotle observes (¹), each one used to have his own field apart from that of others, but all the fruits of the fields were made common property and distributed among all. Hence private ownership among these peoples remained wholly common as regards its use.

2° The adherents of Economic Liberalism, in virtue of the principles of their doctrine, which leads to individualism, do not recognize in a positive manner the existence of the social character of private ownership. Moreover, they deny it at least implicity from the fact that they claim for the individual a liberty in economic matters which is too absolute.

3° According to the opinion of Aristotle and St. Thomas (²), and also according to the social doctrine set forth by Leo XIII in *Rerum Novarum* and by Pius XI in *Quadragesimo Anno*, private property remains in some way common as regards its use. Private property is also private as regards its use, because it is destined for the utility and perfection of its owner; never-

---

(1) *In Politic.*, l. II, l. 4.
(2) Unde manifestum est quod multo melius est quod sint propriae possessiones secundum dominium, sed quod fiant communes aliquo modo quantum ad usum.— *In Politic.*, l. II, l. 4.

theless, it remains common in as much as a man who possesses external things as his own ought more readily to share them with others who are in need (¹). In other words, « the temporal goods which God grants us are ours as to the ownership, but, as to the use of them, they belong not to us alone, but also to such others as we are able to succour out of our superfluous goods ». (²) Superfluous goods are goods which are over and above what is *necessary for the person*⁽³⁾, that is to say, over and above what is necessary that a man and those dependent on him live in keeping with their social station and condition (⁴).

1103. Statement of the thesis.

THESIS. — PRIVATE PROPERTY REMAINS IN SOME WAY COMMON AS REGARDS ITS USE.

1° If private property is destined for the end of civil society, it remains in some way common as regards its use. But private property is destined for the end of civil society. Therefore private property remains in some way common as regards its use.

Major. — If private property did not remain common in any way as regards its use, it would not be destined for the end of civil society, which is the common good, but only for a private good.

Minor. — Private property is a good proper to the members of civil society, i.e., proper to the individual person or to the family. But the good proper to the individual person and to the family is, as we saw in the preceding article, destined for the end of civil society. Therefore.

2° Private property was instituted, in order that external things attain their essential end, which is the common utility

---

(1) II-II, q. 66, a. 2, c.
(2) II-II, q. 32, a. 5, ad 2.
(3) *Ibidem*, c. Necessary to the person, i.e., the official necessities of a person in position.
(4) II-II, q. 32, a. 6, c.

of men. But, in order that external things attain their essential end, which is the common utility of men, private property must remain in some way common as regards its use. Therefore private property remains in some way common as regards its use.

Major.— Private property was not instituted for the utility of this or that man, but for the common utility of men, for, where this institution obtains, production is intensified, and order and peace among men are safeguarded.

Minor.— If private property did not remain in some way common as regards its use, it would be no longer destined for the common utility of men, but exclusively for the utility of this or that man.

3° According to the distributive justice of God, every man has a right to the goods which are necessary for him. But, if private property did not remain in some way common as regards its use, every man would not have a right to the goods which are necessary for him. Therefore private property remains in some way common as regards its use.

Major.— Every man, according to the ordinance of nature, i.e., of God, the author of nature, has a right to his life, and even to a virtuous life. Hence, according to the distributive justice of God, Who is the supreme Lord, every man has a right to the goods necessary for life, and even for a virtuous life.

Minor.— If private property did not remain in some way common as regards its use, the poor and needy, as is evident, would have no right to the goods necessary for life, or, a fortiori, for a virtuous life.

1104. Scholia.— 1° Private ownership is the power of producing and of distributing external goods, and is distinct from the use of external goods.

a) Private ownership, i.e., the right of ownership, is not forfeited or lost by the misuse or even by the non-use of this right ([1]).

---

(1) *Rerum Novarum.*— *Quadragesimo Anno.*

b) The property owner cannot be forced, in virtue of commutative justice, to make the use of his goods common except in the case of extreme necessity; for the indigent, outside the case of extreme necessity, have no strict right to the goods of the property owner (¹), who is free to distribute his goods as he will, provided that in doing so he does not act in violation of the common good.

The common use of private property is demanded by other virtues, viz., friendship, liberality, mercy, magnanimity, and especially Christian charity. Nevertheless, it is specifically required by legal or social justice, which directs all acts of the other virtues to the common good.

2° The obligation of almsgiving results from the common use, i.e., from the social function, of private property. But almsgiving is not the only obligation imposed by this function of private property.

According to Pius XI, « the investment of superfluous income in searching favorable opportunities for employment, provided the labor employed produces results which are really useful, is to be considered...an act of real liberality particularly appropriate to the needs of our time » (²).

The use of private property is also made common by the foundation and endowment of hospitals, schools, universities, and institutions destined for the support of the poor, the orphan, etc.

3° Superfluous goods are not unlawful (³), but should be directed to the common good.

4° Since the common use, i.e., the social function, of private property is required by social justice, the civil authority should make laws governing private ownership that will protect the common good⁽⁴⁾. The legislator, nevertheless, must always

---

(1) *Quadragesimo Anno.*
(2) *Ibidem.*
(3) Quinimo potest esse summa perfectio cum magna opulentia.— II-II, q. 185, a. 6, ad 1.
(4) *In Politic.*, l. II, l. 4.— CAJETANUS, in II-II, q. 118, a. 4, n. III.

act with prudence, even though sometimes with firmness and courage.

POINTS FOR REVIEW

1. Name and briefly explain the principal acts which men can exercise in regard to external things. Define ownership.

2. State the teaching of absolute Communism and also of moderate Communism on private ownership.

3. Is private ownership a useful and necessary institution? Explain.

4. Distinguish between primitive and derived modes of acquiring ownership; and name and explain the primitive modes of the acquisition of ownership.

5. Under what aspect does private property remain in some way common? Explain.

ARTICLE III

NATIONALITY

1105. Description of the nation.— The nation may be described: *a large community of men who, because of their descent from a common stock, are in certain physical characteristics and intellectual and moral qualities to some extent distinct from all other men.*

Hence the nation is distinct from the State, from the people, and from the fatherland.

The State has two meanings.

a) It signifies the supreme authority in civil society, on which every other authority is dependent. It has the same meaning as polity (politia) in Aristotle.

b) It signifies civil society in its totality. In this sense, the State is the civil community as embracing individual citizens and their rulers, and also private societies.

The people is the community united politically. Since the men who comprise a nation, or at least the greater part of it, very often live in the same territory and under the same civil authority, it sometimes happens that the terms nation and people are used indiscriminately.

The fatherland, in the restricted sense of the term, means the place in which we were born, grew up, and received, at least up to the age of reason, the first impressions of this life. In the full sense of the term, it means civil society and the territory over which it extends, in as much as it is the principle of our being.

1106. Philosophical definition of the nation.— The nation is defined philosophically: *the unity in certain characteristic qualities of a large community of men.*

a) The unity which constitutes the nation is unity in being, not unity in operation, although the nation can be united for the purpose of working for the common good, v.g., for the preservation of the qualities which properly characterize it.

b) The qualities in which the members of a nation are united are above all dispositions, v.g., figure, patible quality, or habits.

It is chiefly by unity in disposition that a nation is constituted in its physiological aspect, and chiefly by habits that it is constituted, as they say, in its psychological or psychic aspect.

1107. Causes of the nation.— The causes of the nation are the causes of those common qualities in which the members of a large community of men share. It is evident that specific nature cannot be the cause of the nation, because, if it were, all men would belong to the same nation.

Nevertheless, the causes of the nation should be general, and are those causes on which its production and conservation mainly depend. The chief causes of the production of a nation are the following:

a) food;

b) climatic conditions;

c) geographical conditions;

d) political, religious, and social institutions;

e) common tradition;

f) customs and social environment.

The first three causes directly determine the physiological character of a nation, and indirectly its psychological or psychic character; the other three causes are directly concerned with its physiological formation. It should be observed, however, that the indirect influence of the first three in the determination of the psychic character of a nation may be greater than that of the other three.

The causes chiefly concerned with the conservation of a nation are:

a) heredity;

b) language.

The influence of food on the character of a nation is admitted by all medical doctors and physiologists; it is exaggerated by materialists and determinists. The same may be said of climatic conditions.

Geographical conditions to a very great extent determine the kind of labor proper to a place. It is in accordance with the kind of daily labor that bodily dispositions, as, for example, patible qualities, i.e., health, strength, color, are determined, and that habits are engendered in the soul, v.g., the habits of fortitude, audacity, tenacity, and temperance.

Juridical, political, and social institutions exercise an influence on the habits and customs of a nation. They are, nevertheless, mutually interdependent. Hence we have the rhetorical questions:

What is the use of laws without customs?

What is the use of customs without laws?

Among some peoples, sense of justice and practice of vengeance are ascribed to juridical organization.

Common tradition, customs, and habits exercise an influence on the character of a nation because they constitute the environment in which successive generations receive their education. Successive generations, therefore, inherit the thoughts, aspirations, and desire for the conservation of the national character of their forbears.

The importance of language in the preservation of the character of a nation is twofold.

a) First, language is a sign of nationality, because it is an adequate means, and, for a large community of men, the only adequate means, of the expression of its proper personality or characteristics.

For the bond between a nation's sentiments, thoughts, and aspirations and its language is so close that it is only by its own language that those sentiments, thoughts, and aspirations can be adequately expressed.

b) Secondly, language preserves the psychic qualities of a nation. For the cultural treasures of a nation are found in formulas of its own language, which are, as it were, equivalent to self-evident principles.

Heredity, too, has a great influence on the preservation of a nation.

Heredity is defined: *the transmission by generation of the organic dispositions which determine the individual nature of parents.*

We can arrive at a more accurate notion of heredity from a consideration of human generation. Parents produce offspring similar to themselves *in species*, not by producing the human soul, which is spiritual, but by disposing matter to receive it.

Therefore parents do not transmit personal acts, because actions are proper to supposits, which are not transmitted; nor do they transmit these things which directly appertain to personal acts, as, for example, knowledge; but, because they can dispose matter to receive the soul, they can propagate these things which pertain to natural dispositions.

Therefore they can directly propagate by heredity: *a)* national qualities, which are dispositions of nature, as health, physical weakness, figure, etc.; *b)* good or evil dispositions of the organs used by the sensitive faculties: good eyesight, soft skin, good or bad dispositions of the sensitive memory, imagination, estimate faculty, and irascible and concupiscible appetite.

Since man's spiritual faculties are objectively dependent on the senses, heredity exercises an indirect influence on the habits of the spiritual faculties. Hence different nations have different dispositions for arts, sciences, etc.

Moreover, since the soul is proportionate to the matter into which it is received,— whatever is received is received according to the mode of its recipient,— heredity exercises an influence on the souls of the men who constitute a nation, in as much as their souls can possess a greater or lesser degree of perfection than the souls of the men of another nation.

But, since this diversity of souls results from the dispositions of matter, we must be careful to observe that this diversity is not essential, i.e., specific,— form is the principle of species,— not merely accidental, but *substantial and individual* — matter is the principle of individuation. In other words, men of different nations are not essentially distinct, for all have the same specific nature; but they have different accidental and substantial perfections or characteristics. Hence entirely untenable is the opinion of National Socialists, who teach that the races of men are so different in their perfections or characteristics, which are both native and immutable, that the lowest race of men is farther removed from the highest than it is from the highest species of brute. For men are not specifically distinct from each other; and national characteristics are not immutable, for they are dependent on the dispositions of matter, which is always mutable.

1108. Definition of nationalism.— Nationalism is defined: *love of natural friendship towards one's own nation.*

Nationalism is called *love*, because its object is a known good, i.e., national qualities which are the foundation of likeness between certain men: likeness is the cause of love, as the proper disposition of a subject ([1]).

It is called *love of friendship*, because it implies a sharing in the same thing, i.e., in the same national character.

And it is called love of *natural* friendship, for it is from heredity that it has its origin.

1109. Principle of nationality. — 1° *Preliminaries.* — *a)* The principle of nationality is a principle which declares that every nation should form a civil society of its own.

b) In the beginning, scarcely any one proposed this principle without certain restrictions.

Thus Robert von Mohl (1799-1875) recognized the right of a nation to form a civil society of its own, if this seemed neces-

---

(1) I-II, q. 27, a. 3.

1112. Opinions.— 1° In ancient times, a ruler was commonly regarded as taking the place of God. Thus no one was concerned with the question of the origin, i.e., of the efficient cause, of civil authority.

Positivists do not deal with this question, for they consider authority as a human fact, i.e., as a fact of dominant physical power. There are others also, as Hegel, who are not concerned with this question, for they hold that civil authority is a divine fact, i.e., a supreme autodetermination of the objective spirit.

2° Hobbes, Rousseau, Kant, and others deal with the efficient cause of civil authority, and conclude that its cause, like the cause of society, is a human cause, namely, the will of the people as freely expressed in a social contract.

From the social contract, according to Rousseau, results the public person, i.e., civil society, which has a common will. This common will is the civil authority (¹), which is *inalienable* in as much as the ruler can exercise power only in the name of the people, who can limit, change, or revoke it at will (²).

Rousseau's principles were far-reaching in their influence, and found juridical expression at the beginning of 1789 (³).

3° The Fathers of the Church, as St. Augustine, St. John Chrysostom, and St. Gregory the Great, the early Protestants, as Melanchton, Calvin, Grotius, and Pufendorf, and in general all Catholic philosophers, scholastic and non-scholastic, hold that civil authority as such derives immediately from God.

1113. Statement of the thesis.

> **THESIS.**— CIVIL AUTHORITY AS SUCH DERIVES IMMEDIATELY FROM GOD, THE AUTHOR OF NATURE.

That which necessarily results from the nature of civil society derives immediately from God, the author of nature.

---

(1) *Contrat*, l. I, c. 6.
(2) *Ibid.*, l. III, c. 1.
(3) Nul homme ne peut être soumis qu'à des lois consenties par lui ou ses représentants.— *Déclaration des droits de l'homme.*

sary for its well-being, and if it was probable that it could attain this by political autonomy.

Likewise, Bluntschli (1818-1881) accorded this right to a nation capable of political autonomy and of effecting it by force.

c) Today, however, National Socialists have adopted this principle without any restrictions in as much as they maintain that the nation itself is a civil society, and therefore that any civil society which is not a single nation is unlawful. Hence, in their opinion, the efficient cause of civil society is the instinct of the race or nation, which, therefore, is the first source and the supreme rule of the whole juridical order; and its final cause is the character of the nation, which is the supreme good for which education is primarily intended. In their opinion, then, everything which is conducive to this end is thereby lawful.

In other words, National Socialists teach that civil society is from nature and by nature, i.e., has its origin in and by means of the instinct of the race, whereas, in reality, civil society has its origin, as we have already shown, in nature and in human industry, i.e., in reason under the impulse of nature.

2° *In the light of the foregoing observations*, we shall now prove the propositions which follow.

1) *The principle of nationality, in its unrestricted acceptation, is contrary to the natural law.*— A principle which is founded on a false notion of human nature, and consequently of civil society, is contrary to the natural law. But the principle of nationality is founded on a false notion of human nature, and consequently of civil society. Therefore the principle of nationality, in its unrestricted acceptation, is contrary to the natural law.

The *major* is self-evident.

Minor.— Since the principle of nationality, in its unrestricted acceptation, declares that the nation itself is a civil society, it denies man's reason and liberty, i.e., his rational nature, or at least it subordinates them to racial instincts: for it declares that the proximate efficient cause of civil society is the nation's instincts, not reason; and that its final cause is the nation's well-being, not the good of reason, i.e., happiness. Hence the principle of nationality, in its unrestricted acceptation, is founded, as is evident from what we have already established, on false notions of both human and civil society.

2) *The principle of nationality, even with certain restrictions, is contrary to the common good of society.*— A principle which *a)* leads to the destruction of the lawful political order and *b)* provides opportunities for continual political trouble and disorder is contrary to the common good of society. But the principle of nationality, even with certain restrictions, *a)* leads to the destruction of the lawful political order and *b)* provides opportunities for continual political trouble and disorder. Therefore the principle of nationality, even with certain restrictions, is contrary to the common good of society.

The *major* is self-evident.

Minor.— *a)* This is evident from the fact that many lawfully subsisting States are not constituted in accordance with the principle of nationality.

b) Nationality in the concrete is very indeterminate; hence, if nationality were accepted as the constituent principle of civil society, continual wars and revolutions would be engendered as a result of the difficulties involved in the determination and extension of nationality.

3) *Every nation, or every considerable part of a nation, has a right to self-preservation within the civil society of which it forms a part.*— A good of citizens, and especially a good which is anterior to the existence of civil society, has a right to self-preservation within civil society. But nationality is a good of citizens which is anterior to the existence of civil society. Therefore.

Major.— It is the duty of civil society to protect and foster, not to abolish, whatever appertains to the good of its citizens.

Minor.— Experience and the very notion of the nation, which is unity in certain qualities, have shown that nationality is a good of citizens. Moreover, it is evident that nationality is a good which is anterior to the existence of civil society:

CHAPTER III

CIVIL AUTHORITY

Prologue.— In this chapter, we shall deal with the questions of the origin and the subject of civil authority. Hence the chapter will contain two articles.

Origin of civil authority
- Statement of the question
- Opinions
- Thesis: Civil authority as such derives immediately from God, the author of nature
- Scholion
- Capital punishment

Subject of civil authority
- Statement of the question
- Opinions
- Thesis: According to the order of nature, the people are the first subject from which civil authority naturally results; and its immediate subject is determined by human institution
- Scholion
- Polities and forms of government
- Suffrage
- Resistance of tyranny

it has its origin in a common stock, and hence properly belongs to men before they become members of civil society.

1110. Corollaries.— 1° Therefore the political authority should see to it that its institutions and laws are such as will give assurance that the nations subject to it will work together in peace and harmony for the common good.

2° Therefore the nations in the body politic have a right to their national language, because the existence of nationality is so intimately connected with language that it will gradually disappear if it loses its language.

3° The civil authority may, for a grave reason, take prudent steps to gradually remove national or racial differences which are an impediment to the attainment of the common good.

4° Nationality is not the proximate efficient cause of civil society, but can be an excellent remote preparation for it ([1]).

POINTS FOR REVIEW

1. What is a nation? Give its philosophical definition.
2. Define: heredity, nationalism.
3. Explain why the principle of nationality is contrary to the natural law.

---

(1) *In Politic.*, l. III, l. 2.

ARTICLE I

ORIGIN OF CIVIL AUTHORITY

1111. Statement of the question.— 1° Civil authority, as used here in the sense of power, may be defined: *the faculty of moving and directing civil society to its end.*

The faculty of moving and directing signifies *essentially* the faculty of coercing *morally*, and *consequently* the lawful faculty of using physical coaction in dealing with those who offer resistance.

2° Authority, i.e., power, in itself is distinct from its principle, i.e., from the way in which one acquires authority, and from its use, i.e., from the exercise of authority.

We are concerned at present only with the origin of authority as such.

3° In the thesis, we state that civil authority as such derives immediately from God, the author of nature.

a) Civil authority as such: hence civil authority derives immediately from God not only in as much as it is authority, but also in as much as it is *civil* authority.

b) Derives immediately from God: thus civil authority does not derive from God merely as He is its first and universal cause, for, under this aspect, any power given immediately to a man by a king or by the Pope derives from God; but it derives from God as He is its proximate and proper cause (¹).

c) Derives from God, the author of nature: hence civil authority is not conferred by a positive act of God acting as the author of the supernatural order, as it is, for example, in the case of the authority of the Pope.

---
(1) SUAREZIUS, *De Primatu Summi Pontificis*, l. 3, c. 2.

But civil authority as such necessarily results from the nature of civil society. Therefore civil authority as such derives immediately from God, the author of nature.

Major.— Civil society has its origin in reason under the impulse of nature. But the necessary resultants of the nature of civil society do not derive from *free* reason, nor are they constituted by it, as is evident, but derive immediately from nature, i.e., from God, the author of nature, because the author of a thing is the author also of the thing's necessary adjuncts; v.g., the author of the soul is the author of the intellect and will.

Minor.— Civil society is a heterogeneous society whose end is the common good, which is a good specifically distinct from the private good of its members. Hence authority is of necessity required in civil society, in order that its members be directed to the same end.

1114. Scholion.— Civil authority consists in the power of exacting anything necessary or useful for the end of civil society. In the exercise of this authority are found three functions to which any exercise of authority may be reduced.

For the end of society is attained:

1° by the act of proposing in an obligatory manner, by means of suitable laws, means which are useful and necessary, in order that all may contribute to the common good by working together in harmony — *legislative power;*

2° by the act of defining with authoritative judgment rights disputed in particular cases, and also of decreeing that legally established penalties be imposed on those guilty of the violation of rights — *judicial power;*

3° by the act of pressing the application, i.e., of promoting the execution, of what has been established by laws or legal sentences, using, if necessary, coercive force in the case of the reluctant and contumacious — *executive power.*

Executive power has three functions:

a) government, i.e., the ruling of persons in conformity with the law;

b) administration, i.e., the care and protection of means of production and of goods;

c) coaction, i.e., the coercion and punishment of transgressors of the law.

1115. Capital punishment. — 1° *Preliminaries.* — *a)* Punishment in general may be defined: *an evil inflicted on an agent against his will for a crime.*

The power of inflicting punishment derives from the very nature of civil society, for its ultimate end is the conservation and right government of civil society.

b) Punishment, considered in its effects, may be *reparative, medicinal,* or *exemplary.*

Punishment is *reparative,* in as much as it restores the order injured by the commission of crime; *medicinal,* for, as *statutory,* it engenders fear in the delinquents and withholds them from crime; and, as *inflicted,* it weakens the audacity of criminals and restrains them from returning to their crimnal ways; *exemplary,* in as much as it deters the wicked from crime: they see that other criminals are severely punished for their misdeeds.

c) Now the question arises: does the power of coaction of civil society sometimes extend to the punishment of criminals by death? In other words, it is sometimes lawful for the civil authority to inflict capital punishment on criminals?

d) Beccaria, H. Bentham, the Encyclopedists, the adherents of Liberalism, Lombroso, Ferri, and others deny that the civil authority has the right to inflict the death penalty.

We, on the contrary, hold that the civil authority has the right to inflict capital punishment on those guilty of certain crimes.

2° *Proposition.* — *The civil authority has the right to inflict capital punishment on persons guilty of certain crimes.*— The civil authority has the right to inflict capital punishment on persons who are dangerous to the community in as much as they are a menace to the public peace. But persons guilty of certain crimes are dangerous to the community in as much as they are a menace to the public peace. Therefore the civil authority has the right to inflict capital punishment on persons guilty of certain crimes (1).

Major.— A person entrusted with the good of a whole has the right to cut off a part which is dangerous to the whole in as much as it is a menace to the common good: wherefore we observe that, if the health of the whole human body requires the excision of a member which is, for example, decayed, and infectious to others members, it will be praiseworthy and advantageous to bodily health to excise it. But, on the one hand, the civil authority is entrusted with the welfare of the whole community and the care of the public peace, which is formally the common good of civil society; and, on the other hand, the criminal, like any other individual person, is related to civil society as the part to the whole. Therefore.

The *minor* is evident from examples: persons guilty of homicide or parricide are a menace to the order of the community, which is bound to protect individual persons; and they are, moreover, dangerous to the whole community.

NOTE.— Since a man participates in society, as a part in a whole, by the operation of his will, the civil authority may put to death only such persons as voluntarily abandon their part in the life of society. Hence it is not lawful for the civil authority to put an innocent person to death, even though the safety of the whole State would result from his death.

POINTS FOR REVIEW

1. Define civil authority, and explain under what aspect it derives immediately from God, the author of nature.

2. Has the civil authority the right to inflict capital punishment? Explain and prove your answer.

---

(1) II-II, q. 64, a. 2 et 3.— *Contra Gentes*, l. III, c. 40.

ARTICLE II

SUBJECT OF CIVIL AUTHORITY

1116. Statement of the question.— 1° The question of the subject of civil authority is entirely distinct from the question of the origin of civil society. The former question is concerned with the material cause of civil society, and the latter with its efficient cause.

2° In this article, we shall consider civil authority as such, and not parental or ecclesiastical authority.

3° Subject is defined: *a principle which is capable of receiving a form.*

4° Authority is a power, and therefore it appertains to the *order of operation.* Hence, in order to attain an accurate notion of the subject of civil authority, we must consider the order of operation of the organic world. Now, in the organic world, there are two kinds of subject, i.e., of principle, capable of receiving an organic faculty:

a) the first subject from which an organic faculty results by natural emanation, or, as it is called, the *total* subject: this subject is a complete supposit, i.e., a plant or an animal;

b) the immediate subject into which an organic faculty is received and by which the first subject exercises its operations, or, as it is called, the subject *quo*, the subject of inherence: it is a part of a total subject or an organ, as the eye, but sometimes can be coextensive with the total subject; v.g., the power of assimilation is diffused throughout the whole of the plant.

Similarly, in dealing with civil authority, we must make a distinction between the first subject from which civil authority naturally results and the immediate subject by which it is exercised. Hence we find ourselves confronted with two questions in regard to the subject of civil authority:

first, what, according to natural law, is the first subject from which civil authority results by natural emanation?

secondly, granted that this subject is a complete multitude politically united, i.e., a people, what, according to natural law, is the immediate subject of civil authority?

1117. Opinions.— 1° The people, according to Rousseau, is the efficient cause of civil authority, and therefore civil authority does not derive immediately from God. The people, moreover, is in an inalienable manner the immediate subject of civil authority, and consequently rulers and deputies are merely delegates or mandataries of the people.

2° According to the Sillonists (école du Sillon), civil authority derives from God, but the proximate subject in which it is inalienably vested is the people, and therefore rulers and deputies are nothing more than delegates or mandataries of the people. This is the opinion held by Marc Sangnier and others.

3° Many, especially the Monarchists, hold that the political power of kings derives immediately from God; in other words, they hold that a king is immediately constituted in the regal office by God. Hence they deny that the proximate subject of civil authority is determined by the will of man. This was the opinion held by King James I of England (¹), against whom St. Robert Bellarmine (²) and Suarez wrote. This opin-

---

(1) *Basilicon Doron.* 1599.
(2) King James I, who embraced Anglicanism, imposed an oath of allegiance on all Catholics. On 22 Sept., 1606, this oath was condemned by Pope Paul V as containing many things contrary to the Catholic faith and to the salvation of souls. King James published an anonymous reply entitled: *Triplici nodo triplex cuneus, sive apologia pro juramento fidelitatis adversus duo brevia Pauli PP. Quinti et Epistulam Cardinalis Bellarmini ad G. Blackwellum archipresbyterum nuper scriptam.* London, 1607.

Bellarmine, under the name of his chaplain, wrote a response entitled: *Matthaei Torti responsio ad librum inscriptum: Triplici modo triplex cuneus.*

It is to be observed that in the Middle Ages a distinction was made between civil power and imperial dignity. For, granted the unity of Christendom, the rule of the world was an ideal and free subordination of Christian peoples (who retained their supremacy) in respect to the emperor who, under

ion was held also by Luther, Melanchton, Calvin, King Louis XIV (¹), probably by Bossuet (²), and, in general, by all Gallicans.

4° Many of the older philosophers, as Hugh of St. Victor (d. 1141) and Alexander of Hales (d. 1245), held that the supreme civil authority derives from God through the Church.

5° Scholastics commonly hold that the people, i.e., the whole community politically united, is the first subject from which civil authority results by natural emanation (³).

But they do not agree on what is civil authority's immediate subject.

a) Some, as Liberatore, Schiffini, Meyer, Cathrein, Zigliara, and Lortie simply state, against Rousseau, that the people cannot be the subject of authority.

b) Others hold that the first immediate subject of civil authority is the people, and therefore that the people transfer it to the person of their ruler. This is the opinion held by Costa-Rossetti (⁴), Castelein (⁵), Marcellus of the Child Jesus (⁶), and

---

the Pope, was concerned with the common good of the entire Christian world and protected the Cnurch, its Head, and ecclestiastical dignitaries. Hence an emperor was already constituted in his regal office, i.e., in his civil power in regard to his own people, before he received the office of emperor.

(1) *Mémoires*, vol. 2, p. 285.
(2) *Politique tirée de l'Ecriture Sainte*, 1. 2, a. 4, prop. 1. Avertissements aux Protestants, c. 49.
(3) Dieu est le principe de l'autorité, la multitude est son objet, et sa fin est d'établir l'unité dans le multiple: si le multiple n'existait pas, ou s'il ne devait pas être ramené à l'unité, l'autorité n'aurait plus sa raison d'être et c'est dans ce sens que la multitude est cause que l'autorité existe. Au surplus, le concept de société suppose, dans toute réunion légitime, une autorité qui la conduise à la fin qu'elle s'est proposée, et une autorité qui existe essentiellement, nécessairement; une autorité, comme le remarque Gerdil, que les individus ne peuvent détruire, par la raison qu'ils ne peuvent rien contre l'essence des choses.

Ainsi, l'autorité qui est destinée à unir la multitude, a son origine dans la multitude, elle y prend naissance quand les individus s'associent; car, s'ils ne s'associaient pas, l'autorité ne pourrait les régir; mais on ne peut dire pour cela que c'est la multitude qui crée l'autorité, que l'autorité n'est pas autre chose que la volonté de tous.— TAPARELLI, *Essai théorique de droit naturel*, vol. I, nn. 484-485.
(4) *Phil. Moral.*, p. IV, sect. 2.
(5) *Phil. Moral. et Soc.*, Thes. 31.
(6) *Phil. Moral. et Soc.*, Disp. III, q. 2, a. V, & 2.

others, who attempt to defend the opinion of Cajetan, Bellarmine, Suarez, etc.

c) But, in our opinion, this is not exactly the teaching of Suarez, who, as all agree, gives the best presentation of scholastic tradition in this matter.

First, he maintains that, according to the order of nature, the people are the first subject from which civil authority derives.

Secondly, he holds that nature is negatively related to the proximate subject by which authority is exercised, and therefore that this subject is determined by the will and institution of men. Gredt holds almost the same opinion. This is the opinion which we follow.

1118. Statement of the thesis.

THESIS.— ACCORDING TO THE ORDER OF NATURE, THE PEOPLE IS THE FIRST SUBJECT FROM WHICH CIVIL AUTHORITY NATURALLY RESULTS; AND ITS IMMEDIATE SUBJECT IS DETERMINED BY HUMAN INSTITUTION.

First part.— *According to the order of nature, the people is the first subject from which civil authority naturally results.*— This is evident, because civil authority necessarily derives from the nature of the people, i.e., of the community politically united, as its property.

Second part.— *The immediate subject of civil authority is determined by human institution.*— The immediate subject of civil authority is determined either by the natural law or by human institution. But it is not determined by the natural law. Therefore the immediate subject of civil authority is determined by human institution.

Minor.— According to the natural law, there is no reason why civil authority is vested in one part of a community rather than in another, that is to say, not only is there no reason why it is vested in this particular person rather than in another, but also no reason why it is vested in one person rather than in a senate or legislative body, and vice versa; in one ruler rather than in deputies, and vice versa, as is evident from practice: for peoples adopt different forms of government, and, in doing so, they do not act in violation of the natural law.

1119. Scholion.— Since civil authority results from the nature of the people, it does not derive from the will of the people, nor is it the will of the people, as Rousseau contended, but it is derived immediately from nature, i.e., from God, the author of nature. Hence civil authority as civil or political, whether vested in the people as a whole, or in a ruler, or in a legislative body, is immediately derived from God. But the proximate subject in which it is vested, as a ruler, a legislative body, etc., is determined by human institution.

In other words, authority as civil is immediately derived from God, but civil authority becomes, for example, regal by human institution, as Suarez wrote in condemnation of the teaching of James I; but yet authority as regal is derived from God as from its first cause.

1120. Polities and forms of government.— A polity or constitution is defined by St. Thomas: *the organization or disposition of a state as regards its first and supreme governing body under which its citizens are ruled, and on whose authority the authority of inferior governments are dependent* (¹).

Therefore a constitution is the organization of a state considered under three aspects:

a) the disposition of the supreme governing body, i.e., of the supreme authority;

b) the disposition of inferior authorities which are dependent of the supreme authority;

c) the disposition of the citizens, who are ruled under this authority.

---

(1) *In Politic.*, l. III, l. 5.

The notion of form of government is similar to the notion of constitution, although the latter is more profound. A form of government is defined by modern philosophers: *the disposition of the supreme authority in regard to the proximate subject in which it exists.*

Constitutions or polities are divided into proper constitutions and improper constitutions as they are directly concerned with the common good or with their own good.

The following are proper constitutions:

a) Monarchy: rule of one individual in the interest of the common good;

b) Aristocracy: the rule of the elite few — more than one — in the interest of the common good. The aristocracy is called « status optimatum » (government of the aristocracy, i.e., of the best), either because rulers of this kind are the best, or because this kind of polity has virtue as its object.

c) Democracy: the rule of the people in the interest of the common good.

The following are improper constitutions:

a) Tyranny: the rule of one individual who is concerned with his own good.

b) Oligarchy: the rule of the elite few in the interest of the good of the rich.

c) Anarchy (democracy in a bad sense): the rule of the people in the interest of the good of the poor.

There can be mixed forms of government, i.e., forms which are a combination of the foregoing politics or forms of government.

1121. Suffrage. — 1° The right of suffrage is defined: *the power enjoyed by a people of electing civil officials by whom their State is governed, at least in part.*

We say: *the power of electing civil officials*, because suffrage does not establish authority which derives immediately from God, but determines who may exercise it (Leo XIII, *Diuturnum*).

We say too: *by whom the State is governed, at least in part:* for a country can have a mixed government, whose officials are not all elected by suffrage.

2° Those who hold that civil society and consequently civil authority do not derive from nature, but merely from the consent of the people, teach that the right of suffrage necessarily belongs to all individuals; hence they proclaim that *universal suffrage is a natural right.* Such is the teaching of the disciples of Rousseau, called Liberal Democrats.

We do not admit this opinion: we maintain that the right of suffrage is not a natural right to which all are entitled.

a) If universal suffrage were a natural right, all other methods of choosing civil officials would be unlawful.

b) The Democrats teach the necessity of universal suffrage, because they contend that civil authority belongs inalienably to the people, and consequently that the people must elect their civil officials. But civil authority is neither inalienably in the people, nor from the people, but from God.

3° In order that suffrage be universal, it could not be merely individual, but would have to be exercised by the heads of families as such, by associations, v.g., professional associations, by universities, etc.

4° Some may perhaps hold that suffrage, and, in particular, universal suffrage, is in theory the best way of electing civil officials. But what is best in theory is not necessarily best in practice, and hence the value of suffrage must be judged from circumstances, that is to say, from the education of the people and from the resultant advantages to society.

In a word, the advantages or disadvantages of suffrage depend, as St. Augustine points out (¹), on the civic education of the people and their interest in the common good.

---

(1) Si populus sit bene moratus et gravis, communisque utilitatis diligentissimus custos, recte lex fertur qua tali populo liceat creare sibi magistratus per quos respublica administretur. Porro, si paulatim idem populus depravatus habeat venale suffragium, et regimen flagitiosis sceleratisque committat, recte adimitur populo tali potestas dandi honores, et ad paucorum bonorum redit arbitrum.— *De Lib. Arb.*, l. I, c. 6.

1122. Resistance of tyranny.— 1° *Preliminaries.*— *a)* Tyrant originally meant a governor who had full power over his subjects. Nowadays, however, tyrant signifies a governor who imposes his own will on a people by force, or oppresses a people by unjust laws.

b) Resistance, in general, is opposition to another's activity. It is to two kinds: *active* and *passive.*

Passive resistance is morally the same as disobedience.

Active resistance is of two kinds: *peaceful* or *non-violent,* which is opposition to unjust laws and the violence of governors by means of writings, peaceful demonstrations, etc.; *armed* or *violent,* which is opposition by physical force for the overthrow of tyranny.

c) Both passive resistance and peaceful active resistance to manifestly unjust laws are certainly lawful; moreover, at least passive resistance is obligatory in the case of laws which are manifestly opposed to divine or natural good. But what must be said of violent active resistance?

d) To answer this question, we must make a distinction between *tyrant by usurpation* and *tyrant by oppression.*

A *tyrant by usurpation* or *title* is one who attains supreme authority by the use of illegal means of any kind whatsoever.

A *tyrant by oppression* is one who has a just title to supreme authority, but governs his subjects by manifestly unjust laws.

2° *In the light of the foregoing observations,* we may now set forth our teaching on the violent active resistance of tyrants in the propositions which follow.

1) *At the time of the act of usurpation, both the rightful ruler and people have the right of defending themselves against a tyrant by usurpation.*— This is evident, for, if an individual man may use violence in self-defence against an unjust aggressor in the act of aggression, the people and the person in whom is vested the care of the people have a fortiori a similar right.

Therefore, *while war is actually being waged,* the rightful ruler *may,* and the people not only may, but *should* resist an unjust aggressor, and, if necessary, put him to death, provided that the moderation of a blameless defense is observed.

A private citizen may do the same, provided that he acts not on his private authority, but on the *express* or *tacit* authority of his ruler (¹).

2) *After the usurper has established his rule, both the rightful ruler and the people have, absolutely speaking, the right to dethrone a tyrant by usurpation.*— This is evident, for no one may lawfully become a ruler by the use of violence (²).

We say *absolutely speaking*, for if the people would suffer greater evils as a result of war against the tyrant, and there is no probable hope of overthrowing him, the exercise of rights should be suspended and submission made to the tyrant: for in this case, the public safety of the people, which is the supreme law, is at stake.

Therefore, after a usurper has established himself in power, citizens are bound to submit to his decrees if they are in the interest of the common good, for otherwise there would be no legislator, and the State would perish.

3) *A tyrant by usurpation can become the lawful ruler.*— It is not in virtue of violence, as is evident, but because of the necessity of peace and public security that a usurper can become the lawful ruler. For, if the rule of the usurper is looked upon as unlawful, public peace will be endangered as long as the people regard him as a usurper and question the lawfulness of his authority.

4) *In the case of the tyrant by oppression, we should be guided by the following principles:*

a) When the tyranny is not excessive, it is more advantageous to tolerate the tyrant for a time than to oppose him and thereby become victimized by evils worse than his tyrannous rule.

Public security or the common good, indeed, requires that

---

(1) CAJETANUS, in II-II, q. 64, a. 3.
(2) *In II Sent.*, d. 44, q. 2, a. 2, ad 5.

we suffer small evils, in order that greater ones may be avoided (¹).

b) In the case of tyranny which is intolerable, there are four possible remedies:

First, if there exists a superior authority in whom is vested the right of providing for the government of the people, appeal may be made to him for redress against the tyranny.

Secondly, if the people have the right of making provision for their own government, they may either depose the tyrant, or limit his power, if he is guilty of abuse in its exercise.

Thirdly, if the ruler is not determined by the vote of the people, nor by a higher authority, and if tyranny is evident and excessive, the people very probably have, *because of the common good*, the right of deposing the tyrant: for the safety of the country as a whole is the supreme law.

Fourthly, if no human help can be found to restrain the tyrant, recourse must be had to Almighty God, the King of Kings, Who ever comes at the opportune moment to the aid of those who are suffering tribulation, and Who, moreover, is able to change the cruelty of the tyrant's heart into clemency.

But, in order to obtain this divine favor, the people must give up the sinfulness of their lives, because it is in punishment of sin that Almighty God permits the rule of the people to pass into impious hands (²).

POINTS FOR REVIEW

1. Explain how there is a twofold question in regard to the subject of civil authority.
2. State the teaching of Rousseau and the Sillonists on the subject of civil authority.
3. Give St. Thomas' definition of polity.
4. Define: form of government, right of suffrage.
5. Explain why the right of suffrage is a natural right.

---
(1) *De Reg. Princ.*, l. I, c. 6.
(2) *Ibid.*

BOOK II

The restoration of society

Prologue.— There is no one who does not see that great disorder obtains in civil society at the present time. Hence we may speak of the restoration of society that must be achieved according to the doctrine of the Church and the principles of sound philosophy. In order that this restoration be accomplished, the reformation of morals above all else is necessary. But the Church proposes a means admirably suited for this reformation of society which facilitates the exercise of justice and also the reformation of morals. This means is the professional association. In our discussion of the restoration of society, we shall examine the chief errors in regard to society. Hence there will be two chapters in this book.

Chapter I. Professional associations.

Chapter II. Errors in regard to society.

CHAPTER I

PROFESSIONAL ASSOCIATIONS

Prologue.— First, we shall deal with the ends of the professional association; secondly, with its lawfulness; thirdly, with the complete professional association, which is the corporation. When we have completed our study of these topics, we shall discuss salary and capitalism. Hence there will be five articles in this chapter.

Ends of professional associations	Statement of the question Opinions Thesis: The proximate end of the professional association is the common good of the profession and its members; and its remote end is the common good of civil society
Lawfulness of professional associations	Statement of the question Opinions Thesis: The professional association is in conformity with the natural law
Complete professional associations	Notion of corporatism Corporate associations Political corporatism and social corporatism State corporatism and corporatism of association Syndicates within corporate associations Teaching of the Church on syndicates
Salary or wages	Statement of the question Thesis: Salary in itself is lawful; and the absolute family wage is due in strict justice to workmen The absolute family wage is due in commutative justice Difficulties Scholia Collective labor contracts Strikes Scholia Contracts of partnership

Capitalism

- Statement of the question
- Opinions.
- Capitalism in itself is not intrinsically evil; but today it is beset with many evils, which only great prudence and discretion can remove

ARTICLE I

ENDS OF PROFESSIONAL ASSOCIATIONS

1123. Statement of the question.— 1° The professional association, according to its nominal definition, is a union of persons who practice the same profession.

A profession is defined: *a permanent kind of employment chosen by a person for the support of himself and his family, and at the same time conducive to the common good of civil society.*

A profession is a *permanent* kind of work, for a man who is only temporarily engaged in an employment does not practice a profession.

The end of a profession is not merely the private good of the individual, but the common good as well, for there must needs be a division of labor by which a man helps his neighbor, each making his contribution to the commonweal; v.g., one must be a farmer, another a doctor, another a cook, etc. Therefore professions have their origin in nature, even though each one is free to choose his own particular profession.

2° The professional association is defined: *an organic union of persons of the same profession for the pursuit of their common interests, and for better work on behalf of the common good of civil society as a whole;* v.g., a college of doctors, of lawyers, an association, i.e., a syndicate, of workmen, employers, etc.

3° The professional association may be incomplete, i.e., *syndical,* or complete, i.e., *corporate.*

An incomplete professional association is one which unites only a part of those engaged in the production of a finished commodity, or in the supplying of a complete service; v.g., labor unions, in which only workmen are united; associations of employers.

A complete or corporate professional association is one which unites all engaged in any way in the production of a finished commodity, or in the supplying of a complete service, i.e., employers, managers, workmen, etc.

4° A distinction must be made between the proximate end and the remote end of a professional association.

The proximate end is the common good of both the association and its members.

The remote end is the common good of civil society.

In both cases, the association must protect, i, e., defend, the common good against transgressors, and also promote it in a positive manner.

1124. Opinions.— 1° Revolutionary socialism holds that the end of professional associations is revolution. Associations of workmen, according to this opinion, are instruments of class warfare, and intended to paralyze employers and capitalists.

2° Individualism teaches that the end of the professional association is merely the good of its members.

3° According to the Catholic opinion, the end of the professional association is the common good of the profession and its members, and also of civil society. Hence, in this opinion, professional associations are designed for the establishment of peace and order in society.

1125. Statement of the thesis.

THESIS.— THE PROXIMATE END OF THE PROFESSIONAL ASSOCIATION IS THE COMMON GOOD OF THE PROFESSION AND ITS MEMBERS; AND ITS REMOTE END IS THE COMMON GOOD OF CIVIL SOCIETY.

First part.— *The proximate end of the professional association is the common good of the profession and its members.*— The proximate end of every society is the common good of those who are united in it. But the professional association is a society: for it is a society of persons of the same profession. Therefore the proximate end of the professional association is the common good of the profession and its members (¹).

Second part. — *The remote end of the professional association is the common good of civil society.*— The remote end of a part of civil society is the common good of civil society as a whole. But the professional association is a part of civil society. Therefore the remote end of the professional association is the common good of civil society (²).

Major.— Civil society is a whole which is not an absolute unit, i.e., which has not absolute unity, but which has unity of order. Hence each of its parts has its own proper operation, and therefore its own proper proximate end; and this end has the good of civil society as its remote end: the part is for the whole.

POINTS FOR REVIEW

1. Define: profession, professional association, complete professional association, and incomplete professional association.

2. What is the teaching of Socialism on the end of professional associations?

3. State the proximate end of the professional association, and explain why its remote end is the common good of civil society as a whole.

---

(1) Speaking summarily, we may lay it down as a general and perpetual law that Workmen's Associations should be so organized and governed as to furnish the best and most suitable means for attaining what is aimed at, that is to say, for helping each individual member to better his condition to the utmost, in body, mind, and property.— *Rerum Novarum.*

(2) Order, as the Angelic Doctor well defines, is unity arising from the apt arrangement of a plurality of objects; hence, true and genuine social order demands various members of society, joined together by a common bond. Such a bond of union is provided on the one hand by the common effort of employers and employees of one and the same group joining forces to produce goods or give service; on the other hand, by the common good which all groups should unite to promote, each in its own sphere, with friendly harmony. Now this union will become powerful and efficacious in proportion to the fidelity with which the individuals and the groups strive to discharge their professional duties and to excel in them.

From this it is easy to conclude that in these associations the common interest of the whole group must predominate: and among these interests the most important is the directing of the activities of the group to the common good.— *Quadragesimo Anno.*

ARTICLE II

LAWFULNESS OF PROFESSIONAL ASSOCIATIONS

1126. Statement of the question.— 1° Having dealt with the questions of the nature and ends of the professional association, we turn now to the question of its lawfulness.

2° A thing is lawful, as the very term suggests, which is in conformity with law. Law is either natural or positive.

The professional association is lawful in as much as it is in conformity with the natural law.

3° A thing is in conformity with the natural law either because it is from nature, i.e., is imposed by nature, or because it is in accordance with nature.

A thing is imposed by nature, in the case of man, when man cannot attain his natural ends without it. A thing is in accordance with nature when it is most advantageous to man for the attainment of his natural ends.

Professional associations are said to be lawful not in as much as they are imposed by nature, but in as much as they are in accordance with nature (1).

1127. Opinions.— 1° Liberal individualism holds that professional associations are unlawful, because they are opposed to individual liberty. In the days of the French Revolution, this false opinion led to the dissolution of the corporations, i.e., of the professional associations, of that day.

---

(1) For as nature induces those who dwell in close proximity to unite into municipalities, so those who practice the same trade or profession, economic or otherwise, combine into professional groups. These groups, in a true sense autonomous, are considered by man to be, if not essential to civil society, at least its natural and spontaneous development.— *Qusadragesimo Anno*.

2° The Catholic Church teaches that professional associations are lawful, and, from the point of view of the natural order, most useful. Moreover, the Holy Father teaches that, in conditions such as obtain in the world today, the setting up of professional associations is necessary for the restoration of peace and order in society (¹).

1128. Statement of the thesis.

THESIS.— THE PROFESSIONAL ASSOCIATION IS IN CONFORMITY WITH THE NATURAL LAW.

1° Every society whose end is the attainment of a lawful good is in conformity with the natural law. But the professional association is a society whose end is the attainment of a lawful good. Therefore the professional association is in conformity with the natural law.

The *major* is evident from the fact that man is a social animal, and therefore is natural y inclined to set up societies for the attainment of the common good (²).

The *minor* is evident from what we said on the ends of professional associations.

2° Any association which is suited for the pursuit of an end of natural institution is in conformity with the natural law. But the professional association is suited for the pursuit of an

---

(1) To this grave disorder which is leading society to ruin a remedy must evidently be applied as speedily as possible. But there cannot be question of any perfect cure, except this opposition be done away with, and well-ordered members of the social body come into being anew, vocational groups namely, binding men together not according to the position they occupy in the labor market, but according to the diverse functions which they exercise in society.— *Quadragesimo Anno*.

(2) The experience of his own weakness urges man to call in help from without. We read in the pages of Holy Writ: « It is better that two should be together than one; for they have the advantage of their society. If one fall, he shall be supported by the other. Woe to him that is alone, for when he falleth, he hath none to lift him up » (Eccles. IV, 9-10). And further: « A brother that is helped by his brother is like a strong city » (Prov. XVIII, 19). It is this natural impulse which unites men in civil society; and it is this also which makes them band themselves together in associations of citizen with citizen; associations which, it is true, cannot be called societies in the complete sense of the word, but which are societies nevertheless.— *Rerum Novarum*.

end instituted by nature. Therefore the professional association is in conformity with the natural law.

Major.— If an end is natural, anything which is suited for its attainment is in accordance with the natural law.

Minor.— The end of the professional association is the common good of the profession and of civil society; and this good is of nature's institution. For the professional association, of its very nature, has as its end the pursuit of this common good in a suitable manner, i.e., in a manner in conformity with nature.

1129. Corollary.— Since professional associations are in conformity with the natural law, the State not only should permit that they be established, but should foster and protect them (1).

If, however, any professional association or any private society pursues ends opposed to justice, or to the well-being of civil society, the State, in such a case, has the right to dissolve and abolish it.

---

(1) This is the primary duty of the State and of all good citizens: to abolish conflict between classes with divergent interests, and thus foster and promote harmony between the various ranks of society. The aim of social legislation must therefore be the re-establishment of vocational groups.— *Quadragesimo Anno.*

Societies which are formed in the bosom of the State are called *private*, and justly so, because their immediate purpose is the private advantage of the associates. « Now, a private society », says St. Thomas, « ... is one which is formed for the purpose of carrying out private business; as when two or three enter into partnership with the view of trading in conjunction » (*Contra impugnantes Dei cultum et religionem, Cap. II*). Particular societies, then, although they exist within the State, and are each a part of the State, nevertheless, cannot be prohibited by the State absolutely and as such. For to enter into a « society » of this kind is the natural right of man; and the State must protect natural rights, not destroy them; and if it forbids its citizens to form associations, it contradicts the very principle of its own existence; for both they and it exist in virtue of the same principle, *viz.*, the natural propensity of man to live in society.— *Rerum Novarum.*

ARTICLE III

COMPLETE PROFESSIONAL ASSOCIATIONS

1130. Notion of corporation.— 1° A distinction must be made between corporatism in the broad sense of the term, and corporatism in its restricted meaning, i.e., as signifying professional corporatism.

2° Corporatism, in its wide meaning, is the doctrine of those who conceive civil society not only as a grouping of individuals, but above all as a union of groups or associations of various institutions and social bodies, the chief of which are families, universities, religious institutions, and, in general, all the professions.

Corporatism, in this sense, is the opposite of individualism and statism (State omnipotence).

It is opposed to *individualism,* because it considers civil society not as constituted solely of individuals, but as a union of inferior groups, each pursuing its own particular ends as directed to the common good of civil society as a whole.

It is opposed to *statism,* because it grants inferior groups a certain autonomy and also rights of their own for the pursuit of their special ends, while at the same time it safeguards the power of civil society over the common good.

Corporatism, in this sense, is doctrinally true.

3° Professional corporatism is nothing more or less than the application of corporatism in its broad meaning to the professions. It is the doctrine of those who recommend the organization of the professions into complete professional associations, i.e., into corporate associations or corporations.

1131. Corporate associations.— The corporate association, i.e., the complete professional association, is defined: *a public association, intermediary between private enterprise and the State, charged with the common good of a profession.*

a) Public association: the corporate association is not an organ of the State, and, under this aspect, is a private association; but it has juridical authority to make and enforce regulations for a profession, and, under this aspect, is a public association.

b) Intermediary between private enterprise and the State: the corporate association, though subordinate to the State, is distinct from the State, because it pursues particular ends, and therefore performs functions distinct from the functions of the State.

On the other hand, the corporate association permits private enterprise arising from private activity and personal freedom. Hence it is intermediary between the State and private enterprise.

c) Charged with the common good of a profession, i.e., with the common good of the profession and its members. It is the duty of the corporate association to regulate competition between the members of a profession; to deal with and settle problems pertaining to the advantages or disadvantages of the members of a profession which require attention and protection; and also to make sure that the members are faithful to the practice of their profession, and give a superior quality of professional service, by supplying the *social services* with which the profession is charged.

1132. Political corporatism and social corporatism. — *Political corporatism* is quite distinct from *social corporatism.*

Political corporatism is concerned with the organization of political or civil society as such.

Political corporatism makes two demands:

a) the legal and juridical status of corporate associations;

b) participation of corporate associations in the authority of the State, particularly in its legislative power, in either a deliberative or an advisory capacity.

Social corporatism is not concerned with the organization of civil society as such, and hence does not demand a participation of corporate associations in the authority of the State. It does demand, however, such legal and juridical status and recognition of corporate associations as will enable them to settle authoritatively problems bearing upon the particular ends of a profession.

Political corporatism is a special form of political government. Therefore the Church is entirely neutral in the matter of political corporatism, raising its voice neither in condemnation nor in approval. It simply regards it as a lawful form of government, and leaves all peoples free to choose it, if they will. But such is not the Chuch's attitude towards social corporatism: it highly recommends this kind of corporatism as the chief remedy for the social ills of our day.

1133. State corporatism and corporatism of association.— In State corporatism, it is the State which sets up syndicates and complete professional associations.

In corporatism of association, the members of the profession set up syndicates and complete professional associations. The State has only to give recognition to the organs of the profession by giving them legal status, by fostering them, and by directing and controlling them according to exigencies of the common good of society as a whole.

State corporatism is not unlawful. Moreover, it can be a necessity in certain circumstances. But corporatism of association is preferable, because it gives greater encouragement to private activity in matters pertaining to it.

1134. Syndicates within corporate associations.— The corporate association, i.e., the complete professional association, has authority over all matters which pertain to the common good of the profession and its members.

But the members of a profession differ from one another according to the diversity of their functions, duties, and advantages; v.g., employers and employees.

Hence we are confronted with the problem of whether incomplete professional associations, i.e., distinct syndicates or unions, are permissible within the corporate association; v.g., syndicates of employers and syndicates of employees.

According to State corporatism, generally only one syndicate should be permitted within the corporate association, so that all the members of a profession, employers and employees, would be united in one and the same syndicate.

According to corporatism of association, distinct syndicates may be set up within the corporate association; v.g., syndicates for employers, syndicates for employees, etc. Hence we have the formula: « free syndicates within organized professions.»

Hence, in order to set up a corporate association, the members of a profession may take the following steps:

first, syndicates, i.e., incomplete professional associations, are organized;

secondly, a *corporate council* is set up. This council should have power to settle all matters pertaining to the profession. Moreover, each branch of the profession should have equal representation in the council, i.e., each branch should have the same number of representatives; v.g., employees should have equal representation with employers in the council.

Each profession should have three classes of corporate councils: local councils, regional councils, and national councils.

The final step in corporate organization consists in setting up an *intercorporate* council, into which admission should be given to delegates of different professions, for the purpose of settling matters pertaining to harmony between the professions and to the common good of society as a whole.

1135. Teaching of the Church on syndicates.— In a letter dated 5 June, 1929, and addressed to H. E. Cardinal Lienart, the Sacred Congregation of the Council set forth in the following seven propositions the teaching of the Church on syndicates:

I.— The Church recognizes and affirms the right of employers and employees to set up syndical associations, either separate or mixed, and sees in them an effective means for the solution of the social question.

II.— The Church deems the setting up of such syndical associations as morally necessary in present conditions of the world.

III.— The Church urges the establishment of such syndical associations.

IV.— The Church desires that syndical associations be set up according to the principles of Christian faith and morality.

V.— The Church desires that syndical associations be instruments of peace and concord, and, to this end, recommends the establishment of mixed Commissions as a means of union between them.

VI.— The Church desires that syndical associations set up by and for Catholics be established among Catholics, with regard, however, for practical exigencies which may necessitate a different course.

VII.— The Church recommends the union of all Catholics for a common work in the bonds of Christian charity.

This doctrine of the Church received its completion in the encyclical letter *Quadragesimo Anno* (15 May, 1931), in which Pope Pius XI points out that syndicates should be made integrant parts of the complete professional association or corporate organization.

POINTS FOR REVIEW

1. Define: corporatism in the wide sense, corporate association, political corporatism, social corporatism, state corporatism, and corporatism of association.

2. Is it permissible to set up distinct syndicates within a corporate association? Explain.

ARTICLE IV

SALARY OR WAGES

1136. Statement of the question.— 1° Salary in general is defined: *the reward owed, in virtue of a bilateral contract, to the employee by the employer for services rendered.*

Salary, then, presupposes an onerous bilateral contract, i.e., a labor contract, by which the workman gives up his rights to his labor and its fruits, and acquires the right to a reward which the employer must make good, in order that he may acquire a right to the workman's labor.

2° Salary is divided into *individual* or *personal* salary and *family* salary.

The *personal* salary is a wage sufficient for the support of the wage-earner himself.

The *family* salary is a wage sufficient for the support of the wage-earner and his family.

Family salary is divided into *relative* family salary and *absolute* family salary.

The *relative* family salary is a wage which must be increased in proportion to the number of children and needs of the family.

The *absolute* family salary is a wage determined by taking into account the ordinary and common constitution of the family, without making it subject to the differences in number of children, health, and special needs of any particular family.

3° Socialists hold that the labor contract and consequently salary or wages are unlawful: the salary system is a form of thievery, and the workingman has a right to the full fruits of his labor.

The Liberal school teaches that a salary agreed upon between employer and employee is a just salary.

The Catholic doctrine, as presented by Pope Leo XIII in his memorable encyclical letter *Rerum Novarum*, affirms, against Liberals, that salary, from natural justice, i.e., justice which antecedes all free bargaining between employer and wage-earner, ought to be sufficient to support the wage-earner in reasonable and frugal comfort. The wage-earner is ordinarily a married man, i.e., the head of a family; and, in every case, the salary should be the absolute family salary.

Pope Pius XI, especially in the encyclical *Divini Redemptoris*, affirms that the family salary is due *in strict justice* to the workingman (¹).

The doctrine stated in the thesis which follows must be understood as applicable to the case of the normal workingman, i.e., a man who has reached full physical development and is engaged full time in his work under conditions of normal production.

1137. Statement of the thesis.

THESIS. — SALARY IN ITSELF IS LAWFUL; AND THE ABSOLUTE FAMILY WAGE IS DUE IN STRICT JUSTICE TO WORKMEN.

First part. — *Salary in itself is lawful.* — 1° If a workman may justly place his labor or activity at the service of another person, salary in itself is lawful. But a workman may in justice place his labor or activity at the disposal of another man. Therefore salary in itself is lawful.

Major. — Salary is a reward for labor, a certain price paid for it.

Minor. — The workman is free, and therefore may place his activity at the disposal of another man.

---

(1) Cf. nn. 31 and 49.

2° Socialists hold that salary is unjust, because they regard labor as the sole cause of production. But labor is not the sole cause of production. Therefore.

Major. — Socialists, in virtue of their teaching that labor is the sole cause of production, conclude that all the fruits of production are due to the workman.

Minor.— Capital, as well as labor, makes a most important contribution to production: the various machines and instruments used in production are the efficient cause of production, whereas the material and its powers supplied by the holders of capital are its material cause. Moreover, capitalists pay workmen their hire before the sale of the goods manufactured by them, and thus take the risk of loss. Hence it is only fair that they receive a major portion of the profits of production, because of their greater contributions to it.

Second part.— *The absolute family wage is due in strict justice to workmen.*— 1° The workman has a strict right to what is necessary for his own self-preservation and for the propagation of the species. But the absolute family wage is necessary for the workman for his own self-preservation and for the propagation of the species. Therefore the workman has a strict right to the absolute family wage, i.e., the absolute family salary is due in strict justice to workmen.

Major.—His own self-preservation and the propagation of the species are the natural ends of the workmen, just as they are the natural ends of all other men. Hence workmen have a strict right to what is required for the attainment of these ends.

Minor.— His wage or salary is ordinarily the only means the workman has at his disposal for the support of himself and his family.

2° The workman's labor has a social as well as an individual or personal aspect, for, in contributing to production, it makes a contribution to the happiness of civil society. Hence, just as the workman contributes to the happiness of civil society, i.e., to the common good, so he has a strict right to a share in the common good; and for this the absolute family salary is required.

3° Production is necessary. But production is not possible without the cooperation of workmen. Therefore workmen are necessary, and hence salary must be sufficient for the support and propagation of workmen, i.e., workmen must be paid the absolute family wage.

1138. The absolute family wage is due in commutative justice.— 1° We have already proved that the absolute family salary or wage is due in strict justice to the workman.

But justice, as we know, is of three kinds: *social justice, distributive justice,* and *commutative justice.*

Social justice is *justice which determines the relations of citizens to civil society, as of parts to the whole.*

Distributive justice is *justice which determines the relations of civil society to its citizens, in as much as it regulates the distribution of the common goods and social burdens.*

Commutative justice is *justice which regulates exchange between private persons, i.e., individuals.*

2° All Catholics hold that the absolute family wage is due in justice to the workman. Some claim it is due in social justice; others maintain that it is due in distributive justice; we, for our part, hold that it is due in commutative justice.

The employer is bound in social justice to pay the absolute family wage, in as much as he has the obligation of directing all his acts to the common good. But is is in commutative justice towards him that the employer is formally under obligation to pay the absolute family wage *to the workman.*

In other words, the act by which the employer pays the absolute family wage is an act *elicited* by commutative justice, and *commanded* by social justice (¹).

---

(1) But social justice cannot be said to have been satisfied as long as workingmen are denied a salary that will enable them to secure proper sustenance for themselves and their families.— *Divini Redemptoris,* n. 52.

3° In the light of the foregoing considerations, we shall now prove that the absolute family wage is due in commutative justice.

1) Contracts are regulated by commutative justice. But the absolute family wage is due in virtue of a contract. Therefore the absolute family salary is due in commutative justice.

The *major* is evident, for a contract is a bilateral exchange.

The *minor* also is evident, because the employer pays salary in return for his employee's labor.

2) The kind of justice which regulates the relations between capital and labor, i.e., between employers and employees, is commutative justice (¹). But the absolute family wage is due from the kind of justice which regulates the relations between capital and labor, i.e., between employers and employees. Therefore the absolute family wage is due in commutative justice.

Major.— The employer and the employee are private persons.

Minor.— Salary is owed the employee by the employer.

1139. Difficulties.— 1° The object of commutative justice is the equality of one thing to another. But there is not necessarily equality between the workman's labor and the absolute family wage. Therefore the absolute family wage is not due in commutative justice.

Major.— If we take all elements into account, *I concede*; if we do not take all elements into account, *I deny*.

Minor.— If we take into account the natural end of labor, which is the support of the workman and his family, *I deny*; if we do not take this end into account, *I concede*.

2° Equality measured according to one's condition is due in distributive justice. But the absolute family wage is an equality or right measured according to the condition of the father of a family. Therefore the absolute family salary is due in distributive justice.

Major.— Measured directly according to one's condition, *I concede*; measured indirectly according to one's condition, *I deny*.

---

(1) In the first place, due consideration must be had for the double character, individual and social, of capital and labor, in order that the dangers of Individualism and of Collectivism be avoided. The mutual relations between capital and labor must be determined according to the laws of strictest justice, called commutative justice, supported, however, by Christian charity. —*Quadragesimo Anno*.

Minor.— Measured directly according to the condition of the father of the family, *I deny;* measured indirectly, *I concede.*

The condition of the father of a family is considered, in order to determine the value of the workman's labor. When the value of his labor has been settled, then the absolute family wage is due according to the equality of one thing to another. Therefore the condition of the father of a family is not the direct measure of the equality between the workman's labor and the absolute family wage, but only its indirect measure. Hence the absolute family wage is due in commutative justice.

3° One who distributes a part of the common good performs an act of distributive justice. But the employer who pays the absolute family wage distributes a part of the common good: capital is a part of the common good. Therefore the employer who pays the absolute family wage performs an act of distributive justice, i.e., the absolute family wage is due in distributive justice.

Major.— One who distributes a part of the common good, which is still a common good, when there is no exchange (for services rendered), *I concede*; one who distributes a part of the common good, which is a private good, when there is an exchange, *I deny.*

Minor.— The employer distributes a private good in exchange for the workman's labor, *I concede*; gives a common good without an exchange for the workman's labor, *I deny.*

When the employer pays the absolute family wage, there is an exchange. When there is an exchange, we have a case of commutative justice, not of distributive justice.

On the other hand, capital, although a part of a common good, is a private good, i.e., private property. And we must hold firmly to this teaching in opposition to certain Catholics who maintain that the absolute family wage is due in distributive justice. In this regard, we should give ear to the words of Pope Pius XI: « On the one hand, if the social and public aspect of ownership be denied or minimized, the logical consequence is Individualism, as it is called; on the other hand, the rejection or diminution of its private and individual character necessarily leads to some form of Collectivism (1). »

4° What is due on account of the common good is due in social justice. But the absolute family wage is due on account of the common good. Therefore the absolute family wage is due in social justice.

Major.— In as much as it is due on acccount of the common good *I concede*; in as much as it is due a private person from a lawful title, *I deny'*

Minor.— Is due only on account of the common good, *I deny*; is due also on account of the service rendered, *I concede.*

The act by which the employer pays the absolute family wage is, as we have said, *commanded* by social justice, and *elicited* by commutative justice. The same is true of acts of all the other virtues which are commanded by social justice, but which are always elicited by some particular virtue.

1140. Scholia.— 1° In fixing wages, three considerations must be taken into account: *a)* the support of the workingman and his family; *b)* the condition of business; *c)* the exigencies of the common good, for a scale of wages which is too high or too

---

(1) *Quadragesimo Anno.*

low is contrary to the common good, in as much as it causes unemployment (¹).

2° Since the absolute family wage is due in commutative justice, an employer who pays a lower wage than this is held to restitution. But *prudence,* which takes into account all the circumstances of a human act in a given case, is required for the determination of when an employer is bound to restitution.

3° The duty of paying a salary sufficient to provide for the needs of the workingman and his family rests in the first place on the employer. Later, if necessity requires it, assistance will have to be given, in the first place, by the professional association and, in the last place, by civil society, by family allowance, insurance, etc.

1141. Collective labor contracts.— 1° *Preliminaries.* — *a)* Labor contract in general is an agreement by which a workman hires his services to an employer for a fixed wage.

b) There are two kinds of labor contract: *individual* labor contract and *collective* labor contract.

The individual labor contract is made between two individuals, viz., an employer and an employee.

The collective labor contact is *an agreement between an employer or association of employers and a professional association or union of workingmen, which determines the general conditions for each party under which later individual labor contracts must be entered.*

The collective labor contract, of its nature, does not impose an obligation on the employer of hiring a particular workman or of providing work for him, but only of observing certain general conditions in the event of his hiring workmen or providing jobs for them.

Therefore the collective labor contract is preliminary to the individual labor contract.

---

(1) *Quadragesimo Anno.*

c) The collective labor contract contains, as a general rule, stipulations in regard to the quantity and quality of the labor required of the workman and the wages he should receive for it; the right of making collective demands, the right of dealing with employers through workingmen's agents; the rights of the professional association on behalf of workingmen; conditions of labor and wages, settlement of disputes, etc.

2° *In the light of the foregoing observations,* we shall now epitomize our teaching on collective labor contracts in the proposition which follows.

The collective labor contract is a highly recommended institution.

1° It is a guarantee of justice for individual labor contracts:

a) The worker, left to rely solely on himself, cannot satisfactorily defend his rights in dealing with employers on problems of the quality and quantity of labor and of the wage he should receive for it.

b) The collective contract moderates and regulates competition among the workers themselves. Moreover, it moderates and regulates competition even among employers.

2° It is a means of fostering friendly relations between employee and employer:

a) Where there is a collective contract, the general conditions of labor and wages are more freely and intelligently fixed between employer and employee; and thus many disputes are avoided, and the dignity of labor is safeguarded.

b) It often determines very definitely a period of time during which no change may be made in the contract; and this gives greater security to both the employee and the employer.

c) Finally, it provides a means for the peaceful quelling and amicable settlement of incipient disputes, and is thus a safeguard against strikes and other lesser cessations of work.

1142. Strikes.— 1° *Preliminaries.*— *a)* A strike is an organized cessation of work on the part of a large number for the purpose of obtaining certain advantages, as better working hours or redress of other grievances. Hence a strike is a kind of economic war.

b) Strikes lead to many great evils:

workmen receive no wages, and have to spend the money saved by thrift over a long period of time and intended for the support of themselves and their families;

employers not only make no profits, but often have to bear heavy expenses, in order to protect and repair their buildings and instruments of labor; moreover, they lose their markets for their merchandise not only during the time of the strike, but often for the future, for many of their customers are wont to find new sources of supplies and later to retain them;

railways and certain manufactories which are dependent on the work of the strikers suffer heavy losses;

sometimes the industry and commerce of a whole Province or State become paralyzed, and, in consequence, the ranks of the country's paupers become swelled;

and, finally, many moral evils are engendered, as hatreds, which bring estrangement among citizens, the corruption of morals, which naturally results from protracted idleness, blasphemy against religion, acts of violence and injustice against persons and things, and other such evils.

c) Since strikes are attended by such dire consequences, the question arises: is a strike ever lawful, i.e., not contrary to the natural aw?

The reply to this important question i, contained in the proposition which follows.

2° *Statement of the proposition.*— *Strikes are lawful under certain conditions.*

Strikes are lawful if they are not unjust in themselves, and if workmen are justified in making use of them. But strikes are not unjust in themselves, and, under certain conditions, workmen are justified in making use of them. Therefore strikes are lawful under certain conditions.

The *major* is evident.

Minor.— a) *Strikes are not unjust in themselves,* for a strike is a cessation of labor in accordance with an agreement among workmen. But a cessation of labor is not unjust, for a workman is under no obligation to work for a particular employer; an *agreement* is not unjust, because workmen may agree to cease work at the same time for the pursuit of the common good.

b) *Under certain conditions, workmen are justified in making use of strikes.* Since strikes are attended by evil effects, certain conditions must be fulfilled, in order that workmen who make use of them be not morally responsible for these effects. These conditions are the following:

1) *A grave reason* is required for recourse to a strike. For the cause of the strike must be proportionate to the evil consequences which can result from it.

2) The strike must be the *only means* of obtaining a just settlemen of the workmen's grievances. A strike is a kind of war, which is never lawful, except when no other means is available which can bring an end to it, which is the restoration of justice.

3) The workmen must not be *under contract* for their labor. If such a contract exists, a strike is a violation of it, and is therefore unjust.

4) *No violence* may be used against other workmen who without any violation of justice, refuse to strike; and the property of employers must be respected.

1143. Scholia.— 1° The dismissal of workmen in lockouts can be lawful, just as a strike can be lawful, provided that certa n conditions are fulfilled.

2° Since the strike is lawful, public authority may not suppress it as something unjust in itself. Nevertheless, on account of the common good, which is greater than the private good, the civil authority has both the right and the duty of seeking suitable means to settle the conflict, so that society may be spared serious harm.

3° A strike which is directly opposed to the common good, as for example, a strike in public services, is unlawful.

1144. Contracts of partnership.— 1° The contract of partnership (labor-management contract) is defined: *an agreement by which employer and employees are made sharers in the ownership and management as well as in the profits of a business.*

The contract of partnership is a free agreement between employer and employees, because the employer has the ownership of the capital.

Under the contract of partnership, the workman or employee does not receive a wage from the employer, but, as a co-owner and co-manager of a business, is a sharer not only in the profits, but also in the risks of the business.

2° All who hold that the wage contract is essentially unjust maintain that only the contract of partnership is lawful. This error was condemned by Pope Pius XI ([1]), who, holding that both the wage contract and the contract of partnership are lawful, points out how the wage contract should be governed according to the principles of justice.

Nevertheless, the same Sovereign Pontiff deems it advisable that, when possible, the wage contract should be modified by certain elements borrowed from the contract of partnership.

These elements, which have already been tried in various ways and found advantageous to both wage-earners and employers, are the following:

    a) a sharing in the ownership of business;

    b) a sharing in the management of business;

---

(1) And first of all, those who hold that the wage contract is essentially unjust, and that in its place must be introduced the contract of partnership, are certainly in error. They do a grave injury to Our Predecessor, whose Encyclical not only admits this contract, but devotes much space to its determination according to the principles of justice.— *Quadragesimo Anno.*

c) a sharing in the profits which business yields (¹).

POINTS FOR REVIEW

1. Define: salary, personal salary, absolute family salary, relative family salary, collective labor contract, and contract of partnership,

2. What is the teaching of Socialism on salary?

3. Prove that salary is lawful in itself, and that the absolute family salary is due in strict justice and in commutative justice.

4. Explain why the absolute family salary must be determined by taking into account the condition of the head of the family.

5. State what is meant by a strike, and prove that it is lawful under certain conditions.

---

(1) In the present state of human society, however, we deem it advisable that the wage contract should, when possible, be modified somewhat by a contract of partnership, as is already being tried in various ways to the no small gain both of the wage-earners and of the employers. In this way wage-earners are made sharers of some sort in the ownership, or the management, or the profits.— *Quadragesimo Anno.*

ARTICLE V

CAPITALISM

1145. Statement of the question.— 1° Capitalism, in its etymology, is derived from the word *capital*.

Capital, according to its strict meaning in Economics, is defined: *the part of produced wealth reserved or in actual use for new production;* v.g., instruments and machines of every kind, the various kinds of primary products required for production, and the whole gamut of economic operations.

In modern usage, any kind of wealth is called capital; and capital is divided into social capital and juridical capital.

Under the heading of social capital come all wealth and material goods of all kinds.

Under the heading of juridical capital come money and things of pecuniary value.

2° Capitalism in general, i.e., in itself, must be distinguished from capitalism in its pejorative meaning.

Capitalism in itself signifies capitalistic production, i.e., production in which all agencies distinct from capital are more or less under the sway of capital. It is an economic system, then, in which capital plays a preponderant role, and in which the function of capital is separate from the function of labor ([1]).

Capitalism, in its pejorative meaning, may be described: *systems of economic and social relations, born of capitalistic production, in which the holders of economic and social capital, and especially of juridical capital, i.e., of money, in their eagerness for excessive profits, play not only a preponderant but an unlawful and abusive role.*

---

(1) Cf. GRENIER, *Cours De Philosophie*, n. 555, 2°.

Under the rule of capitalism thus understood, capital, especially in the form of money, becomes, as it were, an omnipotent producer, buyer, seller, and consumer, if not the universal monopolist of all economic transactions.

1146. Opinions.— 1° Economic Liberalism, exaggeratiug individual liberty, holds that capitalism, even in its pejorative meaning, is lawful. Moreover, capitalism and its abuses are logical consequences of Liberalism.

2° Communism and Socialism hold that capitalism is essentially unlawful.

3° Capitalism, according to the teaching of the Catholic Church, is not intrinsically evil in itself, but today is beset with many evils, which only great prudence and discretion can remove. Therefore capitalism, in its pejorative sense, is condemned.

It is to be observed that capitalism is not a system imposed upon us by the natural law, as is the system of private ownership, and therefore it may be lawfully abandoned, provided that justice and the common good are safeguarded by the substitution of an equally good or more advantageous economic system.

1147. Statement of the thesis.

  THESIS.— CAPITALISM IN ITSELF IS NOT INTRINSICALLY EVIL; BUT TODAY IT IS BESET WITH MANY EVILS, WHICH ONLY GREAT PRUDENCE AND DISCRETION CAN REMOVE.

First part.—*Capitalism in itself is not intrinsically evil.*— Capitalism is characterized by three notes: in it money fructifies; the wage contract is in force; and capital assumes the major part of the responsibility for the administration of business, and receives the greater part of profits. But these things are not intrinsically evil. Therefore capitalism in itself is not intrinsically evil.

Minor.— *a) The fructification of money is not intrinsically evil.*— A person who makes his money surety for another may lawfully receive interest on it, i.e., may receive a certain compensation; for, under conditions such as obtain today, everyone has the opportunity of earning profits with his money; therefore, by risking his money as surety for another, he deprives himself of profits which he could otherwise make, and hence may lawfully receive compensation for his service.

b) The wage contract is lawful.— A man who demands a living wage in return for services on behalf of others does not act in violation of any natural law.

c) Capital is justified in assuming the major part of the responsibility for the administration of business, and in receiving the greater part of the profits, provided that abuses are avoided.— This is evident, for capital greatly increases the possibilities of business, and runs a greater risk than labor. Moreover, capitalists have a right to remuneration as property-owners, as managers-directors of business, and often as employees.

Second part.— *Today capitalism is beset with many evils, which only great prudence and discretion can remove.*— It will be sufficient to give an enumeration of these evils or abuses: the unbridled desire for gain and lust for riches, which destroy all sense of justice and charity towards others, and especially towards workingmen; ignorance of the social character of economic activity, of the exigencies of the common good; inadequate wages, ill-befitting work required of women and children; unfair distribution of economic agencies, with the result that in production workmen especially, and sometimes managers-directors, are completely dependent on the will of capitalists who hold a monopoly of it; the dictatorship of the few in economic life, and consequently in political life as a whole; unjust playing of the stock market and excessive profits therefrom, etc.

CHAPTER II

ERRORS IN REGARD TO SOCIETY

Prologue.— In this chapter, we shall deal with the three chief errors in regard to society, viz., Communism, Socialism, and Economic Liberalism. Hence there will be three articles in this chapter.

Communism
- Statement of the question
- Thesis: Communism, under its three aspects: materialism, dialectical materialism, and historical materialism, is false

Socialism
- Statement of the question
- Thesis: Socialism is untenable

Economic Liberalism
- Statement of the question
- Historical sketch
- Economic Liberalism is inadmissible

ARTICLE I

COMMUNISM

1148. Statement of the question — 1° Communism, according to the etymology of the term, is a doctrine which denies private persons the ownership of material goods, i.e., of external things.

2° Modern communism has its foundation in Marxism, i.e., in the philosophical teaching presented and developed by Karl Marx (1818-1883) and Friedrich Engels (1820-1895). Communism, in its strict sense, is but a part of Marxism; for Communism, according to Marx himself (¹), is only a phase or period of the historical evolution conceived in Marxism.

Nevertheless, Marxism is commonly called Communism. Hence, unless otherwise indicated, we shall speak of Communism as being one and the same as Marxism.

3° The fundamental theory of Communism is *dialectical materialism*.

The application of dialectical materialism to the study of social life is called *historical materialism*.

Hence, in order to understand Communism, we must study its elements:

materialism;
dialectical materialism;
historical materialism.

---

(1) Le communisme... est une phase réelle de l'émancipation et de la renaissance humaines, phase nécessaire pour l'évolution historique prochaine. Le communisme est la force nécessaire et le principe énergique de l'avenir prochain. Mais le communisme n'est pas, en tant que tel, la fin de l'évolution humaine, il est une forme de la société humaine. — Karl MARX, *Morceaux Choisis*, NRF, 4e édition, Gallimard, p. 228.

4° Materialism, as presented by Communism, does not deny the existence of knowledge and of spirits, but affirms that matter, which is called nature, is the first and fundamental reality from which all other realities derive and on which they depend (¹).

Hence Communism teaches:

a) knowledge is objective, because it attains external realities;

b) spirits cannot exist independently of matter, because they have their origin in matter;

c) no spirits, as the spiritual soul, angels, and God, can be subsistent;

d) spirits are homogeneous with matter: they are of the same nature as matter, because they are derived from matter and are intrinsically dependent on it.

5° The materialism of Communism is called *dialectical* because of the principles which Marx and Engels borrowed from Hegel.

According to Hegel, the principle of contradiction is not the first law of intellective knowledge, but, on the contrary, every idea contains its contradiction in itself, so that human

---

(1) The material, sensuously perceptible world to which we ourselves belong is the only reality; and... our consciousness and thinking, however supersensuous they may seem, are the product of a material, bodily organ, the brain. Matter is not a product of mind, but mind itself is merely the highest product of matter.— ENGELS, *Ludwig Feuerbach And the Outcome of Classical German Philosophy*, p. 54.

With me... the idea is nothing else than the material world reflected by the human mind, and translated into forms of thought.— Karl MARX, *Capital*, New York, The Modern Library, 1906, Preface To The Second Edition, p. 25.

Contrary to idealism, which regards the world as the embodiment of an « absolute idea », a « universal spirit », « consciousness », Marx's philosophical materialism holds that the world is by its very nature material, that the multifold phenomena of the world constitute different forms of matter in motion, that interconnection and interdependance of phenomena, as established by the dialectical method, are a law of the development of moving matter, and that the world develops in accordance with the laws of movement of matter and stands in no need of a « universal spirit ». — Joseph STALIN, *Dialectical and Historical Materialism*, International Publishers, New York, 1940, p. 15.

knowledge is undergoing a constant evolution in passing from affirmation to negation, and so on (¹).

But, whereas Hegel looks upon the dialectical method as a law of logic and knowledge, Communism regards it as the first law of all reality (²).

Hence dialectical materialism teaches:

a) a contradiction is inherent in nature, and consequently every reality contains a contradictory reality, i.e., all reality is self-contradictory (³);

---

(1) In what does the movement of pure reason consist? To pose, oppose and compose itself, to be formulated as thesis, antithesis and synthesis, or, better still, to affirm itself, to deny itself and to deny its negation.

How does reason act, in order to affirm itself, to place itself in a given category? This is the affair of reason itself and of its apologists.

But once it has placed itself in thesis, this thesis, this thought, opposed to itself, doubles itself into two contradictory thoughts, the positive and the negative, the yes and the no. The struggle of these two antagonistic elements, comprised in the antithesis, constitutes the dialectic movement, the yes becoming no, the no becoming yes, the yes becoming at once yes and no, the no becoming at once no and yes, the contraries balance themselves, neutralise themselves, paralyse themselves. The fusion of these two contradictory thoughts constitutes a new thought which is the synthesis of the two. This new thought unfolds itself again in two contradictory thoughts which are confounded in their turn in a new synthesis. From this travail is born a group of thoughts. This group of thoughts follows the same dialectic movement as a simple category, and has for antithesis a contradictory group. From these two groups is born a new group of thoughts which is the synthesis of them.

As from the dialectic movement of simple categories is born the group, so from the dialectic movement of the group is born the series, and from the dialectic movement of the series is born the whole system.— Karl MARX, *The Philosophy Poverty*, London, Twentieth Century Press, 1900, p. 86.

(2) My dialectic method is not only different from Hegelian, but is its very opposite. To Hegel, the life-process of the human brain, i.e., the process of thinking, which, under the name of « the Idea », he even transforms into an independent subject, is the demiurgos of the world, and the real world is only the external, phenomenal form of « the Idea ». With me, on the contrary, the ideal is nothing else than the material world reflected by the human mind, and translated into forms of thought.— Karl MARX, *Capital*, New York, The Modern Library, 1906, Preface To The Second Edition, p. 25.

Engels gives the following description of Dialectics: The great basic thought that the world is not to be comprehended as a complex of ready-made *things*, but as a complex of *processes*, in which the things apparently stable no less than their mind-images in our heads, the concepts, go through an uninterrupted change of coming into being and passing away.— *Ludwig Feuerbach And the Outcome of Classical German Philosophy*, p. 54.

(3) Contrary to metaphysics, dialectics holds that internal contradictions are inherent in all things and phenomena of nature, for they all have their negative and positive sides, a past and a future, something dying away and something developing; and that the struggle between these opposites, the struggle between the old and the new, between that which is dying away

b) nature, all reality, evolves by means of a struggle between contradictories;

c) no natures are stable, but are ever evolving; in other words, evolution, i.e., universal mobilism, is the only reality.

6° *Historical materialism* is the application of dialectical materialism to society and to man.

Since matter, according to Communism, is the first and fundamental reality, man should first be considered under the aspect of his material life. But man, from this point of view, is distinct from other things by his capacity to produce material goods which are necessities for him.

Hence historical materialism teaches:

a) man is essentially a being capable of production, i.e., he is essentially a *producer* (¹).

b) society, which is a union of men, is a union in production and all production must be social (²), and therefore the private

---

and that which is being born, between that which is disappearing and that which is developing, constitutes the internal content of the process of development, the internal content of the transformation of quantitative changes into qualitative changes.— Joseph STALIN, *op. cit.*, p. 11.

In its proper meaning, dialectics is the study of the contradiction *within the very essence of things.*— LENIN, *Philosophical Notebooks*, Russian edition, p. 318.

(1) Men can be distinguished from animals by consciousness, by religion or anything else you like. They themselves begin to distinguish themselves from animals as soon as they begin to *produce* their means of subsistence, a step which is conditioned by their physical organization. By producing their means of subsistence men are indirectly producing their actual material life.— Karl MARX, *The German Ideology*, New York, International Publishers, 1939, p. 7.

(2) The *instruments of production* wherewith material values are produced, the *people* who operate the instruments of production and carry on the production of material values, thanks to a certain production experience and, *labor skill* all these elements jointly constitute the *production forces* of society.

But the productive forces are only one aspect of production, only one aspect of the mode of production, an aspect that expresses the relations of men to the objects and forces of nature which they make use of for the production of material values. Another aspect of production, another aspect of the mode of production, is the relation of men to each other in the process of production, men's *relations of production*. Men carry on a struggle against nature and utilize nature for the production of material values not in isolation from each other, not as separate individuals, but in common, in groups, in societies. Production, therefore, is at all times and under all conditions *social* production.— Joseph STALIN, *op cit.*, p. 28.

ownership of productive goods should be abolished;

c) The evolution of society and of man is merely the evolution of matter; and, although human ideas and institutions can exercise an influence on the evolution of society, this evolution ever remains the evolution of matter, because human ideas and institutions are only certain aspects of matter;

d) the evolution of society is brought about by the struggle between its opposite elements, i.e., by class-struggle; and and hence this struggle is necessary and the cause of a more and more perfect evolution of society;

e) man attains his perfection to the degree in which he perfects production, i.e., man is his own ultimate end; thus Communism is *integrated humanism;*

f) since society must continually evolve by means of the struggle of its contradictorily opposite elements, Communism, in the strict sense, which would abolish all classes, is only a phase or period in the evolution of society.

It is evident from what has been said that Communism is a complete theory on nature, man, and society. The complete refutation of the infamous teachings of this satanic scourge of Christian civilization, which is often concealed under the most seductive trappings (¹), would require more and longer arguments than the limits of our present study allow, and therefore we must be satisfied with showing very briefly that Communism, under its three aspects of materialism, dialectical materialism, and historical materialism, is false.

1149. Statement of the thesis.

> **THESIS.**— COMMUMISM UNDER ITS THREE ASPECTS: MATERIALISM, DIALECTICAL MATERIALISM, AND HISTORICAL MATERIALISM, IS FALSE.

First part.—*Communism, under the aspect of mate ialism, is false.*— A theory which teaches that the human soul is not

---

(1) Cf. *Divini Redemptoris,* nn. 7 and 9.

subjectively independent of matter, i.e., is not spiritual, and which, in consequence, subscribes to pantheism, is false. But Communism, under its aspect of materialism, is a theory which teaches that the human soul is not subjectively independent of matter, i.e., is not spiritual, and which, in consequence, subscribes to pantheism. Therefore Communism, under the aspect of materialism, is false.

Major.— We have already proved that the human soul is spiritual, i.e., subsistent (n. 458), and that pantheism is untenable (n. 767).

Second part.— *Communism, under the aspect of dialectical materialism, is false.*— 1° A theory which teaches universal mobilism is false. But Communism, under the aspect of dialectical materialism, teaches universal mobilism. Therefore Communism, under the aspect of dialectical materialism, is false.

Major.— According to universal mobilism, everything is changing. But the proposition: everything is changing, i.e., everything is movement, means: *motion is motion*, which is mere tautology; or it means: *motion changes into something else*, which is a denial of universal mobilism, for, if motion changes into something other than itself, it is no longer motion. Therefore.

The *minor* is evident from what has been already said.

2° A theory which teaches that knowledge is objective and at the same time denies the existence of determinate natures is false. But Communism, under the aspect of dialectical materialism, is a theory which teaches that knowledge is objective and at the same time denies the existence of determinate natures. Therefore Communism, under the aspect of dialectical materialism, is false.

Major.— If determinate natures do not exist, man is not man, the producer is not a producer, and being is not being: thus the principle of contradiction is denied, and all objective and certain knowledge becomes impossible.

sion of the most excessive kind; and, on the other hand, it fosters a false liberty. Therefore Socialism is untenable.

Antecedent — a) Society is impossible and inconceivable without the use of compulsion of the most excessive kind.— According to Socialism, the possession of the greatest possible amount of temporal goods is esteemed so highly that man's higher goods, not excepting liberty, must be subordinated and even sacrificed to the exigencies of efficient production.

b) Society fosters a false liberty.— Society, according to the Socialistic conception of it, is based solely on temporal and material advantages. From this it follows that neither society nor its members are subject to God, the wellspring of all authority. In other words, Socialism, in which no place is found for true social authority, destroys all authority.

We may add that Socialism cannot, in virtue of its principles, abolish class welfare.

POINTS FOR REVIEW

1. Name the two sections into which Socialism is divided, and point out in what they are distinct from each other.

2. Are we justified in stating that Socialism is entirely oblivious of man's eternal happiness? Explain.

3. Show why society, as conceived by the Socialist, is impossible and unthinkable without the use of compulsion of the most excessive kind, and, moreover, why it fosters a false liberty.

The *minor* is evident from the statement of the question.

3° A theory which holds that natural, i.e., spatio-temporal, being is a compound of contradictory principles is false. But Communism, under the aspect of dialectical materialism, holds that natural being or nature is a compound of contradictory principles. Therefore Communism, under the aspect of dialectical materialism, is false.

Major.— The principles of natural being in the state of becoming, i.e., the principles of generation, are *privation, first matter,* and *form.* Privation is opposed privatively, but not contradictorily, to form, because it has the same subject as form, i.e., first matter; although first matter without form is opposed to form, first matters of itself is not in opposition to form, because form is the perfection to which it tends, and nothing has an inclination to its opposite. Therefore natural, i.e., spatio-temporal, being is not a compound of opposite principles (Cf. n. 219).

The *minor* is clear from the statement of the question.

Third part.— *Communism, under the aspect of historical materialism, is false.*— 1° A theory which teaches that man is essentially and specifically a producer is false. But Communism, under the aspect of historical materialism, teaches that man is essentially and specifically a producer. Therefore Communism, under the aspect of historical materialism, is false.

Major.— Man produces the instruments of production and the things necessary or useful for his existence, in as much as he makes use of external things, i.e., material goods, and disposes of them. But man makes use of material goods and disposes of them by an act of his own over which he has dominion, i.e., dominative power. In other words, man makes use of material goods and disposes of them, because he is endowed with liberty, which has its roots in reason. Therefore man is not essentially and specifically a producer, but he is essentially and specifically a *rational animal.*

2° Production is not necessarily a social function, but one which primarily belongs to private activity and personal freedom. Moreover, union in production is not union in political society, but union in a private society. Hence Communism, which teaches that production is a *social* or *political* function, is false.

3° Communism, under the aspect of historical materialism, strips man of his true liberty, destroys the notion of spirituality, denies the existence of the spiritual soul and of God, refuses to admit the natural right of the private ownership of productive goods, robs man of his human dignity, and refuses to acknowledge that true happiness consists in the practice of the virtues. Therefore it is false.

POINTS FOR REVIEW

1. Name and briefly explain three distinct aspects of Communism.
2. Explain the difference between dialectical materialism and historical materialism.
3. Prove that man is not essentially and specifically a producer.

ARTICLE II

SOCIALISM

1150. Statement of the question.— 1° Socialism is divided into two sections:

a) the more violent section, which is Communism (¹), with which we dealt in the preceding article;

b) the moderate section, which has retained the name of Socialism.

It is with the more moderate section of Socialism that we shall deal in the present article.

2° Socialism is much less radical than Communism, from which it is distinguished in two ways:

a) it condemns recourse to physical force for the attainment of its ends;

b) it mitigates and moderates to some extent class warfare and the abolition of the private ownership of property, though it does not reject them entirely.

3° Some Catholics have unwarrantably wondered about the possibility of a « middle course » between mitigated Socialism and the principles of Christian truth, so that Socialism could be met, as it were, upon common ground.

For, *first,* they have felt, class warfare, on condition that it refrains from enmities and mutual hatred, can gradually become an honest discussion of differences, which is a principle of social restoration and peace.

---

(1) One section of Socialism has undergone approximately the same change through which, as We have described, the capitalistic economic regime has passed; it has degenerated into Communism.— *Quadragesimo Anno.*

Secondly, the war declared upon the ownership of private property, if attenuated, can be directed not towards the abolition of the possession of productive goods, i.e., the means of production, but towards the restoration of order in society, namely, when, according to the principles of sound philosophy, certain forms of property are reserved to the State, the private ownership of which would be at variance with the common good.

Pope Pius XI settled very definitely any doubts in this matter by solemnly declaring that Socialism, even in its more moderate form, is irreconcilable with the teachings of Christianity (¹).

1151. Statement of the question.

THESIS.— SOCIALISM IS UNTENABLE.

1° Man must live in society, in order to attain temporal and eternal happiness. But, according to Socialism, man's only purpose in living in society is the acquisition of an abundance of temporal goods. Therefore.

Major.— The end of civil society is the temporal happiness of this life as directed to eternal happiness.

Minor.— For Socialism, in declaring even an attenuated kind of war on private ownership, is concerned only with the acquisition of an abundance of material goods, and thus shows no solicitude either for man's higher goods, or for his liberty. For it teaches that man must be completely subject to civil society, in order that he acquire an abundance of material goods.

2° Society, as conceived by the Socialist, is, on the one hand, impossible and inconceivable without the use of compul-

---

(1) Whether Socialism be considered as a doctrine, or as a historical fact, or as a movement, if it really remain Socialism, it cannot be brought into harmony with the dogmas of the Catholic Church, even after it has yielded to truth and justice in the points We have mentioned; the reason being that it conceives human society in a way utterly alien to Christian truth.— *Quadragesimo Anno.*

ARTICLE III

ECONOMIC LIBERALISM

1152. Statement of the question.— 1° Liberalism in general is the teaching of those who assert the absolute autonomy of human liberty, and of individual liberty in particular. According to this teaching, the moral law and all authority have their foundation, as Rousseau imagined, in the will of man, so that every man is a law unto himself.

Liberalism is divided into religious liberalism, political liberalism, and economic liberalism.

Religious liberalism claims that civil society is completely independent of the Church and religion.

Political liberalism teaches that civil authority comes from the people, and may be exercised only in the name of and by the people.

Economic liberalism proclaims the absolute autonomy of individual liberty in economic, commercial, and industrial life.

It is with economic liberalism that we are concerned in this article.

2° Economic liberalism maintains that the control of material goods is a strictly private, personal, and individual right. Its fundamental principles are the following:

a) Private utility is the chief and almost the sole stimulus of economic life, and especially of production, for it is the individual who can best seek, know, and promote his own interests or utility.

b) Therefore, in economic life, private liberty must be strictly safeguarded. Hence the State's only function in economic matters consists in the protection of private rights; and it must abstain from all positive intervention in the settlement of the economic problems of society (State police or night watchmen).

Moreover, all associations, especially workmen's associations, should be abolished, because they are a restraint on individual liberty.

c) Economic life should be governed by free competition. In other words, the first law of economic activity is free competition, i.e., *the free play of economic individualities seeking, by any lawful means, the greatest possible advantages, respecting at the same time, of course, the equal rights of others to do the same.*

d) The consequence of free competition is *responsibility;* and hence each one not only must provide for his own needs entirely through his own initiative and industry, but becomes solely responsible for the happiness or unhappiness that may be his (1).

1153. Historical sketch.— 1° In the eighteenth century, the physiocrats proclaimed the principle of absolute liberty for all human activities. Hence they held that all or almost all intervention on the part of the State should be abolished, and advocated that all phases of economic life should be conducted in accordance with the forces or laws of nature, and solely under the dicates of human sense.

2° Adam Smith (1723-1790) systematically and scientifically applied the principle of absolute or almost absolute liberty to social economics in particular. Hence he is considered to be father and framer of economic Liberalism.

3° Adam Smith's teachings were adopted and changed to some small extent by David Ricardo (1804-1863) and John Bright (1811-1850), who, with the assistance of their mutual friend Robert Peel (1788-1850), succeeded in having the British Parliament vote for freedom in both national and internation-

---

(1) For by an inexorable economic law, it was held, all accumulation of riches must fall to the share of the wealthy, while the workingman must remain perpetually in indigence or reduced to the minimum needed for existence.— *Quadragesimo Anno.*

al trade, and also by J. B. Say (1767-1832), Frederic Bastiat (1801-1850), de Molinari (1819-1912), Michel Chevalier (1806-1878), etc.

4° In the latter part of the nineteenth century, and especially after the publication of the Encyclical Letter *Rerum Novarum* in 1891, certain writers began to advocate a more moderate application of the principles of economic Liberalism. Prominent among these writers were the following: in France, Paul Leroy-Beaulieu (1843-1916), Cauvès (1843-1912), and Charles Gide (1847-1932); in Italy, Luzzati (1841-1927), Marco Minghetti (1818-1886), and Luigi Cossa (1831-1896); in Germany, Karl Heinrich Rau (1792-1870); in Belgium, Em. Lavely, (1822-1892), etc.

1154. Statement of the thesis.

THESIS.— ECONOMIC LIBERALISM IS INADMISSIBLE.

1° A doctrine which ignores man's natural sociability and which is subversive of the very notion of civil society is inadmissible. But economic Liberalism ignores man's natural sociability and is subversive of the very notion of civil society. Therefore economic Liberalism is inadmissible.

The *major* is evident from what we have already said, and also from its very terms.

Minor.— a) *Economic Liberalism ignores man's natural sociability.*— According to the order of nature, men are destined, because of their needs as individuals, to live in society, in order that they may mutually assist one another in the pursuit of the temporal happiness of this life. But, according to economic Liberalism, men should not render assistance to one another, but, in accordance with the law of free competition, the highly skilled and talented should surpass and overcome the weak, and hence some may acquire material goods in very great abundance, whereas many others must live in indigence. Therefore.

b) *Economic Liberalism is subversive of the very notion of civil society.* — Civil society is a heterogeneous society, and in it the civil authority should direct the activity of all individual citizens to the common good, not only negatively, by removing obstacles to the common good, but positively, by stimulating private activity, by supplying it where it is lacking, and by overseeing and directing it, as circumstances permit and necessity demands. But economic Liberalism teaches that the State, i.e., the civil authority, should refrain from all positive intervention in the economic life of its citizens. Therefore.

2° Since economic Liberalism holds that free competition is the supreme law of economic activity, it denies the social aspect of private property and of labor, and denies or ignores the existence of either legal or distributive justice; in a word, it refuses to recognize the subjection of economic activity to the moral law. Moreover, economic Liberalism entails disastrous consequences: increased hardships and poverty for the wage-earning class, i.e., for the workingman, economic dictatorship which enslaves civil authority and makes it the docile instrument of the passions and ambitions of a few men of great wealth, or, as it is said, of the vested interests; economic nationalism, or even, in the other extreme, internationalism, i.e, international imperialism, whose guiding principle may be stated thus: the country which offers the greatest advantages to me is my fatherland. Finally, economic Liberalism prepares the way for class warfare, Socialism, and Communism. As an economic doctrine, it contradicts itself, for, in order to safeguard liberty, it refuses the liberty of organizing associations. Therefore economic Liberalism is entirely inadmissible.

POINTS FOR REVIEW

1. Distinguish between religious, political, and economic Liberalism.
2. State the teaching of economic Liberalism, and show why it ignores man's natural sociability and is subversive of the very notion of civil society.

BOOK III

Relations between societies

Prologue.— In this book, we shall discuss the relations between civil societies, and also the relations between civil society and the Church.

Hence there will be two chapters in this book.

Chapter I. Relations between civil societies.

Chapter II. Relations between civil society and the Church.

CHAPTER I

RELATIONS BETWEEN CIVIL SOCIETIES

Prologue.— In the first chapter, we shall deal with international law, international society, and war. Hence there will be three articles in this chapter.

International law
- Statement of the question
- Thesis: There exists an international law derived from the natural law

International society
- Statement of the question
- Thesis: International society is founded in nature, and is directed to the good of all nations

War
- Statement of the question
- Opinions
- Thesis: War, both defensive and offensive, is lawful under certain conditions

ARTICLE I

INTERNATIONAL LAW

1155. Statement of the question.— 1° International law is that body of laws which determines the relations of civil societies to one another.

International law may be private or public.

Private international law regulates the relations between the citizens of different States.

Public international law regulates the relations between different States as such, i.e., as moral persons.

The existence of private international law is evident, for justice requires that everyone be given his due, without making any distinction between compatriots and aliens.

Hence we are concerned with public international law in the thesis.

2° The requisites for the existence of a public international law are two in number:

a) a plurality of mutually independent States which, as moral persons, have relations to one another;

b) the unity of all mankind in relation to some common good: for international law is an ordinance of reason for the common good of many States, i.e., of the human race.

3° Many modern economists, denying, at least in practice, the existence of the natural law, maintain that international law is derived either from the common express consent of civilized nations, or from the enactment of other rules accepted on the universal conviction of the civilized world, according to the principle: pacts must be respected and observed.

We maintain that international law not only exists, but is derived from the natural law.

1156. Statement of the thesis.

THESIS.— THERE EXISTS AN INTERNATIONAL LAW DERIVED FROM THE NATURAL LAW.

There exists an international law derived from the natural law if there exist conclusions of the natural law which determine the mutual relations of States, and which have the characteristics of true laws. But there exist conclusions of the natural law which determine the mutual relations of States, and which have the characteristics of true laws. Therefore there exists an international law derived from the natural law.

The *major* is evident from its very terms, for laws which are conclusions of the natural law are principles which have their force from, and are just as inviolable as, the natural law itself.

Minor.— a) *There exist conclusions of the natural law which determine the mutual relations of States.*— These conclusions are of two orders:

first, conclusions necessarily deriving from the natural law which place communities under obligation to act according to the dictates of reason; v.g., agreements must be respected and observed; the killing of the innocent is unlawful; it is unlawful to wage war without a just cause;

secondly, conclusions not necessarily annexed to principles of the natural law, but manifested by custom ([1]).

b) *These conclusions of the natural law have the characteristics of true laws.*— They are ordinances of reason, because they are conclusions which are lawfully deduced from the natural law; they are in the interest of the common good of rational beings as such; they derive from a superior, because they are

---

(1) I-II, q. 97, a. 3.

derived, at least in their principles, from natural reason, and therefore from God, the author of nature, and, in consequence, impose an obligation.

Hence all the conditions of a true law are verified in these conclusions.

POINTS FOR REVIEW

1. Define international law in general; and distinguish between public and private international law.

2. State the requisites for the existence of public international law.

ARTICLE II

INTERNATIONAL SOCIETY

1157. Statement of the question.— 1° International society is defined: *a society which comprises all States, and directs them to their common good, i.e., to the common good of all mankind.*

International society neither absorbs nor abolishes States, but leaves them their independence and autonomy in their own order.

International society, as directing all States to the common good of mankind, must possess true authority, superior to the authority of any individual States.

The subject of this authority must be determined by man, just as the organization and constitution of international society must be determined by him.

2° All who deny the specific unity of the human race conceive international society as unlawful and impossible.

Moreover, all who consider the State as the source of all rights, in doing so, deny that international society has its foundation in nature.

Again, all who conceive a perfect society as absolutely autonomous and independent hold that the State cannot be subject to the authority of an international society.

But we have already learned that a perfect society is a society which pursues a perfect good, i.e., the fulness of happiness in life.

Hence we teach that international society is founded in nature, and is directed to the good of all civil societies, i.e., of all States or nations.

1158. Statement of the thesis.

THESIS. — INTERNATIONAL SOCIETY IS FOUNDED IN NATURE, AND IS DIRECTED TO THE GOOD OF ALL NATIONS.

First part. — *International society is founded in nature.* — International society is founded in nature if all States are naturally united by mutual moral and juridical bonds, and must tend to the common good of all mankind. But all States are naturally united by mutual moral and juridical bonds, and must tend to the common good of all mankind. Therefore (¹).

Major. — In this case, we have all the requisites of an international society: *a)* the pursuit of a specific common good, i.e., the common good of all mankind; *b)* the juridical union of all States for the pursuit of the common good of the whole human race.

Minor. — *a) All States are united by mutual moral and juridical bonds.* — This is so because, as we have already proved, international law exists.

b) All States must tend to the common good of all mankind. Mankind, i.e., the human race, has unity of origin, unity of nature, and unity of territory or habitation, which is the whole world. Hence all men, all groups or communities of men, and all States must tend to the common good of all mankind.

Second part. — *International society is directed to the common good of all nations, i.e., of all States.* — 1° International society leaves each State its autonomy in its own order, and directs the common good of each State to a more perfect common good, which is the common good of all nations.

---

(1) A disposition, in fact, of the divinely-sanctioned natural order divides the human race into social groups, nations or States, which are mutually independent in organization and in the direction of their internal life. But for all that, the human race is bound together by reciprocal ties, moral and juridical, into a great commonwealth directed to the good of all nations and ruled by special laws which protect its unity and promote its prosperity. — PIUS XII, *Summi Pontificatus*, n. 65.

2° International society fosters peace and harmony among nations, because the enforcement of international law belongs to a superior authority, just as the enforcement of laws governing the relations between individual persons is reserved to the political authority. Hence States can, without recourse to war, settle their quarrels according to the principles of justice.

ARTICLE III

WAR

1159. Statement of the question. — 1° War is defined: *the state of active hostility and conflict of two or more nations as such, waged by force of arms.*

War is a *state*, i.e., a general state, as distinct from battles by which war is waged.

War is an armed conflict between *nations as such*, as distinct from armed conflict of men of different States who do not wage their conflict in the name of their States, and from conflict of citizens of the same State,— rebellion, i.e., civil war,— which is improperly called war.

2° War may be *offensive* or *defensive*.

An offensive war is a war undertaken to repair the violation of rights, i.e., in reparation for harm done and in punishment of injury inflicted.

A defensive war is a war undertaken to repel aggression.

1160. Opinions — 1° There are some, as Tolstoi and so-called conscientious objectors, who hold that war is unjust.

2° Others hold that all wars useful to the State are just.

3° Others maintain that war is justified in virtue of a tacit agreement between the belligerents, in as much as they hold that victory settles quarrels and provides the solution to questions of rights.

4° Catholics teach that war can sometimes be just, i. e., is just under certain conditions, not, however, in virtue of a tacit pact or agreement between the belligerents, but because the natural law has provided rights with sanctions destined to make them respected, or, in other words, in virtue of vindicative justice.

1161. Statement of the thesis.

THESIS.— WAR, BOTH DEFENSIVE AND OFFENSIVE, IS LAWFUL UNDER CERTAIN CONDITIONS.

It is lawful under certain conditions for a State to use physical force to prevent or to avenge the violation of rights. But defensive war is war undertaken to prevent the violation of rights, and offensive war is war undertaken to avenge the violation of rights. Therefore war, both defensive and offensive, is lawful under certain conditions.

Major.— Coercion, i.e., the use of physical force, is a property of right, and, under the conditions we have stated, the exercise of this coercion belongs to the State, for there is no higher authority to which recourse is possible.

1162. Scholia.— 1° War, objectively considered, cannot be just on the part of both of the opposing belligerents; but, subjectively considered, it is possible for each of the opposing belligerents to consider it just. But war can, because of different motives, be objectively unjust on the part of both of the belligerent nations.

2° War may be undertaken against a State which is guilty of some act of injustice. But it is not required that this act of injustice be morally imputable, in as much as the State which violates a right is conscious, i.e., has subjective knowledge, of having violated a certain right of another nation. It is sufficient, as they say, that the act of injustice be juridical.

3° Nowadays, it would seem that war between civilized nations should be avoided, because the evils caused by it are so great that scarcely any temporal good can be attained which is worth the price that must be paid for it in war.

CHAPTER II

RELATIONS BETWEEN CIVIL SOCIETY AND THE CHURCH

Prologue.— This chapter contains two articles, the first of which deals with the State and religion, and the second with the relations between the State and the Church.

The State and religion
- Statement of the question
- Thesis: The State is bound to profess and to protect the true religion

Relations between the State and the Church
- Statement of the question
- Thesis: The State is subject to the Church; in the juridical order, the State is indirectly subordinate to the Church
- Separation of Church and State
- Liberty as conceived by Liberals
- Tolerance
- Scholia

ARTICLE I

THE STATE AND RELIGION

1163. Statement of the question.— 1° We are at present concerned with the question of the relation of civil society as such, and consequently of the civil authority, i.e., of governments, to religion.

2° Political or State atheism teaches that the State should take no interest whatsoever in God and religion.

Naturalism denies the existence of revealed religion, because it is beyond the powers of human reason; and it holds that the State is bound only to support any form of religion which is correspondent to man's natural instincts.

Indifferentism maintains that the State should look with equal favor upon all religions and grant all of them protection, so that all may make their contribution towards the good of public tranquillity and morality.

3° We hold all these opinions as utterly erroneous, and teach that the State is bound to profess and to protect the true religion, which, as we know, is the supernatural religion revealed by God.

1164. Statement of the thesis.

THESIS.— THE STATE IS BOUND TO PROFESS AND TO PROTECT THE TRUE RELIGION.

First part.— *The State is bound to profess religion.*— 1° Individual men are bound to worship God, because God is the author, sustainer, and end of their being. But God is the author, sustainer, and ultimate end of civil society. Therefore civil society, i.e., the State, is bound to worship God, that is to say, to profess religion (¹).

2° The welfare of society is possible only when harmonious relations obtain between subjects and rulers. But religion is the only efficacious means which has been found capable of keeping the citizens of a country, subjects and rulers, within the bounds of duty, honesty, and justice; and, if these bounds are transgressed, order and harmony among citizens cease to exist. Therefore religion is most necessary for society, i.e., society is bound to profess religion.

The *major* is evident.

Minor.— If religion is removed, there is removed also man's relation to God and to the eternal law, which is the supreme rule of the duties of rulers and subjects.

Second part.— *The State is bound to profess the true religion.*- The State is bound to worship God. But it is only by the true religion that the State can pay God the worship due Him: it is absurd to hold that God can be honored by a false worship and a superstitious religion, or in any manner man may choose (²).

---

(1) To have in public matters no care for religion, and in the arrangement and administration of civil affairs to have no more regard for God than if He did not exist, is a rashness unknown to the very pagans; for in their heart and soul the notion of a divinity and the need of public religion were so firmly fixed that they would have thought it easier to have a city without foundation than a city without God. Human society, indeed, for which by nature we are formed, has been constituted by God the Author of nature; and from Him, as from their principle and source, flow in all their strength and permanence the countless benefits with which society abounds. As we are each of us admonished by the very voice of nature to worship God in piety and holiness, as the Giver unto us of life and of all that is good therein, so also and for the same reason, nations and States are bound to worship Him; and therefore it is clear that those who would absolve society from all religious duty act not only unjustly but also with ignorance and folly.— LEO XIII, *Humanum Genus.*

(2) We are bound absolutely to worship God in the way which He has shown to be His will. All who rule should hold in honor the holy name of God, and one of their chief duties must be to favor religion, to protect it, to shield it under the credit and sanction of the laws, and neither to organize nor enact any measure that may compromise its safety. This is the bounden duty of rulers to the people over whom they rule... Care must be taken to preserve unharmed and unimpeded the religion whereof the practice is the link connecting man with God.— LEO XIII, *Immortale Dei.*

Third part.— *The State is bound to protect the true religion.*— The State is bound to protect whatever promotes in great measure the unity, peace, and tranquillity of civil society and the perfection of its citizens. But the true religion promotes in great measure the unity, peace, and tranquillity of civil society and the perfection of its citizens. Therefore.

ARTICLE II

RELATIONS BETWEEN THE STATE AND THE CHURCH

1165. Statement of the question.— 1° The Church is a society whose end is man's spiritual good, which is eternal happiness.

Civil society, i.e., the State, is a society whose end is the temporal happiness of this life.

2° Neither the Church nor the State, from the point of view of the moral order, may be called a perfect society, as we have already seen. For a perfect society is a society whose end is man's complete good, and which embraces all other societies as its parts. But the Church does not embrace all other societies as its parts,— civil society is not a part of the Church; and its end is not man's complete good, but rather his highest good.

3° Nevertheless, from the point of view of the juridical order, the Church and State may be called perfect societies.

A juridically perfect society is a society whose end is the complete good of its own order, and which posseses in itself the means necessary and useful for the attainment of this end.

A juridically perfect society, in as much as its end is the complete good of its own order, is not a part of another society; as possessing in itself the means necessary and useful for the attainment of this good, it is independent, i.e., autonomous, in its own order.

The State, it is evident, is a juridically perfect society, for its end is the temporal happiness of this life, i.e., the complete good of its own order, and it possesses in itself the means necessary and useful for the attainment of this end.

The Church is also a juridically perfect society, for its end is man's absolutely highest good; and it possesses, as endowments of its Divine Founder, the authority and all the means necessary for the attainment of this end.

4° The State is subject to the Church, because the end of the Church is the absolutely ultimate end to which the end of the State is directed; but, in the juridical order, the State is only indirectly dependent on the Church, because the State is a juridically perfect society and possesses *proper rights of its own*.

A society is indirectly dependent on another society when *its end is subordinate to the end of the other society, not as a means or a part, but only as a good inferior in nature to the good of a higher order*.

The chief consequences of this indirect dependence, i.e., subordination, are the following:

a) the subordinate society must not, in the pursuit of its end, place any obstacle in the way of the attainment of the end of the superior society, and, in the case of collision of rights, must yield to, i.e., abandon its claims in favor of, the superior society;

b) the subordinate society enjoys freedom and independence of action in everything formally related to the pursuit of its own end, provided that it always respects the subordination of its own end to the end of the superior society.

1166. Opinions.— 1° Atheists and the exponents of indifferentism, who refuse recognition to the Church, hold that the State is in no way subordinate to the Church.

2° *Rigorous* Liberals, who maintain that the State is the only juridical society and the source of all rights, hold the same opinion.

3° *Moderate* Liberals do not deny that the Church is a true society; nevertheless, they hold that the State has no duties towards the Church, and therefore that the State should ignore the Church.

All the foregoing opinions are untenable; and, against them, we present the thesis which follows.

1167. Statement of the thesis.

THESIS. — THE STATE IS SUBJECT TO THE CHURCH; IN THE JURIDICAL ORDER, THE STATE IS INDIRECTLY SUBORDINATE TO THE CHURCH.

First part. — *The State is subject to the Church.* — A society whose proper end is a relatively ultimate end is subject to that society whose proper end is the absolutely ultimate end. But the proper end of the State is a relatively ultimate end, whereas the proper end of the Church is the absolutely ultimate end. Therefore the State is subject to the Church ([1]).

Major. — That whose proper end is the absolutely ultimate end must always direct all others whose activities, i.e., operations, are directed to the absolutely ultimate end: for the order or relation of agents is determined by the order or relation of their ends. But a relatively ultimate end is directed to the absolutely ultimate end. Therefore.

Minor. — The proper end of the State is the temporal happiness of this life, whereas the proper end of the Church is eternal happiness, i.e., the beatific vision.

Second part. — *In the juridical order, the State is indirectly subordinate to the Church.* — A society whose end is a complete good of its own order is, in the juridical order, only indirectly subordinate to a superior society. But the end of the State is a complete good of its own order. Therefore, in the juridical order, the State is only indirectly subordinate to a superior society, i.e., to the Church.

Major. — A society whose end is a complete good of its own order is a juridically perfect society, because it possesses in

---
(1) *De Reg. Princ.*, l. I, c. 14.

itself all the means necessary for the attainment of its end, and hence is independent and supreme in its own order. Therefore it cannot be directly subordinate to another society in as much as its end is a part of the end of a superior society, or serves as a means for the attainment of the end of the superior society, but is only indirectly subordinate to it in as much as its end is subordinate to the end of another order.

Minor.— The end of civil society, i.e., of the State, is the temporal happiness of this life. But the temporal happiness of this life is a complete good in its own order: for it is not a part of eternal happiness, nor is it of its nature a means of directly attaining eternal happiness, for there can be no natural proportion between natural good and supernatural good.

1168. Separation of Church and State.—1° *Preliminaries.*— a) The system of separation of Church and State is that system which claims full autonomy of the State, which should be in no way concerned with religious rights, that is to say, which should pay no more heed to the Church than if it did not exist.

b) The patrons of this system are called Liberals. There are three main forms of Liberalism: *rigorous* or *pure Liberalism, moderate Liberalism,* and *Liberal Catholicism* (Ecclesiastical Liberalism).

Rigorous or *pure Liberalism* holds that the State is the source of all rights. Hence the Church is not of its nature a juridical society with which the State should have juridical relations. Hence we have the slogan: « The Church from the State and in the State. »

Moderate Liberalism recognizes the Church as a juridical society, but holds that the State is not subordinate to the Church. Hence it proposes the slogan: « A free Church in a free State. »

Moderate Liberalism proposes its system as a means of protecting the liberty of citizens: *liberty of conscience under the protection of law.*— It recommends to the protection of the

State, in addition to liberty of conscience, liberty of *thought*, liberty of *speech*, and liberty of *worship*.

Liberal Catholicism admits *in theory* the superiority of the Church and the subordination of the State; but, *in practice*, insists upon the separation of the Church and State as the system by which the Church can best adapt itself to the times and conform to what is required by modern systems of government. Therefore, in practice, Liberal Catholicism adopts as its slogan: « A free Church in a free State. »

2° In refutation of the tenets of Liberalism, we shall prove the proposition which follows.

Proposition.— *The separation of the Church and State is unlawful.*

1) A system which is at variance with the ordinances of the divine law and prejudicial to the peace and unity of the members of civil society is unlawful. But the separation of the Church and State is at variance with the ordinances of the divine law and is prejudicial to the peace and unity of the members of civil society. Therefore the separation of the Church and the State is unlawful.

The *major* is evident from its very terms.

Minor.— a) *The separation of the Church and State is at variance with ordinances of the divine law.*— The Church is a society whose proper end is the absolutely ultimate end, and which should, by its supreme authority, direct all human societies to eternal happiness.

Moreover, according to the ordinances of the divine law, civil society should offer to God the worship due to Him, i.e., Christian worship, which the Church alone can determine and ordain. But, if the Church and State are separated, the State is not directed by the Church to eternal happiness, nor is the State subject to the Church in the all-important matter of divine worship.

b) *The separation of the Church and State is prejudicial to the peace and unity of the members of civil society.*—The Church and State have as their subjects the same persons, living in the same territory, and, moreover, often legislate for them on the same matters, though under a different aspect. But, if the Church and State were completely separated, they would make laws and give commands on the same matter which would be irreconcilable, with the result that the peace and unity of civil society would be jeopardized: the Church would declare certain marriages as both unlawful and invalid, whereas the State would pronounce them lawful; the Church would prohibit work on a certain day, whereas the State would exact it, etc. Therefore.

2) In practice, the separation of the Church and State is deleterious to souls, and results in the limitation of the rights of the Church. Moreover, it makes the Church dependent on the State, as lamentable experience has clearly shown. Hence the separation of the Church and State is entirely untenable.

1169. Liberty as conceived by Liberals. — 1° *Preliminaries*.— Liberals conceive liberty as the absolute autonomy of the human will not only in the physical order but also in the moral order, attributing to it complete independence from all human and divine authority.

In virtue of this concept of liberty, Liberals proclaim as sacred rights three so-called modern liberties: *liberty of conscience, liberty of speech,* and *liberty of worship*.

Liberty of conscience is the moral power of holding any opinion of one's choosing in moral and religious matters.

Liberty of speech, which includes liberty of the press, is the moral power of teaching, by the spoken or written word, whatever one wishes.

Liberty of worship is the moral power of offering to God any kind of worship one may wish, or no worship at all; in other words, it is the moral power of professing any religion one may wish, or no religion at all.

2° The so-called liberties which we have just described are not liberties at all, but various forms of license, pernicious to both civil and religious society, as we shall point out in what follows.

1) *The notion of liberty proposed by Liberals is wholly false.* — Liberty, as we have already shown, is the moral power of choosing between several particular goods, or between a particular good and the universal or infinite good known to us in an incomplete and imperfect manner. Therefore liberty always presupposes imperfection either in the good which is the object of liberty, or in the free being, i.e., in the subject possessed of imperfect knowledge of the infinite good. Thus God is free only in regard to particular or imperfect goods; the creature, however, and man in particular, is free in regard to the infinite good, on account of the subjective imperfection of the created intellect, which can know the infinite good only by comparing it to finite things. Hence man's liberty in relation to his ultimate end, i.e., in the moral order, is of its nature imperfect because of its dependence on the imperfection of the human intellect, which is incapable of full and adequate knowledge of God, and also because of its dependence on the imperfection of man's imperfect will, which is not wholly absorbed in love of God. In order that liberty may not become irremediably detrimental to man, the order of nature requires an authority, i.e., divine law and human law, which will recall man from evil and direct him to good.

2) Liberty of conscience has a variety of meanings. It may mean:

a) *immunity from physical necessity or from violence by which a person is prevented from observing the moral order in his internal acts.*— Everyone enjoys this kind of liberty, i.e., physical liberty, for no one can directly impede another person's internal acts.

b) *the right which protects a person against all coercion by which he could be compelled to act contrary to the dictates of conscience.*— This kind of liberty, i.e., liberty of conscience, is sacred since God forbids man to act in violation of the certain dictates of conscience, even though they may be erroneous.

But, if the dictates of an erroneous conscience conflict with the certain rights of other persons, these persons may defend their rights if no other circumstances forbid their doing so.

c) the right which safeguards a person against all legal obstacles to his acting as he wills within the limits of the moral order, i.e., at least to his acting in a becoming manner in his public or private life.— This kind of liberty is a natural right, but a right which, in matters not commanded, but only permitted by the natural law, may sometimes be subject to certain restrictions for the sake of the common good.

d) the right of holding any opinions one wishes in religious and moral matters.— This kind of liberty of conscience, loudly proclaimed and defended by Liberals, is utterly untenable, for it is a denial of the whole moral order, of God's supreme dominion over creatures, and of divine Revelation.

3) *Liberty of speech, as conceived by Liberals, is impious, false, and absurd.*— In the first place, this so-called liberty presupposes that error and vice, which are evils of the intellect and will, have the same rights as truth and virtue, which are goods of the intellect and will.

Moreover, such liberty is an insult to God, for it authorizes man to deny in speech and writing the truths of divine Revelation; and this, of course, is both impious and irrational.

Finally, if liberty of speech is permitted even in the discussion of what is false and unseemly, civil society is exposed to great moral and intellectual jeopardy, for men are victimized by strong inclinations to evil, and the unlettered are incapable of detecting the gross errors of the specious arguments of the wicked.

4) *Liberty of worship, in relation both to the individual and to society, is impious.*— Liberty of worship is an insult to God, Who must be worshipped in the manner which He has determined. Moreover, it supports the cause of religious indifferentism, and promotes the cause of atheism.

1170. Tolerance. — *Tolerance is a disposition of soul by which we patiently submit, for various reasons, to things which* are hurtful or troublesome to us, and which do not meet with our approval.

Tolerance, then, formally consists in something negative: for things which are tolerated are things of which we do not approve, but which we allow, because we cannot, or, for serious reasons, should not prevent them.

In principle, tolerance of false religions is never permissible. Hence tolerance of false worship in a Catholic State is permissible only when there are serious reasons to justify it.

These serious reasons are the following: *a*) the *moral impossibility* of using coercive means to prevent the practice of false religions: to use such means would result, for example, in wars, seditions, and persecutions of the innocent faithful; *b*) a *motive of prudence* which requires the patient bearing of that evil, in order that greater evils may be avoided.

What we have just said in regard to liberty of worship is applicable also to liberty of conscience and liberty of speech.

1171. Scholia.— 1° In a Catholic State, the faithful should strive to prevent the separation of the Church and State. This is evident from what has been already said.

But, if the separation of the Church and State becomes inevitable, Catholics should strive most earnestly to preclude by laws a condition in which the State of separation would be tantamount to a state of opposition.

Therefore the following precautions should be observed:

a) that the Church be recognized as a lawful body, and that it possess all the rights enjoyed by other corporations with the status of juridical person;

b) that it be given full freedom to exercise untrammeled its own proper prerogatives in the direction of souls;

c) that full freedom be given for both the private and public practice of its Catholic worship;

d) that Catholics have the right to open their own schools (confessional or separate schools), that the instruction imparted in them receive the same official recognition as that accorded to instruction received in public schools, and that no obligation be imposed on Catholics either to support or to attend atheistic schools;

e) that the Church have the right and the freedom to acquire, own, and administer temporal goods, and that this right be granted not only to itself, but also to moral persons, as religious communities, subject to it, at least to the same extent as this right is possessed by other reputable civil bodies or associations;

f) that the faithful be entirely free to enter the religious life without losing, as religious, their civil rights ([1]).

2° Heretics and schismatics, because of their Baptism, are, in principle, subject to the laws of the Church. Therefore the Church has the right to make the same demands of a heretical or schismatical State as it does of a Catholic State.

In practice, however, the Church does not exercise this sovereign right.

A heretical or schismatical State may be considered as it exists in the act of rebellion, or in the state of complete apostacy from the faith and Catholic unity.

When such a State is in the act of rebellion, the Church exercises its rights to prevent the complete collapse of Catholic life; hence it punishes heretics, and, if necessity requires, it has recourse to disciplinary or punitive measures in dealing with rulers.

In the case of complete apostacy, i.e., when rulers and people are separated from the Church because of the apostacy of their ancestors, the Church, in practice, restricts the exercise of its rights in so far as the sacredness of its office permits and circumstances require.

Nevertheless, there are certain demands which the Church must make.

---

(1) OTTAVIANI, *Inst. Juris Publici Eccles.*, vol. II, p. 100.

a) In virtue of its rights, the Church must be recognized as a moral person enjoying all the rights of a lawful society, i.e., the right of possessing and employing the services of the civil authority against internal and external enemies who act in violation of its rights or accepted regulations.

b) In accordance with the principles proclaimed by the heretical or schismatical State, as, for example, in accordance with the principle of liberty of worship, the Church may lay claim to its right to practice, unrestricted and unmolested, its own religion; in accordance with the principle of liberty of conscience, it may demand its right to preach the Catholic religion with a view to propagating it by making converts to the Catholic Church.

c) Moreover, the Church makes sure of the recognition of its rights by entering into agreements with the heterodox State.

3° In dealing with pagan States, the Church may claim the natural rights claimed by all lawful associations, namely, the right of using the means necessary for the attainment of its end, the right of holding sacred places, and the right of acquiring, owning, and administering temporal goods.

Since pagans cannot reasonably deny that there is at least the probability that the teachings of Christianity are true, a pagan State which prohibits the preaching and spread of the Christian religion acts unreasonably and in violation of natural rights.

Therefore the Church, in consideration of its specific mission to preach religion, may claim special rights so that, as a religious society, it may spread throughout the whole world, may practice its worship, and may be free to apply with maternal solicitude the benign rules of its saving religion to all who may become its spiritual children through the regenerating waters of Christian Baptism ([1]).

([1]) OTTAVIANI, l. c.

END OF POLITICS

ALPHABETICAL INDEX

(Numbers refer to sections)

A

Abjectness, excessive. 1013, 1°.
Abortion. 969.
Acts. Elicited and commanded acts of the will, 855, 856; commanded act and command, 859. Cf. command.
Acts, human. Are directed to an end, 825, 826, 827;— to the ultimate end, 828, 829, 830, 831, 832; goodness and evil of human acts, 863, 864; intrinsically good and intrinsically evil human acts, 865, 866, 867;— primary goodness and evil 876;— morality and circumstances, 877, 878, 879, 880;— in the abstract, can be morally indifferent, but not in the concrete, 881; consequences of morality, 882-891; imputability of human acts, 887, 887, 888. Cf. merit.
Adulation. 973.
Adultery. 926, 1005.
Affability. 968, 6°.
Alcoholism. 997.
Ambition. 981.
Anarchism. 1038, 2°.
Anger. 1010, 2°; lack of anger, 1010.
Art. And Moral Philosophy, 815;— and prudence, 939;— and morality, 940.
Association, corporative. Notion, 1031;— and syndicates, 1134, 1135. Cf. Corporatism.
Association, professional,. Notion, 1123, 1°; end, 1123-1125; lawfulness, 1126, 1129. Cf. Corporative association.
Astuteness. 945.
Authority. Notion, 1037; opinions, 1038; necessity of authority, 1039, 1042; all authority derives from God, 1041.
Authority, civil. Notion, 1111, 1°; origin, 1111-1113; division, 1114; subject, 1116-1119.
Authority, parental. Notion, 1063; origin, 1065;— resides principally in the husband, 1066.
Avarice. 973.

B

Beatitude, perfect. 842, 1°; objective beatitude 842; formal, 845;—as a state, 845, 2°, 846.

C

Capitalism. 1145-1147.
Caution. 941.
Chastity. Notion and division, 998; virginal chastity, 999-1003.
Circumspection. 941.
Church. And education, 1072; — and State, 1165-1168, 1171.
Clemency. Notion, 1008; opposite vices, 1009.
Command. Notion, 856; necessity of command, 857; relation of command to intellect and will, 858; command and commanded act, 859.
Communism. And private ownership, 1097; modern communism, 1148, 1149.
Concupiscence. Influence on voluntariness and liberty, 853.
Conscience. Notion, 920;—morality and obligation, 922; division, 923; rules, 924.
Continence,. 1007.
Contract, collective labor. 1141.
Contract of partnership. 1144.
Contumely. 966.
Corporatism. Notion, 1130; political corporatism, social corporatism, 1132; State corporatism, corporatism of association, 1133.

ALPHABETICAL INDEX 483

Cruelty. 1009.
Curiosity. 1016.
Cursing. 966.

D

Debt. Legal and moral, 968, 4°.
Derision. 966.
Detraction. 966.
Divorce. 1058-1062.
Docility. 941.
Dominion. 952; subject of dominion, 954; man's dominion, 955, 957.
Drunkenness. 996.
Duties of children. 1068.
Duties, immanent. 956.

E

Economics. Notion, 1030; division, 1031.
Education of children. Notion, 1069;— belongs properly and directly to parents, 1071; erroneous opinions, 1070;— and the Church, 1072;— and civil society, 1073. 1074.
Emancipation of women. 1067.
End, ultimate. And human acts, 828-832.
Epicheia. 974.
Epiky. 974.
Equity. 974.
Eubulia. 943.
Eugenics. 1052.
Eutrapelia. 1017.

F

Family. Notion, 1030, 2°;— and civil society, 1090-1093.
Foresight. 941.
Fortitude. Two meanings, 975; definition, 1076; vices opposed to fortitude, 977; integrant and potential parts of fortitude, 978.
Friendship. Love, love of preference, charity, 1018; definition, 1019; love of neighbor, 1022, 1023; domestic friendship, 1026; political friendship, 1027; friendship, justice, and charity, 1028; internal effects of friendship, 1024; external effects, 1025; vices opposed to friendship, 1029.

G

Glory, God's. 841.
Gluttony. 994, 4°.
Gnome. 943.
Government, forms of. 1120.
Grace. 968, 5°.
Guile. 945.

H

Happiness, natural. 834-836; delight is found in happiness, 837; speculative happiness, active happiness, 838; goods of the body and the society of friends are quasi-instrumental requisites of natural happiness, 839; natural happiness and divine good, 840. Cf. Beatitude.
Heredity. Notion, 1107.
Homicide. 969.
Honesty. As an integrant part of temperance, 992.
Humility. Notion, 1012; vices opposed to humility, 1013.

I

Impatience. 985.
Imprudence. 944.
Imputability of human acts. 886, 887.
Inconstancy. 944.
Incontinence. 1007.
Ignorance. And voluntariness, 854.
Insensibility. 985.
Instruction, monopoly of. 1075 Cf. Education.
Intention. Notion, 856, d); actual, virtual, habitual, interpretative intention, 828, 4°.
Involuntariness. Notion and sources, 850;— and violence, 851;— and fear, 852;—and concupiscence, 853;— and ignorance, 854.

J

Justice. Definition, 961; acts of justice, 962; subjective parts, 963; integrant parts, 967; potential parts, 968; general, legal, social justice, 964; particular justice, 965; distributive and commutative justice, 965; sins against distributive justice, 965, 3°; sins against commutative justice, 966; justice, friendship, and charity, 1028.

L

Law. Notion, 892; definition, 893; — and precept, 894; effects and acts of law, 895; obligation of law, 896; division, 898.

Law, eternal. Notion, 899; existence, 900.

Law, international. 1155-1156.

Law, natural. Notion, 902; existence, 903; precepts of the natural law, 904; immutability of the natural law, 905; dispensation from the natural law, 907; obligation of the natural law, 908; sanction of the natural law, 909;— and human law, 911, 913.

Law, positive. Notion, 910;— and the natural law, 911;— and the divine law, 912; human law is derived from the natural law, 913; necessity of human law, 914; extension of human law, 915; change of human law, 916; human law and custom, 916; penal obligation, 919.

Liberalism, Economic. 1152-1154.

Liberality. 968, 6°.

Liberty. As conceived by liberals, 1169.

Lust. Notion and daughters, 1004; species of lust, 1005.

Lying. 972.

M

Magnanimous persons. Characteristics, 980.

Magnanimity. Definition, 979; vices opposed to magnanimity, 981.

Magnificence. Notion, 982; vices opposed to magnificence, 983.

Materialism. Dialectical and historical, 1148-1149.

Matrimony. Notion, 1043, 1°; opinions, 1044; — is natural to man, 1043-1045; essence of matrimony, 1046; its efficient cause, 1047; its ends, 1048;— is the most natural of all societies, 1049;— is sacred in character, 1050; precept of matrimony, 1053-1054; unity of matrimony, 1055-1057; indissolubility of matrimony, 1058-1062.

Meekness. Notion and opposite vices, 1010.

Memory. And prudence, 941.

Merit of human acts. 899-891.

Modesty. Notion and species, 1011.

Modesty of external movements and dress. 1017.

Mollities. 988.

Monastics. Definition, 823; division, 824.

Morality. Notion, 860; formal constituent, 861; division, 862; existence, 863-864; intrinsic morality of human acts, 865-867; knowledge of morality, 868; rule of morality, 870-874; sources of morality, 875;— and object of human acts, 876;— and circumstances, 877-879; — and end, 880; consequences of morality, 882-891;— and moral obligation, 897;— and conscience, 922;— and art, 940.

Murmuring. 966.

N

Nation. Description, 1105; philosophical definition, 1106; causes, 1107; definition of nationalism, 1108; principle of nationalism, 1109.

Negligence. 944, 1016.

O

Ownership, private. Notion, 1096, 3°; opinions, 1097; ownership is lawful, and even necessary, 1098-1099; modes of acquiring ownership, 1100; social character of private ownership, 1101-1104.

P

Patience. Notion, 984; opposite vices, 985; considerations for acquirement of patience, 986.

Parsimony. 983.

Perseverance. Notion, 987; vices opposed to perseverance, 988.

Personalism. 1094-1095.

Pertinacity. 988.

Philosophy, moral, speculative philosophy, and the mechanical arts: 815; definition, 816;— is an essentially practical science, 817; method, 818;— and speculative philosophy, 819;— and Sacred Theology, 820; division, 821.

ALPHABETICAL INDEX 485

Politics. Notion, 1080; division, 1081;— is wisdom in the order of the practical sciences, 822.
Polities. 1120.
Polygamy. 1055.
Precipitation. 944.
Presumption. 981.
Pride. Notion, 1013; gravity of pride, 1014.
Prodigality. 973.
Property, private. Cf. Ownership.
Prudence. Notion, 936; acts of prudence, synderesis, and moral virtue, 938;— and art, 939; integrant parts of prudence, 941; subjective parts, 942; potential parts, 943; vices opposed to prudence by deficiency, 944;— by excess, 945; prudence of the flesh, 945.
Punishment, capital. And the State, 1115.
Pusillanimity. 981.

Q

Quarreling. 973.

R

Reason. And prudence, 941.
Religion. 968, 3°; 971.
Resistance of tyranny. 1122.
Responsibility of moral agents. 886-888.
Restriction, mental, 972, note.
Revenge. 968, 5°.
Right. Meanings, 947;— is the object of justice, 946; objective right, 948; subjective right, 949; relation between subjective right and objective right, 950; division of objective right, 951; division of subjective right, 952; real right and personal right, 952, 2°; subject of right, 953; right and coaction, 959.

S

Sagacity, personal. 941.
Salary. Notion, 1136, 1°; division, 1136, 2°;— is lawful and due in strict justice, 1137;— is due in commutative justice, 1138-1139; fixing of salary, 1140.
School, neutral. 1076; liberty of the school, 1077.
Seduction. 966, 1005.

Servants, domestic. 1079.
Shame. 992.
Sin. Notion, 882; divisions, 883; distinction of sins, 884; philosophical sin, 885.
Slavery. 1078.
Sobriety. 995.
Socialism. 1150-1151.
Society. Notion, 1032; division, 1036; man is destined by his nature to live in society, 1034; necessity of society, 1035, 1°; formal constituent of society, 1035, 2° and 3°; — is a moral person, 1035, 4°; relation of parts to society as a whole, 1035, 5°.
Society, civil. Notion, 1082, 1°; end, 1082-1084; origin, 1086-1089; persons, families, and society, 1090-1093;— and education, 1073-1074.
Society, international. 1157-1158.
Solicitude, excessive. 945.
State and religion, 1163-1164; — and the Church, 1165-1168.
Strikes. 1142.
Studiousness. Notion, 1015; vices opposed to studiousness, 1016.
Suffrage. 1121.
Suicide. 930.
Synderesis. 868;— prudence and moral virtue, 938.
Syndicates. Notion, 1123, 3°;— and corporative associations, 1134; doctrine of the Church, 1135.
Synesis. 943.

T

Temperance. Definition, 989; rule of temperance, 990; vices opposed to temperance, 991; integrant parts of temperance, 992; subjective parts, 993; potential parts, 1006.
Thoughtlessness. 944.
Truth. 968, 5°.

U

Understanding and prudence. 941.

V

Vainglory. 981.
Vice. 935.
Violence and involuntariness. 851.

Virginity. Notion, 999;— is lawful, 1000;—is more excellent than matrimony, 1002; sins opposed to virginity, 1004-1005.

Virtue. Definition, 926; necessity, 925; subject, 927; division, 928; intellectual and moral virtues, 929; cardinal virtues, 930; parts of the cardinal virtues, 931; moral virtue consists in a mean, 932; connexion between the moral virtues, 933; equality and inequality of the moral virtues, 934; moral virtue, prudence, and synderesis, 938.

Voluntariness. Notion, 848; division, 849.

W

Wages. Cf. Salary.
War. 1159-1162.
Wastefulness. 983.